DIAGNOSTIC IMAGING OF CHILD ABUSE

DIAGNOSTIC IMAGING OF CHILD ABUSE

PAUL K. KLEINMAN, M.D.

Professor of Radiology and Pediatrics
University of Massachusetts Medical School
Director, Pediatric Radiology
University of Massachusetts Medical Center
Worcester, Massachusetts

with 8 contributors

WILLIAMS & WILKINS
Baltimore • London • Los Angeles • Sydney

Editor: Timothy H. Grayson
Associate Editor: Carol Eckhart
Copy Editor: Megan Barnard Shelton
Design: Jo Anne Janowiak
Illustration Planning: Lorraine Wrzosek
Production: Anne G. Seitz

Copyright © 1987
Williams & Wilkins
428 East Preston Street
Baltimore, MD 21202, U.S.A.

Accurate indications, adverse reactions, and dosage schedules for drugs are provided
in this book, but it is possible that they may change. The reader is urged to review
the package information data of the manufacturers of the medications mentioned.

Printed in the United States of America

Library of Congress Cataloging in Publication Data

Kleinman, Paul K.
   Diagnostic imaging of child abuse

   Bibliography: p.
   Includes index.
   1. Battered child syndrome—Diagnosis. 2. Pediatric diagnostic imaging. I. Title.
[DNLM: 1. Child Abuse. 2. Forensic Medicine. 3. Wounds and Injuries—in infancy
& childhood. 4. Wounds and Injuries—radiography. WO 700 K64d]
RA1122.5.K57 1987   617'.10757   86-32490
ISBN 0-683-04655-1

Composed and printed at the   87 88 89 90 91
Waverly Press, Inc.   10 9 8 7 6 5 4 3 2 1

To my family

Foreword

The concept of willful assault upon children by their caretakers is almost incomprehensible. Sometimes the physician needs reassurance that what is seen by physical examination of radiography can be believed. The chapters on the radiologic aspects of child abuse, 2 through 9, present in exquisite detail, with gross microscopic pathologic correlation, the many radiographic findings caused by willful injury to the skeleton and solid organs. The discussion of the incidence and patterns of injury reminds us of the underestimation of the incidence of skeletal injury and that the overall concept of child abuse has been expanded. The discussion of the skeletal survey and the scintigraphic examination of the skeleton shows that each has value; they are less supplementary than complementary.

The chapter dealing with the radiologic dating of fractures is important in the diagnosis of the abused child and also has everyday applicability. The pathophysiology of fracture healing is lucidly presented, as is its modification by repetitive trauma. The discussion of trauma to solid viscera and the central nervous system includes the use of computed tomography and mechanisms of injury; for example, mesenteric injury can result from blunt trauma or sudden deceleration. Involvement of the distal colon and rectum is most often caused by sexual abuse. Inflicted abuse seldom injures the spleen, the kidneys, or the lower urinary tract.

Doctor Kleinman has had a long and fruitful relationship with his colleagues in pathology. The material derived from autopsies is of interest to both disciplines. The value of postmortem radiographic study and of its correlation to the actual pathologic anatomy is persuasively presented. The differential diagnosis of inflicted skeletal injury is discussed in Chapter 11, followed by a chapter dealing with the legal aspects of child abuse.

In the chapter dealing with legal issues, it is stated that "sensitive management of family violence cases requires both medical and legal input." The radiologist has a role in determining the nature and degree of inflicted injury, information that often can be obtained in no other way. Of further interest to the radiologist is the discussion concerned with legal consent, medical records, reporting statutes, and procedures relative to service as a witness or expert witness. This is followed by a chapter on psychological considerations associated with abuse that include the role of the radiologist in the initial detection of skeletal injury, its documentation, and the subsequent support provided for psychological or legal intervention.

The last chapter reviews technical considerations in dosimetry and includes a discussion of radiation risks entailed in the examination as well as methods for the reduction of exposure via appropriate selection of equipment, techniques, and the application of clinical judgment.

All in all, one can be enthusiastic about this work and thankful to Doctor Kleinman and his coauthors for presenting a cogent examination of the radiologic aspects of child abuse; the radiologist may be the first to note the possibility of an unfortunately common occurrence.

John A. Kirkpatrick, Jr., M.D.

Preface

The origins of my interest in the subject of child abuse rest in part with a bizarre incident that occurred during my pediatric residency. The episode began with a middle-of-the-night phone call from a woman who introduced herself as only "Clara." She spoke in an authoritative and well-polished manner and quickly drew me from my groggy state. I asked her to repeat her name, and this time she identified herself as "Mrs. Clara." Without any apology for my inconvenience, she stated that she had a matter of extreme importance to discuss. She said my testimony was required in the proceedings of a child custody case due to occur the following day. The case entailed a dispute between parents who were each seeking to gain custody of several children, one of whom was alleged to have been abused. She indicated that the child had been seen in our acute care clinic by a physician who was not available for testimony and, as I had been assigned to the same clinic, my testimony was required to validate the clinical record describing the visit. As I did not recall seeing the patient and the name of the physician who had seen the child was unfamiliar to me, I suggested she seek the assistance of the director of the Emergency Room. She would not relent and explained in further detail the abusive assaults perpetrated by the mother and the importance of placing this child with the father. The conversation drew to a close only after I pressed her to determine her actual interest in the case. I easily fell back to sleep and when I awoke the next morning, I wondered if I had in fact dreamt the entire incident.

Shortly after morning rounds, I was summoned to the chief of staff's office and was rapidly escorted into a stately mahogany-paneled board room. Seated around a huge table were the chief of staff, the director of the pediatric clinic, a lawyer, and a number of other unfamiliar men and women. They asked if I had been contacted by anyone requesting my testimony in a current child custody case. I provided them with what I could recall from the evening's telephone conversation and asked them to explain what was going on.

They provided me with the details of a custody case presently in court in which child abuse had been alleged, and in which the validity of the medical record was being contested. The clinic director held a copy of a page taken from the child's medical record that detailed the physical laboratory and x-ray findings of one of the children in the custody dispute. The clinical findings read like a page out of Helfer and Kempe's textbook, *The Battered Child Syndrome*; the radiologic descriptions could have been taken directly from Caffey's *Pediatric X-Ray Diagnosis* and included terms such as "corner" fractures and "bucket-handle" lesions. Although much of the terminology was appropriate, the organization of the note, the use of language, and the flow of the discussion clearly indicated that the note had not been written by a physician. The bogus nature of the record was confirmed when it was determined that none of the laboratory studies and x-rays referred to in the note had been performed.

As the various elements of the story were pieced together, it became clear that someone whose interest would have been served if child abuse on the part of the mother were proven had doctored the medical record. This was achieved simply by securing a hospital progress note sheet, entering the historic, physical, and laboratory data, and bolstering the account with suitable language obtained from appropriate textbooks on the subject of child abuse. The papers were then forwarded to the record room and duly added to the patient's existing chart. The true identity of the midnight caller remains a question to this day. However, the father in this case was described as a major figure in high circles with many important friends, and I suspect the caller was one of them.

Over the 15 years since that incident, I have been continually impressed with the variety of ways caretakers have managed to inflict injury upon infants and children. What was viewed as only a medical curiosity 25 years age now permeates the radiologic and pediatric literature, and the ramifications of the problem have spread to many allied scientific disciplines, the legal community, and the population at large. Heightened awareness has led to child abuse legislation throughout the 50 states and to the creation of national and local organizations dealing with the prevention, identification, and management of abuse. Most academic medical institutions are equipped with child abuse teams composed of physicians, social workers, psychologists/psychiatrists, and other specialists. Scientific papers concerning child abuse number in the thousands, and many textbooks are available dealing with the condition in general, as well as specific facets of the problem.

Although the origin of the concept of child abuse as a medical entity rests squarely with Dr. John Caffey, one of the fathers of pediatric radiology, there has been to date no textbook dealing exclusively with the radiologic alterations occurring in this condition. Several excellent discussions of the subject can be found in textbooks dealing principally with child abuse, and most general and pediatric radiology works devote space to the entity. Recent technical advances in nuclear medicine, ultrasonography, and computed tomography, in addition to newer insights gained by anatomic studies in abused infants, have resulted not only in improved diagnostic capabilities, but also in a better understanding of the pathogen-

esis of the various lesions associated with child abuse. The sheer volume of radiologic material dramatizes the need for a textbook dealing specifically with the radiologic alterations in abuse. Additionally, as diagnostic imaging frequently plays a central role in the evaluation of suspected abuse, the radiologist must be prepared to deal with concerns that go beyond the simple monitoring and interpretation of radiologic studies. A variety of social issues may arise as the radiologist seeks to fulfill her/his responsibility in abuse cases and, with increasing prosecutions and civil litigation, the radiologist is called upon to offer testimony related to his/her findings. Other physicians, and personnel in the fields of social work, psychology, and law, may find themselves in need of a single reference source dealing in depth with specific radiologic alterations occurring with abuse. I have attempted in this work, *Diagnostic Imaging of Child Abuse*, to fulfill this need.

Chapters 2 through 5 and 7 through 10 are a distillation of the literature on the radiologic manifestations of child abuse and neglect. In most cases, the abnormalities illustrated are secondary to known child abuse. A few examples of nonabusive injuries are included for the purpose of discussion, and, when provided, these exceptions are clearly stated in the legends. The case material is drawn principally from the files of the University of Massachusetts Medical Center. Dr. John O'Connor of Boston City Hospital, and Drs. Paula Brill and Patricia Winchester of New York Hospital have generously provided me with supplementary illustrative case material. Authorities on the subject of child abuse throughout the world have contributed examples of unusual manifestations of child abuse and neglect that appear in these chapters, and the cases are invaluable additions to the work. Special thanks are in order to Dr. Theodore Vandersalm and Stephen Done for supplying several especially useful radiographs. The other chapters have been contributed by authorities in radiology, orthopaedic surgery, psychology, and law. The final chapter, written by experts in imaging technology and application, provides a background for those readers less familiar with radiologic principles, technique, and dosimetry. These chapters cover a broad range of issues, but in sum dramatize the need for an enlightened role of the radiologist in the diagnosis of child abuse.

In addition to those already mentioned, special thanks are in order to Patricia Belanger for her technical assistance, to Mary Cunnion for her artistic renderings, and to Jean Edmunds for her editoral work, as well as to Sandra Costa, Marilee Caliendo, Cathy Russell, Norman Delongchamp, Jr., James Staruck, Sandy Marks, Brian Blackbourne, Barbara Biber, and Paul Bohdiewicz. Timothy Grayson, Carol Eckhart, and John Gardner of Williams & Wilkins have been of great help and without the support of George Stamathis, formerly of Williams & Wilkins, the project would not have gotten off the ground. I am indebted to my good friends and colleagues, Vassilios Raptopoulos, Edward Smith, and Carl D'Orsi, who have provided unwavering support throughout the project. This work would not have been completed but for the devotion of Kathy Delongchamp, who has done most of the leg work and prepared the manuscript. During the many trying periods, she has performed conscientiously with infinite care and patience.

Of necessity, much of this book has been written at the kitchen table on weekends and evenings. Consequently, my wife and daughter have suffered a form of pediatric radiologist abuse—forced to endure endless descriptions of hideous acts perpetrated against innocent children. Throughout this period, they have exhibited patience and consideration. To my family I owe not only my gratitude, but also my apologies.

Paul K. Kleinman, M.D.

Contributors

Richard Bourne, J. D., Ph.D.
Associate Professor of Sociology, Northeastern University; General Counsel, The Children's Hospital, Boston, Massachusetts

Paula W. Brill, M.D.
Associate Professor of Radiology, Cornell Medical College; Associate Attending in Radiology, Associate Director, Pediatric Radiology, New York Hospital, Cornell Medical Center, New York, New York

Jonathan Cohen, M.D.
Professor of Orthopedic Surgery, Tufts University School of Medicine; Orthopedic Surgeon, Kennedy Memorial Hospital for Children, Brighton, Massachusetts

Andrew Karellas, Ph.D.
Assistant Professor of Radiology, University of Massachusetts Medical School; Director, Radiologic Physics, University of Massachusetts Medical Center, Worcester, Massachusetts

John A. Kirkpatrick, Jr., M.D.
Professor of Radiology, Harvard Medical School; Radiologist-in-Chief, The Children's Hospital, Boston, Massachusetts

Paul K. Kleinman, M.D.
Professor of Radiology and Pediatrics, University of Massachusetts Medical School; Director, Pediatric Radiology, University of Massachusetts Medical Center, Worcester, Massachusetts

John F. O'Connor, M.D.
Professor of Pediatric Radiology and Anatomy, Boston University School of Medicine; Director, Pediatric Radiology, Boston City Hospital, Boston, Massachusetts

Vassilios Raptopoulos, M.D.
Professor of Radiology, University of Massachusetts Medical School, Director, Abdominal Imaging, University of Massachusetts Medical Center, Worcester, Massachusetts

Peter F. Toscano, Ph.D.
Assistant Professor of Psychiatry, University of Massachusetts Medical School; Director, Family Center Project, University of Massachusetts Medical Center, Worcester, Massachusetts

Patricia Winchester, M.D.
Associate Professor of Radiology, Cornell Medical College; Attending Radiologist, Director, Pediatric Radiology, New York Hospital, Cornell Medical Center, New York, New York

Contents

1 Introduction

PAUL K. KLEINMAN, M.D.

In 1946 John Caffey, a pediatrician and radiologist practicing at Babies Hospital in New York, described six infants with subdural hematomas and long bone fractures in the absence of any history of trauma (1). His initial observations prompted speculation of "intentional ill-treatment," and, in the years that immediately followed, he expressed the conviction in conferences, lectures, and personal communications that the findings were manifestations of maltreatment by custodians (2). Although maltreatment of infants and children can be traced throughout recorded history (2–5), Caffey's observations formed the basis upon which a medical entity of child abuse, the battered child syndrome, was eventually formulated (6). In 1987, the literature is replete with literally thousands of publications dealing with child abuse and neglect. The subject has been of intense interest not only to health professionals, but to sociologists, social workers, lawyers, and legislators. The greatest strides in the area of child abuse and neglect have been made in reporting legislation, in management, and in an understanding of the social, psychological, and epidemiologic aspects of the problem.

The diagnostic imaging of abuse has also evidenced important improvements, particularly within the past 15 years. Modern radiographic equipment and film–screen systems provide high-quality images at relatively low exposure. In nuclear medicine the use of gamma ray emitters tagged to a variety of pharmaceuticals results not only in images supplying anatomic information, but also in physiologic data regarding blood flow and organ function. Real-time ultrasonography is a safe, noninvasive means of assessing soft tissue abnormalities, and is of exceptional value in the abdomen. The most significant advance in the diagnostic imaging of abusive injuries rests with cranial computed tomography (CT). Major intracranial abnormalities previously requiring invasive procedures such as pneumoencephalography and cerebral arteriography are now easily diagnosed in a noninvasive fashion. Small subdural hematomas and a variety of intracerebral injuries previously undetectable before death are beautifully delineated by CT. Computed tomography of the abdomen is particularly useful in assessing pancreatic pathology as well as other solid organ injury. Magnetic resonance imaging, a tool that is of great clinical value for a variety of diagnostic problems, should prove useful in certain cases of abuse.

The varied and complex injuries occurring in abused patients as well as the sophisticated technology employed to diagnose these problems warrant an in-depth discussion of the subject of diagnostic imaging of child abuse.

Definition

There is no universal agreement on a definition of child abuse. In the years following the landmark article of Kempe et al., the term "the battered child syndrome" appeared appropriate (6). It characterized a group of children suffering physical harm as a result of intentional acts of violence perpetrated by custodians. As the concept of child abuse has broadened to include sexual assaults, neglect, and adverse psychological consequences of abnormal family interactions, it is apparent that definitions will vary depending upon the professionals involved and the particular population and problem under study (7–10). As this textbook deals principally with physical injury, a definition restricting the subject to the physical consequences of willful assault upon children by caretakers seems appropriate. Miscellaneous entities that do not necessarily fall under this strict definition are covered briefly in Chapter 9.

Incidence

Estimates regarding the incidence of child abuse are fraught with difficulties. They center around variations in reporting procedures, as well as different attitudes regarding what constitutes child abuse. It is safe to assume that official statistics simply reflect the workings of a system as it attempts to characterize the magnitude of the problem. The numbers do not provide a true measure of the extent of abuse and violent behavior in families (7).

Estimates of the incidence of child abuse can be based upon actual reporting or statistical extrapolations drawn from smaller representative sample groups. In 1983 approximately 1 million reports of child abuse and neglect were documented by child protective services in the United States. Because these reports included both families and individual children, approximately 1.5 million children were reported to be abused (11). Straus et al. conducted a national survey employing a representative sample of 2143 individual family members (12). The authors relied upon self-reports of violence and abuse against individual family members. The study was an attempt to avoid biases inherent in offical statistical gathering. The authors estimated that between 1.4 and 1.9 million children were vulnerable to physical injury from their parents during the year of the survey. Interestingly, the survey also estimated that 1.5 million parents of teenagers were severely assaulted by their children each year, and that 500,000 elderly parents (over 65 years of age) were abused by their children. This study properly places child abuse within the overall context of family violence, a concept that must be recognized in order to fully under-

stand the environmental factors leading to child abuse (see Chapter 13).

Childhood fatalities due to abuse are similarly difficult to estimate. This is a particular problem in infancy, when it is likely that many cases of homicide remain undiagnosed (see Chapter 10). Present estimates indicate that between 2000 and 5000 children are killed each year by their parents (13). The wide range of cases in this estimate dramatizes the limitations and uncertainties that exist in the identification and reporting of fatal abuse (14, 15). Helfer has criticized medical examiners who "hide behind" anatomic diagnoses to avoid the issues of abuse (16). Similar criticisms may be justified in instances where radiologists fail to properly label cases of abuse when the radiologic alterations are unequivocal.

The Abused Child

A detailed profile of the abused child, as well as the abuser, is presented in Chapter 13. However, a knowledge of certain facts about the child at risk for abuse is useful in assessing the various radiologic alterations. The average age of the maltreated child is 7.1 years, in contrast to 8.6 for all U.S. children (11). However, major physical injuries are concentrated in very young children. Sixty-four percent of all reported cases of maltreatment evidencing major physical injury are found in patients 0 to 5 years of age. If one looks specifically at children manifesting radiologic evidence of abusive injury, the majority will in fact be less than 2 years of age (17). The injuries in these infants and young children are more frequently occult, and tend to provide more specific information regarding abuse than injuries encountered in older children.

The Radiologist as Consultant

For many years pediatric radiologists have been regarded as important members of pediatric medical and surgical teams. This consultant role derives from the unique character of the pediatric population as well as the standards of practice established by pioneers in the field such as John Caffey and Edward Neuhauser. In recent years, similar attitudes toward the role of the general radiologist as a consultant have flourished (18). The vast array of physical alterations occurring with child abuse and the epidemic proportions of the problem demand this clinical approach by the diagnostic radiologist. Child abuse should be viewed in much the same manner as any other medical problem in which facts are gathered and evaluated, and a medical judgment based upon one's knowledge and expertise is formulated.

REFERENCES

1. Caffey J: Multiple fractures in the long bones of infants suffering from chronic subdural hematoma. *Am J Roentgenol (AJR)* 56:163–173, 1946.
2. Silverman FN: Unrecognized trauma in infants, the battered child syndrome, and the syndrome of Ambroise Tardieu. Rigler lecture. *Radiology* 104:337–353, 1972.
3. English PC, Grossman H: Radiology and the history of child abuse. *Pediatr Ann* 12:870–874, 1983.
4. Robin M: Historical introduction. Sheltering arms: the roots of child abuse. In Newberger EH (ed): *Child Abuse*. Boston, Little, Brown, 1982, pp 1–21.
5. Radbill S: A history of child abuse and infanticide. In Helfer RE, Kempe CH (eds): *The Battered Child*. Chicago, University of Chicago Press, 1974, pp 3–20.
6. Kempe CH, Silverman FN, Steele BF, Droege-mueller W, Silver HK: The battered-child syndrome. *JAMA* 181:105–112, 1962.
7. Gelles RJ: Child abuse and family violence: implications for medical professionals. In Newberger EH (ed): *Child Abuse*. Boston, Little, Brown, 1982, pp 25–41.
8. Gelles R: Community agencies and child abuse: labeling and gatekeeping. In Gelles R (ed): *Family Violence*. Beverly Hills, Sage Publications, 1979, pp 55–72.
9. Gill D: Unraveling child abuse. *Am J Orthopsychiatry* 45:345–356, 1975.
10. Giovannoni JM, Becerra RM (eds): *Defining Child Abuse*. New York, Free Press, 1979.
11. American Association for Protecting Children, Inc.: *Highlights of Official Child Neglect and Abuse Reporting 1983*. Denver, The American Humane Association, 1985, pp 1–36.
12. Straus MA, Gelles RJ, Steinmetz SK: *Behind Closed Doors: Violence in the American Family*. New York, Anchor Press, 1980.
13. National Center on Child Abuse and Neglect: *Executive Summary: National Study of the Incidences and Severity of Child Abuse and Neglect*. DHHS Publication OHDS 81-30329. Washington, DC, US Government Printing Office, 1981.
14. Emerick SJ, Foster LR, Campbell DT: Risk factors for traumatic infant death in Oregon, 1973 to 1982. *Pediatrics* 77:518–522, 1986.
15. Bass M, Kravath RE, Glass L: Death-scene investigation in sudden infant death. *N Engl J Med* 315:100–105, 1986.
16. Helfer RE: Where to now Henry? Commentary on the battered child syndrome. *Pediatrics* 76:993–997, 1985.
17. Merten DF, Radkowski Ma, Leonidas JC: The abused child. A radiological reappraisal. *Radiology* 146:377–381, 1983.
18. Baum S: The radiologic consultant. *AJR* 134:1281, 1980.

2 Skeletal Trauma: General Considerations

PAUL K. KLEINMAN, M.D

Skeletal injuries are frequently central to the documentation of child abuse. In contrast to central nervous system (CNS) and other visceral injuries, they are rarely life threatening. On occasion, these injuries pose difficult orthopedic problems and may ultimately result in significant deformity. However, it is the frequent high specificity for abuse that warrants an in-depth study of these varied skeletal abnormalities.

In 1946, Caffey described a variety of long bone injuries in infants with subdural hematomas (1). Although countless examples of unexplained subdural hematomas in infants had appeared in the literature, it was only after Caffey associated these lesions with certain patterns of skeletal injury that a specific medical entity of child abuse was formulated. In a sense, recognition of the role of skeletal injuries in child abuse became the catalyst for the tremendous interest in the subject following Caffey's original description. In the years to follow, most reports of child abuse relied heavily upon radiologic alterations (2–12). The firm documentation of injury, facilitated by characteristic radiologic alterations, provided enlightened investigators the necessary climate for study of the many other facets of child abuse. It was this blend of the clinical and the radiologic that allowed Drs. Kempe and Silverman and others to bring this condition to the status of the "battered child syndrome" (13).

As the concept of the battered child syndrome has expanded and surveillance dramatically improved, there has been a predictable and progressive decrease in the percentage of patients evidencing fractures in large series of abused patients (14). This phenomenon may be producing an unfortunate trend wherein the importance of documentation of skeletal injury in cases of abuse is underestimated. There is no greater tragedy than when a child is seriously injured or murdered, or a sibling suffers a similar fate, as the result of a failure to document an earlier abusive episode. These concerns warrant familiarity with these skeletal injuries by all professionals dealing with child abuse. The radiologist, as the ultimate authority on diagnostic imaging of abuse, must possess in-depth knowledge on this subject as well as ensure the technical quality of appropriate radiologic studies.

INCIDENCE

Reports of the frequency of fractures in cases of abuse vary from 11% to 55% (15–21). Skeletal injuries are significantly more common in the younger age groups. Herndon found long bone injuries in only 11% of 273 cases of abuse (15). However, 94% of the fractures occurred in patients less than 3 years of age, although only 58% of the children were under 3. Ebbin et al. found fractures in 42% of 50 abused children (18). Although 20% of the patients were over 5 years of age, no fractures were identified in children over age 4. Akbarnia et al. reviewed the radiographs in 217 abused children (22). They found that 50% of the fractures occurred in patients less than 1 year of age, and 78% occurred in children less than 3 years of age.

Other factors that influence the reported incidence of skeletal injury include the type of population from which the samples are drawn. Centers with large orthopedic services may see larger proportions of abused children with fractures. Studies that fail to differentiate neglect and sexual assaults from cases of physical abuse will likely show smaller percentages of fractures (23).

Finally, a major factor affecting the frequency with which skeletal injury is detected relates to the utilization and expertise of diagnostic imaging services. Studies of large numbers of abused children show that skeletal surveys are performed variably in 59% to 95% of cases (16, 21). Great variation in the technical quality and the thoroughness of skeletal surveys exists. Although the tendency to obtain a "baby gram" (single film of the entire infant) has diminished, variations on this theme are still practiced, particularly in centers without pediatric radiologists. The regions of interest and the number of films obtained similarly vary between centers. Technical problems such as under- or overexposures and patient motion frequently hinder studies in young and uncooperative patients. Finally, some film–screen combinations may provide images of insufficient quality to identify the subtle alterations that have a high specificity for abuse.

Patterns of Skeletal Injury

A variety of skeletal injuries occur in abused infants and children (Table 2.1). Based upon their nature, location, and chronicity, relative specificities can be applied to these various skeletal injuries (Table 2.2).

PERIOSTEAL NEW BONE FORMATION

The periosteum is comprised of two layers, a relatively thick osteogenic layer and a thin outer fibrous layer. In the older patient, abundant Sharpey's fibers anchor the periosteum along the shaft. There is a paucity

Table 2.1
Patterns of Skeletal Injury

Periosteal new bone formation
Metaphyseal lesions
Epiphyseal plate injuries
Diaphyseal fractures
Dislocations
Miscellaneous injuries

Table 2.2
Specificity of Radiologic Findings

High specificity
  Metaphyseal lesions
  Posterior rib fractures
  Scapular fractures
  Spinous process fractures
  Sternal fractures
Moderate specificity*
  Multiple fractures, especially bilateral
  Fractures of different ages
  Epiphyseal separations
  Vertebral body fractures and subluxations
  Digital fractures
  Complex skull fractures
Common, but low specificity*
  Clavicular fractures
  Long bone shaft fractures
  Linear skull fractures

* Moderate- and low-specificity lesions become high when history of trauma is absent or inconsistent with injuries.

of these attachments in infants (24). As the periosteum passes beyond the growth plate, it is referred to as the perichondrium. LaCroix demonstrated the strong attachment of the fibrous layers of periosteum to the epiphyseal cartilage (25). Subperiosteal hemorrhage of any cause produces elevation of the periosteum. This results in separation of the bony cortex from the osteogenic layer of periosteum by intervening blood clot of varying amounts (Fig. 2.1). The perichondral attachments are usually preserved, which results in maximal hemorrhage thickness along the diaphysis, with gradual tapering toward the epiphyses (Fig. 2.2).

Except for soft tissue swelling, radiographs are initially negative. In 5 to 14 days, a thin layer of subperiosteal new bone will be formed (Fig. 2.3A). If massive bleeding is

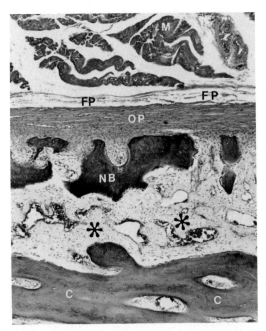

Figure 2.1. Periosteal reaction—histopathology. A medium power photomicrograph of the tibial shaft resected at autopsy from an abused infant reveals the periosteum, which is comprised of a thick osteogenic layer (*OP*) and a thinner fibrous layer (*FP*), to be elevated from the original cortex (*C*). The hemorrhage has been resorbed and replaced by highly vascular immature fibrous tissue (*). Subperiosteal new bone formation (*NB*) is evident corresponding to the band of density on the radiograph. *M* = muscle.

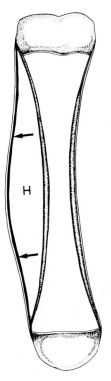

Figure 2.2. Schematic representation of a subperiosteal hematoma. The hematoma (*H*) lies between the cortex and the periosteum. The earliest new bone formation (*arrows*) occurs beneath the osteogenic layer of periosteum.

present, ultrasonography may clearly elucidate the morbid anatomy (Figs. 2.3*B* and *C*). In most cases, periosteal reaction is related to the injury of the metaphyseal-epiphyseal complex and will be greatest along the metaphysis and diaphysis adjacent to this region. With major injury, the hemorrhage will elevate the periosteum throughout its length. When epiphyseal displacement is present, the periosteal attachment will usually be maintained, and the subsequent periosteal new bone will create a "new" cortex aligned in a normal fashion to the displaced epiphysis. This factor accounts for the remarkable remodeling capacity evident in massively injured infant long bones (see Chapter 3).

When severe, the preceding injuries are

often evident clinically and are manifest by substantial swelling and occasional deformity. In contrast, isolated subperiosteal new bone formation, occurring principally along the diaphysis of multiple long bones, is generally silent. The radiographic alterations are often subtle and may be detectable on only one of several views of an extremity. Because a minimum of 5 days is required to see visible radiologic changes, radionuclide bone scanning is extremely useful in detecting early subperiosteal hemorrhage (Fig. 2.4). Although a frequent finding in abused infants, focal or generalized periosteal new bone formation is in itself a nonspecific finding and can be noted in infectious, traumatic, metabolic, and a variety of miscellaneous entities (see Chapter 11). On occasion, fine diaphyseal periosteal new bone formation, particularly in the tibia, may point to a subtle underlying fracture (Fig.

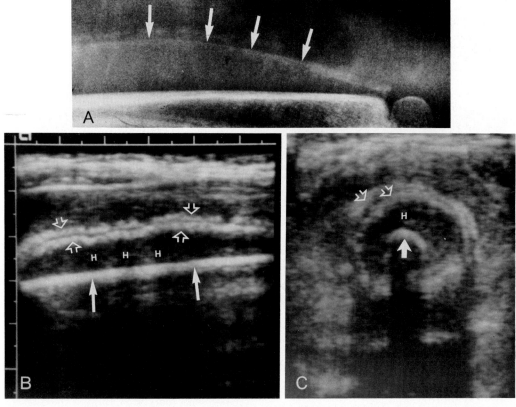

Figure 2.3. Subperiosteal hematoma. This infant presented with a swollen thigh and no history of trauma. *A,* Lateral projection of the right femur demonstrates a fine rim of periosteal new bone (*arrows*). Sagittal (*B*) and transverse (*C*) ultrasonographic images of the femur demonstrate a hypoechoic hematoma (*H*) situated between the echogenic cortex (*solid arrows*) and two lamellated layers of subperiosteal new bone (*open arrows*). Other studies revealed metaphyseal-epiphyseal lesions typical of abuse. (Courtesy of Roy McCauley, Tufts New England Medical Center, Boston, Massachusetts.)

2.5) (12). For this reason, any region of abnormality detected on a standard skeletal survey should be radiographed in a second projection, and coned-down views should be obtained if deemed useful.

A variety of physical forces give rise to subperiosteal hemorrhage. The early articles of Snedecor and others provide invaluable insights into the pathogenesis of subperiosteal hemorrhage, as well as the metaphyseal lesions, which will be discussed subsequently (26, 27). Snedecor et al. found bony alterations resembling those noted in abused infants in neonates delivered with difficulty from breech presentations. They described excessive tractional and torsional forces applied in attempts to rotate and ex-

tract the fetus. Injuries were noted in both upper and lower extremities, and typically the involved extremities were swollen following the day of delivery. Radiographs obtained at birth were initially interpreted as normal. Radiographic changes were first noted between the fifth and seventh days. Although these injuries are more dramatic than those usually encountered in abused infants, the types of forces inducing these injuries are likely the same.

Drawing on these earlier observations and his extensive experience, Caffey formulated his views on the pathogenesis of these injuries in abused infants (1). He postulated that manually administered severe forces result in stripping of the loosely at-

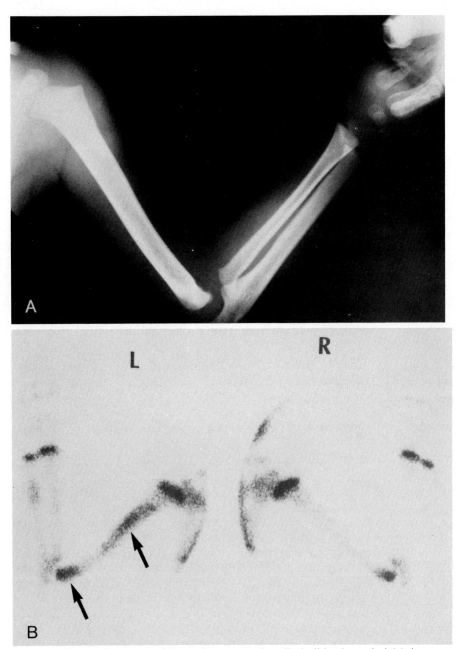

Figure 2.4. *A*, Initial radiographs of the left upper extremity in this abused child show no abnormalities. *B*, Technetium bone scan shows several areas of increased activity consistent with subperiosteal hemorrhage (*arrows*). (Reproduced with permission from Sty JR, Starshak RJ: The role of bone scintigraphy in the evaluation of the suspected abused child. *Radiology* 146:369–375, 1983.)

tached periosteum along the shafts of the long bones. Such forces are applied as a child is grabbed by an extremity and pulled or twisted. When the extremities are used as a "handle" for shaking, similar forces are applied. These injuries, however, do not require direct application of force via the extremity. Identical lesions can be encoun-

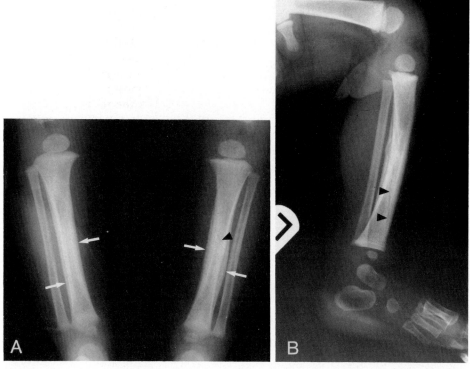

Figure 2.5. *A*, AP views of the lower legs of a 7-month-old abused infant demonstrate periosteal reaction along both tibial diaphyses (*arrows*). A faint radiolucency (*arrowhead*) is noted in the left tibial diaphysis. *B*, A lateral view of the lower leg confirms a nondisplaced oblique fracture (*arrowheads*). Beaking of the posterior and medial aspects of the left proximal tibial metaphysis is likely related to a healed metaphyseal injury.

tered in infants who have been shaken while being gripped around the thorax. The massive accelerational and decelerational forces developed as the extremities flail about produce substantial bony alterations. As will be noted, this concept of infant shaking either by the extremities or the thorax is a recurrent theme throughout the various aspects of infant abuse. Of course, direct blows to the extremity may result in subperiosteal hemorrhage; however, it is these indirect torsional, accelerational, and decelerational forces that account for the majority of skeletal injuries noted in child abuse.

THE METAPHYSEAL LESIONS

For those physicians and other professionals dealing with cases of child abuse, there is a proverbial question that inevitably arises. Is there a radiologic alteration that, regardless of history in an otherwise normal patient, can be viewed as "diagnostic" of nonaccidental injury? The classically described metaphyseal lesions of the long bones satisfy this definition more closely than any other skeletal or visceral abnormality occurring in cases of child abuse. The author agrees with numerous other authorities that the classic metaphyseal "corner" fracture and "bucket-handle" lesions are virtually pathognomonic of infant abuse (20, 28–30). Other terms that are commonly employed to describe these injuries include metaphyseal infractions, avulsion fractures, and metaphyseal flags. Although metaphyseal injuries may vary in location, extent of involvement, and degree of separation of fragments, and can be strikingly influenced by technical factors, the fundamental anatomic alterations are similar in most cases.

Until recently, conclusions regarding the essential nature of these lesions have been derived from speculation. Some authors have even suggested that an underlying state of metaphyseal fragility leads to these injuries (31, 32). This view, however, is not held by a significant number of authorities on the subject.

According to Caffey, "much of the morbid anatomy and causal mechanisms can be inferred from the radiographic changes" (24). Caffey believed these metaphyseal injuries were closely tied etiologically to traumatically induced periosteal separation. Stressing the anchoring of the periosteum to the epiphyseal cartilage, he stated: "After the application of injuring force to the bone, it is transmitted to these terminal levels of tightest attachment, where, when the injuring force is sufficiently strong, bits of cartilage and bone are torn off and displayed in a variety of patterns" (24). He suggested that when a "small chunk" of bone is avulsed from the peripheral margin of the metaphysis, it projects as a discrete metaphyseal fragment. This pattern is generally referred to as a corner fracture. When a crescentic fragment is pulled from the zone of provisional calcification, and tipped into an oblique plane, a bucket-handle appearance results. Caffey thus concluded that metaphyseal infractions noted in young infants are a consequence of avulsion of peripheral metaphyseal fragments of variable size at the point of insertion of the periosteum. This view has received wide acceptance, and Caffey's classic diagram depicting the findings has been repeatedly reproduced in journals and textbooks (20, 33–37). In 1984, the author and coworkers undertook an in-depth study of the pre- and postmortem radiologic features combined with histologic analyses of metaphyses from a group of abused infants. This work, which was subsequently published, provides some insights into the nature of these peculiar lesions (38).

The fundamental histologic lesion is a series of microfractures occurring in a planar fashion through the most immature portion of metaphyseal primary spongiosa (Fig. 2.6). There is disruption of the delicate trabeculae and central calcified cores that traverse this region (Fig. 2.7). Consequently, the cellularity and the trabecular density in the subepiphyseal zone is diminished. At high magnification remodeling is evident, with numerous osteoclasts aligned along the scalloped trabecular margins. The fracture plane is through the most immature metaphyseal bone, and thus the resultant fracture fragment encompasses two contiguous mineralized regions, the zone of calcified cartilage of the epiphyseal plate and a thin metaphyseal zone of primary spongiosa. Because the plane of injury extends to the periphery of the bone, a characteristic histologic pattern is evident (Fig. 2.8). The plane tends to undermine an isolated osseous peripheral fragment that encompasses the subperiosteal collar of bone. The resultant peripheral fragment will thus be of greater thickness than the central portion. The actual size of this peripheral margin will depend upon the point at which the planar fracture intersects the subperiosteal bone. The result is separation from the metaphysis of a mineralized mass consisting of a thin disc centrally and a variably thicker peripheral margin.

Although periosteal new bone formation may be present in lesions with significant displacement, it is frequently absent in milder injuries. Lesions may extend across the entire metaphysis, resulting in a round or ovoid mineralized disc fragment. However, incomplete lesions may be seen where the plane of injury extends only partially across the metaphyseal surface. The age of the lesion will influence the cellularity of the injured region, and the amount of remodeling present. In most cases, hemorrhage is conspicuously absent, and staining for iron is negative. Presumably, hemorrhage occurring at the time of injury is rapidly cleared. Although radiologic changes are usually present, lesser microscopic injury may be associated with minimal or no radiologic abnormalities (Fig. 2.9).

Radiologic Alterations

As the fundamental histologic lesion is a transmetaphyseal disruption of the primary spongiosa, an analysis of the radiographic features must be consistent with this micro-

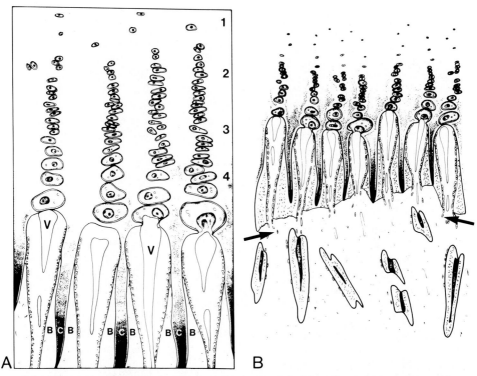

Figure 2.6. The metaphyseal lesion in abused infants. *A*, Schematic representation of the normal metaphyseal-epiphyseal junction. The zones of resting (*1*), proliferating (*2*), hypertrophying (*3*), and calcified (*4*) cartilage are evident. Cartilage cells degenerate and vascular (*V*) ingrowth occurs. The primary spongiosa is formed as columns of new bone (*B*) are deposited around central calcified cartilaginous cores (*C*). *B*, The metaphyseal lesion is a planar injury (*arrows*) through the immature primary spongiosa.

scopic pattern of injury. The most subtle indication of injury is a transverse lucency within the subepiphyseal region of the metaphysis (Fig. 2.10). Adjacent to this lucency is a linear radiodensity that abuts the epiphyseal plate. The region represents both the zone of provisional calcification and a minute thickness of metaphysis that remains attached to the epiphysis. This radiolucency is the actual plane of disruption occurring within the primary spongiosa. The lucency may be vague with indistinct margins, or may appear as a sharply defined radiolucent band (Fig. 2.11). This lucency may be apparent in one projection and invisible in another. Its appearance is influenced by the severity of the bony injury, the degree of displacement of the fragments, and the chronicity of the process. If there is insufficient trabecular disruption to produce

significant alterations in regional bone density, the radiographs may be normal.

These metaphyseal lucencies may be indistinguishable from those noted in patients who are chronically stressed, in particular those with leukemia. However, the lucencies in these cases are generally symmetrical, often associated with diffuse demineralization, and not accompanied by other bony alterations suggesting abuse (39, 40).

Given the planar nature of the metaphyseal lesion, a model of the resultant fragment can be constructed (Fig. 2.12). The fracture fragment will be comprised of epiphysis, physis, and a thin layer of metaphyseal bone. The radiographically visible calcium density will consist of the zone of calcified cartilage and a thin layer of primary spongiosa. The peripheral margin of the fragment will encompass the periosteal

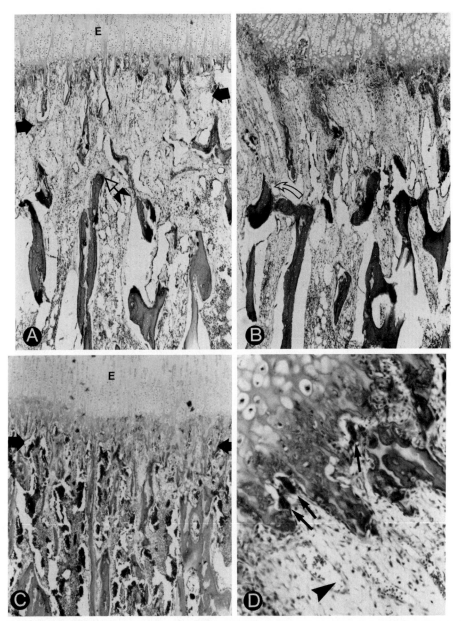

Figure 2.7. Distal right tibia of a 3-month-old abused infant with comparison section from normal infant. *A*, Photomicrograph of the right distal epiphyseal plate (*E*) and the metaphysis. Note that the subepiphyseal zone (*solid arrows*) differs from the remainder of the metaphysis, as evidenced by fewer nucleated cells and a paucity of trabeculae (*open arrow*). Hematoxylin and eosin (H&E) ×160. *B*, Photomicrograph of another region of the same section as *A*, Trabecular (*open arrow*) disruption and discontinuity are more striking. *C*, Photomicrograph of normal tibial metaphysis of a 3-month-old child with no history of abuse. Note continuity of metaphyseal trabeculae with chondrocyte columns of epiphyseal plate (*E*) and cellularity of subepiphyseal zone (*arrows*). H&E ×160. *D*, Subepiphyseal zone of same specimen as *A* and *B* reveals numerous osteoclasts (*arrows*) and subepiphyseal zone (*arrowhead*) containing loose fibrous tissue with little bone and few trabeculae. H&E ×560.

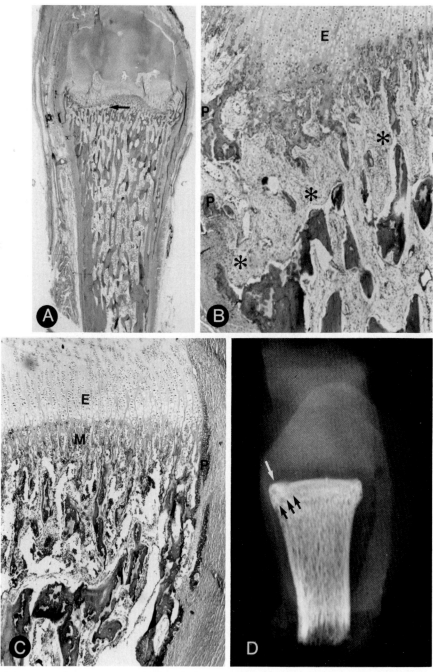

Figure 2.8. Distal left ulna of a 5-month-old abused infant (*A* and *B*) and comparable region of a normal 3-month-old infant (*C*). At lower power (*A*), a faint metaphyseal separation is evident (*arrow*). At intermediate magnification (*B*), plane of separation (*) veers away from the epiphyseal plate (*E*) and undermines the periosteal collar (*P*). *C*, Demonstrates intact trabeculae and periosteal collar (*P*) at junction of epiphyseal plate (*E*) and metaphysis (*M*) in normal infant. H&E ×12, ×160, ×160, respectively. *D*, Corresponding radiograph of specimen shows only subtle metaphyseal radiolucency (*black arrows*) that appears to undermine a metaphyseal fragment (*white arrow*).

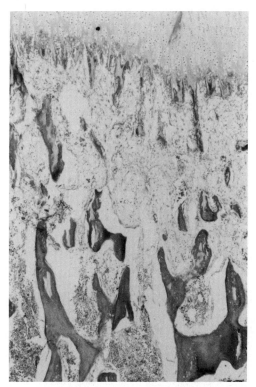

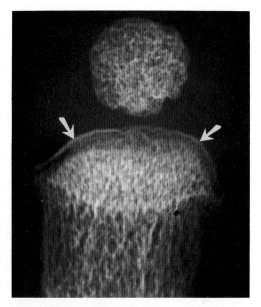

Figure 2.10. Specimen radiograph of right humerus from 3-month-old abused infant corresponding to histologic material in Figure 2.9. Note ill-defined radiolucency in subepiphyseal region of the metaphysis. A resultant mineralized fragment consisting of immature metaphyseal bone and calcified cartilage is produced (*arrows*).

Figure 2.9. Medium power photomicrograph of right proximal humerus of a 3-month-old abused infant. Note trabecular amputation and paucity of cells in the subepiphyseal region.

collar, a circumferential band of subperiosteal bone that extends a variable distance beyond the zone of provisional calcification. Excluding this relatively thick peripheral margin, the remainder of the disc-like fragment will possess minimal radiodensity. It is this relatively thick peripheral margin of bone that produces the corner fractures and bucket-handle configurations, and has led authors to conceive of this lesion as involving only a peripheral rim of bone rather than a plane of injury across the metaphysis.

The radiographic projection will influence the appearance of the disc-like metaphyseal fragment. If viewed tangentially the fragment, as defined by its dense, rounded peripheral margin, will be seen as a linear density separated from the metaphysis by a radiolucent band. If the orientation of the metaphysis and the radiographic projection are appropriate, the margin of this fragment

will be viewed end-on at the periphery of the bone as a discrete fragment. The resultant appearance has been termed the corner fracture (Fig. 2.13). A similar discrete appearing fragment will often be noted on the lateral projection, which provides an indication that these two apparently separate triangular fragments are in fact portions of the same larger disc of bone that has been separated from the metaphysis (Fig. 2.14). A view of the epiphyseal plate in oblique rather than tangential projection results in a continuous crescentic bone density that is, in fact, the dense peripheral margin of the disc-like fragment that has been separated from the metaphysis (Fig. 2.15). Although the disc contains mineralized cartilage and bone across this entire surface, it is only the dense peripheral margin of this disc that is visualized radiographically. This arc-like bony fragment has been referred to as the bucket-handle lesion. Thus, in one projection a fragment may appear as a corner

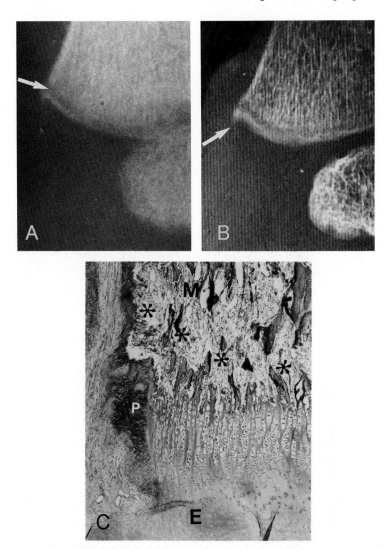

Figure 2.11. Lateral aspect of the distal femur of a 5-month-old abused infant. *A,* Antimortem radiograph demonstrates metaphyseal radiolucency (*arrow*). *B,* Specimen radiograph demonstrates a more clearly defined metaphyseal radiolucency and a peripheral extension of subperiosteal bone (*arrow*). *C,* Corresponding histologic material oriented to provide comparison. A plane of disrupted and bent trabeculae (*) extends across the metaphysis (*M*). As the plane of cleavage extends peripherally, it undermines the periosteal collar (*P*). This results in a separate mineralized fragment that is thin centrally with a thicker peripheral component. *E* = epiphysis.

fracture, and in another view a bucket-handle appearance may be noted (Fig. 2.16).

In addition to the projection, a variety of other factors can influence the radiographic appearance. Although many of these lesions extend across the entire metaphyseal margin resulting in a complete disc-like fragment, incomplete injuries that separate only a fragment of this disc can also occur. The resultant lesion may appear as a corner fracture, or simply a radiolucency extending across a portion of the metaphysis (Fig. 2.17). The shape of the specific metaphysis involved will also influence the radiographic appearance. If the metaphyseal margin is relatively straight, such as in the tibia, a nearly flat disc will result in a continuous fragment of bone that is seen as a

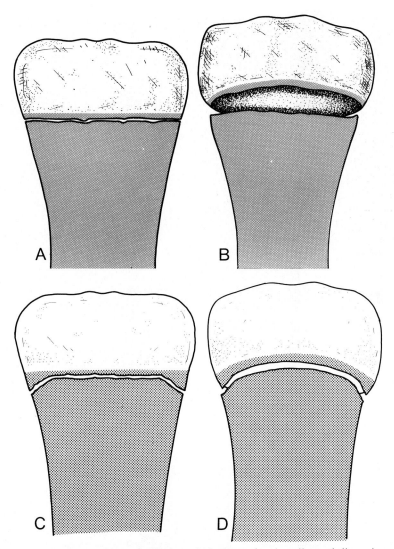

Figure 2.12. Model of the metaphyseal lesion. *A,* A planar fracture through the primary spongiosa produces metaphyseal lucency. *B,* If the metaphysis is tipped or simply projected at an obliquity to the x-ray beam, the margin of the resultant fragment is projected with a bucket-handle appearance. *C,* If the peripheral fragment is substantially thicker than the central fragment and the plane of injury is viewed tangentially, a corner fracture appearance will result. *D,* If the metaphysis is displaced or projected at an obliquity, as in *B,* a thicker bucket handle will be apparent.

crescent or bucket-handle lesion. The biconvex shape of the distal femur is less likely to allow a projection of any resultant fragment in its entirety, and the radiographic appearance is more likely to be that of a corner fracture (Fig. 2.18*A*). However, if the knee is flexed, the corner fracture will appear to be continuous with a larger arc of bone, producing the pattern of a bucket-handle lesion (Fig. 2.18*B*).

The age and degree of healing of the lesion will also influence the radiographic features. The presence of new bone formation and bone resorption may produce indistinctness of the margins of the fragments. The planar lucency may be obscured by

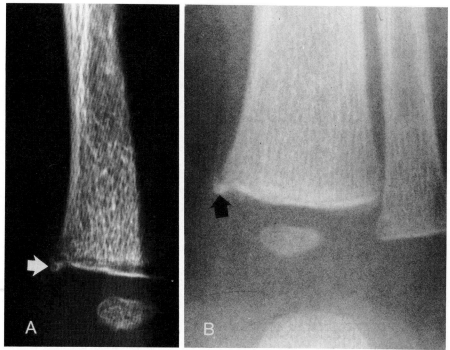

Figure 2.13. Distal tibia of a 3-month-old abused infant. *A,* Specimen radiograph reveals a corner fracture medially (*arrow*) in addition to a conspicuous metaphyseal radiolucency. *B,* Antimortem radiograph tangential to the metaphyseal margin also demonstrates the corner fracture (*arrow*) with the suggestion of a radiolucent band.

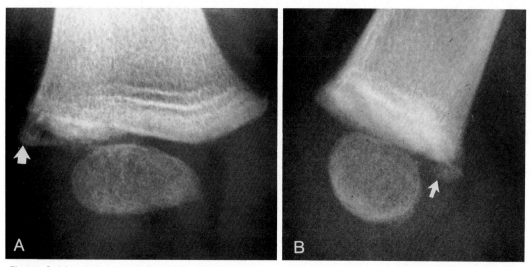

Figure 2.14. Anteroposterior (*A*) and lateral (*B*) views of the distal femur of a 5-month-old abused infant. A corner fracture appearance is noted on both AP and lateral projections (*arrows*). Although the appearances suggest two discrete triangular fragments, they are, in fact, portions of a larger mineralized disc viewed tangentially. Note sclerosis and radiolucency extending across the entire metaphyseal surface on the lateral projection.

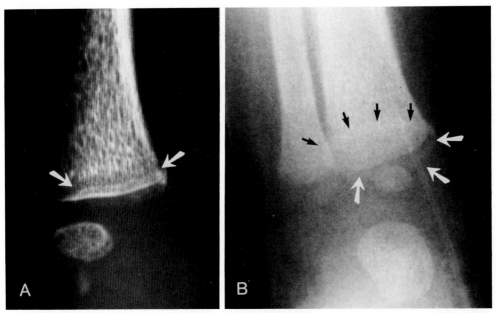

Figure 2.15. Distal right tibia of a 3-month-old abused infant. Corresponding histologic material is presented in Figure 2.7. *A*, Radiograph of postmortem specimen reveals only zone of transverse radiolucency in the subepiphyseal region (*arrows*). *B*, Antimortem radiograph obtained at slight obliquity to the metaphyseal surface reveals a bucket-handle pattern (*arrows*). An indwelling venous catheter is present.

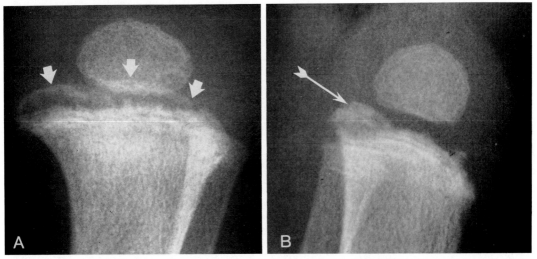

Figure 2.16. Anteroposterior (*A*) and lateral (*B*) views of the proximal tibia of an abused infant. A bucket-handle pattern is present in the AP projection (*arrows*) and a corner fracture configuration is present on the lateral view (*arrow*). These fragments are portions of the same mineralized disc, viewed in different projections. Note sclerosis and irregularity along the metaphyseal surface, indicating a healing lesion.

surrounding sclerosis (see Fig. 2.16*B*). The size of the peripheral fragment may vary substantially, and on occasion a thick peripheral fragment will dominate the radio-

graphic picture (Fig. 2.19). In the absence of additional injury, the radiolucency will become less distinct. As the cartilage is preserved, normal endochondral bone forma-

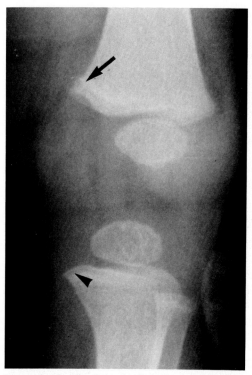

Figure 2.17. Radiologically incomplete lesions at the knee in an abused infant. Sclerosis is noted about a metaphyseal lucency, extending only across the medial half of the distal femur (*arrow*). A similar incomplete zone of radiolucency with less bone production is noted in the proximal tibia (*arrowhead*).

tion will continue, and no growth disturbance will result. The radiographic appearance will thus return to normal within several weeks. If there is repeated injury, however, continued disruption of trabeculae will result in a gross disorganization of the metaphyseal-trabecular architecture (Fig. 2.20). Periosteal new bone formation is frequently absent, but, when present, it is generally modest in degree and may simply produce a haziness in the adjacent cortical contour. When extensive periosteal reaction is present, it reflects either displacement of the resultant fracture fragment or an actual stripping of the periosteum with associated subperiosteal hemorrhage. In such cases, the cloak of periosteal reaction will be continuous with the bucket-handle lesion at the metaphysis (Fig. 2.20). With healing, the periosteal new bone is incorporated within the original cortex, and this may lead to a blocking or squaring of the metaphysis.

The histologic alterations, and associated radiologic changes as defined, indicate that the basic pattern of injury is not circumferential but planar. Fragments are not simply avulsed from the periphery of the metaphysis, as suggested by Caffey, but rather a transmetaphyseal disruption of trabeculae of the primary spongiosa occurs. The resultant fracture fragment is a slab of bone and calcified cartilage. The density is greatest in the periphery due to more bony trabeculae, as well as bone laid down beneath the periosteal collar. Variations in position, projection, and size and shape of the fragment will result in the characteristic patterns classically associated with metaphyseal injury.

Although the histopathologic features are at variance with Caffey's speculations, his views regarding the types of injuries giving rise to these lesions are entirely consistent with the anatomic alterations. The accelerational and decelerational forces occurring as an infant is shaken by the extremities or the thorax, and the torsional and tractional forces applied as an infant is twisted or pulled by an extremity, subject the metaphyses to stresses that the immature bony trabeculae are incapable of withstanding. The result is disruption of the earliest complete unit of endochondral ossification, a cartilage core arising from the epiphyseal plate, surrounded by a fine layer of trabecular bone.

EPIPHYSEAL PLATE INJURIES

Silverman has stressed the importance of cartilaginous epiphyseal plate injuries in child abuse (41, 42). As noted, most metaphyseal-epiphyseal lesions involve the primary spongiosa of the metaphysis. However, there are undoubtedly instances of epiphyseal separation that occur as a result of disruption of the cartilage of the epiphyseal plate. These fractures have been studied extensively by Salter and Harris, who have produced the lesion experimentally in rabbits (43). These laboratory studies revealed the plane of injury to course principally through the zone of hypertrophying carti-

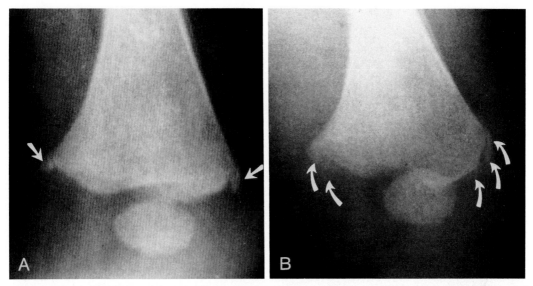

Figure 2.18. Anteroposterior views of the distal femur of an abused infant. *A*, A standard frontal projection obtained tangential to the metaphysis reveals typical corner fractures (*arrows*). *B*, A view with the knee flexed, resulting in a projection oblique to the metaphysis, reveals a bucket-handle configuration (*arrows*). Note periosteal reaction along the femoral shaft.

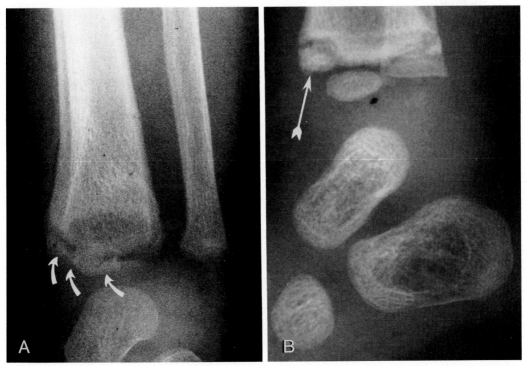

Figure 2.19. Oblique (*A*) and lateral (*B*) views of the distal tibia of a 5-month-old abused infant demonstrate that bucket-handle fragment (*arrows*, part *A*) and corner fracture (*arrow*, part *B*) are all portions of a continuous disc of bone. Fracture plane undermines a thicker portion of bone peripherally, accounting for the conspicuous appearance in this patient. Note extensive periosteal reaction along the medial aspect of the tibial shaft, which is continuous with the bucket-handle fragment.

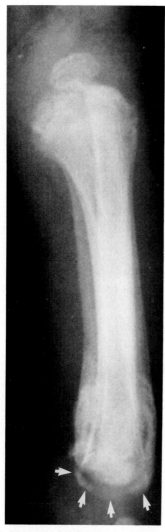

Figure 2.20. Chronic injuries involving the tibia in an abused infant. Proximally, there is mixed radiolucency and sclerosis involving a substantial thickness of metaphysis, probably related to repeated trauma. There is extensive periosteal new bone formation along the shaft. This cloak of periosteal reaction is continuous with a distal bucket-handle lesion (*arrows*).

lage (Figs. 2.21*A* and *B*). In humans, this line of injury may be more undulating, and may extend variable distances into the primary spongiosa (Fig. 2.21*C*). The fracture margins may encompass large fragments of epiphysis and/or metaphysis, in which cases they are readily diagnosed. The fracture may, however, be purely cartilaginous

in nature, making diagnosis prior to signs of healing very difficult (see Chapter 3). The frequency of these injuries in cases of accidental injury prompted Salter and Harris to devise a classification that has proven to be quite useful in assessing the prognosis of injuries involving the epiphyseal plate (Fig. 2.22). The vast majority of these fractures occur in patients beyond infancy and are accidental in nature. True Salter-Harris type fractures are unusual with child abuse, but a knowledge of this classification is useful in an analysis of the occasional cases that fulfill the appropriate criteria.

DIAPHYSEAL FRACTURES

A variety of patterns of diaphyseal injury occur in infants. None possesses a specificity comparable to metaphyseal lesions for abuse, and factors such as the patient's age and an absent or inconsistent history provide clues to the diagnosis. The pattern of injury (e.g., the spiral fracture), although not specific, should suggest the possibility of abuse (see Chapter 3). Fractures involving the shaft may be extremely subtle and, much like accidental "toddler's" fractures, may be visible only with healing (see Fig. 2.5). These fractures may, in fact, extend to the metaphyseal region and coexist with typical lesions in these areas.

DISLOCATIONS

Dislocations are rarely encountered in abused children. Malalignment of bones sharing an articulation usually indicates metaphyseal-epiphyseal injury rather than dislocation (see Chapter 3). When dislocations do occur, they are likely secondary to massive injury, and are accompanied by adjacent fracture. Presumably, the ligamentous and capsular supports of most joints are stronger than the adjacent metaphyseal-epiphyseal complexes.

MISCELLANEOUS INJURIES

In infants and young children, certain fractures have a high specificity for abuse owing to their unusual locations. Scapular injuries (see Chapter 4), injuries involving

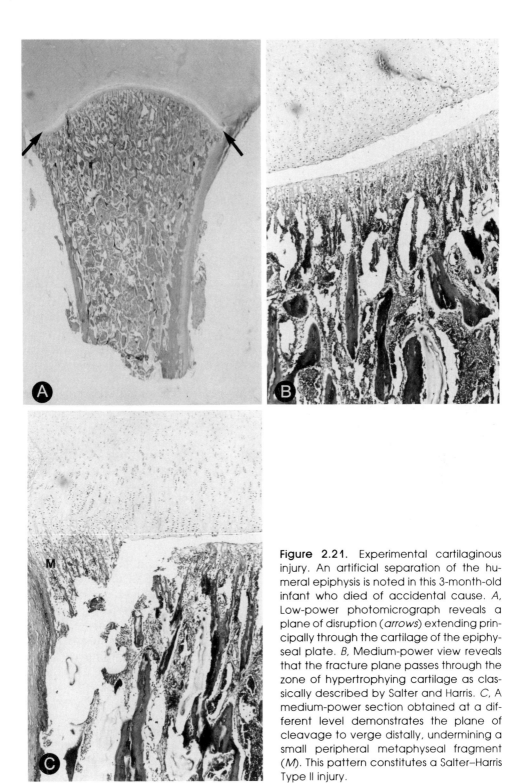

Figure 2.21. Experimental cartilaginous injury. An artificial separation of the humeral epiphysis is noted in this 3-month-old infant who died of accidental cause. *A*, Low-power photomicrograph reveals a plane of disruption (*arrows*) extending principally through the cartilage of the epiphyseal plate. *B*, Medium-power view reveals that the fracture plane passes through the zone of hypertrophying cartilage as classically described by Salter and Harris. *C*, A medium-power section obtained at a different level demonstrates the plane of cleavage to verge distally, undermining a small peripheral metaphyseal fragment (*M*). This pattern constitutes a Salter–Harris Type II injury.

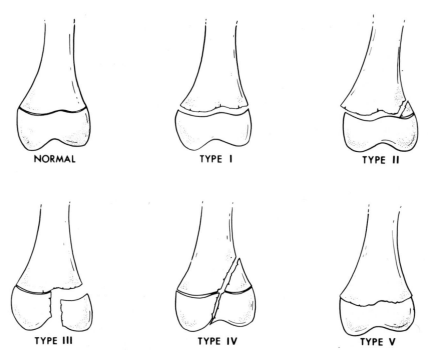

Figure 2.22. Salter–Harris classification of epiphyseal plate injuries. Type I: Cartilaginous injury only. Type II: Plane of fracture encompasses a metaphyseal fragment. Type III: Plane of fracture encompasses an epiphyseal fragment. Type IV: Both epiphyseal and metaphyseal fragments are produced. Type V: A crush injury with compression of the epiphyseal plate. Types IV and V carry the greatest likelihood of growth arrest and subsequent deformity.

the small bones of the hands and feet (see Chapter 3), and spinal injuries (see Chapter 5) in otherwise normal children provide a level of specificity for abuse approximating that accompanying the classic metaphyseal lesions.

Several authors have reported diffuse bony sclerosis or "chalkiness" involving the long bones of abused children (24, 44). Silverman believes, however, that the sclerosis is secondary to bone reaction resulting from repetitive traumatic stress (45).

Skeletal Survey versus Bone Scintigraphy

A problem that continues to plague diagnostic imaging of occult skeletal injury relates to the choice of primary screening modality. Traditionally, skeletal surveys have been used for this purpose. In recent years, bone scintigraphy has gained increas-

ing popularity as an adjunct to skeletal survey, and in some centers it is used as a primary screening tool. Studies comparing the relative utility of these examinations in cases of suspected abuse are limited and often hindered by small numbers of patients, variation in imaging protocols, different degrees of technologist and interpreter expertise, and bias of the investigators. A variety of factors influence the suitability of either procedure as a screening tool, including availability, cost, and radiation exposure, but the primary consideration in this issue should be which study ultimately provides the most information relating to the presence or absence of physical injury.

Despite being a subject of wide debate (46–51), there have been relatively few studies specifically assessing the respective value of radiography versus scintigraphy as a screening tool for child abuse (52–56). The largest and best controlled study on the subject originated from the Children's Hospital of Milwaukee, a large pediatric facility where radiologic and nuclear medicine studies were performed by experienced pediatric radiologists. The study included 261 infants and children suspected of being abused who underwent radiographic skeletal surveys and bone scintigraphy. Scintigraphy was performed with meticulous attention to technique and converging collumation in small infants. Sedation was required in uncooperative patients. Complete radiographic skeletal surveys were obtained, including frontal and lateral views of the thoracolumbar spine. Assessment of the skull by scintigraphy was not included in the study, and the authors emphasized the superiority of radiography in the assessment of skull fractures.

Of 261 children examined by both techniques, 120 demonstrated scintigraphic abnormalities at one or more sites, and 105 demonstrated one or more radiologic abnormalities. Radiography yielded false-negative results in 32 patients; scintigraphy yielded two false-negative studies. Although no "gold standard" could be applied to the cases where abnormalities were apparent only on scintigraphy, the study clearly demonstrates the superior sensitivity of scintigraphy to radiography under the conditions described by the authors. Other studies have shown higher percentages of false-negative bone scans (20, 55, 56). Merten et al., in a multicenter study, reviewed the radiologic findings in 563 abused infants and children (20). In the limited number of cases undergoing both scintigraphy and skeletal surveys, a false-negative rate of 27% was encountered. The studies of Sty and Starshak (52) and Merten et al. (20) prompted a useful exchange of views in the editorial section of *Radiology* (47–51). On the basis of these communications and other relevant sources in the literature, the relative merits of these two studies as screening procedures can be assessed (Table 2.3).

Sensitivity. Bone scans are more sensitive than skeletal surveys in detecting abnormalities. Lesions found on scintigraphy and not on radiography can only be assumed to be indicative of occult trauma, because no "gold standard" is available. Undoubtedly, some of these false-negative

Table 2.3
Comparison of Skeletal Surveys and Bone Scintigraphy

	Skeletal Survey	Bone Scintigraphy
Sensitivity	Moderate	High
Specificity	High	Low
Sedation	Rare	Common
Dose		
Gonadal	Very low	Low
Metaphyseal	Very low	Moderate
Availability	High	Varies
Need for additional studies	Occasionally	Always
Cost	Low	70–300% higher
Technical factor dependency	Moderate	High
Interpreter dependency	Moderate	High

radiologic studies may in fact be false-positive radionuclide exams. Despite these limitations, on theoretical grounds it is reasonable to assume that a physiologic study such as bone scintigraphy will, under ideal circumstances, be more sensitive than an anatomic one. The superior sensitivity of scintigraphy is most evident in the assessment of rib fractures, particularly those involving the costovertebral junction, acute nondisplaced long bone fractures, and subperiosteal hemorrhage (54). Skeletal surveys are clearly more sensitive in the detection of skull fractures, and in subtle bilateral metaphyseal injury. Spinal fractures and scapular fractures are probably best assessed with radiography.

Specificity. Radiography provides a high level of specificity. Most traumatic injuries can be determined to be such with radiography. Beyond this, certain lesions such as the bucket-handle or corner fracture are virtually diagnostic of abuse. Other patterns of injury as outlined in this text provide varying levels of confidence for the diagnosis of abuse. Although scintigraphic patterns may provide some hints to underlying etiology, in most cases they are either "negative" or "positive." Radiography of all areas positive on bone scans is essential to provide optimal diagnostic accuracy.

Sedation. Skeletal surveys rarely require sedation because proper restraints and use of rapid exposure times will overcome most problems of patient motion. Scintigraphy demands a motionless patient, and to avoid a limited study sedation is frequently employed.

Dose. Scintigraphy provides substantially greater exposure to the metaphyses, the gonads, and the whole body as compared to skeletal surveys performed with customary low- and ultra-low-dose rare earth film–screen combinations (see Chapter 14).

Availability. In most cases, a skeletal assessment can be performed during routine working hours, but on occasion the clinical situation may warrant an emergency study. Although nuclear medicine may be available, the radiographic study is generally performed with more ease in a timely fashion.

Need for Additional Films. Skull films must always supplement a bone scan, and any positive scintigraphic abnormality must be subsequently assessed radiographically. This usually requires a separate visit to the radiology department. Skeletal surveys can be reviewed while the patient remains in the department, and any additional films can be obtained at that time.

Cost. In most centers, radionuclide studies are substantially more costly than skeletal surveys. At various centers, the cost of a bone scan is between 70% and 300% more than the radiographic skeletal survey. In addition, the cost of the routine skull films and any further radiographs will inflate the cost of evaluation.

Technical Factors Dependency. Both scintigraphic and radiographic methods require technically near-perfect studies to optimize detection of abnormalities. Radiographic studies of this quality can generally be obtained in most radiology departments that maintain an overall high technical quality of their examinations. A similar quality of bone scan is harder to achieve in a general nuclear medicine department performing relatively limited numbers of examinations in young patients. Problems of patient motion, improper collimation, and a variety of other difficulties may add to substantial degradation of images.

Interpreter Dependency. Technical problems are further compounded by limited expertise of the interpreting physician. Most radiologists are familiar with the various patterns of injury encountered in abused children, and can be expected to identify radiologic abnormalities with a high level of proficiency. In contrast, detection of subtle alterations on scintigraphy, as well as recognition of the technical limitations of the study, may be difficult for all but the most experienced pediatric radiologists. Perhaps the most specific indicators of abuse, the various metaphyseal lesions, can be extremely difficult to assess scintigraphically, especially when bilateral. The globular rather than ovoid appearance of the epiphysis, an abnormal scintigraphic finding, may be evident to the expert but remain overlooked by the usual interpreter.

These comments should in no way detract from the great value of scintigraphy in the evaluation of child abuse. Not only should it continue to be performed as a primary tool in centers that have shown it to be superior to radiography, but all institutions should attempt to bring the quality of these studies to the highest possible level. However, in those departments where the quality of such examinations cannot be ensured, scintigraphy should not be a primary screening method.

At the University of Massachusetts, a general hospital with a busy pediatric department with nuclear medicine performed by capable nonradiologists, skeletal surveys are the primary investigative study in cases of abuse (see Table 2.4). They are routinely performed in infants and young children. In older children, studies are chosen on an individual basis, depending upon the clinical findings and index of suspicion. Scintigraphy is a valuable adjunct in cases where limited or equivocal findings are encountered radiographically. In instances where a strong clinical suspicion of abuse is present, and the skeletal survey is negative, scintigraphy will also be performed.

The issue of scintigraphy versus radiography as the primary investigative tool in cases of abuse is not likely to be resolved in

Table 2.4
The Skeletal Survey

AP supine chest†
Lateral chest*†
AP humeri
AP forearms
PA hands
AP pelvis
Lateral lumbar spine*
AP femurs
AP tibias
AP feet
AP skull
Lateral skull

Note: All positive sites should be viewed in at least two projections.
* In infants.
† Bone technique.

these pages. Each center needs to make its own decision based upon the local expertise, technical resources, and patient population. As usual, Dr. Walter Berdon of Babies Hospital in New York City has neatly summarized his views on the subject: "so, Sty and Starshak have clearly shown that in the best of worlds, the scintigraphic approach is excellent and probably surpasses radiography.... Unfortunately most of us do not live in the best of worlds" (51).

REFERENCES

1. Caffey J: Multiple fractures in the long bones of infants suffering from chronic subdural hematoma. *Am J Roentgenol (AJR)* 56:163–173, 1946.
2. Meneghello J, Hasbun J: Hematoma subdural y fractura de los huesos largos. *Rev Chil Pediatr* 22:80–83, 1951.
3. Marquezy RA, Bach C, Blondeau M: Hematome sous-dural et fractures multiples des os longs chez un nourrisson de 9 mois. *Arch Fr Pediatr* 9:526–531, 1952.
4. Kugelmann J: Uber symmetrische Spontanfrakturen unbekannter Genese beim Saugling. *Ann Pediatr (Paris)* 178:177–181, 1952.
5. Bakwin H: Roentgenologic changes in the bones following trauma in infants. *J Newark Beth Israel Hosp* 3:17–25, 1952.
6. Bakwin H: Multiple skeletal lesions in young children due to trauma. *J Pediatr* 49:7–15, 1956.
7. Jones HH, Davis JH: Multiple traumatic lesions of the infant skeleton. *Stanford Med Bull* 15:259–273, 1957.
8. Woolley PV Jr, Evans WA Jr: Significance of skeletal lesions in infants resembling those of traumatic origin. *JAMA* 158:539–543, 1955.
9. Neimann N, Beau A, Antoine M, Pierson M, Manciaux M, de Kersauson MC: Les alterations des os long au cours de l'hematome dural chronique du nourrisson. *J Radiol Electr* 39:576–581, 1958.
10. Smith MJ: Subdural hematoma with multiple fractures. Case report. *Am J Roentgenol (AJR)* 63:342–344, 1950.
11. Marie J, Apostolides P, Salet J, Eliachar E, Lyon G: Hematome sous-dural du nourrisson associe a des fractures des membres. *Ann Pediatr (Paris)* 30:1757–1763, 1954.
12. Silverman FN: The roentgen manifestations of unrecognized skeletal trauma in infants. *Am J Roentgenol (AJR)* 69:413–427, 1953.
13. Kempe CH, Silverman FN, Steele BF, Droegemueller W, Silver HK: The battered-child syndrome. *JAMA* 181:105–112, 1962.
14. Buchanan MF: The recognition of non-accidental injury in children. *Practitioner* 229:815–819, 1985.
15. Herndon WA: Child abuse in a military population. *J Pediatr Orthop* 3:73–76, 1983.
16. Kogutt MS, Swischuk LE, Fagan CJ: Patterns of injury and significance of uncommon fractures in the battered child syndrome. *Am J Roentgenol (AJR)* 121:143–149, 1974.
17. Galleno H, Oppenheim WL: The battered child syndrome revisited. *Clin Orthop* 162:11–19, 1982.
18. Ebbin AJ, Gollub MH, Stein AM, Wilson MG: Battered child syndrome at the Los Angeles County General Hospital. *Am J Dis Child* 118:660–667, 1969.
19. Ryan MG, Davis AA, Oates RK: One hundred and eighty-seven cases of child abuse and neglect. *Med J Aust* 2:623–628, 1977.
20. Merten DF, Radkowski MA, Leonidas JC: The abused child. A radiological reappraisal. *Radiology* 146:377–381, 1983.
21. Lauer B, Broeck ET, Grossman M: Battered child syndrome: review of 130 patients with controls. *Pediatrics* 54:67–70, 1974.
22. Akbarnia B, Torg JS, Kirkpatrick J, Sussman S: Manifestations of the battered-child syndrome. *J Bone Joint Surg* 56A:1159–1166, 1974.
23. Caniano DA, Beaver BL, Boles ET Jr: Child abuse. An update on surgical management in 256 cases. *Ann Surg* 203:219–224, 1986.
24. Caffey J: Some traumatic lesions in growing bones other than fractures and dislocations: clinical and radiological features. *Br J Radiol* 30:225–238, 1957.
25. LaCroix P: Origin of the perichondrial osseous ring. First example of a phenomenon of induction in skeletal development. In LaCroix P (ed): *The Organization of Bones.* Philadelphia, The Blakiston Company, 1951, pp 90–97.
26. Snedecor ST, Knapp RE, Wilson HB: Traumatic ossifying periostitis of the newborn. *Surg Gynecol Obstet* 61:385–387, 1935.
27. Snedecor ST, Wilson HB: Some obstetrical injuries to the long bones. *J Bone Joint Surg* 31A:378–384, 1949.
28. Leonidas JC: Skeletal trauma in the child abuse syndrome. *Pediatr Ann* 12:875–881, 1983.
29. Cameron JM, Rae L: The radiological diagnosis. In *Atlas of the Battered Child Syndrome.* London, Churchill Livingstone, 1975, pp 20–50.
30. Hilton S: The accidentally injured and abused child. In Hilton SVW, Edwards DK, Hilton JW

(eds): *Practical Pediatric Radiology*. Philadelphia, WB Saunders, 1984, pp 443–485.

31. Astley R: Multiple metaphyseal fractures in small children (metaphyseal fragility of bone). *Br J Radiol* 26:577–583, 1953.

32. Hiller HG: Battered or not—A reappraisal of metaphyseal fragility. *Am J Roentgenol Radium Ther Nucl Med (AJR)* 114:241–246, 1972.

33. Altman DH, Smith RL: Unrecognized trauma in infants and children. *J Bone Joint Surg* 42A:407–413, 1960.

34. Caffey J: The bones: parent-infant trauma syndrome (PITS; Caffey-Kempe syndrome; battered babe syndrome). In *Pediatric X-Ray Diagnosis*, ed 7. Chicago, Year Book Medical Publishers, 1978, vol 2, pp 1335–1351.

35. Lloyd-Roberts G: The diagnosis of injury of bones and joints in young babies. *Proc R Soc Med* 61:1299–1300, 1968.

36. Krige HN: The abused child complex and its characteristic x-ray findings. *S Afr Med J* 40:490–493, 1966.

37. Straus P, Compere R, Livchitz J, Prot D, Kaplan M: L'apport de la radio-pediatrie au depistage des enfants maltraites. Ses limites. *Ann Radiol (Paris)* 11:159–169, 1968.

38. Kleinman PK, Marks SC, Blackbourne B: The metaphyseal lesion in abused infants: a radiologic-histopathologic study. *AJR* 146:895–905, 1986.

39. Rosenfield NS: Bone manifestations at diagnosis. In *The Radiology of Childhood Leukemia and its Therapy*, ed 2. St Louis, Warren H. Green, Inc., 1982, pp 5–19.

40. Silverman FN: The skeletal lesions in leukemia. Clinical and roentgenographic observations in 103 infants and children, with a review of the literature. *Am J Roentgenol (AJR)* 59:819–844, 1948.

41. Silverman FN: Radiologic aspects and special diagnostic procedures. In Kempe CH, Helfer RE (eds): *The Battered Child*, ed 3. Chicago, University of Chicago Press, 1980, pp 215–240.

42. Silverman FN: The bones. In *Caffey's Pediatric X-Ray Diagnosis*, ed 8. Chicago, Year Book Medical Publishers, 1985, vol 1, pp 780–791.

43. Salter RB, Harris WR: Injuries involving the epiphyseal plate. *J Bone Joint Surg* 45A:587–622, 1963.

44. DeSmet AA, Kuhns LR, Kaufman RA, Holt JF: Bony sclerosis and the battered child. *Skeletal Radiol* 2:39–41, 1977.

45. Silverman FN: Unrecognized trauma in infants, the battered child syndrome, and the syndrome of Ambroise Tardieu. Rigler lecture. *Radiology* 104:337–353, 1972.

46. Diament MJ: Should the radionuclide skeletal survey be used as a screening procedure in suspected child abuse victims? Letters to the editor. *Radiology* 148:573, 1983.

47. Sty JR, Starshak RJ: Should the radionuclide skeletal survey be used as a screening procedure in suspected child abuse victims? Letters to the editor. *Radiology* 148:573–574, 1983.

48. Merten DF, Radkowski MA, Leonidas JC: Should the radionuclide skeletal survey be used as a screening procedure in suspected child abuse victims? Letters to the editor. *Radiology* 148:574, 1983.

49. Conway JJ: Should the radionuclide skeletal survey be used as a screening procedure in suspected child abuse victims? Letters to the editor. *Radiology* 148:574–575, 1983.

50. Merten DF, Radkowski MA, Leonidas JC: Should the radionuclide skeletal survey be used as a screening procedure in suspected child abuse victims? Letters to the editor. *Radiology* 148:575–576, 1983.

51. Berdon WE: Should the radionuclide skeletal survey be used as a screening procedure in suspected child abuse victims? Letters to the editor. *Radiology* 148:576, 1983.

52. Sty JR, Starshak RJ: The role of bone scintigraphy in the evaluation of the suspected abused child. *Radiology* 146:369–375, 1983.

53. Haase GM, Ortiz VN, Sfakianakis GN, Morse TS: The value of radionuclide bone scanning in the early recognition of deliberate child abuse. *J Trauma* 20:873–875, 1980.

54. Smith FW, Gilday DL, Ash JM, Green MD: Unsuspected costo-vertebral fractures demonstrated by bone scanning in the child abuse syndrome. *Pediatr Radiol* 10:103–106, 1980.

55. Pickett WJ, Faleski EJ, Chacko MA, Jarrett RV: Comparison of radiographic and radionuclide skeletal surveys in battered children. *South Med J* 76:207–212, 1983.

56. Jaudes PK: Comparison of radiography and radionuclide bone scanning in the detection of child abuse. *Pediatrics* 73:166–168, 1984.

3 Extremity Trauma

PAUL K. KLEINMAN, M.D

The Lower Extremity

THE FEMUR

Between 1946 and 1952, Caffey and others described the association of femoral fractures with subdural hematomas in infants (1–3). Femoral fractures in infants were also described in several other reports published in the 1950s, and many of those accounts pointed to abuse as a possible cause of injury (4–10). The first chapter on these lesions came to a close with Kempe et al.'s grouping of these and other radiographic and clinical manifestations under the concept of the "battered child syndrome" (11).

The femur and the humerus are the two most frequently fractured long bones in abused children. A review of fractures cited in five large series of abused children reveals the overall incidence of femoral fractures to be 20% (12–16). Several series indicate a close relationship between the etiology of femoral fractures and the age of the injured child. Femoral fractures in infants have a strong association with abuse, whereas similar fractures in older children are usually determined to be accidental (17–19). Beals and Tufts analyzed 80 femoral fractures in children under 4 years of age and found that 8.5% of the fractures were caused by violent (accidental) trauma, 12.5% were pathologic in nature, and 30% were caused by child abuse (19). The remainder occurred from lesser accidental trauma to otherwise normal children. They found femoral fractures secondary to abuse to be more common in children under 1 year of age who were firstborns and had preexisting brain damage. The fractures, which were often bilateral, occurred with two peak incidences, the first at 6 months of age and the

second at 3 years. Anderson reviewed 117 patients with 122 femoral fractures (18). Of 18 children under 13 months of age with femoral fractures, 15 (83%) were abused. Of 24 children under 2 years of age, 19 (79%) were abused. Of these 24 children, two-thirds evidenced only a fractured femur as an indication of abuse. In older children, accidental injuries predominated. Gross and Stranger analyzed 74 femoral fractures occurring in children under 6 years of age (17). Of these fractures, 34 (46%) occurred with confirmed or suspected abuse. In infants under 1 year of age, 17 of 26 fractures (65%) were associated with abuse. Indication of abuse was not always present on the initial admission, and required subsequent admissions and investigation for confirmation.

The Proximal Femur

As in other regions, evaluation of the soft tissues may provide a clue to a traumatic insult. Soft tissue swelling is often difficult to assess about the hips, but may be appreciated as loss of normal fat planes or localized increased soft tissue density. Deviation of the fat planes about the hips can occasionally provide a clue to injury, but minor degrees of rotation and improper positioning may simulate soft tissue injury. Myositis ossificans may subsequently develop in the thigh. A biopsy of evolving myositis can be easily confused with osteogenic malignancy, with disastrous consequences. Rarely, soft tissue foreign bodies such as sewing needles may be identified in a battered child (20).

According to Anderson (18) and Beals and Tufts (19), fractures of the proximal metaphyseal-epiphyseal regions of the femur are much less common than those involving the

29

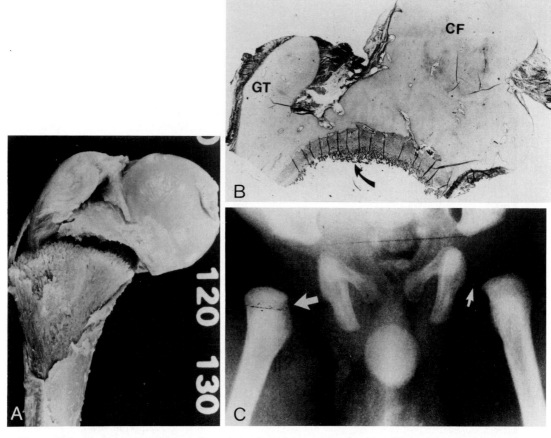

Figure 3.1. *A*, Experimentally produced proximal femoral fracture in stillborn human. A transverse fracture has occurred across the entire physeal-metaphyseal interface. The cartilaginous femoral head and greater trochanter have migrated medially with respect to the neck, resulting in a varus deformity. *B*, Histologic section of fracture fragment that encompasses the capital femur (*CF*) and greater trochanter (*GT*). Although the plane of the fracture is somewhat variable, its principal location is within the primary spongiosa (*arrow*). *C*, AP view of the hips in a 5-week-old abused infant. There is lateral displacement of the right femoral neck (*large arrow*) as compared with the normal left side (*small arrow*). The normal acetabular development weighs against a congenital dislocation of the hip. *D*, Right hip arthrogram reveals a normally positioned femoral head. The metaphysis (*black arrow*) is laterally displaced secondary to a fracture through the physeal-metaphyseal junction. Note confinement of contrast material within the joint, indicating maintenance of capsular attachments (*white arrows*). *E*, At 5 months of age, an irregular metaphysis (*arrows*) is laterally displaced and there is no ossification within the femoral head. *F*, At 8 months of age, coxa vara deformity is present (*arrow*). The femoral head is somewhat dysplastic but seated within the acetabular cavity. A valgus osteotomy was performed. *G*, Despite osteotomy, coxa vara developed at 5 years of age. (Reproduced with permission from Ogden JA, Lee KE, Rudicel SA, Pelker RR: Proximal femoral epiphysiolysis in the neonate. *J Pediatr Orthop* 4:285–292, 1984.)

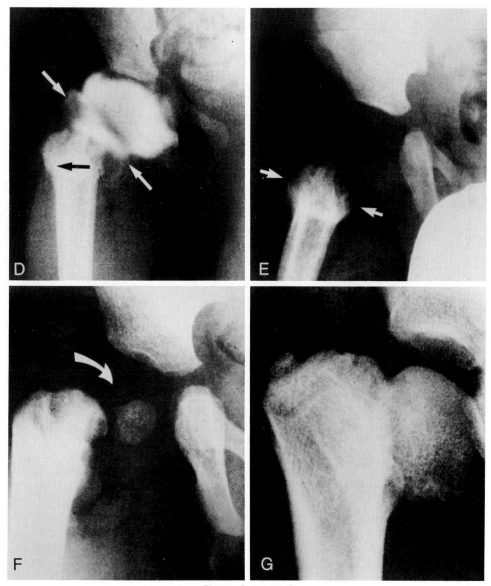

Figure 3.1. *D–G.*

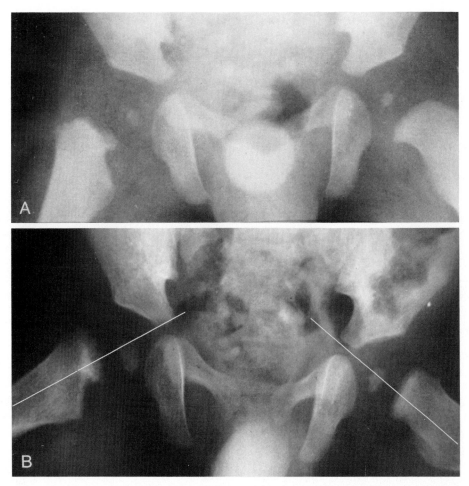

Figure 3.2. An abused infant with proximal femoral fracture. *A,* The right femoral metaphysis is displaced laterally with respect to the femoral head. Femoral heads are similar in size and acetabular development is normal. *B,* A follow-up frog-lateral view of the hip demonstrates persistent displacement. A line drawn through the long axis of the femur intersects the femoral head on the left, but not on the right.

shaft and distal metaphyseal-epiphyseal complexes. Of a total of 48 femoral fractures associated with abuse in these two studies, only 1 involved the femoral neck. This contrasts with the earlier patterns of involvement described by Silverman (5), Woolley and Evans (7), and others in which injuries of the proximal femur appeared to be much more common.

Of all fractures associated with child abuse, none is more interesting or more likely to be associated with long-term orthopedic deformity than injury to the proximal femoral growth plate. The fracture is usually indistinguishable from that arising

as a result of birth injury (see Chapter 11). Descriptions of this fracture and its consequences predate the radiologic literature and have been the subject of many publications. In 1907, Reginald Cheyne Elmslie delivered a lecture for the Royal College of Surgeons of England entitled "Injury and Deformity of the Epiphysis of the Head of the Femur (Coxa Vara)" (21). Elmslie summarized the prior 18 years of discussion on the subject of coxa vara and emphasized the importance of a traumatic etiology, not only in the adolescent but also in the infantile form. He indicated that both accidental injury and birth trauma could result in epiphyseal plate injury, with consequent decrease in the neck shaft angle or coxa vara.

By 1944, 21 cases of traumatic separation of the upper femoral epiphysis due to birth injury had been recorded. Kennedy, in an excellent review of the subject, pointed out that all but one fracture reported in the literature occurred during breech presentation and extraction, or version and breech extraction (22). There was frequent mention of a difficult or prolonged delivery and of the application of strong traction to the legs. Kennedy emphasized that, because the proximal femoral epiphysis was not ossified at birth, the findings were often mistaken for a traumatic subluxation of the hip, a rare occurrence in infancy (22). Only with serial radiographs was it apparent that the ossification center of the femoral head was situated within the acetabulum, and that the fundamental alteration was a traumatic separation of the metaphysis from the epiphysis.

In 1969, Blockey emphasized that many cases of so-called congenital coxa vara were in fact secondary to trauma (23). His four cases clearly established the role of injury in the development of coxa vara, and he speculated as to the role of child abuse in this lesion. Although many articles have illustrated proximal femoral epiphyseal separations, the development of coxa vara and the possible confusion with what is likely a rare developmental condition have not been emphasized (5, 7, 10, 11, 24–35).

Ogden et al. studied proximal femoral epiphyseolysis in six neonates, concluding that injuries related to delivery (five cases) and child abuse (two cases) were essentially identical (36). They also produced neonatal epiphyseal separations in six stillborn human cadavers. The fracture was produced by sudden compression or traction applied to the distal femur until an audible snap was heard (Fig. 3.1A). Histologic examination usually revealed disruption of the hypertrophying cartilage cells as classically described in a Salter–Harris Type I fracture. Interestingly, however, the fracture was noted to propagate into the primary spongiosa of the metaphysis in one case (Fig. 3.1B). This pattern of involvement of the

immature trabeculae of the metaphysis is the characteristic picture associated with metaphyseal lesions elsewhere. In general, periosteal disruption occurred anteriorly but was maintained posteriorly, allowing the displaced metaphysis to "buttonhole" through the tear. Maintenance of the posterior attachment of the periosteum is critical in providing intrinsic stability to the fracture, minimizing the amount of residual deformity.

Radiographically, a fracture of the unossified proximal femur can only be established if displacement of the femoral shaft with respect to the acetabulum has occurred. If the capital femoral epiphysis is unossified, differentiation between a fracture separation and a congenital subluxation of the hip cannot be made with certainty (Fig. 3.1C). A normal-appearing acetabulum weighs against a congenital hip dysplasia and, as noted earlier, true traumatic subluxations of the hip are extremely rare in infancy. Occasionally arthrography is performed in this situation, and contrast material will define a normally positioned, unossified femoral head (Fig. 3.1D). Varying degrees of coxa vara can develop, and val-

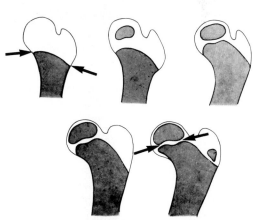

Figure 3.3. Ossification pattern of the proximal femur. At birth (*upper left*), the femoral head, greater trochanter, and much of the femoral neck are composed of cartilage. The fracture at this age occurs through the lower portion of the femoral neck (*arrows*). With increasing age, the fracture is more proximally situated. In the older patient (*right lower*), the fracture will occur in the subcapital region (*arrows*).

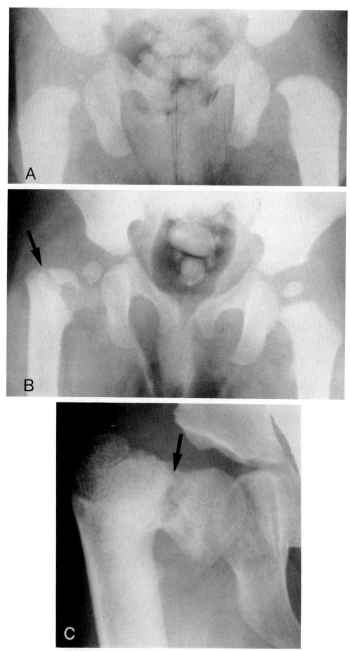

Figure 3.4. Posttraumatic coxa vara. *A*, Initial hip films at age 5 months show normal femoral-acetabular relationships. Other radiographic evidence of abuse was present at this time. *B*, AP view of the hips 2 years later demonstrates right coxa vara deformity with a femoral neck fracture just above the greater trochanter (*arrow*). Sclerosis about the fracture site is evident and the femoral neck is dysplastic. *C*, At age 7, the fracture line has healed, but there is severe coxa vara deformity. Sclerosis and irregularity are noted about the epiphyseal plate (*arrow*). (Reproduced with permission from Blockey NJ: Observations on infantile coxa vara. *J Bone Joint Surg* 51B:106–111, 1969.)

gus osteotomy may be required (Figs. 3.1E–G). Ultrasonography has been shown to be useful in evaluating the position of the femoral head in congenital subluxation of the hip. It should prove to be of benefit in the initial evaluation of these cases and may obviate the need for arthrography.

When the femoral head is ossified, and substantial displacement is present, the diagnosis is simplified. Typically, the femoral neck migrates laterally and proximally with the resultant varus deformity. Mild cases will show only slight lateral displacement of the femoral shaft, which is best appreciated on a frog-lateral projection (Figs. 3.2A and B). A useful sign for detecting minor differences in the position of the femoral heads with respect to the metaphyses can be created by drawing a line through the medullary cavities of the shafts of the femurs. These lines should intersect the femoral heads at identical sites. If there is asymmetry, the more medially displaced epiphysis, with respect to the line, indicates the side of injury. As with Salter–Harris Type I fractures elsewhere, a nondisplaced fracture will be virtually impossible to identify. In

such cases, radionuclide scintigraphy should provide useful information.

With healing, the nature of the underlying anatomic alteration becomes apparent. This repair may display several patterns depending on the degree of displacement, periosteal disruption, and age of the patient. The extent of ossification of the femoral neck and head varies with the patient's age and, since the fracture invariably occurs at the metaphyseal-epiphyseal junction, the site of injury will vary with the patient's age (Fig. 3.3). In infancy, the fracture occurs in the distal portion of the femoral neck (Figs. 3.1A and B). With healing, irregular ossification develops within the femoral neck, with associated varus deformity (Figs. 3.4A–C). At the site of fracture, a persistent radiolucent line is often noted between the irregular new bone formation within the femoral neck and the more normal-appearing bone in the femoral shaft. This vertical lucency may persist for months, but when a stable state is reached union will occur (23). Periosteal new bone formation may be minimal or lacking, in which case these lesions are often erroneously considered to

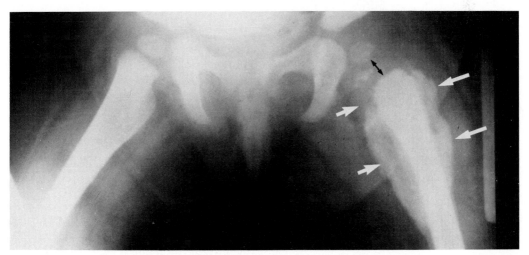

Figure 3.5. Anteroposterior view of the hips and pelvis in an 8-month-old abused infant reveals exuberant callus formation (*white arrows*) about the proximal shaft of the left femur. A biopsy of this lesion was interpreted as an osteogenic sarcoma, but additional radiographs revealed other evidence of abuse. Careful assessment reveals the typical lateral displacement of the femoral neck with respect to the head (*black arrow*) indicating an epiphyseal-metaphyseal injury. (Reproduced with permission from Galleno H, Oppenheim WL: The battered child syndrome revisited. *Clin Orthop* 162:11–19, 1982.)

represent a congenital, rather than a traumatic, injury. When exuberant callus formation occurs and typical displacements are present, the traumatic nature of this lesion will be evident (Fig. 3.5). The growth disturbance at the epiphyseal plate may result in substantial shortening and/or bowing of the extremity. When epiphyseal separation occurs in the older infant and child, the fracture will lie in the subcapital region (Fig. 3.3).

Metaphyseal corner fractures and bucket-handle lesions commonly noted in other regions are rare in the hips. The explanation for this is not readily apparent, but it may relate to the more frequent cartilaginous nature of proximal femoral injuries, in contrast to the more common involvement of the primary spongiosa at other sites. An early sign that suggests injury is a radiolucent line within the metaphysis (Fig. 3.6). Although nonspecific, in the context of

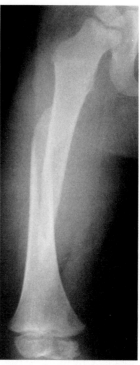

Figure 3.7. Spiral fracture of the femoral shaft. Although these fractures typically occur in abused patients as a result of indirect torsional forces, they can occur with accidental injury, as in this case.

other indications of abuse such abnormalities may widen the overall spectrum of involvement in individual cases.

Swischuk described an unusual case of cortical irregularity, periosteal reaction, and myositis ossificans around the lesser trochanter in a 2-year-old with associated spinal cord injury (37). He believed these findings were related to avulsion of the iliopsoas muscle insertion.

The Femoral Shaft

In contrast to metaphyseal-epiphyseal lesions, which are characteristic of abuse, fractures of the femoral shaft have a much lower specificity. This type of fracture is quite common and, in fact, is probably more frequent than the classic lesions at the ends of the bone. Three of the six femoral fractures noted by Caffey in 1946 involved the shafts of the femurs (1). One of these cases

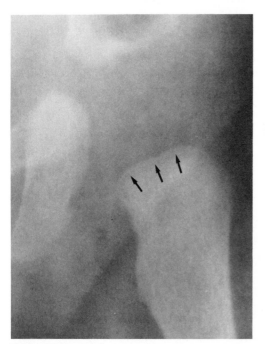

Figure 3.6. Faint zone of lucency (*arrows*) is noted in the subepiphyseal region of this 2-month-old abused infant. This is a nonspecific finding that can be seen in stressed infants, particularly those with underlying malignancy. This patient evidenced typical metaphyseal injuries at other sites.

had a spiral configuration. Kogutt et al. found twice as many transverse and spiral fractures as metaphyseal-epiphyseal fractures in 95 abused children (38). Others have emphasized the frequency of spiral and oblique fractures of the femur with abuse (15–17, 39). The fractures usually occur with a rotational force applied to the extremity during vigorous handling and twisting. Although spiral fractures do occur with accidental injury in children, a severe torsional force developed during a major fall would be required to produce such an injury (Fig. 3.7). Thus, any spiral fracture in an infant, particularly with an incongruous history, should be regarded as highly suspicious of abuse. In contrast to spiral fractures, transverse fractures are usually caused by direct injury. These fractures tend to be more common in the older patient.

Unlike metaphyseal lesions, shaft fractures are frequently associated with a large amount of soft tissue swelling and limitation of movement. Failure to seek immediate attention for such an injury is in itself evidence of neglect. Substantial callus formation will occur around a femoral fracture that has not been immobilized (Fig. 3.8). The extent of periosteal new bone may be so impressive as to simulate a malignancy. A biopsy of this exuberant callus may, in fact, further support the diagnosis of an osteogenic sarcoma (see Fig. 3.5) (40).

These fractures, if untreated, often heal spontaneously with little positional deformity. Malalignment of the fracture site may lead to angular deformity (Fig. 3.8B). As rotation is often present at the fracture sites, a substantial torsional deformity may develop. If there is significant overriding, a shortened extremity will develop. If there is no overriding, an actual increase in extremity length may occur secondary to increased longitudinal growth at the physis. As with other long bones, periosteal new bone formation may be an indication of abuse. However, in the young infant, symmetrical periosteal new bone formation frequently occurs as a normal finding (see Chapter 11).

In summary, fractures of the femoral shaft are quite common in abused children, but in and of themselves do not allow a

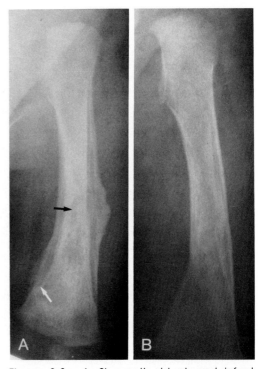

Figure 3.8. *A,* Six-month-old abused infant with an ill-defined fracture of the midshaft of the femur (*black arrow*) with accompanying periosteal new bone formation. A second healing fracture is seen in the distal shaft (*white arrow*) with associated varus angulation. *B,* A follow-up study reveals healing with persistent varus angulation.

radiologic diagnosis of abuse. An incongruous history, evidence of healing at the time of initial diagnosis, and/or association with other injuries are necessary to confirm child abuse.

The Distal Femur

In contrast to fractures of the femoral shaft, metaphyseal injuries provide highly specific information regarding abuse. The reported frequency of metaphyseal versus diaphyseal involvement in abusive femoral fractures is variable. Anderson found that only 4 of 16 femoral fractures involved the metaphysis (18). Beals and Tufts noted that 25% of 86 femoral fractures of the femur involved the distal third as compared to 65% involving the middle third (19). It is likely, however, that the frequency of me-

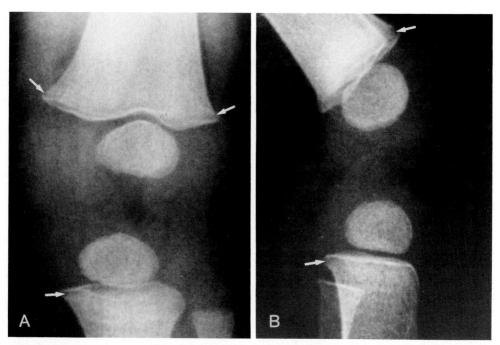

Figure 3.9. Anteroposterior (*A*) and lateral (*B*) views of the knee of a 4-month-old abused infant. Ill-defined transverse metaphyseal radiolucencies are noted in the subepiphyseal regions (*arrows*). Although nonspecific, these findings are common in abused patients. This infant had multiple central nervous system injuries.

taphyseal involvement is greater than these reports suggest. Studies based primarily on referrals to orthopedic services will be biased in favor of those fractures of the shaft that require orthopedic management. Metaphyseal infractions rarely require any specific therapy. Additionally, as has been previously emphasized, metaphyseal lesions are easily overlooked and require the highest quality of radiographic images.

The earliest sign of metaphyseal injury is a transverse radiolucency extending from the medial to the lateral aspect of the distal femoral metaphysis (Figs. 3.9*A* and *B*). In the anteroposterior (AP) projection, the medial and lateral cortices will be disrupted by this lucent line. This is a nonspecific sign but should, in the proper context, raise strong suspicion. As has been pointed out in Chapter 2, the metaphyseal lucency, corner fracture, and bucket-handle appearances of metaphyseal injury are all related to the same histologic lesion. Thus, the corner fracture appearance may coexist with a metaphyseal lucency (Fig. 3.10; see also Fig. 3.14). More advanced lesions will show

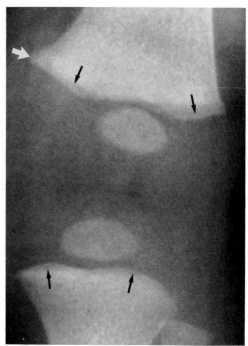

Figure 3.10. Anteroposterior view of the left knee in a 2-month-old abused infant. Metaphyseal lucencies are noted in the femurs and tibias (*black arrows*). A corner fracture appearance is present medially (*white arrow*).

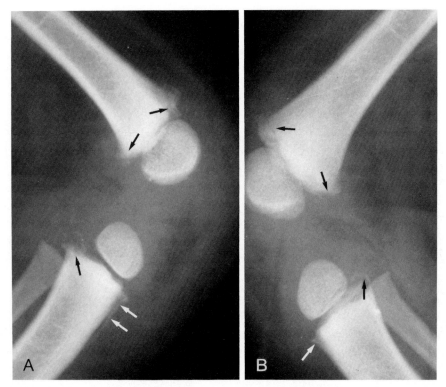

Figure 3.11. Lateral views (*A* and *B*) of both knees of a 2-year-old abused child demonstrate fragmentation and sclerosis along the distal femoral and proximal tibial margins (*black arrows*). There is new bone formation along the tibial tubercle apophyses (*white arrows*).

fragmentation and sclerosis along the metaphyseal margin (Figs. 3.11*A* and *B*).

When severe injury is present, it may produce arrested or diminished growth in the central segment of the epiphyseal plate. This will result in the progressive development of a cupped pattern of the distal femoral metaphyseal margin. This deformity presumably relates to injury of the central segment of the proliferating cartilage of the physis. This is a result of a severe injury, because growth deformity is uncommon with the usual metaphyseal infractions. Rarely, an actual distal femoral epiphyseal separation (Salter–Harris Type I fracture) may occur. As the lesser lesions involving the distal femurs often relate to shaking, they are frequently symmetrical. The more catastrophic injuries associated with gross epiphyseal separation are usually unilateral.

THE TIBIA

The frequency of tibial fractures as compared to other skeletal injuries in abused children varies from 12% to 17% (13–15, 41). In contrast to the femur, metaphyseal injuries predominate in this bone. Fractures of the shaft do occur but, in general, severe deformity resulting from abusive tibial injuries is uncommon. In contrast to femoral fractures, which are commonly suspected clinically at presentation, tibial lesions are more frequently identified during routine radiologic investigation of suspected abuse. Early reports by Caffey (1), Woolley and Evans (7), Lis and Frauenberger (42), and Neimann et al. (43) included a total of 15 tibial fractures.

The Proximal Tibia

Typical bucket-handle fractures are commonly observed involving the proximal tibial metaphysis. This appearance will be accentuated if the plane of the projection is oblique to this region (see Chapter 2). If the plane of the metaphyseal fracture incorporates a larger peripheral fragment of bone, the appearance of a discrete fragment or corner fracture will be present (Fig. 3.12). Other patterns of involvement include fraying and irregularity of the metaphyseal surface (Fig. 3.13). As at other sites, a vague metaphyseal lucency may be the only indication of injury, but histologic examination

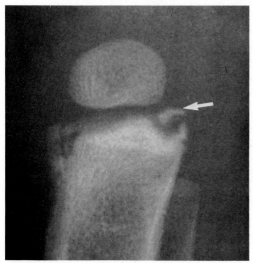

Figure 3.12. Lateral view of the proximal tibia of an 8-month-old abused infant. A healing corner fracture pattern (*arrow*) is present along the posterior aspect of the proximal tibia. There is surrounding sclerosis that extends across the metaphysis. There is fragmentation of the anterior cortex as well.

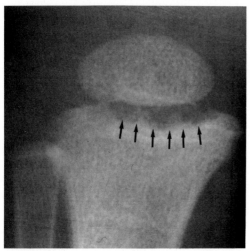

Figure 3.13. An 8-month-old abused infant with fraying and irregularity of the central portion of the tibial metaphysis (*arrows*).

will reveal the typical injury of primary spongiosa. These changes are frequently bilateral and are often associated with lesions involving the ipsilateral distal femur (see Fig. 3.9A and B).

A fracture involving the metaphysis of the proximal tibia may extend to involve the region of the unossified tibial tubercle apophysis (see Fig. 3.10). An actual epiphyseal separation may occur, with anterior displacement of the epiphysis and tibial tubercle (Fig. 3.14) (44). If this fracture is associated with a large metaphyseal fragment (Salter–Harris Type II) and displacement has occurred, an open reduction with internal fixation may be necessary (Fig. 3.15). Substantial angular deformity may develop

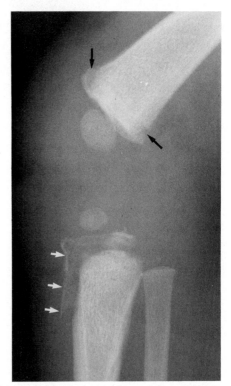

Figure 3.14. Lateral view of the knee in an abused infant. There is a displaced fracture through the epiphyseal-metaphyseal junction of the proximal tibia with extension to the tibial tubercle apophysis (*white arrows*). In addition, corner fractures (*black arrows*) involve the distal femur. These are not discrete fragments but rather the thicker peripheral margins of a disc of bone resulting from a transmetaphyseal injury.

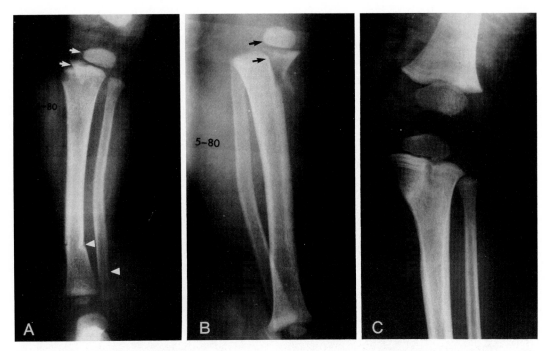

Figure 3.15. Anteroposterior (*A*) and lateral (*B*) views of the proximal tibia of a 7-month-old abused infant reveal a fracture through the anteromedial aspect of the proximal tibial metaphysis. The fracture extends to the growth plate, resulting in anterior and lateral displacement of the combined epiphyseal-metaphyseal fragment (*arrows*). This is a Salter–Harris Type II fracture. Non-displaced fractures of the distal tibia and fibula (*arrowheads*) are also noted. At 5 months of age (*C*), following open reduction and internal fixation, the epiphyseal plate is aligned, but residual valgus deformity is present. (Reproduced with permission from Thompson GH, Gesler JW: Proximal tibial epiphyseal fracture in an infant. *J Pediatr Orthop* 4:114–117, 1984.)

without actual fusion of the growth plate. Corrective osteotomy is required to reduce this angulation.

Buckle fractures of the proximal tibial metaphysis are unusual consequences of abuse. They tend to occur beyond infancy and are probably due to sudden varus stress. They may be difficult to identify, because an actual break in the cortex is not evident. Bone scintigraphy and follow-up films will confirm initial suspicions (Fig. 3.16).

The Tibial Shaft

Periosteal reaction is a common finding along the tibial diaphyses in abused children. This is related to subperiosteal hemorrhage and may not be associated with a visible fracture (Fig. 3.17). A thin radiolucent line may be noted within the tibial shaft (Fig. 3.18). This type of fracture may occur

with unintentional injury and has been referred to as a "toddler's fracture" because it is known to be related to torsional stress in newly ambulating infants (45). An identical fracture may be encountered in abused children, probably caused by similar torsional stress applied by twisting the infant's extremity. More severe forces may result in a displaced spiral or oblique fracture, but these injuries are considerably less common in the tibia than in the femoral shaft. Tibial shaft fractures may be encountered in the healing phase, and will produce diffuse sclerosis of the diaphysis and cortical thickening (Fig. 3.19).

The Distal Tibia

Distal tibial metaphyseal fractures are very common in abused infants. The appearance is similar to that seen in other

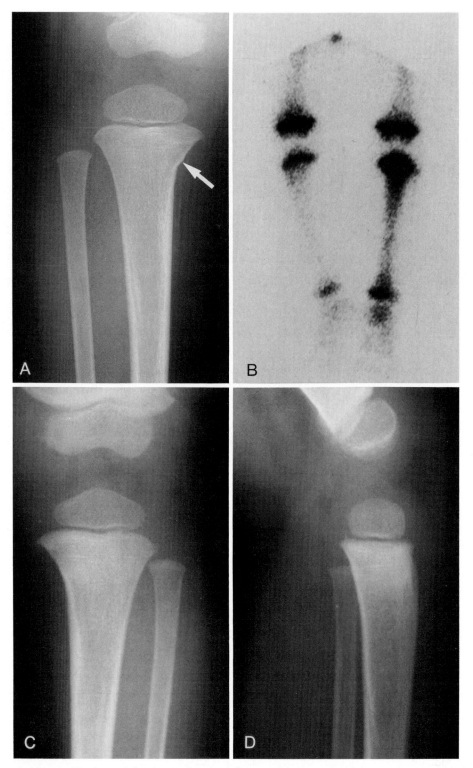

Figure 3.16. *A*, AP view of the lower leg in a 2-year-old abused child reveals a buckle in the proximal cortex (*arrow*). *B*, ^{99m}Tc:methylene diphosphonate bone scan reveals increased activity in the proximal and distal left femur. *C* and *D*, Follow-up views 1 month later demonstrate sclerosis of the proximal tibia, confirming the suspected fracture.

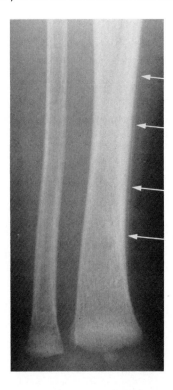

metaphyses. Although a corner fracture appearance is often encountered, careful examination shows this apparently triangular fragment to actually represent the margin of a larger planar fragment of bone (Fig. 3.20). A view that tips this fragment off of the plane of the radiographic projection will reveal a bucket-handle configuration. If the fracture is new and results in a small fragment, the "handle" will be thin. If the fragment is thicker, or the lesion older, the handle will be larger (Fig. 3.21). As at other sites, periosteal reaction may be present and may result in a "squared" appearance of the distal tibial metaphysis (Fig. 3.22). With extensive periosteal new bone formation and thickening of the distal metaphyseal frag-

Figure 3.17. Anteroposterior view of the lower tibia and fibula in a 4-month-old infant with a history of abuse reveals fine periosteal reaction along the medial aspect of the tibial shaft (*arrows*).

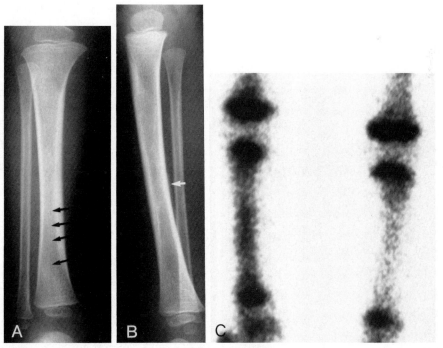

Figure 3.18. *A,* AP view of the tibia in a 20-month-old abused infant reveals a long intramedullary vertical radiolucency in the distal diaphysis representing a fracture (*arrows*). *B,* Lateral projection demonstrates fine periosteal new bone formation along the posterior cortex (*arrow*). *C,* Anterior view of a radionuclide bone scan demonstrates increased activity throughout the right tibial diaphysis.

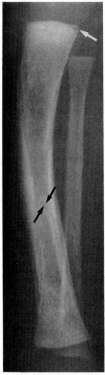

Figure 3.19. Lateral view of the tibia in a 6-month-old abused infant demonstrates an oblique fracture through the mid-diaphysis (*black arrows*) with surrounding sclerosis and moderate periosteal reaction. A metaphyseal injury is noted proximally (*white arrow*).

ment due to additional appositional bone, a characteristic appearance results. The tibial shaft will appear cloaked with periosteal reaction. This shell of bone will be continuous with the distal metaphyseal fragment (Fig. 3.21). With healing there will be incorporation of the subperiosteal new bone into the cortex, and the distal metaphyseal fragment will gradually unite with the remainder of the bone. There is usually little resultant deformity. However, if severe injury is present and the germinal layers of cartilage are involved, a growth disturbance may occur, with resultant diminished endochondral ossification in the central portion of the metaphysis. This can lead to the development of metaphyseal cupping and overall shortening of the extremity (46).

THE FIBULA

Although lesions of the proximal and distal tibia are very common, fractures of the fibula are unusual (1, 5, 7, 9, 14, 32, 41, 43, 47). The reason for this sparing of the fibula is unclear. The patterns of fractures of the fibula are similar to those in other bones, with metaphyseal lesions both proximally (Fig. 3.23) and distally (Fig. 3.24). Fractures of the shaft do occur, however, particularly when tibial shaft fractures are also present

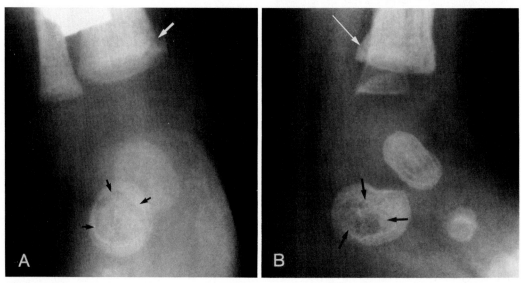

Figure 3.20. Anteroposterior (*A*) and lateral (*B*) views of the distal tibia in a 2-month-old abused infant demonstrate a corner fracture pattern (*white arrow*) projecting medially and posteriorly. These fragments are actually components of a larger disc of metaphyseal bone with a thin central portion and a thicker peripheral margin. Note impressive central demineralization of the calcaneus (*black arrows*).

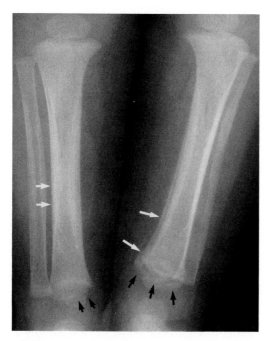

Figure 3.21. Anteroposterior views of the lower legs in a 5-month-old abused infant reveal bilateral bucket-handle fractures (*black arrows*) of the distal tibias. There is bilateral periosteal new bone formation (*white arrows*) that is continuous with the bucket-handle lesion on the left.

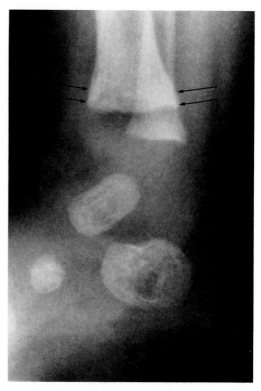

Figure 3.22. Lateral view of the ankle in a 2-month-old abused infant reveals periosteal new bone formation posteriorly and anteriorly (*arrows*), leading to a "squared appearance" of the tibial metaphysis.

(see Fig. 3.15). It is important not to confuse a normal cupped appearance of the fibula metaphysis related to the radiographic projection with that occurring in abused infants. Also, a double contour of the cortex may simulate periosteal reaction in the fibula (48). Careful evaluation of the radiographic images should prevent this confusion.

THE FEET

Fractures involving the bones of the feet are uncommon, but because of a high specificity for abuse these fractures should be sought in any case of suspected child abuse. They tend to involve the metatarsals, and there is usually little, if any, clinical indication of injury (39, 49, 50). Although metatarsal fractures may be identified if the foot is included on a view of the lower extremity, optimal assessment for these subtle fractures involving the small bones of the feet requires separate, well-coned radiographs of the feet (Fig. 3.25).

THE PELVIS

Fractures of the pelvis in abused children are extremely unusual (10, 14, 51, 52). Merten et al. identified two pelvic fractures in 494 abused patients (52). They recommended close scrutiny of the pubic rami for subtle injury. Akbarnia et al. also found two fractures involving the pelvis (14). Jones and Davis noted periosteal reaction along the ischium and pubic bones in a 2-year-old with other evidence of metaphyseal injury (10). This author has noted periosteal new bone formation along the iliopectineal line of the pelvis in one infant. In light of the frequency of femoral injuries, it is likely that injuries to the pelvis are more common than this paucity of reports suggests.

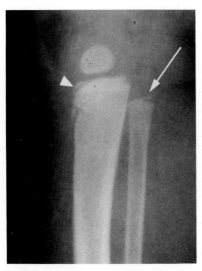

Figure 3.23. Lateral view of the lower leg of a 3-month-old abused infant. A planar fracture through the proximal fibula is evident (*arrow*). There is an accompanying proximal tibial metaphyseal fracture (*arrowhead*). (Courtesy of Professor C. Faure, Hôpital Trousseau, Paris, France.)

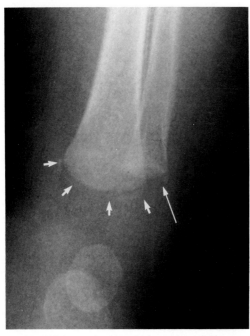

Figure 3.24. Anteroposterior view of the ankle, tipped at an obliquity, of a 6-month-old abused infant. There are bucket-handle fractures of the tibia (*short arrows*) and the fibula (*long arrow*).

The Upper Extremity
THE HUMERUS

The humerus is one of the most frequently injured bones in abused children. There was bilateral involvement of the humeri in three of Caffey's six original cases (1). His correspondence with Ingraham revealed an additional case of a humeral fracture with subdural hematoma. Most of the reports that shortly followed included examples of humeral lesions (3–5, 8–10, 45, 53).

The frequency of humeral involvement is not at all unexpected considering the proposed mechanism of injury of these lesions. It is likely that many injuries to the humerus occur by grabbing the infant by the forearm or wrist and suddenly pulling or twisting the extremity. These may occur during attempts to pull the child from a supine to upright position or, in extreme cases, while swinging the infant from one upper extremity. Using the forearms as "handles" during an episode of shaking will subject the humeri to excessive tractional and torsional forces. Finally, holding the infant by the thorax with violent to-and-fro shaking will allow the upper extremities to flail about the axis of the shoulder joint, resulting in a variety of abnormal stresses to this region (see Chapter 4). As at other sites, direct blows, particularly in older children, may result in injuries to the shaft.

Anatomy of the Humerus

An understanding of some of the unique anatomic aspects of the humerus is helpful in grasping the observed pathologic alterations. At birth, the proximal humeral epiphysis is entirely cartilaginous in nature. Its distal end demonstrates a concave contour with a resultant conical shape of the metaphysis. Subsequently, two ossification centers develop, the largest becoming the capital humeral center, the smaller the center of the greater tuberosity. The larger center is normally evident by 4 months of age, and the greater tuberosity appears between 6 and 18 months (54). These two ossification centers and the surrounding cartilaginous structures move as a unit, and displacements following epiphyseal-metaphyseal

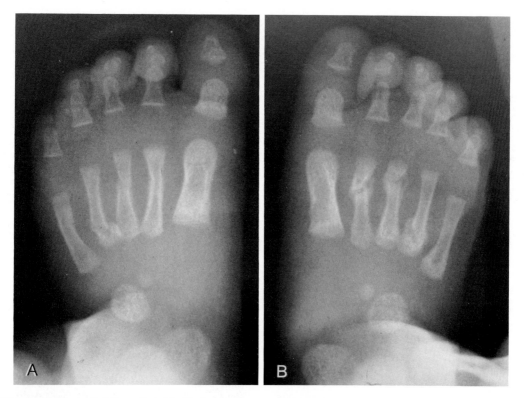

Figure 3.25. Left (*A*) and right (*B*) feet of a 6½-month-old abused infant. There are healing fractures of the 2nd through 5th metatarsals bilaterally. Note extensive callus formation about the displaced fractures of the 2nd and 3rd metatarsals on the right. There were no physical findings related to the feet, and the fractures were identified during a routine skeletal survey performed for suspected abuse. (Reproduced with permission from Jaffe AC, Lasser DH: Multiple metatarsal fractures in child abuse. *Pediatrics* 60:642–643, Copyright 1977.)

injury will result in identical migration of both ossification centers.

The periosteum of the proximal humerus is thicker posteriorly, a factor that influences displacements following fracture. Approximately 80% of the growth of the humerus occurs proximally; therefore, injuries affecting the growth mechanism in this region will produce deformity and/or shortening of the extremity (54).

The distal humeral epiphysis is unossified at birth. The capitellum appears at 3 to 4 months, the medial epicondyle at 4 to 6 years, the trochlea at 8 to 9 years, and the lateral epicondyle at 9 to 11 years (55). During infancy, injuries to this region may be difficult to diagnose because of the lack of ossification within the epiphysis. Ossification often progresses in an irregular fashion, particularly within the trochlea, also leading to difficulties in diagnosis.

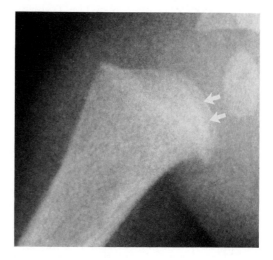

Figure 3.26. A faint metaphyseal lucency (*arrows*) is present in the proximal humerus of this 2-month-old fatally abused infant. Characteristic histologic abnormalities were present.

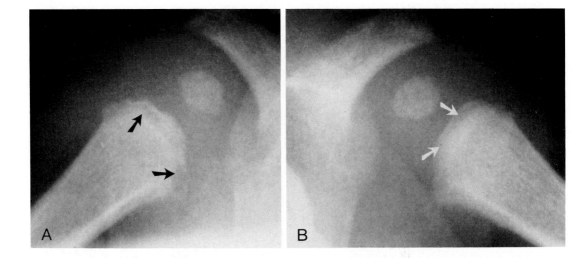

Figure 3.27. Right (*A*) and left (*B*) proximal humeral metaphyseal lucencies are present in this abused infant (*arrows*). Sclerosis and irregularity indicating chronicity are more pronounced on the right.

The Proximal Humerus

As pointed out, injuries to the proximal humerus may not be apparent radiographically, but histologic evaluation will show impressive and characteristic alterations. The most subtle indication of metaphyseal injury is a vague lucency adjacent to the physis (Fig. 3.26). As at other sites, this is a nonspecific finding but may be significant if associated with other more characteristic lesions. This radiolucent band can be more conspicuous and is often associated with metaphyseal irregularity (Fig. 3.27). If no displacement is present, identification of this lesion will be difficult in the acute phase. If the periosteal attachments are torn, periosteal new bone formation will occur with healing (Fig. 3.28).

When the normal relationship of the humeral head to the metaphysis is altered due to a displaced fracture, early diagnosis will be possible (Fig. 3.29). The humeral head normally lies roughly centered or just slightly lateral to the shorter plateau of the metaphyseal margin. When displacement occurs, the epiphysis lies more laterally, and is usually centered over the apex formed between the medial and lateral metaphyseal margins of the humerus (Fig. 3.29*B*). A chest x-ray examination, performed with the arms

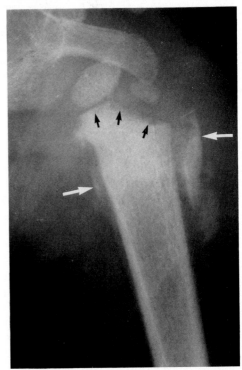

Figure 3.28. Metaphyseal irregularity (*black arrows*) and extensive periosteal reaction (*white arrows*) are evident in the proximal humerus in this 2-year-old abused child.

elevated in the routine fashion, may create a superimposition of the displaced proximal humeral ossification centers over the meta-

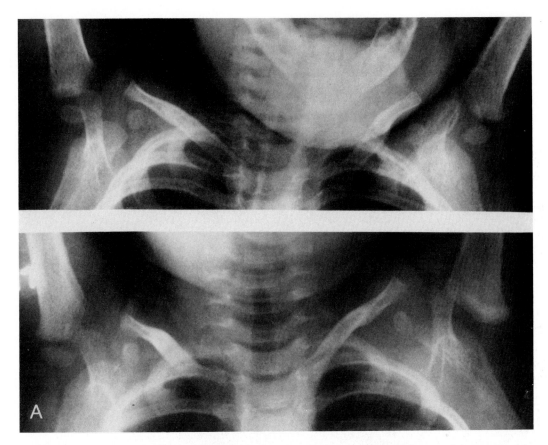

Figure 3.29. Displaced Salter–Harris Type I fracture of the proximal humerus in an 18-month-old child. The mother indicated that she had pulled the child's right forearm, producing sudden forward flexion at the shoulder. *A, (Lower frame)* Upper portion of a chest film obtained at admission demonstrates apparent absence of the left proximal humeral epiphysis. *(Upper frame)* Chest film obtained 6 months earlier shows normal proximal humeral ossification center. *B,* Subsequent external rotation view of the shoulder demonstrates anterolateral displacement of the ossification centers of the humeral head *(arrow)* and greater tuberosity. *C,* This injury occurs by sudden forward flexion of the shoulder resulting in anterior slippage of the epiphysis. The projection of the beam with a standard chest film *(arrow)* causes superimposition of the humeral head over the metaphysis, resulting in "absence" of the ossification centers. *D,* Follow-up film 2 weeks later in the axillary projection demonstrates epiphyseal displacement *(black arrow)* and periosteal reaction *(white arrows)*. (Reproduced with permission from Kleinman PK, Akins CM: The "vanishing" epiphysis: sign of Salter Type I fracture of the proximal humerus in infancy. *Br J Radiol* 55:865–867, 1982.)

physis and result in an apparent absence of the proximal humeral epiphysis (Figs. 3.29A and C). A follow-up film will reveal periosteal reaction and epiphyseal displacement (Fig. 3.29D).

When the humeral head is not ossified, apparent displacement of the humerus from the glenoid cavity may be the only abnormal radiologic finding, and, in this instance, an arthrogram will reveal an epiphyseal sepa-

ration (56) (Fig. 3.30). With healing, considerable periosteal reaction may be noted, although since a substantial portion of the proximal humerus lies within the joint capsule, periosteal reaction may extend only to the point of capsular attachment. If the periosteum remains firmly anchored to the physeal region, the new bone will converge on the metaphyseal margin (Fig. 3.29D). If it has been torn from its attachment, the

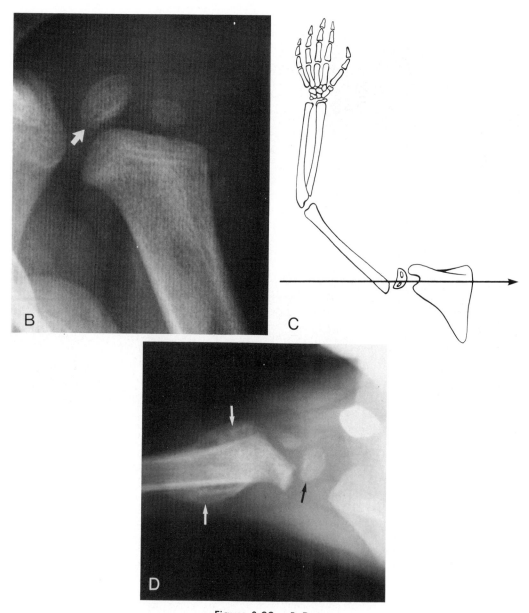

Figure 3.29. *B–D.*

new bone will tend to end abruptly in the nearby soft tissues (Fig. 3.31). Nicastro and Adair reported a unique example of a fracture–dislocation of the shoulder in a 32-month-old child suspected of being abused (57). As is usually encountered, the ossified epiphysis was displaced from the shaft (Fig. 3.32). However, the epiphysis was also noted to be "buttonholed" anteriorly through the capsule, and to lie in a subglenoid position. An open reduction with in-

ternal fixation was performed, with excellent results.

Humeral Shaft

Most humeral shaft fractures tend to be oblique or spiral (Fig. 3.33) as a result of indirect torsional forces, but transverse fractures do occur (Fig. 3.34). Occasionally a direct blow, such as with an iron bar, will result in a transverse shaft fracture (58). Periosteal reaction may be noted secondary

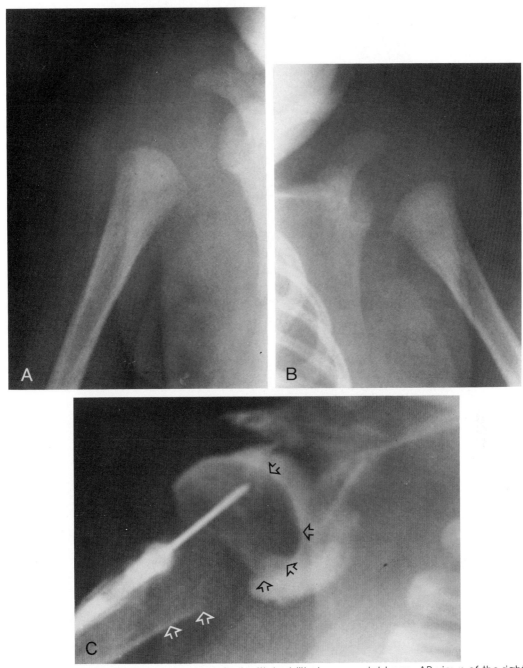

Figure 3.30. Three-week-old abused infant with inability to move right arm. AP views of the right (*A*) and left (*B*) shoulders reveal lateral displacement of the right humerus from the glenoid fossa. C, Right shoulder arthrogram reveals medial displacement of the metaphysis (*white arrows*) with respect to the unossified humeral head (*black arrows*). Humeral head is normally seated in the glenoid fossa. (Reproduced with permission from Merten D, Kirks DR, Ruderman RJ: Occult humeral epiphyseal fracture in battered infants. *Pediatr Radiol* 10:151–154, 1981.)

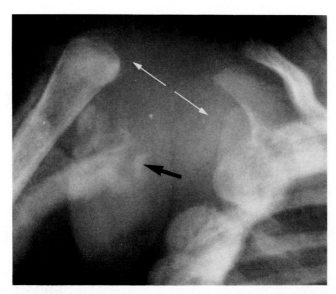

Figure 3.31. Salter–Harris Type I fractures of the right proximal humerus in an abused infant. The humeral metaphysis is severely displaced (*white arrows*). There is massive periosteal reaction that ends abruptly in the medial soft tissues (*black arrow*). Note healing rib fractures.

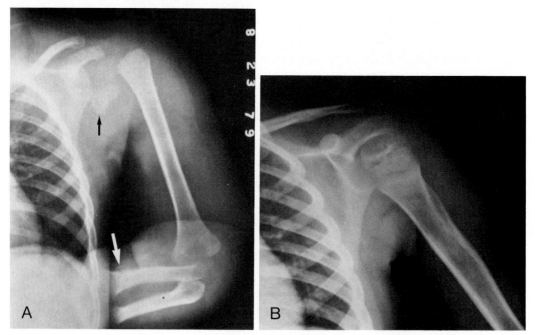

Figure 3.32. Fracture-dislocation of the proximal humerus in a 32-month-old child suspected of being abused. *A,* There is separation of the humeral metaphysis from the proximal epiphysis, which is dislocated anteriorly to a subglenoid position (*black arrow*). There is also a distal radial fracture (*white arrow*). *B,* Excellent results were achieved following open reduction and internal fixation. (Reproduced with permission from Nicastro JF, Adair DM: Fracture-dislocation of the shoulder in a 32-month-old child. *J Pediatr Orthop* 2:427–429, 1982.)

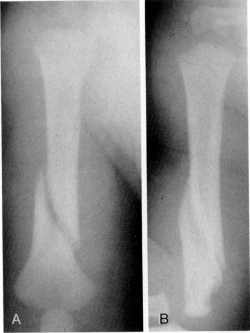

Figure 3.33. Anteroposterior (*A*) and lateral (*B*) views of the right humerus in a 7-month-old abused infant reveal a spiral diaphyseal fracture.

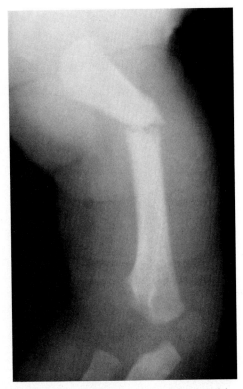

Figure 3.34. Healing transverse humeral fracture in a 3-month-old abused infant.

to traumatic separation; however, care should be exercised in differentiating this from "physiologic" new bone in early infancy (see Chapter 11).

Distal Humerus and Elbow

The unique anatomy of the distal humeral epiphysis results in a characteristic fracture when sufficient abnormal stresses are applied. This injury was first noted by Smith in 1850 (59). Even in the preradiographic era, distinction was made between distal humeral epiphyseal separation and a more common supracondylar fracture. Little attention was directed to the radiology of this lesion until Rogers and Rockwood's description in 1973 (60). The youngest of their cases was a 7-month-old girl who was "allegedly" found in a crib with elbow deformity. In 1974, Chand described an epiphyseal separation in a 7-month-old battered infant who also had a femoral neck fracture (61). Others have stressed the importance of this lesion in battered infants (56, 62).

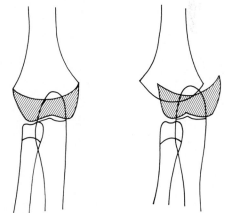

Figure 3.35. Distal humeral epiphyseal separation. The epiphysis (*hatched region*) is displaced medially with maintenance of radial and ulnar relationships.

Injuries to the distal humeral metaphyseal-epiphyseal complex present a variety of interesting radiologic patterns. The most difficult injury to recognize is separation of

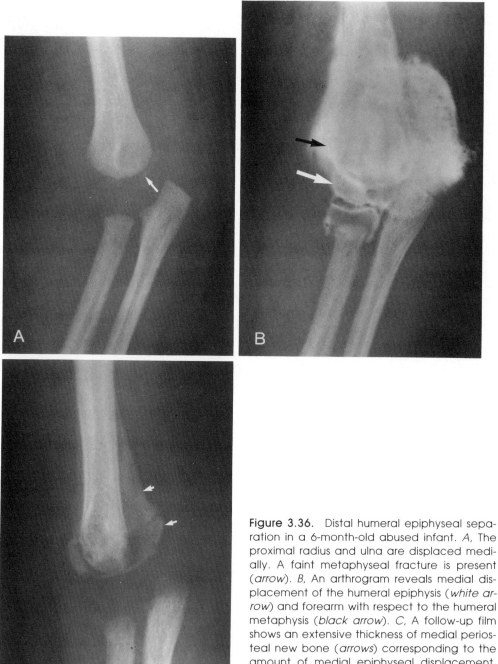

Figure 3.36. Distal humeral epiphyseal separation in a 6-month-old abused infant. *A,* The proximal radius and ulna are displaced medially. A faint metaphyseal fracture is present (*arrow*). *B,* An arthrogram reveals medial displacement of the humeral epiphysis (*white arrow*) and forearm with respect to the humeral metaphysis (*black arrow*). *C,* A follow-up film shows an extensive thickness of medial periosteal new bone (*arrows*) corresponding to the amount of medial epiphyseal displacement. (Reproduced with permission from Merten D, Kirks DR, Ruderman RJ: Occult humeral epiphyseal fracture in battered infants. *Pediatr Radiol* 10:151–154, 1981.)

the unossified distal epiphysis (Fig. 3.35). This injury has been well described in association with birth injury, and an identical pattern occurs in young abused infants (54, 56, 60, 61, 63). On radiologic grounds, differentiation of a fracture separation from a dislocation can be difficult. However, as this is a rare injury in infancy, a fracture is much

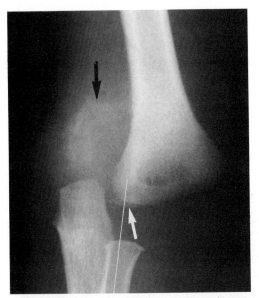

Figure 3.37. Distal humeral epiphyseal separation in an abused infant. There is marked medial displacement of the ossified capitellum (*white arrow*) and the proximal forearm. Extensive new bone formation due to medial periosteal elevation is present (*black arrow*). Despite displacements, a line drawn through the radial shaft intersects the capitellum.

through the long axis of the radial shaft will always intersect the capitellum regardless of the position, confirming the cartilaginous nature of the injury (Fig. 3.37). Diagnosis is additionally simplified if an associated distal humeral metaphyseal fracture fragment is present (Fig. 3.38). On occasion, a long arc of distal humerus comprised of zone of provisional calcification and primary spongiosa may be noted, with a typical bucket-handle configuration (60) (Fig. 3.39).

With healing, the displaced epiphysis and physis will initiate the ossification of what is essentially a new metaphysis in a more medial posterior position. The pattern of periosteal new bone formation will reflect the initial displacements of the fracture fragment. As the distal humeral epiphysis is displaced medially and posteriorly, the degree of separation of the periosteum, and thus the thickness of the ensuing subperiosteal new bone, will be greatest medially and

more likely. In addition, the displacement of the forearm with respect to the humerus is sufficiently characteristic to avoid any confusion with a dislocation. The proximal portion of the olecranon, which should normally superimpose over the distal humerus, will lie medial in location when epiphyseal separation is present (Fig. 3.36). On occasion, arthrography may be useful in defining the unossified distal humeral epiphysis lying in an abnormal location with respect to the humerus, without disruption of the elbow articulation (56) (Fig. 3.36*B*). Although this fracture is generally assumed to be cartilaginous in nature, careful scrutiny may reveal a thin shell of metaphyseal bone on initial films (Fig 3.36*A*).

When ossification within the capitellum is present, there should be little difficulty in recognizing this lesion. Regardless of the degree of posteromedial displacement of the distal humeral fragment, the normal relationship will be maintained between the capitellum and the radius. A line drawn

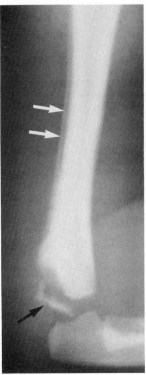

Figure 3.38. A metaphyseal fragment (*black arrow*) is associated with a distal humeral fracture in this abused infant. Note periosteal reaction along the shaft (*white arrows*).

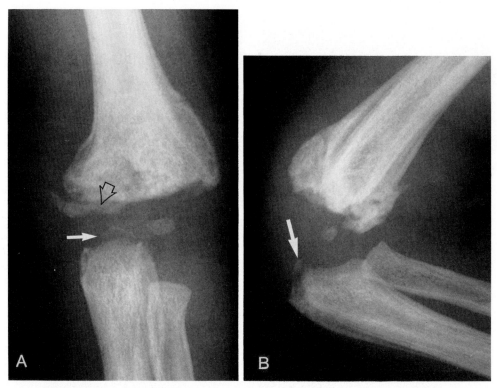

Figure 3.39. Anteroposterior (*A*) and lateral (*B*) views of the elbow in an abused child demonstrate an epiphyseal separation of the distal humerus with typical medial displacement. Note that alignment of the capitellum and the radius is maintained. A crescentic metaphyseal fragment is noted (*open arrow*) with a bucket-handle configuration. There is also a fracture of the proximal ulna (*white arrow*) in the region of the unossified olecranon apophysis. Substantial callus formation is noted involving both fracture sites.

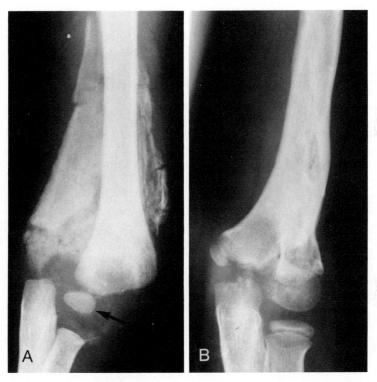

Figure 3.40. *A,* Severely displaced epiphyseal separation of the distal humerus in an abused child. There is marked medial displacement of the radius and ulna as well as the capitellum (*arrow*). The radiocapitellar and radioulnar relationships are maintained. The thickness of the medial periosteal new bone formation roughly corresponds to the degree of displacement of the distal humeral epiphysis. *B,* The follow-up film demonstrates healing with a predictable varus deformity.

posteriorly. Further periosteal cloaking will occur, and the newly formed cortex will gradually blend with the original cortical margins (Fig. 3.40). The significant orthopedic deformity will be a cubitus varus and posterior angulation of the distal humeral shaft.

With these typical patterns of distal humeral fractures in mind, a review of the literature reveals that these injuries are more common than the limited number of reports indicate. Either the cartilaginous nature of the fracture is simply overlooked, or confusion with a dislocation occurs (34, 41, 45).

An unusual lesion noted in abused infants is a "punched out" defect in the distal humeral metaphysis. Although the nature of this injury is unclear, it may result from avulsion of the anterior capsular attachment with associated periosteal reaction. Based solely upon the radiographic appearance,

an erroneous diagnosis of osteomyelitis could be made (Fig. 3.41).

Supracondylar fractures of the humerus are the most common accidental injury of the distal humerus in children, and identical injuries can occur in the abused child. However, the radiologic abnormalities provide no specificity for child abuse. A variety of types of supracondylar fractures occur; the reader is referred elsewhere for a thorough discussion (55).

THE FOREARM

As the forearms are frequently used as "handles" for shaking, pulling, or twisting

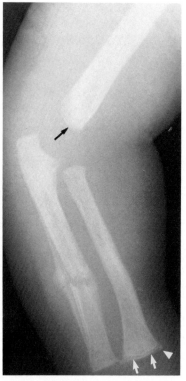

Figure 3.42. Oblique view of the elbow and forearm in this 2-month-old abused infant demonstrates multiple injuries. There is a supracondylar fracture with a bucket-handle fragment (*black arrow*). There is a healing transverse fracture of the ulna with substantial periosteal reaction. There is cortical thickening in the adjacent radius, probably due to a healed fracture. A distal radial metaphyseal injury is present with features of both a discrete metaphyseal lucency (*white arrows*) and a corner fracture (*arrowhead*).

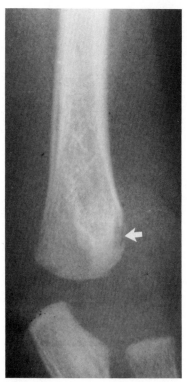

Figure 3.41. An oblique view of the elbow in this 2-month-old infant demonstrates a radiolucent defect in the ventral supracondylar region (*arrow*). Periosteal reaction is noted posteriorly. This pattern suggests osteomyelitis; however, this infant was the victim of abuse.

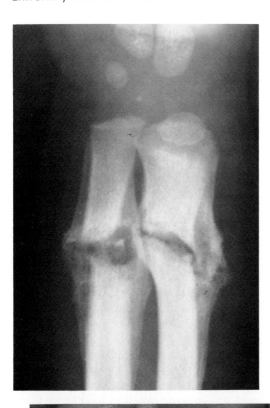

Figure 3.43. Paired healing transverse fractures of the distal radius and ulna are noted in this abused child, with a second major injury at the elbow (see Fig. 3.40).

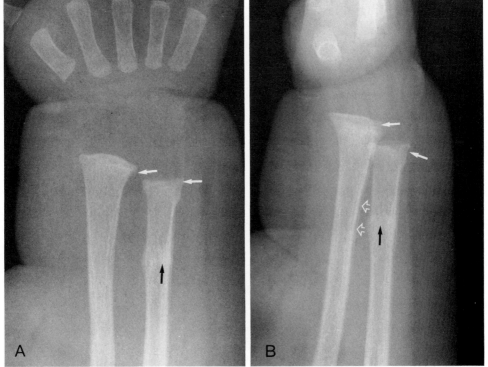

Figure 3.44. Anteroposterior (*A*) and lateral (*B*) views of the forearm and wrist in this 5-month-old infant demonstrate metaphyseal injuries of the distal radius and ulna (*white arrows*), a healing transverse fracture of the distal ulna (*black arrow*), and periosteal new bone formation along the distal shaft of the radius (*open arrows*).

infants, it is no surprise that radial and ulnar fractures are common in abused children. Incidences of radial or ulnar fractures among all abusive skeletal injuries range from 10% to 20% (13–15). In 1939, Ingra-

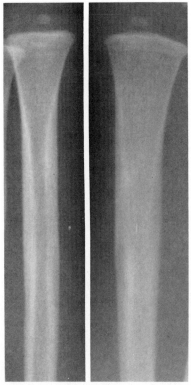

Figure 3.45. Anteroposterior (A) and oblique (B) views of the distal radius demonstrate regular cortical thickening of the radius in this 20-month-old abused child. This abnormality was noted on routine skeletal survey as well as a radionuclide bone scan. The studies provided important evidence of old injury.

ham and Heyl reported fractures of both radii and ulna in both forearms of an infant with a subdural hematoma (64). Subsequently, Caffey described two fractures of the radius and four ulnar fractures in three infants with subdural hematomas (1). Additional reports during the following decade demonstrated the frequent occurrence of forearm fractures in abused children (2, 7, 8, 53).

Fractures of the proximal radius and ulna are unusual sequelae of abuse, especially in infancy. This is peculiar considering the frequency of fractures involving the distal humerus. As injuries about the elbow are generally due to indirect trauma, the distal humeral metaphyseal-epiphyseal complex is presumably the weakest region absorbing the various indirect traumatic forces. However, an associated fracture of the olecranon process may be noted (Fig. 3.39). This can be regarded as a "metaphyseal equivalent" lesion, involving the region of the olecranon apophysis. In contrast, shaft fractures of the forearm are common and tend to be transversely oriented (Fig. 3.42). Frequently, paired fractures of radius and ulna are noted at similar points along the shafts in identical stages of healing, indicating simultaneous injuries. In children, these fractures may result from a direct blow to the forearm as the victim attempts to shield himself/herself from a violent blow (Fig. 3.43). In infants, the common association of these findings with other lesions generally associated with indirect injury and the frequent bilaterality of these fractures suggest that they occur when the infant is grabbed by the extremity

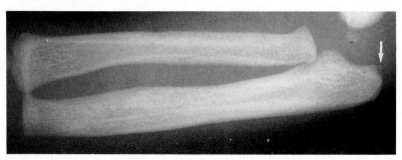

Figure 3.46. View of the forearm of an 8-month-old abused infant demonstrates regular cortical thickening along the radius and ulna. This pattern is similar to that noted in Caffey's disease, but this child had evidence of traumatic injuries elsewhere. Note fracture of olecranon (arrow).

and is shaken or twisted (Figs. 3.42 and 3.44). In the acute phase, these fractures are accompanied by a large amount of soft tissue swelling; therefore failure to seek attention for this sort of injury should immediately raise suspicion of abuse. Without immobilization, extensive easily palpable callus formation develops about the fracture sites. With further healing and remodeling, little evidence of prior injury may be present. If the initial fracture is simply a linear nondisplaced fracture, it may be easily overlooked and be identified only with a routine skeletal survey or bone scan (Fig. 3.45).

As at other sites, periosteal new bone formation secondary to subperiosteal bleeding may be the only indication of injury. When new bone formation involves both radius and ulna bilaterally, a pattern similar to that noted in infantile cortical hyperostosis, or Caffey's disease (see Chapter 11),

will develop (Fig. 3.46). However, evaluation of other skeletal regions, in particular the mandible, should allow exclusion of this rare condition.

Transverse metaphyseal lucencies and corner fracture patterns commonly involve the distal radius and ulna (see Figs. 3.42 and 3.44). The bucket-handle appearance, however, is uncommon at the wrist. Healing lesions may manifest periosteal new bone formation and metaphyseal fraying (Figs. 3.47 and 3.48). A mild cupping and spurring of the margins of the distal ulnar metaphysis should not be misinterpreted as a traumatic injury. This appearance can occur as a normal variant, and is substantially influenced by the projection of the radiographic beam (48). Occasionally, torus or buckle fractures of the distal radius or ulna, common accidental injuries in childhood, may be noted in abused infants (Fig. 3.49).

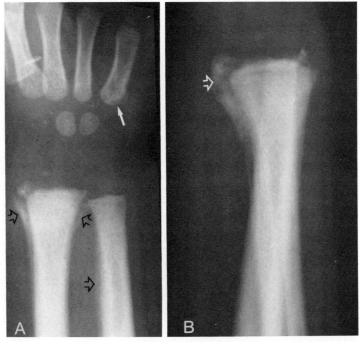

Figure 3.47. Anteroposterior (*A*) and lateral (*B*) views of the wrist in this 2-year-old abused child demonstrate periosteal reaction along the distal radius and ulna (*open arrows*). There is fragmentation of the ventral and lateral aspect of the distal radius. On the lateral view, the extensive periosteal reaction along the volar surface of the radius suggests that there has been ventral displacement of the epiphysis. Also note healing fracture of the base of the 5th metacarpal (*solid arrow*).

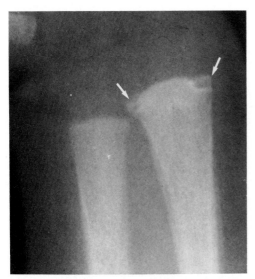

Figure 3.48. The view of the wrist in this abused infant demonstrates fraying of the medial and lateral margins of the distal radial metaphysis (*arrows*). These changes are likely related to repeated trauma with a resultant growth disturbance in the primary spongiosa. There is also periosteal reaction along the radial shaft.

THE HAND

Injuries to the digits are occasionally reported, with incidences varying from 0% to 3% in larger series (13, 15, 38, 41, 52). In 1955, Woolley and Evans described fractures of the terminal phalanges in a 9-month-old infant (7). Fisher illustrated a fracture-dislocation at the proximal interphalangeal joint of the fourth finger in a 10-year-old (27). Scattered additional reports of metacarpal and phalangeal injuries have been published (58, 65, 66).

When substantial digital injuries are present, they may be noted clinically by fusiform swelling of the digits suggesting an arthritis (31, 66, 67). Metacarpal fractures may involve the shafts or the metaphyseal-epiphyseal regions, with periosteal new bone formation in the healing phases (65, 68) (Figs. 3.50 and 3.51). Intravenous lines in the hand and feet may obscure the bony structures, but their presence should not preclude radiographs of these important regions (Fig.

3.50). Multiple chip fractures of the metacarpals, with associated sclerosis, have been noted by Barrett and Koslowski (41). Interesting irregularities along the distal portions of the proximal and middle phalanges of the digits have been noted, with subsequent dense sclerosis in the healing phase (69) (Fig. 3.52). Posnanski has described injuries of the small bones of the hands secondary to "knuckle beating" as a form of punishment in children (70). As in the feet, fractures of the hands are likely more common than the paucity of reports in the literature suggests. It is common practice either to exclude the hands and wrists from a skeletal survey, or simply to include them on a view of the entire upper extremity. For optimal assessment it is recommended that coned-down posteroanterior (PA) views of the hands be obtained in all infants and young children suspected of abuse. Older patients should be radiographed if there is any clinical or historic finding to suggest injuries to the hand and wrist (52).

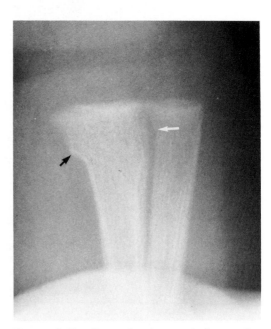

Figure 3.49. Torus fractures of the radius (*black arrow*) and ulna (*white arrow*) are noted in this 2-month-old abused infant. Periosteal reaction is present along the ulnar aspect of the distal radius.

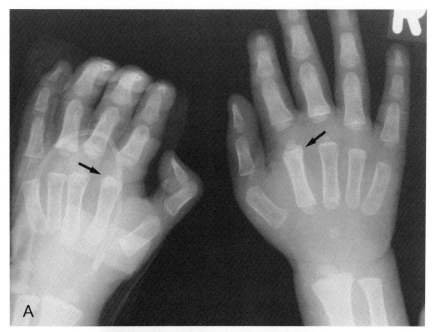

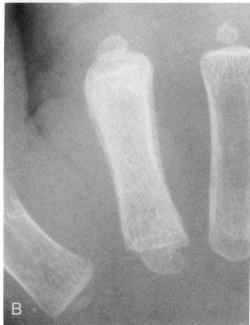

Figure 3.50. Metacarpal fractures. *A,* PA view of the hands in this 2-year-old child with a duodenal hematoma reveals bilateral healing fractures of the heads of the 2nd metacarpals (*arrows*). Although an intravenous apparatus is present on the left hand, the healing fracture is still apparent. *B,* Coned-down view of the right 2nd metacarpal demonstrates sclerosis within the metaphysis, and periosteal new bone formation.

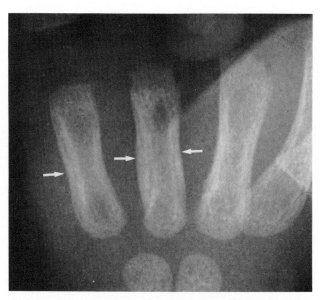

Figure 3.51. Periosteal new bone formation (*arrows*) is noted about the 4th and 5th metacarpals in this 8-month-old abused infant.

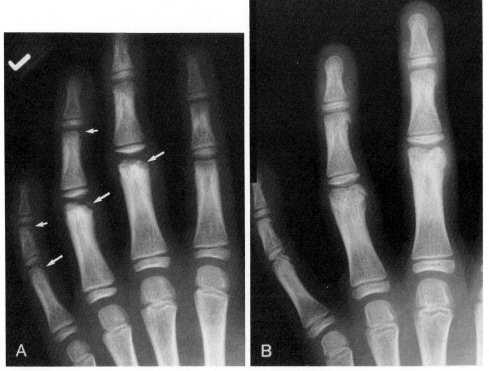

Figure 3.52. *A,* View of the digits of a 10-year-old child with multiple unexplained bruises on her back and hands. Irregularity and fragmentation are noted, involving multiple phalanges (*arrows*). *B,* Follow-up film 14 months later shows further healing, but residual deformities are present. (Reproduced with permission from Rao KS, Hyde I: Digital lesions in non-accidental injuries in children. *Br J Radiol* 57:259–260, 1984.)

REFERENCES

1. Caffey J: Multiple fractures in the long bones of infants suffering from chronic subdural hematoma. *Am J Roentgenol (AJR)* 56:163–173, 1946.
2. Marquezy R-A, Bach C, Blondeau M: Hematome sous-dural et fractures multiples des os longs chez un nourrisson de 9 mois. *Arch Fr Pediatr* 9:526–531, 1952.
3. Kugelmann J: Uber symmetrische spontanfrakturen unbekannter genese beim saugling. *Ann Pediatr (Paris)* 178:177–181, 1952.
4. Bakwin H: Roentgenologic changes in the bones following trauma in infants. *J Newark Beth Israel Hosp* 3:17–25, 1952.
5. Silverman FN: The roentgen manifestations of unrecognized skeletal trauma in infants. *Am J Roentgenol (AJR)* 69:413–427, 1953.
6. Astley R: Multiple metaphyseal fractures in small children (metaphyseal fragility of bone). *Br J Radiol* 26:577–583, 1953.
7. Woolley PV Jr, Evans WA Jr: Significance of skeletal lesions in infants resembling those of traumatic origin. *JAMA* 158:539–543, 1955.
8. Marie J, Apostolides P, Salet J, Eliachar E, Lyon G: Hematome sous-dural du nourrisson associe a des fractures des membres. *Ann Pediatr (Paris)* 30:1757–1763, 1954.
9. Bakwin H: Multiple skeletal lesions in young children due to trauma. *J Pediatr* 49:7–15, 1956.
10. Jones HH, Davis JH: Multiple traumatic lesions of the infant skeleton. *Stanford Med Bull* 15:259–273, 1957.
11. Kempe CH, Silverman FN, Steele BF, Droegemueller W, Silver HK: The battered-child syndrome. *JAMA* 181:105–112, 1962.
12. O'Neill JA Jr, Meacham WF, Griffin PP, Sawyers JL: Patterns of injury in the battered child syndrome. *J Trauma* 13:332–339, 1973.
13. Galleno H, Oppenheim WL: The battered child syndrome revisited. *Clin Orthop* 162:11–19, 1982.
14. Akbarnia B, Torg JS, Kirkpatrick J, Sussman S: Manifestations of the battered-child syndrome. *J Bone Joint Surg* 56A:1159–1166, 1974.
15. Herndon WA: Child abuse in a military population. *J Pediatr Orthop* 3:73–76, 1983.
16. Rosenberg N, Bottenfield G: Fracture in infants: a sign of child abuse. *Ann Emerg Med* 11:178–180, 1982.
17. Gross RH, Stranger M: Causative factors responsible for femoral fractures in infants and young children. *J Pediatr Orthop* 3:341–343, 1983.
18. Anderson WA: The significance of femoral fractures in children. *Ann Emerg Med* 11:174–177, 1982.
19. Beals RK, Tufts E: Fractured femur in infancy: the role of child abuse. *J Pediatr Orthop* 3:583–586, 1983.
20. Bhaskaran CK: Insertion of a sewing needle as a form of child abuse. *Arch Dis Child* 53:968, 1978.
21. Elmslie RC: Erasmus Wilson Lecture on injury and deformity of the epiphysis of the head of the femur: Coxa vara. *Lancet* 1:410–417, 1907.
22. Kennedy PC: Traumatic separation of the upper femoral epiphysis: a birth injury. *Am J Roentgenol Radium Ther Nucl Med (AJR)* 51:707–719, 1944.
23. Blockey NJ: Observations on infantile coxa vara. *J Bone Joint Surg* 51B:106–111, 1969.
24. Caffey J: Some traumatic lesions in growing bones other than fractures and dislocations: clinical and radiological features. *Br J Radiol* 30:225–238, 1957.
25. Silverman FN: Radiologic aspects and special diagnostic procedures. In Kempe CH, Helfer RE (eds): *The Battered Child*, ed 3. Chicago, University of Chicago Press, 1980, pp 215–240.
26. Horan FT, Beighton PH: Infantile metaphyseal dysplasia or "battered babies?" *J Bone Joint Surg* 62B:243–247, 1980.
27. Fisher SH: Skeletal manifestations of parent-induced trauma in infants and children. *South Med J* 51:956–960, 1958.
28. El Fehaiel A, Tabbane C: Syndrome de Silverman: a propos d'une observation. *Tunis Med* 52:223–229, 1974.
29. Fessard C, Maroteaux P, Lamy M: Le syndrome de Silverman. "Fractures multiples du nourrisson" (etude de seize observations). *Arch Fr Pediatr* 24:651–666, 1967.
30. MacFarlane IJA: Hip problems in battered children: a case report. *Aust NZ J Surg* 49:107–108, 1979.
31. Maroteaux P, Fessard C, Aron J-J, Lamy M: Les sequelles du syndrome de Silverman (fractures multiples du nourrisson, syndrome dit des "enfants battus"): etudes de seize observations. *Presse Med* 75:711–716, 1967.
32. Moyson F, Sevens-Rocmans C: Fractures meconnues et enfants maltraites. *Bruxelles-Medical* 46:857–871, 1966.
33. Silverman FN: The battered child. *Manitoba Med Rev* 45:473–477, 1965.
34. Blount JG: Radiologic seminar CXXXVIII: The battered child. *J Miss State Med Assoc* 15:136–138, 1974.
35. Silverman FN: Unrecognized trauma in infants, the battered child syndrome, and the syndrome of Ambroise Tardieu. Rigler lecture. *Radiology* 104:337–353, 1972.
36. Ogden JA, Lee KE, Rudicel SA, Pelker RR: Proximal femoral epiphysiolysis in the neonate. *J Pediatr Orthop* 4:285–292, 1984.
37. Swischuk LE: Spine and spinal cord trauma in the battered child syndrome. *Radiology* 92:733–738, 1969.
38. Kogutt MS, Swischuk LE, Fagan CJ: Patterns of injury and significance of uncommon fractures in the battered child syndrome. *Am J Roentgenol (AJR)* 121:143–149, 1974.
39. Norman MG, Smialek JE, Newman DE, Horembala EJ: The postmortem examination on the abused child. Pathological, radiographic, and legal aspects. *Perspect Pediatr Pathol* 8:313–343, 1984.
40. Brailsford JF: Ossifying haematomata and other simple lesions mistaken for sarcomata: the responsibility of biopsy. *Br J Radiol* 21:157–170, 1948.
41. Barrett IR, Kozlowski K: The battered child syndrome. *Australas Radiol* 23:72–82, 1979.
42. Lis EF, Frauenberger GS: Multiple fractures associated with subdural hematoma in infancy. *Pediatrics* 6:890–892, 1950.
43. Neimann N, Beau A, Antoine M, Pierson M, Manciaux M, de Kersauson MC: Les alterations des os

long au cours de l'hematome dural chronique du nourrisson. *J Radiol Electr* 39:576–581, 1958.

44. Thompson GH, Gesler JW: Proximal tibial epiphyseal fracture in an infant. *J Pediatr Orthop* 4:114–117, 1984.

45. Ogden JA: Tibia and fibula. In *Skeletal Injury in the Child*. Philadelphia, Lea & Febiger, 1982, pp 555–620.

46. Caffey J: Some traumatic lesions in growing bones other than fractures and dislocations: clinical and radiological features. *Br J Radiol* 30:225–238, 1957.

47. Meneghello J, Hasbun J: Hematoma subdural y fractura de los huesos largos. *Rev Chil Pediatr* 22:80–83, 1951.

48. Glaser K: Double contour, cupping and spurring in roentgenograms of long bones in infants. *Am J Roentgenol (AJR)* 61:482–492, 1949.

49. Jaffe AC, Lasser DH: Multiple metatarsal fractures in child abuse. *Pediatrics* 60:642–643, 1977.

50. Hiller HG: Battered or not—A reappraisal of metaphyseal fragility. *Am J Roentgenol Radium Ther Nucl Med (AJR)* 114:241–246, 1972.

51. Faure J, Cau G, Couderc P, Yacoub M, Faure H: Le syndrome de Silvermann ou syndrome des enfants battus. A propos d'un cas. *Med Leg Dommage Corporel (Paris)* 1:139–141, 1968.

52. Merten DF, Radkowski MA, Leonidas JC: The abused child. A radiological reappraisal. *Radiology* 146:377–381, 1983.

53. Smith MJ: Subdural hematoma with multiple fractures. Case report. *Am J Roentgenol (AJR)* 63:342–344, 1950.

54. Ogden JA: Humerus. In *Skeletal Injury in the Child*. Philadelphia, Lea & Febiger, 1982, pp 221–282.

55. Ogden JA: Elbow. In *Skeletal Injury in the Child*. Philadelphia, Lea & Febiger, 1982, pp 283–296.

56. Merten D, Kirks DR, Ruderman RJ: Occult humeral epiphyseal fracture in battered infants. *Pediatr Radiol* 10:151–154, 1981.

57. Nicastro JF, Adair DM: Fracture-dislocation of the shoulder in a 32-month-old child. *J Pediatr Orthop* 2:427–429, 1982.

58. Cameron JM, Rae L: The radiological diagnosis. In *Atlas of the Battered Child Syndrome*. London, Churchill Livingstone, 1975, pp 20–50.

59. Smith RW: Observations on disjunction of the lower epiphysis of the humerus. *Dublin Q J Med Sci* 9:63–74, 1850.

60. Rogers LF, Rockwood CA Jr: Separation of the entire distal humeral epiphysis. *Radiology* 106:393–399, 1973.

61. Chand K: Epiphyseal separation of distal humeral epiphysis in an infant: a case report and review of literature. *J Trauma* 14:521–526, 1974.

62. DeLee JC, Wilkins KE, Rogers LF, Rockwood CA: Fracture-separation of the distal humeral epiphyses. *J Bone Joint Surg* 62A:46–51, 1980.

63. Siffert RS: Displacement of the distal humeral epiphysis in the newborn infant. *J Bone Joint Surg* 45A:165–169, 1963.

64. Ingraham FD, Heyl HL: Subdural hematoma in infancy and childhood. *JAMA* 112:198–204, 1939.

65. Weigel W, Kaufmann HJ: Der verschleierte Pflegeschaden. *Rontgenblatter* 28:463–470, 1975.

66. Fairburn AC, Hunt AC: Caffey's "third syndrome"—A critical evaluation ("the battered baby"). *Med Sci Law* 4:123–126, 1964.

67. Krivine F, Deffez JP: Le syndrome de Silverman en stomatologie. *Rev Stomatol Chir Maxillofac* 74:343–352, 1973.

68. Radkowski MA, Merten DF, Leonidas JC: The abused child: criteria for the radiologic diagnosis. *RadioGraphics* 3:262–297, 1983.

69. Rao KS, Hyde I: Digital lesions in non-accidental injuries in children. *Br J Radiol* 57:259–260, 1984.

70. Posnanski AK: Specific congenital malformation syndromes. Lipoid proteinosis (hyalinosis cutis et mucosae, lipoid proteinosis of urbach and wiethe). In *The Hand in Radiologic Diagnosis with Gamuts and Pattern Profiles*. Philadelphia, WB Saunders, 1984, pp 470.

4 Bony Thoracic Trauma

PAUL K. KLEINMAN, M.D.

The Rib Cage

In 1946, when Caffey first described the connection between subdural hematomas and long bone fractures in abused children, he made no mention of rib fractures (1). In fact, it was not until the early 1950s that the importance of rib fractures in the radiologic spectrum of child abuse was appreciated (2–6).

Countless examples of rib fractures have since been described, and the presence of these lesions is now often central to the radiographic diagnosis of child abuse. Rib fractures comprise between 5% and 27% of all fractures occurring in abused children (7–9). They are probably more common than these statistics suggest, owing to technical factors that will be discussed subsequently. Rib fractures have even been reported as the result of prenatal abuse. Gee described multiple healing rib fractures in a newborn whose mother had presumably attempted to abort the fetus by banging her abdomen against tables and by falling downstairs (10).

Rib fractures in infants and young children are unusual, and any such injury should be regarded with suspicion. When causes such as prematurity, birth injury, metabolic disorders, and bone dysplasias are excluded, most rib fractures in infants are caused by nonaccidental injury (11). The assertion that rib fractures may have occurred as a result of vigorous cardiopulmonary resuscitation (CPR) can often cloud the investigation of suspected abuse. However, rib fractures are rarely the result of compression during CPR. Feldman and Brewer studied the radiographs of 113 children categorized into three groups: victims of abuse, children who had undergone CPR, and children with incidentally identified rib fractures (12). They found no rib fractures in any of the children who had undergone closed chest massage. Half of the fractures identified were found in the group of abused children, and the rest were caused by motor vehicle accidents, rickets, osteoporosis, surgery, and osteogenesis imperfecta. The authors concluded that, in the absence of radiologic evidence of intrinsic bone disease or obvious major trauma, unexplained rib fractures are specific for abuse.

In contrast to appendicular fractures, which are often suspected clinically, rib fractures are usually occult. In a series reported by Merten et al., only 20% of rib injuries were suspected, in contrast to 57% of extremity fractures (13). Rib fractures were significantly more common before 1 year of age and were considered specific for abuse.

ANATOMY AND MECHANISM OF INJURY

An appreciation of the anatomic relationships of the ribs to the spine, the sternum, and one another is helpful in understanding the variety of injuries affecting the rib cage. The rib head articulates with the costal facet of the vertebra anteriorly, and posteriorly the rib tubercle articulates with the transverse process facet (Fig. 4.1). Each rib can be regarded as a lever, the fulcrum lying at the costotransverse articulation. These relationships provide the slight gliding movement that accompanies excursion of the rib cage during respiration. Anteriorly, the 1st ribs are directly united to the sternum by a

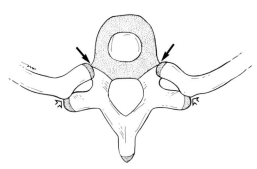

Figure 4.1. The costovertebral articulations. The rib head articulates with the costal facet of the vertebra anteriorly (*solid arrows*). Posteriorly, the rib tubercle articulates with the transverse process facet (*open arrows*).

synchondrosis. The 2nd through 7th ribs are attached to the sternum by a costal cartilage of progressively increasing size. The 8th rib is attached to the 7th by facets and interchondral ligaments, and the 9th and 10th ribs are secured in a similar fashion. The 11th and 12th ribs are free floating (14).

Most fractures involve the posterior arc of the ribs; they are frequently multiple and bilateral (11–13, 15, 16). The majority of posterior rib fractures occur near the costotransverse process articulation. Cameron and Rae believe that these fractures occur with lateral compression during violent squeezing of the chest from side to side (15). Smith et al. believe this type of fracture is usually caused as a child is struck from behind or trodden upon (3). However, on the basis of clinical observations as well as recent radiologic and histologic studies, there is little evidence to support these views.

An analysis of the anatomic alterations associated with these fractures provides a mechanism of injury that is consistent with anterolateral thoracic compression that occurs during shaking (17). The radiographs in Figure 4.2 reveal over 30 rib fractures that were inflicted during a 6-week period in a 6-month-old abused infant. A precise history provided by the abuser described multiple episodes of shaking with anteroposterior (AP) thoracic compression. The infant was held by the chest with the abuser's

palms situated laterally, the thumbs extended anteriorly near the midline, and the fingers positioned posteriorly. Compression was from front to back, and the infant was shaken in a to-and-fro fashion in an AP direction. Multiple old and new fractures involving the posterior and lateral aspects of the 2nd through 10th ribs are evident (Figs. 4.2*A* and *B*). Computed tomography, obtained to assess the associated intrathoracic injuries, reveals several enlightening findings (Fig. 4.2*C*). First, several of the posterior rib fractures are situated ventral to the transverse processes, clearly shielded from any direct blows to the back. Second, the posterior fractures evidence periosteal reaction only along the ventral (inner) aspects of the ribs. Even in cases of comminution, where a fragment of dorsal cortex is displaced, callous formation is noted only along the ventral surface of the rib.

A pathologic analysis of a posterior rib fracture reveals identical features. Figure 4.3*A* displays healing fractures of the posterior aspect of the left 3rd and 4th ribs in another abused infant. These regions are evident in the specimen resected at postmortem examination (Fig. 4.3*B*). The histologic cross-section through the 3rd rib reveals that the fracture has actually occurred at a point medial to the costotransverse process articulation (Figs. 4.3*C* and *D*). Periosteal disruption and new bone formation are situated only along the ventral aspect of the rib, and the dorsal cortex is intact.

On the basis of these facts, a plausible mechanism of injury consistent with AP thoracic compression can be formulated (Fig. 4.4). As the chest is compressed front to back, the rib is levered over the fulcrum of its transverse process. Stress is applied to the ventral cortex at the costovertebral junction and along the posterior arch of the rib. If sufficient force is developed, the ventral cortex and periosteum are disrupted. If greater force is applied, a fracture fragment may arise from the dorsal cortex of the rib. The absence of periosteal reaction dorsally may be explained by an actual extrusion, or "buttonholing," of the bony fragment through the overlying periosteum.

If the rib cage is viewed as a functional unit comprised of a series of parallel struts attached anteriorly to the sternum and posteriorly to the spine, complex patterns of rib injury can be explained. Because forces are distributed along the entire posterior arc of the rib, multiple fractures of similar ages within the same rib can be explained by this theory. Because this mechanism assumes similar forces applied to adjacent ipsilateral ribs, it explains the frequent occurrence of a row of posterior fractures involving numerous ribs. As will be discussed, fractures occurring along the lateral arcs are also secondary to AP compression, and thus a single mechanism of injury provides a unifying

concept for most rib fractures occurring in young infants (Fig. 4.4).

RADIOLOGIC MANIFESTATIONS

In the acute phase, costovertebral junction rib fractures are often invisible on standard AP radiographs (Fig. 4.2A). Because they overlie the region of the transverse process, they can be extremely difficult to identify, even with healing. The slightly oblique lateral projection will often provide clearer delineation of the healing fracture (15). A common appearance of these healing fractures at the costovertebral junction is a slight widening of the neck of the rib due to subperiosteal appositional

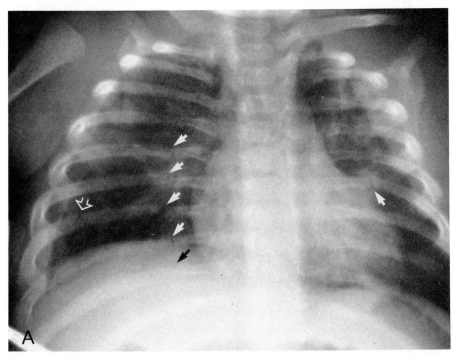

Figure 4.2. Six-month-old infant with multiple rib fractures occurring over a 6-week period. *A,* The initial chest film demonstrates multiple fresh fractures involving the posteromedial aspects of the ribs (*solid arrows*) and a fracture of the posterolateral aspect of the right 7th rib (*open arrow*). *B,* Approximately 3 weeks later, the rib fractures show evidence of healing. Multiple other fractures are seen involving the posterior and lateral aspects of the ribs, not demonstrable on the original film. Note in particular fractures in the region of the costovertebral junctions (*black arrows*). An acute fracture is present involving the right posterior 3rd rib (*white arrow*). *C,* CT scan through the midthoracic region. Two fractures are noted at and just lateral to the left costotransverse process articulation. Note that the periosteal reaction occurs only ventrally (*white arrows*). On the right, there is a comminuted fracture with periosteal new bone formation ventrally. A small bone fragment is displaced posteriorly but there is no adjacent periosteal reaction (*black arrow*). Note pleural fluid on right and parenchymal disease on left. *V* = vertebral body; *T* = transverse processes.

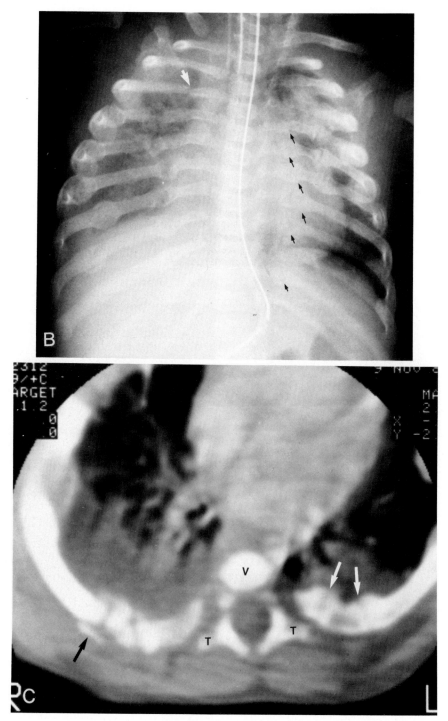

Figure 4.2. *B* and *C.*

bone (Fig. 4.5). The appearance is one that may be easily overlooked or attributed to normal anatomic variation (Fig. 4.6). Any asymmetry in the appearance of the necks of the ribs from right to left should be viewed with suspicion. Occasionally, the proximal end of the rib will evidence fragmentation and sclerosis (Fig. 4.7). These

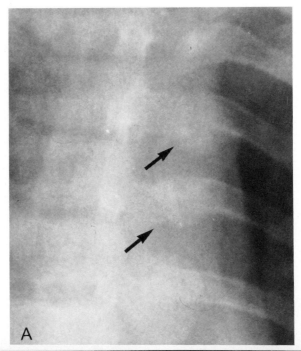

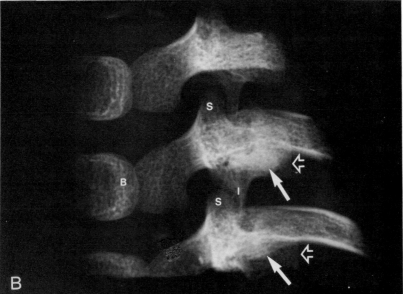

Figure 4.3. *A*, Two-month-old abused infant with healing fractures of the posteromedial aspect of the left 3rd and 4th ribs (*arrows*). The infant died as a result of central nervous system injuries, and an en bloc resection of the 2nd through 4th costovertebral junctions was performed. *B*, A radiograph of the specimen demonstrates callus formation along the inferior aspects of the 3rd and 4th ribs (*solid arrows*). The callus is situated medial to the lateral extent of the transverse processes (*open arrows*). *B* = vertebral body; *S* = superior articular facet; *I* = interior articular facet. *C*, A low-power histologic section of the left 3rd rib demonstrates a healing fracture of the posterior rib. The fracture is situated between the cartilaginous head of the rib (*H*) and the costotransverse process articulation (*CT*). Periosteal new bone formation (*arrows*) is noted only along the ventral aspect of the rib. *V* = vertebral body. *D*, Medium-power view of the region indicated by arrows demonstrates extensive periosteal new bone (*P*) as well as cartilage (*C*) within the internal callus of the fracture.

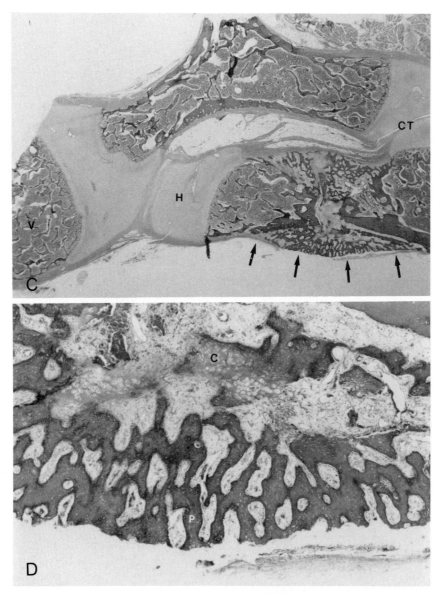

Figure 4.3. *C* and *D*.

fractures are rarely severely displaced, and healing and remodeling can be expected within 1 or 2 months without any radiologic residua.

More laterally situated posterior rib fractures are easier to identify, but can still be missed in the acute phase (Fig. 4.8). In Thomas's study, fresh fractures were rarely noted unless they occurred in association with other healing fractures (11). In light of the frequency of healing fractures noted radiologically in large groups of abused chil-

dren, the infrequent identification of acute rib fractures in infants suggests that these fractures are usually overlooked in the acute phase.

The earliest radiologic sign of healing is a faint area of increased density localized to a short arc of the rib (Fig. 4.8). This early callus formation shows indistinct margins and may be misinterpreted as a parenchymal density (Figs. 4.9 and 4.10). The association with other rib fractures at a more advanced phase of healing points to the true nature of these findings (see Fig. 4.5). With further callus formation, an area of nodular thickening of the rib develops, often with a vertical radiolucency that represents the fracture line (Fig. 4.7). In some cases, with further bridging of callus across the superior and inferior margins of the rib, all that remains of the fracture line is the central area of radiolucency. This rounded, central lucent defect may suggest a benign neo- plasm of bone such as an enchondroma rather than a healing fracture (Fig. 4.11). As with rib fractures elsewhere, further remod- eling occurs, and ultimately a normal ap- pearance will result.

Lateral rib fractures are less common than

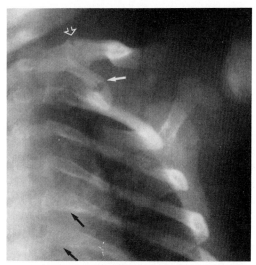

Figure 4.6. Healing fractures produce widen- ing of the neck of the ribs (*black arrows*) in this abused infant. There is an unusual acute frac- ture of the left 1st rib (*solid white arrow*), and a healing fracture of the proximal aspect of the clavicle (*open white arrow*).

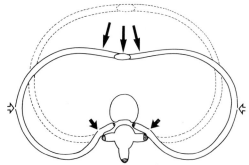

Figure 4.4. Mechanism of production of pos- teromedial rib fracture. Anterior compression of the chest (*long arrows*) produces excessive le- vering of the rib over the fulcrum of its trans- verse process. Stresses are applied along the ventral surface of the rib resulting in fracture (*short arrows*). Similar anteropostero-compres- sive forces will produce more laterally situated fractures as well (*open arrows*).

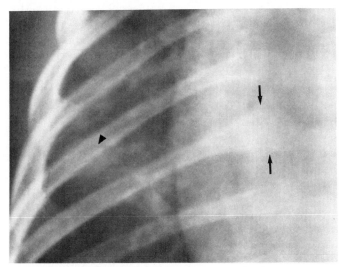

Figure 4.5. Healing posterior rib fracture in an abused infant results in apparent widening of the neck of the rib (*arrows*). A more recent fracture is noted posterolaterally (*arrowhead*), with faint surrounding periosteal new bone formation.

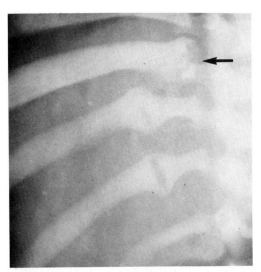

Figure 4.7. A costovertebral fracture of the right 9th rib in this abused infant is manifested as fragmentation and sclerosis (*arrows*). Older fractures of the 10th and 11th ribs are manifest by extensive callus formation. Bone resorption about the fracture site is present, greatest in the 11th rib.

those situated posteriorly. They are generally assumed to occur from AP compression of the chest (see Fig. 4.4) (11, 12, 15). The degree of compression must be greater than the amount generally used in CPR, since fractures from CPR are rare. The degree of callus formation produced depends on the amount of displacement of the fracture, as well as on subsequent movement at the fracture site. The amount of callus formation produced may be quite abundant, and, on the AP view, the actual fracture lines may be obscured (Fig. 4.12A). Oblique views, however, will generally demonstrate the fracture line as well as associated displacement and angular deformity (Figs. 4.12B and C). Lateral fractures may be associated with more posteriorly situated fractures within the same ribs (Fig. 4.12; also see Fig. 4.1). These multiple fractures may result in a "flail chest." Any infant with multiple lateral and posterior rib fractures has undoubtedly been subjected to a severe forceful injury, and other associated skeletal injuries should be expected.

The reported frequency of anterior and costochondral junction fractures varies considerably. Feldman and Brewer found 18 rib fractures situated anteriorly, as compared to 24 that were located posteriorly (12). In another series, however, Merten et al. described 31 rib fractures of which 25 were posterior and 6 were lateral; none were described as anteriorly situated (13). It is likely that anterior rib fractures are quite common with abuse, but detection of the injuries is often difficult. Costochondral injury can be regarded as a "metaphyseal equivalent" lesion, that is, an injury occurring at or adjacent to a cartilaginous growth plate. In the acute phase, radiologic abnormalities are generally lacking. It is only in the healing phase that fragmentation and irregularity will be noted (Fig. 4.13). These findings may be quite subtle on a posteroanterior (PA) view, and Cameron and Rae recommend oblique projections to better assess costochondral fractures (15). When multiple fractures are present bilaterally, the pattern will be difficult to distinguish from a rachitic rosary.

Fractures of the 1st rib are unusual, and when present are usually associated with other injuries about the shoulder girdle (see Fig. 4.6). Similarly, fractures of the 12th rib are unusual and imply a severe traumatic insult. One of Feldman and Brewer's patients with fractures of the 11th and 12th ribs also had a compression fracture of the 2nd cervical vertebra and a laceration of the carotid artery (12).

Although most rib fractures in infants are related to shaking and thoracic compression, in older infants and children direct blows by a clenched fist, kicking, or sudden deceleration by being thrown into a solid object may result in fractures at the site of impact. In these cases, fractures involving the lower ribs may be associated with injuries to the liver, spleen, or hollow viscera. It is curious that, despite the frequency of rib fractures in abused infants, associated pleuroparenchymal injury and pneumothoraces are uncommon (see Chapter 7).

RADIONUCLIDE SCANS VERSUS RADIOGRAPHIC SURVEYS

Radionuclide bone scanning has been shown to be extremely useful in the detec-

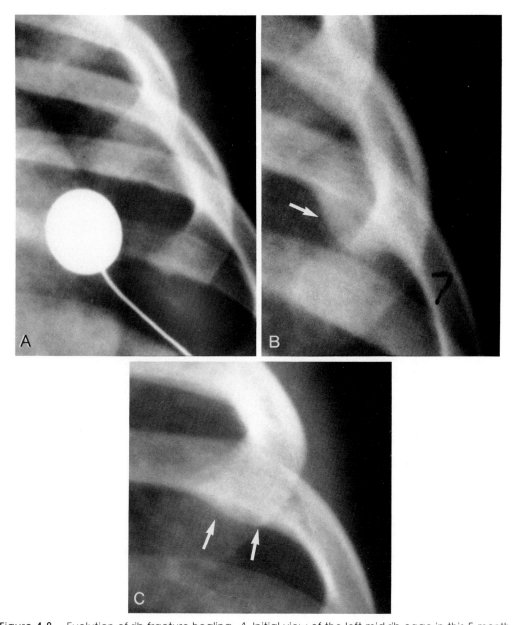

Figure 4.8. Evolution of rib fracture healing. *A,* Initial view of the left mid rib cage in this 5-month-old infant demonstrates no abnormality. *B,* Two weeks later, callus formation (*arrow*) is noted surrounding the left 7th rib. No fracture line is seen. *C,* One month later, the only indication of prior fracture is slight cortical thickening along the under surface of the rib (*arrows*).

tion of rib fractures in abused infants and children (Fig. 4.14) (3, 18–20). In contrast to fractures of the epiphyseal-metaphyseal complexes, which can be extremely difficult to assess and are greatly affected by positioning, rib fractures are highly detectable by radionuclide bone scans. Smith et al.

have shown that bone scanning is especially useful in the identification of costovertebral fractures (3). Although rib fractures were confirmed radiographically in three of four cases, one abused child showed no radiologic alterations corresponding to the abnormalities seen on the bone scan. Jaudes

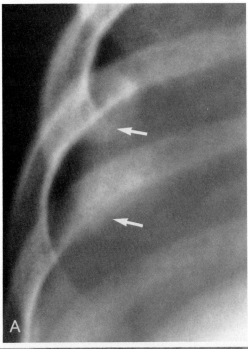

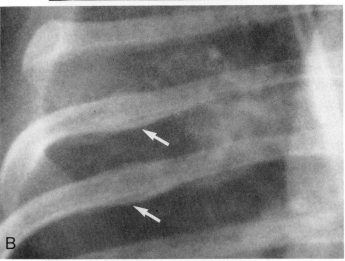

Figure 4.9. *A,* Callus formation is noted along the posterolateral aspects of the ribs (*arrows*) in this 2-month-old abused infant. Fracture lines are not evident. *B,* On the follow-up film, the only indication of fracture is slight cortical thickening inferiorly (*arrows*).

studied a group of patients undergoing both skeletal survey and bone scans (18). In five children with normal radiologic skeletal surveys, subsequent bone scans demonstrated five cases with rib fractures or other old fractures. In four patients with positive skeletal surveys, additional rib fractures were diagnosed. Sfakianakis et al. found disparity regarding rib fractures detected by bone scan and x-rays in eight patients (21). In perhaps the most complete study on the subject, Sty and Starshak performed both radiologic and scintigraphic examinations on 261 children suspected of abuse (19). They found 12 cases of one or more rib fractures that were identified by scintigra-

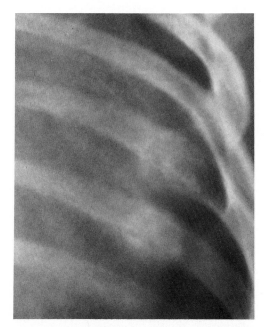

Figure 4.10. "Nodular" thickening of the posterolateral aspects of the fractured ribs in this 5-month-old abused infant could be mistaken for pulmonary nodules.

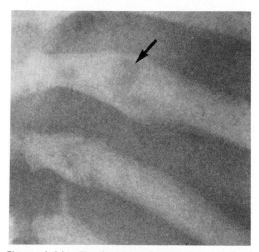

Figure 4.11. The fractures in this abused infant are manifest by radiolucency within the fracture site due to bone resorption. The defect may, in fact, simulate a lytic lesion (*arrow*).

phy but not on standard radiographs (Fig. 4.15).

Other authors have shown less dramatic findings. Pickett et al. showed comparable sensitivity with radiographic and radio-

nuclide studies in five cases of rib fractures (22). This team also described one false-positive radionuclide scan that erroneously pointed to three rib fractures. Merten et al. reported the results of bone scans performed in 23 of 563 abused children (13). Only one patient exhibited fractures by bone scan that were not apparent radiographically. These occult rib lesions occurred in a 4-month-old infant with multiple radiologically identifiable limb fractures.

The arguments presented in favor of radionuclide scans versus radiologic skeletal surveys for detection of rib abnormalities are part of the larger question of scintigraphy versus radiography. The reader is referred to the discussion of this issue in Chapter 2. Suffice it to say that high quality bone scans performed and interpreted by experienced radiologists in active pediatric nuclear medicine divisions will detect greater numbers of rib fractures than skeletal surveys. This sensitivity undoubtedly diminishes as the expertise of the technical staff and those interpreting the scans is reduced (23, 24). Issues related to cost, radiation exposure, availability, sedation, and clinical setting will also bear on this matter (25).

The Clavicle

Fractures of the clavicle have long been recognized as sequelae of child abuse (4, 5, 7, 8, 13, 15, 16, 26–31). The cases of Marquezy et al. (29), Woolley and Evans (4), and Marie et al. (5) were among the earliest reports of this finding. Although the clavicle is one of the most common accidentally fractured bones in childhood, it comprises only 2% to 6% of fractures caused by abuse (8, 13, 27, 30). Thus, a clavicular fracture is usually considered a nonspecific finding. However, there are some anatomic factors that may affect the significance of this type of fracture in any given case of suspected abuse.

The clavicle is firmly attached to the manubrium medially at the sternoclavicular joint and laterally at the acromioclavicular articulation. Located at both ends are cartilaginous growth centers that eventually ossify and fuse. Because of this firm fixation, a sudden applied force to the clavicle will usually result in a fracture of the midshaft. These fractures are often angulated, but generally little displacement is present (Fig. 4.16). Although they can result from a direct impact upon the clavicle, they commonly occur indirectly as a result of landing on an outstretched arm (32). The patient often fails to seek attention, and this fracture may only be discovered incidentally during the healing phase. The midshaft fracture is also the most common type of clavicular injury in the battered child, but, without other associated injury, this fracture cannot be regarded as a specific indication of abuse (13, 33). Fractures involving the medial third of the shaft carry a greater suspicion of abuse. The fracture line may be clearly

delinated (see Fig. 4.6), or obscured by extensive callus formation (Fig. 4.17).

Any injury to the region of the lateral or medial clavicular growth plates may lead to a frayed pattern and, with healing, a club-like appearance of the distal end may result. These medial and lateral injuries are likely analogous to metaphyseal lesions elsewhere, and are usually caused by violent shaking (16).

A problem that often arises relating to clavicular fractures pertains to differentiation from a birth-related injury (26, 34, 35). This subject is covered elsewhere in this text (Chapter 11), but suffice it to say that a healing fracture in the first few days of life may well be an unrecognized consequence of a difficult delivery. However, if a clavicular fracture is encountered greater than 11 days after birth, and shows no evidence of healing, it should be regarded as highly suspicious of abuse (26).

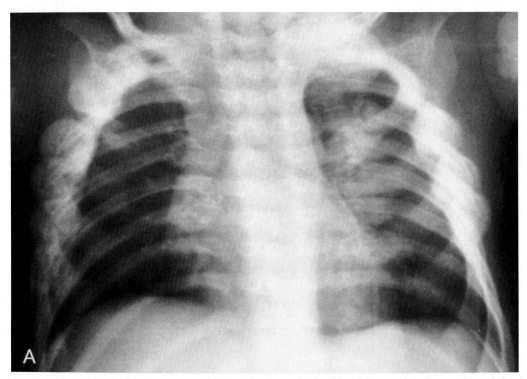

Figure 4.12. Multiple fractures are noted in this abused infant involving mainly the costovertebral junctions and the lateral ribs. *A,* Nodular callus formation laterally obscures the fracture sites. *B* and *C,* Oblique views demonstrate the fracture sites as well as the degree of displacement of the fracture. A fracture of the posterior aspect of the right 8th rib is well demonstrated on the steep right anterior oblique projection (*arrow*).

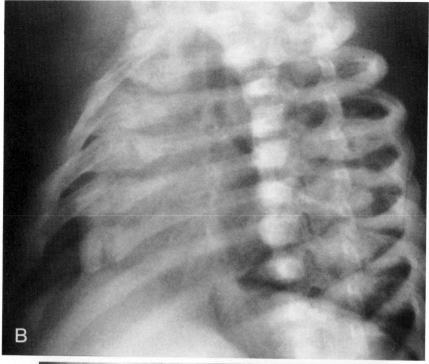

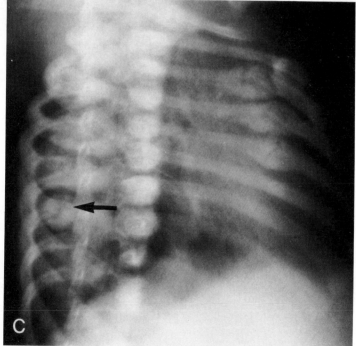

Figure 4.12. *B* and *C*.

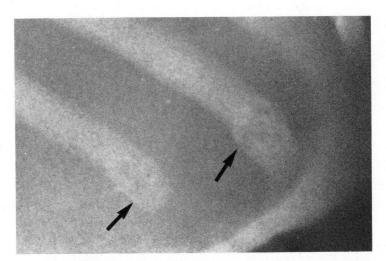

Figure 4.13. Fractures of the costochondral junction (*arrows*) are evidenced by sclerosis and fragmentation in this abused infant.

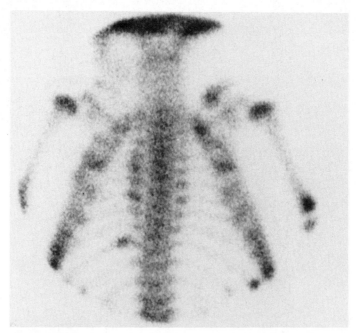

Figure 4.14. ^{99m}Tc: methylene diphosphonate bone scan reveals increased activity at the costo-vertebral junctions, indicating fractures in this abused infant. (Reproduced with permission from Sty JR, Starshak RJ, Hubbard AM: Radionuclide evaluation in childhood injuries. *Semin Nucl Med* 13:258–281, 1983.)

The Sternum

Injuries to the sternum are rare in young children. The sternum is a relatively compliant structure because there is some inherent mobility of the sternoclavicular, ster-

nomanubrial, and sternocostal joints. Fractures secondary to abuse have rarely been described and have been attributed to direct blows (16, 28). They may result in displacement at the sternomanubrial joint or appear only as a defect along the cartilaginous mar-

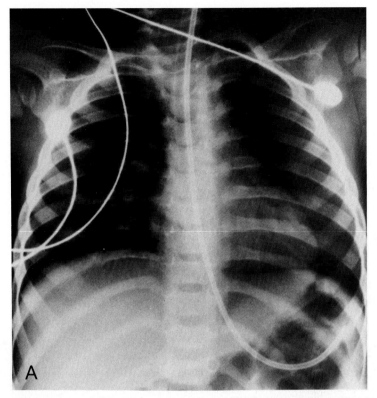

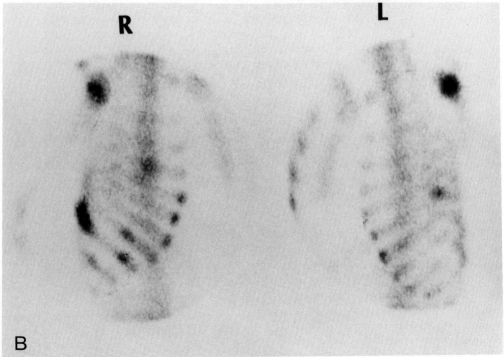

Figure 4.15. *A,* AP chest radiograph of an abused infant reveals no abnormalities. *B,* ^{99m}Tc: methylene diphosphonate bone scan reveals focal areas of increased activity bilaterally consistent with fractures. (Reproduced with permission from Sty JR, Starshak RJ: The role of bone scintigraphy in the evaluation of the suspected abused child. *Radiology* 146:369–375, 1983.)

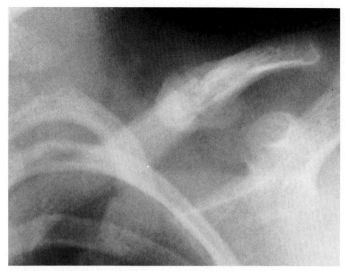

Figure 4.16. Healing nondisplaced fracture of the distal third of the clavicle in a 4-year-old abused child.

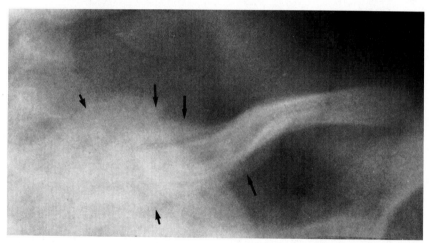

Figure 4.17. Fracture of the medial third of the left clavicle in this abused infant is evidenced by extensive callus formation (*arrows*).

gin of a sternal ossification center (Figs. 4.18 and 4.19). The two illustrated cases were noted incidentally on lateral projections of the chest. It is likely that these fractures result from compression of the chest rather than direct blows. Because lateral views are required for recognition but are not usually obtained with routine skeletal surveys, it is likely that fractures of the sternum are more common than reported. This injury is virtually diagnostic of a massive force applied to the thorax, and is presumptive evidence of abuse. The possibility of such fractures demands a lateral film in all infants suspected of abuse.

The Scapula

Evaluation of the scapula is essential in the workup of children suspected of having been abused. Although these fractures are

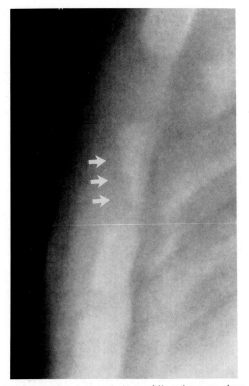

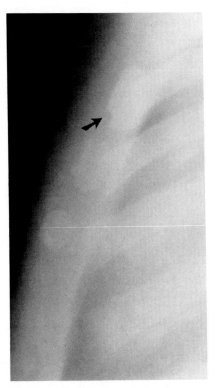

Figure 4.18. Lateral view of the sternum demonstrates a defect involving the 1st sternal segment (*arrows*) in this 4-month-old abused infant.

Figure 4.19. A defect is noted along the anteroinferior margin of the 1st sternal segment (*arrow*) in this 5-month-old abused infant.

considered unusual, a variety of examples have found their way into detailed descriptions of injuries in abused infants (2, 16, 28, 31, 36–41). These fractures are generally difficult to identify, and are probably more common than the paucity of reports suggests. As accidental scapular fractures are rare during infancy, in the absence of a history of massive direct trauma they should be considered specific for abuse.

Some anatomic considerations are useful in understanding the various types of scapular injury (Fig. 4.20) (14). The scapula is a triangular bone that can be viewed as having a head that is joined to a plate-like body by a short neck. The acromion process originates from a spine-like process arising from the upper dorsal surface of the bone. The head gives rise to an anteriorly and laterally oriented process, the coracoid. Ossification centers develop from eight separate cartilaginous sites. The largest center

develops within the body of the scapula. Two centers are present for the coracoid and acromion, and one center is noted in the medial border, inferior angle, and lower part of the glenoid cavity. The deltoid muscle attaches to the acromion process. The coracoclavicular ligament, short head of the biceps, and coracobrachialis muscles attach to the distal portion of the coracoid. The serratus anterior and latissimus dorsi muscles arise from the inferior angle of the scapula.

The acromion is the most commonly injured portion of the scapula. Radiographically, there may simply be irregularity and indistinctness of the acromial margin (Fig. 4.21). However, an actual fracture line extending transversely through the acromion may be noted. With a relatively recent fracture the margin may be indistinct, and this injury can be easily overlooked (Fig. 4.22A). In other cases, a sclerotic fracture line extending through the acromion may be noted

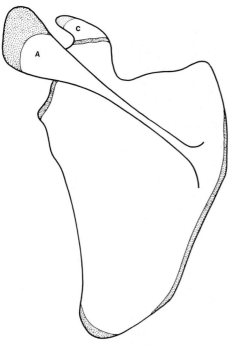

Figure 4.20. Ossification pattern of the scapula in the prepubertal child. Cartilage (*stippled areas*) caps the coracoid (*C*), acromion (*A*), medial border, inferior angle, and glenoid cavity. These areas ossify with skeletal maturity, but are susceptible to injury in infancy and childhood.

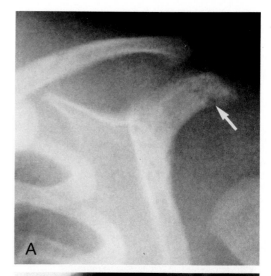

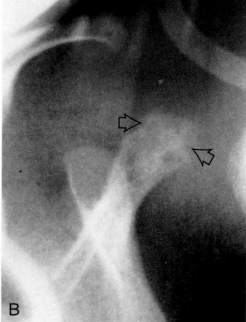

Figure 4.22. Left shoulder of same infant as in Figure 4.21. *A,* An acromial lesion is evidenced by an irregular lucency extending transversely across the bone (*arrow*). *B,* A second view shows patchy areas of bone resorption (*arrows*) without a discrete fracture line.

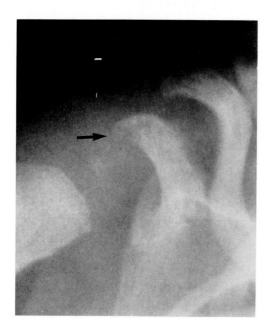

Figure 4.21. An acromial injury is manifest by irregularity and indistinctness of the bony margin (*arrow*) in this 2-month-old abused infant.

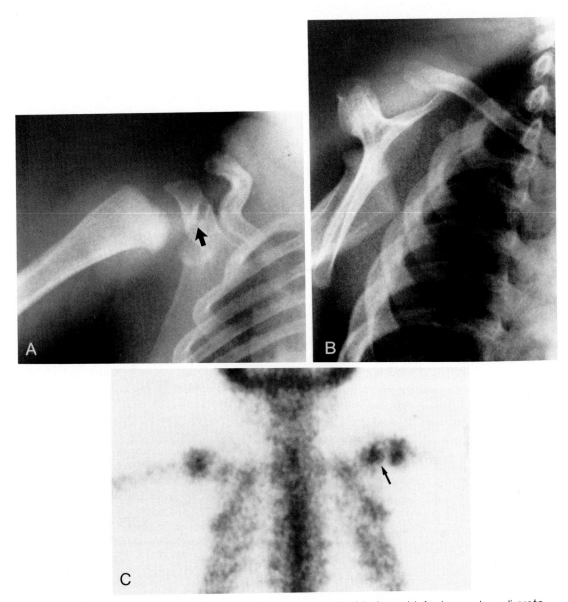

Figure 4.23. *A*, An AP view of the scapula in a 6-month-old abused infant reveals a discrete fracture line with a sclerotic margin (*arrow*). *B*, A lateral view of the scapula fails to show the fracture line and simply reveals extensive callus formation. *C*, A posterior view of a bone scan demonstrates an area of increased activity corresponding to the acromial fracture (*arrow*).

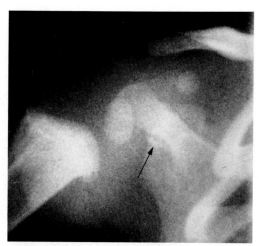

Figure 4.24. An unusual fracture of the inferior aspect of the base of the acromion (*arrow*) is noted in this abused infant. There is also irregularity of the humeral metaphysis.

(Fig. 4.23*A*). The radiographic projection will often influence the appearance of these fractures. What appears as a discrete fracture line in one view may be manifest as patchy areas of bone resorption in another view (Fig. 4.22*B*). The sharply defined, discrete fracture line may be obscured by overlying callus in a second projection (Fig. 4.23*B*). Rarely, a fragment may arise from the inferior margin of the acromion (Fig. 4.24). Radionuclide scanning may show increased activity in this region supporting the diagnosis (Fig. 4.23*C*).

Coracoid fractures are less common than those involving the acromion (2). If the fracture occurs through the cartilaginous junction between the coracoid ossification center and the head of the scapula, a subtle abnormal orientation of the coracoid, as compared to the opposite side, will be evident (Fig. 4.25). Computed tomography is ideally suited to identification of these injuries (Figs. 4.25*C* and *D*), and radionuclide bone scans may support the diagnosis (Figs. 4.25*E*).

Another rare injury to the scapula involves the inferior glenoid margin (16, 28, 41). This fracture bears some similarity to that occurring with anterior glenohumeral dislocation in older patients. Unusual "punched out" lesions of the glenoid have been described by Jones and Davis (39). These may be similar to the other glenoid fractures, with a large amount of surrounding bone resorption. Finally, a unique lesion of the inferior angle and medial aspect of the scapula occurs. The injury is seen as a crescentic rim of bone paralleling the normal contour of the scapula margins (Fig. 4.26).

It is difficult to be certain of the mechanisms of injury of these various scapula fractures; however, because these lesions are most frequently noted in infants who have typical patterns of abuse elsewhere, they most likely occur from indirect forces. The rare fracture of the body of the scapula (16) may be the only exception to this rule. Several authors have stressed the association of scapula injuries and other fractures about the shoulder girdle and upper rib cage (31, 36, 38). It is likely that abnormal forces generated during shaking, or abnormal rotational or tractional forces applied to the shoulder via the upper extremity result in proximal humeral, scapular, clavicular, and upper rib fractures (Fig. 4.27). Avulsion of the distal acromion by the deltoid attachment, or actual impingement of the humeral head upon the acromion is consistent with the noted injuries. The coracoid fracture likely results from abnormal tension applied via the muscles and ligaments attached to this structure. Although glenohumeral dislocation is rare in infancy, it is reasonable to assume that excessive inferior motion of the head may result in a glenoid fracture with spontaneous reduction. The peculiar lesion involving the inferior angle and medial margin of the scapula is harder to explain, but may be secondary to an avulsive injury at the attachment of the serratus anterior or latissimus dorsi muscles.

The complex anatomy of the scapula renders it a difficult structure to fully evaluate. The area will generally be included in the standard skeletal survey on both views of the upper extremity, as well as the chest film. Careful scrutiny of this region is important and, in cases where suspicion exists, coned-down views should be obtained.

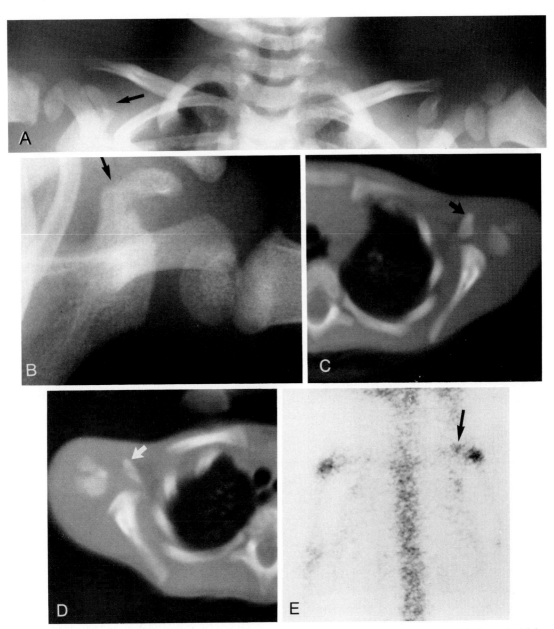

Figure 4.25. Coracoid fracture. *A*, An AP view of the shoulders in an 18-month-old abused child shows a malalignment of the right coracoid process with respect to the head of the scapula (*arrow*) as compared to the left side. *B*, The malalignment of the coracoid (*arrow*) is more evident on this axillary view. Computed tomographic scans through the right (*C*) and left (*D*) shoulders define the anatomic alterations. The right coracoid (*black arrow*, part *C*) is separated from the head of the scapula by a greater distance than the left (*white arrow*, part *D*), indicating an injury through the intervening cartilage. *E*, A posterior view of a bone scan shows increased activity (*arrow*) corresponding to this coracoid injury.

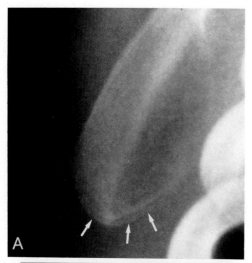

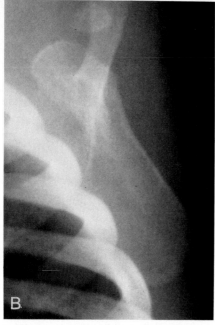

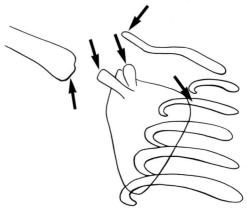

Figure 4.27. Patterns of shoulder girdle injuries in abused infants. Most injuries involving these regions result from forces delivered indirectly via the upper extremity, or associated with violent shaking. Fractures can involve the clavicle, coracoid, acromion, humerus, and upper ribs (*arrows*). Scapular injuries carry the greatest specificity for abuse; however, multiple lesions involving the other sites carry a similar specificity.

Figure 4.26. *A*, View of the right scapula of a 6-month-old abused infant reveals a curvilinear bone density related to the inferior angle of the scapula (*arrows*). *B*, The left scapula is normal.

Radionuclide scintigraphy may be particularly useful in assessing these complex regions. Computed tomography should be reserved for particularly difficult cases. Although these uncommon injuries are usually difficult to identify, the high specificity for child abuse demands thorough assess- ment with compulsive attention to technical quality.

REFERENCES

1. Caffey J: Multiple fractures in the long bones of infants suffering from chronic subdural hematoma. *Am J Roentgenol (AJR)* 56:163–173, 1946.
2. Lis EF, Frauenberger GS: Multiple fractures associated with subdural hematoma in infancy. *Pediatrics* 6:890–892, 1950.
3. Smith FW, Gilday DL, Ash JM, Green MD: Unsuspected costo-vertebral fractures demonstrated by bone scanning in the child abuse syndrome. *Pediatr Radiol* 10:103–106, 1980.
4. Woolley PV Jr, Evans WA Jr: Significance of skeletal lesions in infants resembling those of traumatic origin. *JAMA* 158:539–543, 1955.
5. Marie J, Apostolides P, Salet J, Eliachar L, Lyon G: Hematome sous-dural du nourrisson associe a des fractures des membres. *Ann Pediatr* 30:1757–1763, 1954.
6. Silverman FN: The roentgen manifestations of unrecognized skeletal trauma in infants. *Am J Roentgenol (AJR)* 69:413–427, 1953.
7. Herndon WA: Child abuse in a military population. *J Pediatr Orthop* 3:73–76, 1983.
8. Akbarnia B, Torg JS, Kirkpatrick J, Sussman S: Manifestations of the battered-child syndrome. *J Bone Joint Surg* 56A:1159–1166, 1974.
9. Barrett IR, Kozlowski K: The battered child syndrome. *Australas Radiol* 23:72–82, 1979.
10. Gee DJ: Radiology in forensic pathology. *Radiography* 41:109–144, 1975.

11. Thomas PS: Rib fractures in infancy. *Ann Radiol (Paris)* 20:115–122, 1977.
12. Feldman KW, Brewer DK: Child abuse, cardiopulmonary resuscitation, and rib fractures. *Pediatrics* 73:339–342, 1984.
13. Merten DF, Radkowski MA, Leonidas JC: The abused child. A radiological reappraisal. *Radiology* 146:377–381, 1983.
14. Warwick R, Williams PL (eds): Osteology. Arthrology. In *Gray's Anatomy*. Philadelphia, WB Saunders, 1973, pp 200–385, 388–471.
15. Cameron JM, Rae L: The radiological diagnosis. Differential diagnosis. In *Atlas of the Battered Child Syndrome*. London, Churchill Livingstone, 1975, pp 20–50, 51–64.
16. Kogutt MS, Swischuk LE, Fagan CJ: Patterns of injury and significance of uncommon fractures in the battered child syndrome. *Am J Roentgenol (AJR)* 121:143–149, 1974.
17. Kleinman PK: Radiologic and histopathologic correlates of posterior rib fractures in abused infants: an alternate mechanism of injury. Presented at the Society for Pediatric Radiology, Washington, DC, April 10–13, 1986.
18. Jaudes PK: Comparison of radiography and radionuclide bone scanning in the detection of child abuse. *Pediatrics* 73:166–168, 1984.
19. Sty JR, Starshak RJ: The role of bone scintigraphy in the evaluation of the suspected abused child. *Radiology* 146:369–375, 1983.
20. Haase GM, Ortiz VN, Sfakianakis GN, Morse TS: The value of radionuclide bone scanning in the early recognition of deliberate child abuse. *J Trauma* 20:873–875, 1980.
21. Sfakianakis GN, Haase GM, Ortiz VN, Morse TS: The value of bone scanning in the early recognition of deliberate child abuse. *J Nucl Med* 20:675, 1979.
22. Pickett WJ, Faleski EJ, Chacko MA, Jarrett RV: Comparison of radiographic and radionuclide skeletal surveys in battered children. *South Med J* 76:207–212, 1983.
23. Berdon WE: Editorial. Battered chldren: how valuable are bone scans in diagnosis? *Appl Radiol* 10:12, 124, 1981.
24. Berdon WE: Should the radionuclide skeletal survey be used as a screening procedure in suspected child abuse victims? Letters to the editor. *Radiology* 148:576, 1983.
25. Diament MJ: Should the radionuclide skeletal survey be used as a screening procedure in suspected child abuse victims? Letters to the editor. *Radiology* 148:573, 1983.
26. Cumming WA: Neonatal skeletal fractures. Birth trauma or child abuse? *J Can Assoc Radiol* 30:30–33, 1979.
27. Galleno H, Oppenheim WL: The battered child syndrome revisited. *Clin Orthop* 162:11–19, 1982.
28. Haller JO, Kassner EG: The "battered child" syndrome and its imitators: a critical evaluation of specific radiological signs. *Appl Radiol* 6:88–111, 1977.
29. Marquezy R-A, Bach C, Blondeau M: Hematoma sous-dural et fractures multiples des os longs chez un nourrison de 9 mois. *Arch Fr Pediatr* 9:526–531, 1952.
30. O'Neill JA Jr, Meacham WF, Griffin PP, Sawyers JL: Patterns of injury in the battered child syndrome. *J Trauma* 13:332–339, 1973.
31. Silverman FN: Radiologic and special diagnostic procedures. In Kempe CH, Helfer RE (eds): *The Battered Child*, ed 3. Chicago, University of Chicago Press, 1980, pp 215–240.
32. Ogden JA: Chest and pectoral girdle. In *Skeletal Injury in the Child*. Philadelphia, Lea & Febiger, 1982, pp 202–219.
33. Rosenberg N, Bottenfield G: Fracture in infants: a sign of child abuse. *Ann Emerg Med* 11:178–180, 1982.
34. Forster A: Neonatal metaphyseal injuries: typical changes and an unusual site. *Ann Radiol (Paris)* 14:315–319, 1971.
35. Snedecor ST, Wilson HB: Some obstetrical injuries to the long bones. *J Bone Joint Surg* 31A:378–384, 1949.
36. Merten D, Kirks DR, Ruderman RJ: Occult humeral epiphyseal fracture in battered infants. *Pediatr Radiol* 10:151–154, 1981.
37. Hiller HG: Battered or not—a reappraisal of metaphyseal fragility. *Am J Roentgenol Radium Ther Nucl Med (AJR)* 114:241–246, 1972.
38. Hilton S: The accidentally injured and abused child. In Hilton SVW, Edwards DK, Hilton JW (eds): *Practial Pediatric Radiology*. Philadelphia, WB Saunders, 1984, pp 443–485.
39. Jones HH, Davis JH: Multiple traumatic lesions of the infant skeleton. *Stanford Med Bull* 15:259–273, 1957.
40. Sauer H, Kurz R, Fink M: Uber thoracoabdominale- und knochenverletzungen bei kindesmisshandlungen (battered child-syndrome). *Monatsschr Unfallheilk* 78:533–543, 1975.
41. Astley R: Multiple metaphyseal fractures in small children (metaphyseal fragility of bone). *Br J Radiol* 26:577–583, 1953.

5 Spinal Trauma

PAUL K. KLEINMAN, M.D

The first case of spinal fractures related to probable child abuse was reported by Astley in 1953 (1). Although he attributed these fractures as well as other long bone injuries to an underlying state of metaphyseal fragility, it is apparent that he was describing a group of abused infants. In 1957, Jones and Davis (2) found a fracture involving the lumbar spine in one of the five abused children they studied. Subsequent reports have dealt specifically with spine lesions in abused infants (3–11), and other articles and texts dealing with child abuse have included examples of spinal injuries (12–24).

The true incidence of spine involvement in abused children is difficult to determine. Only 1 of Kogutt et al.'s series of 95 abused children had evidence of spinal injury (25), and only 1 of the 89 fractures noted in Galleno and Oppenheim's study of 36 battered children involved the spine (26). In contrast, Akbarnia et al. (15) noted that 9 of 264 fractures occurring in 74 abused children involved the spine. Merten et al. (27), in a recent large review of 563 cases of child abuse, failed to identify a single spine injury.

A review of the literature reveals 41 cases of spinal injury secondary to abuse. A total of approximately 85 fractures were identified, attesting to the common multiplicity of these lesions. The vast majority of these fractures involved the vertebral bodies, and most fractures of the posterior elements accompanied vertebral body lesions. Only two examples of isolated posterior element injuries are reported (10, 11). The average age of recognition of spinal injury was 22 months, with a range of 2 months to 10 years. Over two-thirds of these injuries occurred in children under 3 years, and half

were in those under a year. Thus, the age distribution tends to follow a pattern similar to that of injuries involving the remainder of the skeleton. Although an accentuated kyphosis is occasionally seen, the large majority of patients show no symptoms referable to the spine. Dramatic degrees of subluxation and vertebral body displacement may be accompanied only by postural abnormality or stiffness (6, 8). Occasionally patients may present with evidence of spinal cord involvement related to compression or contusion (3–6). Although radiologic alterations are the rule, one case of an epidural hemorrhage without associated plain film abnormality has been described (28).

In a letter to *The Lancet*, Towbin (29) described four infants between 2 weeks and 6 months of age dying with spinal epidural hematomas. Hemorrhage was consistently in the cervical and upper thoracic regions and was associated with spinal cord congestion and petechia. The clinical picture was that of the sudden infant death syndrome. No history of trauma was described. The author attributed these hemorrhages to self-induced acute hyperextension or flexion. He presumed that spinal shock with direct suppression of respiration accounted for the clinical pattern of sudden infant death. The relationship of these injuries to those seen in abused infants remains to be clarified.

Concepts regarding the mechanisms of injury of spinal lesions are based upon occasional admissions by the offender, the pattern of radiologic alterations, and the presence of other associated lesions that have well-described causal mechanisms. As with most reports of child abuse, confessions that precisely define the form of inflicted trauma are usually lacking. Gosnold and Sivaloganathan (28) provided a concise description of the mechanism of injury leading to an epidural hemorrhage in the thoracic region of a 9-month-old infant. The infant had been thrown into the air and allowed to drop, striking the right side of the thorax against the knee of the assailant. This acute lateral flexion produced epidural and spinal cord hemorrhage, as well as injury to the liver and thorax. Curphey et al. (13) described the specifics of the injury in a 3-week-old infant with a fracture-dislocation at C2–C3. The father admitted to repeated beatings of the infant because of continual crying. On the day of death, he admitted squeezing and twisting the child's neck and that he heard a "snapping" sound. Thus, in these unusual examples, lateral flexion or torsion resulted in spinal damage.

Most other incidences of spinal injury, however, are more consistent with hyperflexion and/or hyperextension. Romer and Wolff (3) provided a detailed account of the injuries resulting in bilateral pedicle and vertebral body fractures involving T12 in an 18-month-old child. The mother described lifting the child approximately 2 feet above the kitchen table with both hands about the chest. She then forcefully sat the child down on the table. The child immediately developed flaccid paraplegia and incontinence. A fracture of the distal humerus also occurred, presumably as the child attempted to break the fall with an outstretched arm.

Fractures of the pedicles of C2, the so-called hangman's fractures, are well known to occur with hyperextension, and a case of a hangman's fracture secondary to shaking of a 4-month-old infant has been described by McGrory and Fenichel (30). In this case, the mother forcibly shook the child by the shoulders during a period of apnea and cyanosis. This type of mechanism likely explains a case of hangman's fracture noted in an abused infant (10). Many of the infants demonstrating spinal injury will manifest metaphyseal lesions characteristic of abuse. It is well accepted that these metaphyseal lesions occur during episodes of sudden acceleration and deceleration consistent with shaking, and it is reasonable to assume that hyperflexion and extension during these episodes results in the usual spinal injuries as well.

Radiologic Alterations

VERTEBRAL BODIES AND INTERVERTEBRAL DISCS

The most commonly encountered injuries to the spine involve the vertebral bodies. These are manifest as varying degrees of compression deformity. The majority of these lesions occur in the lower thoracic and upper lumbar region. During the hyperflexed state, these vertebrae will lie at the apex of the resultant dorsal lumbar kyphosis. Findings may range from a barely perceptible loss of height of the anterior aspect of the vertebral body (Fig. 5.1) to severe compression deformity (Fig. 5.2). The endplates are intact, and the disc spaces are preserved. When greater loss of height is present, the tendency for multiple-level involvement increases. Although compression injuries are not infrequent with accidental trauma in older patients and in patients with

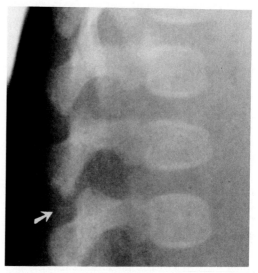

Figure 5.1. Lateral radiograph of the upper lumbar spine in a 2-month-old abused infant reveals compression deformity of the body of L2, associated with avulsion of the spinous process (*arrow*). (Reproduced with permission from Kleinman PK, Zito JL: Avulsion of the spinous processes caused by infant abuse. *Radiology* 151:389–391, 1984.)

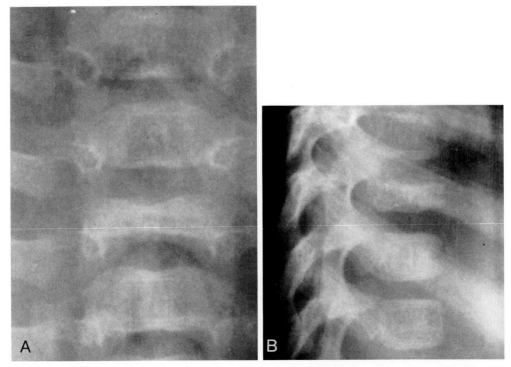

Figure 5.2. Anteroposterior (AP) (*A*) and lateral (*B*) views of the spine reveal severe compression deformity of T8. This abused infant also had a skull fracture, subdural hematomas, and cerebral contusion.

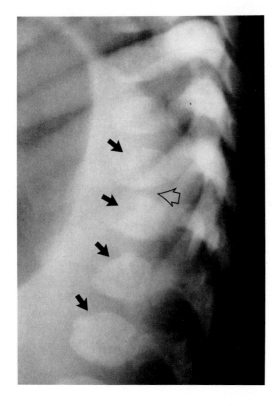

osteoporosis, a compression fracture in an infant or in any child without a history of major trauma is a very suspicious finding.

With severe hyperflexion, herniation of the nucleus pulposus into the vertebral body may occur, with resultant narrowing of the intervertebral disc space. The herniation invariably occurs along the anterior margin of the vertebral endplates and is usually most pronounced superiorly (Fig. 5.3). This disruption of the endplate and replacement of the normal marrow space and trabeculae of the vertebral body by disc material results in a loss of bone at the site of herniation. This leads to a notched appearance that is most commonly observed along the anter-

Figure 5.3. Lateral radiograph of the thoracolumbar junction in an abused infant reveals varying degrees of notching of the anterosuperior endplates of T10 through L2 (*solid arrows*). These defects are secondary to herniation of the nucleus pulposus into the vertebral body. Disc space narrowing is noted at T11-T12 (*open arrow*).

osuperior and occasionally along the anteroinferior margin of the vertebral body. Bone reaction along the margins of this defect will result in sclerosis, and the margins may become quite well defined (Fig. 5.4). This appearance is accentuated if an accompanying compression fracture of the body is associated with the disc herniation. A somewhat similar but less marked appearance can occur in normal infants (31), and occasionally confusion with an inflammatory process may occur. However, the notching noted in abused patients generally involves a large portion of the anterior margin of the vertebral body, a somewhat unusual finding in cases of inflammatory discitis and osteomyelitis. An additional differential feature is relatively mild disc space narrowing when the finding is due to trauma in contrast to severe disc space loss in infectious discitis. On occasion, only the lack of clinical and

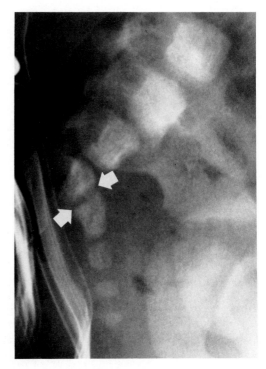

Figure 5.5. Lateral view of the sacrum and coccyx of a 2-year-old abused child. There is a fracture of the lower sacrum with an acute kyphotic angulation (*arrows*). (Reproduced with permission from Dorst JP: Child abuse. *Radiologe* 22:335–341, 1982.)

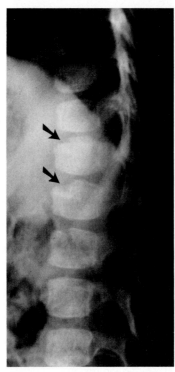

Figure 5.4. Anterosuperior notching of the bodies of T12 and L1 with surrounding sclerosis is noted (*arrows*) in this 33-month-old abused child. (Reproduced with permission from Barrett IR, Kozlowski K: The battered child syndrome. *Australas Radiol* 23:72–82, 1979.)

laboratory findings in the abused patient will allow differentiation from an inflammatory etiology.

Fractures involving the vertebrae of the sacral region have been described by Hilton (24) and by Dorst (20) (Fig. 5.5). Hilton believes this injury occurs as a child is lifted below the axilla and the child's buttocks are then smashed onto a chair, table, or countertop, delivering an axial load to the sacrum with resultant compression deformity.

In contrast to injuries involving the extremities, vertebral body injuries will persist long after the acute insult. Disc herniation may interfere with ossification and ultimate fusion of the ring apophysis anteriorly, resulting in a growth disturbance. Hemorrhage due to bruising in the paraspinal muscles may lead to a scoliotic and an excessive lordotic deformity in the lumbar region, detectable many years after the original injury (9)

POSTERIOR ELEMENTS

Injuries to the posterior elements may involve the bony and/or ligamentous structures. In the author's experience, spinous process fractures are the most common injury involving the posterior elements. In 1984, Kleinman and Zito reported three cases of spinous process injuries in three infants under 5 months of age (11). An earlier report by Hiller (32) described a similar fracture of the spinous process in an infant, but he attributed this to underlying bone fragility rather than to abuse. The spinous process fractures may occur in the mid- and lower thoracic region, as well as the upper lumbar area. Fractures may be solitary (Fig. 5.1), or multiple (Figs. 5.6 and 5.7). They appear to result from avulsion of

cartilage and/or bone at the interspinous ligamentous attachments. If bone is avulsed, the fracture will be evident on initial films. If a portion of the generous cartilaginous apophysis is avulsed, progressive calcification and ossification will be seen on delayed examinations (Fig. 5.7). A similar fracture occurs in older patients at the cervicothoracic junction in association with sudden hyperflexion, the so-called clay shoveler's fracture (33). If the infant is held around the trunk, forceful movement during an episode of shaking would produce sudden extension and flexion that could result in spinous process avulsion (Fig. 5.6B). Posterior ligamentous complex injury due to sudden hyperflexion is well described in older patients, often in association with vertebral body compression (34). Vertebral compres-

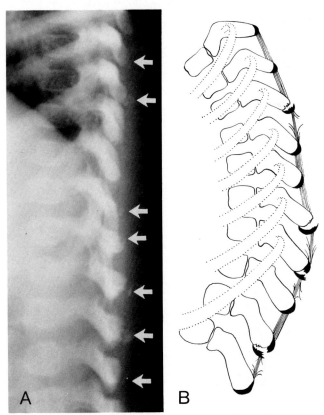

Figure 5.6. *A,* Lateral view of the thoracolumbar spine in a 4 ½-month-old abused infant reveals irregular ossification (*arrows*) adjacent to multiple thoracic and lumbar spinous processes. *B,* Schematic rendering of proposed hyperflexion mechanism of injury. (Reproduced with permission from Kleinman PK, Zito JL: Avulsion of the spinous processes caused by infant abuse. *Radiology* 151:389–391, 1984.)

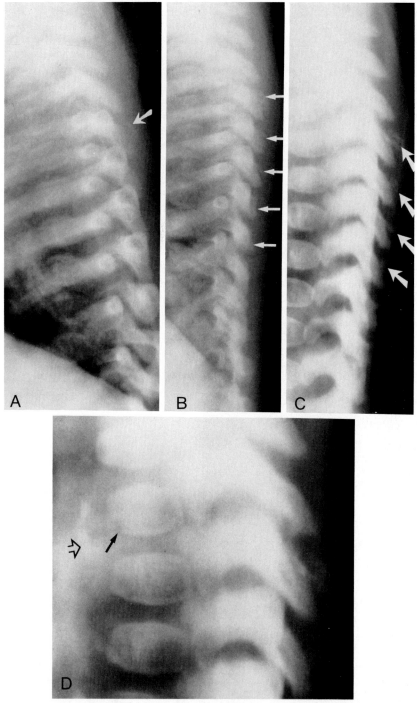

Figure 5.7. *A*, Lateral radiograph of the thoracic spine of a 3-month-old abused infant reveals faint ossification adjacent to a midthoracic spinous process (*arrow*). *B*, Radiograph obtained several weeks later shows increased ossification adjacent to multiple spinous processes (*arrows*). *C*, Lateral tomogram 2 weeks later demonstrates multiple areas of ossification adjacent to irregular spinous processes (*arrows*). *D*, Coned-down lateral tomogram of the midthoracic spine reveals notching of a vertebral body (*closed arrow*) with adjacent prevertebral soft tissue calcification (*open arrow*). (Reproduced with permission from Kleinman PK, Zito JL: Avulsion of the spinous processes caused by infant abuse. *Radiology* 151:389–391, 1984.)

sion deformities were, in fact, present in two of Kleinman and Zito's three spinous process avulsion cases (11). One of these cases also had associated paraspinal soft tissue calcification (Fig. 5.7D).

Despite extensive posterior ligamentous complex disruption, these injuries appear to be quite stable. In contrast, the so-called hangman's fracture, or fracture of the pedicles of C2, possesses some degree of instability. The fracture is often difficult to identify, but it is visible as a vertical lucency just posterior to the body of C2 (Fig. 5.8). The critical atlanto-occipital relationships are maintained because the transverse ligamentous structures are intact. Although this injury requires prompt and secure immobilization, it is usually not associated with a neurologic deficit at presentation.

An extraordinary fracture involving the junction of the neural arch and vertebral bodies has been described by Faure et al.

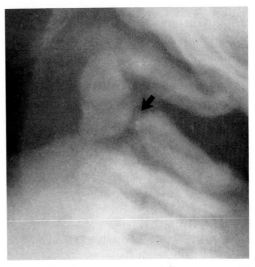

Figure 5.8. Lateral view of the upper cervical spine in this abused infant reveals a hangman's fracture (i.e., fractures of the pedicles of C2) (*arrow*). There is slight anterior tilting of the odontoid process, but the alignment of the posterior elements is maintained.

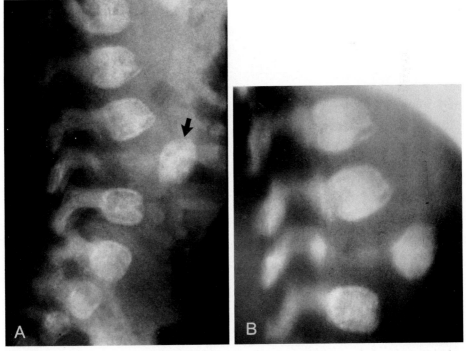

Figure 5.9. *A*, Lateral view of the lumbar spine in a 3-month-old abused infant reveals a fracture through the posterior elements of L4 with marked anterior displacement of the vertebral body (*arrow*). Notching and wedging of L2 and L3 is also present. *B*, Lateral tomogram through this region shows the injuries to advantage. (Reproduced with permission from Faure C, Steadman C, Lelande G, AL Moudares N, Marsault C, Bennet J: The wandering vertebral body. *Ann Radiol* 22:96–99, 1979.)

(8). The so-called wandering vertebral body appeared to be the result of an actual separation of the posterior arch from the vertebral body at the neurocentral synchondrosis (Fig. 5.9). This was associated with marked anterior displacement of the body of L4 and an increase in the interpediculate distance at this level. The lesion was accompanied by notching and/or compression at three other levels, further supporting the hyperflexion theory proposed by the author. There were other associated bony lesions consistent with abuse, in particular one involving the left pubic bone. Unfortunately, the diagnosis of the battered child syndrome was "refused" by the attending pediatrician because of the "high social situation" of the parents.

Vertebral dislocation with or without fracture carries greater import than fracture with maintenance of alignment. During hy-

perflexion or extension, fractures of the posterior elements and/or disruption of the posterior ligamentous complexes may allow anterior or posterior dislocation of vertebrae, with spinal cord compression (Figs. 5.10 and 5.11) (5, 6). Again, the association of paraspinal calcification indicates the concomitant soft tissue hemorrhage. Although the frontal projection may provide some indication of these injuries, lateral projections are essential to document and characterize the extent of the dislocation.

Although most subluxations associated with abuse involve the lower thoracic and lumbar regions, on occasion the cervical spine is involved. Figure 5.12 illustrates a patient with Marfan's syndrome who was allegedly struck in the head, with resultant subluxation (perched facets) at C2–C3. A fracture involving the ring apophysis appeared to limit the reducibility of the sub-

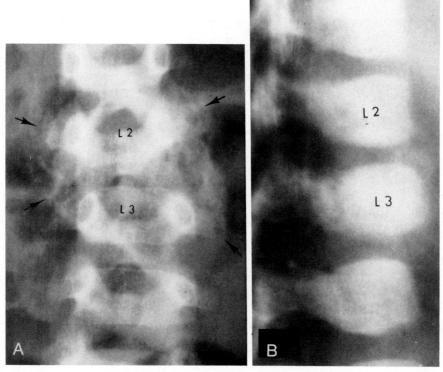

Figure 5.10. Anteroposterior (A) and lateral (B) views of the lumbar spine of a 2-year-old abused child demonstrate a healing fracture dislocation at L2–L3. Note lateral and posterior displacement of L2 upon L3 and extensive calcifying hematoma (arrows). (Reproduced with permission from Swischuk LE: Spine and spinal cord trauma in the battered child syndrome. Radiology 92:733–738, 1969.)

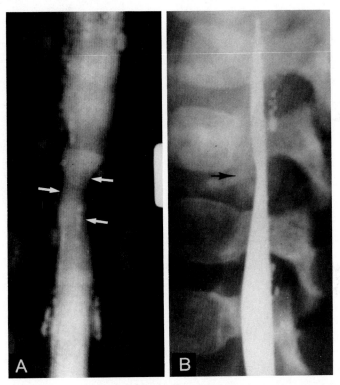

Figure 5.11. Myelogram corresponding to plain films in Figure 5.9. AP (*A*) and lateral (*B*) radiographs demonstrate compression of the thecal sac laterally and anteriorly (*arrows*). Anterior displacement of L2 on L3 is evident. (Reproduced with permission from Swischuk LE: Spine and spinal cord trauma in the battered child syndrome. *Radiology* 92:733–738, 1969.)

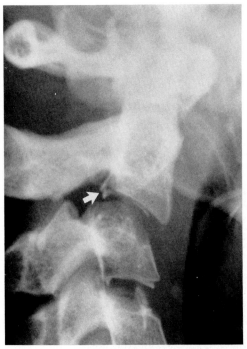

Figure 5.12. Lateral view of the upper cervical spine in a 13-year-old male with Marfan syndrome. Patient was allegedly struck in the head, resulting in subluxation of C2 on C3. There is a fracture of the ring apophysis and posterior vertebral margin of C2 (*arrow*) with perching of the facets of the apophyseal joints at this level.

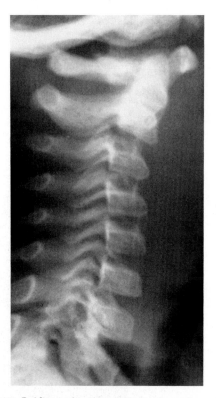

Figure 5.13. Lateral cervical spine of an 18-month-old abused infant with a skull fracture and cervical muscle spasm. C2 is 2 mm anterior to C3, and there is a mild kyphotic deformity at this level. This "pseudosubluxation" is a common finding in patients with muscle spasm and does not signify underlying ligamentous injury. There were no neurologic signs in this patient.

luxation. True C2–C3 subluxation should not be confused with the so-called pseudosubluxation that is commonly noted in young patients with cervical muscle spasm (Fig. 5.13) (35).

Finally, substantial spinal cord injury may occur without associated bony alterations. In most instances this is due to a dislocation or subluxation at the apophyseal joints that has subsequently reduced. Soft tissue swelling, particularly in the pretracheal region, may be the only plain film indication of spinal cord injury. Myelography will document the associated spinal cord contusion or edema (Fig. 5.14) (5).

Summary

Because the mechanism of injury of all of the fractures described above is consistent with hyperflexion-extension, it is not uncommon to encounter multiple lesions involving the posterior elements and the vertebral bodies in a single patient. Identification of an isolated spinal injury makes careful scrutiny of the entire spine mandatory. It is clear that such alterations are more common than the limited number of reports in the literature suggest. In most cases the injuries are silent, and, therefore, routine evaluation of the spine is essential when skeletal surveys for abuse are carried out in infants and young children. At the University of Massachusetts, we routinely radiograph the infant spine in the lateral as well as the anteroposterior projection. Because spinal injuries are likely to be associated with extremely violent assaults, surveillance

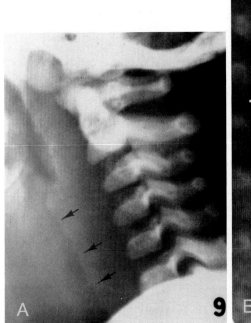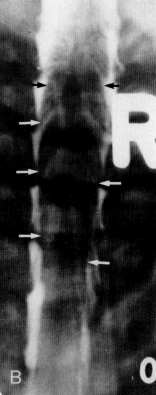

Figure 5.14. *A,* Lateral cervical spine radiograph of same patient as in Figure 5.9 reveals tracheal displacement (*arrows*) indicating prevertebral swelling. *B,* AP view of cervical myelogram shows symmetrical widening of the cervical spinal cord (*arrows*) consistent with hematoma or edema. (Reproduced with permission from Swischuk LE: Spine and spinal cord trauma in the battered child syndrome. *Radiology* 92:733–738, 1969.)

for these injuries is mandatory. The utility of radionuclide studies in the diagnosis of these spinal injuries secondary to abuse is untested, and, at present, standard radiographic studies are the primary method of investigation.

REFERENCES

1. Astley R: Multiple metaphyseal fractures in small children (metaphyseal fragility of bone). *Br J Radiol* 26:577–583, 1953.
2. Jones HH, Davis JH: Multiple traumatic lesions of the infant skeleton. *Stanford Med Bull* 15:259–273, 1957.
3. Romer KH, Wolff F: Uber wirbelsaulenverletzungen durch misshandlung bie kleinstkindern. *Arch Orthop Unfall-Chir (Orthop Trauma Surg)* 55:203–211, 1963.
4. Dahmen G: Zur prognose der traumatischen querschnittslahmung im kindesalter. *Arch Orthop Unfall-Chir* 53:311–314, 1961.
5. Swischuk LE: Spine and spinal cord trauma in the battered child syndrome. *Radiology* 92:733–738, 1969.
6. Cullen JC: Spinal lesions in battered babies. *J Bone Joint Surg* 57B:364–366, 1975.
7. Dickson RA, Leatherman KD: Spinal injuries in child abuse: case report. *J Trauma* 18:811–812, 1978.
8. Faure C, Steadman C, LeLande G, Al Moudares N, Marsault C, Bennet J: The wandering vertebral body. *Ann Radiol (Paris)* 22:96–99, 1979.
9. Wenger DR, Rokicki RR: Spinal deformity secondary to scar formation in a battered child. A case report. *J Bone Joint Surg* 60A:847–849, 1978.
10. Gille P, Bonneville JF, Francois JY, Aubert D, Peltre G, Canal JP: Fracture des pedicules de l'axis chez un nourrisson battu. *Chir Pediatr* 21:343–344, 1980.
11. Kleinman PK, Zito JL: Avulsion of the spinous processes caused by infant abuse. *Radiology* 151:389–391, 1984.
12. McHenry T, Girdany BR, Elmer E: Unsuspected trauma with multiple skeletal injuries during infancy and childhood. *Pediatrics* 31:903–908, 1963.
13. Curphey TJ, Kade H, Noguchi TT, Moore SM: The

battered child syndrome. Responsibilities of the pathologist. *Calif Med* 102:102–104, 1965.

14. Maroteaux P, Fessard C, Aron J-J, Lamy M: Les sequelles du syndrome de Silverman (fractures multiples du nourrisson, syndrome dit des "enfants battus"): etudes de seize observations. *Presse Med* 75:711–716, 1967.

15. Akbarnia BA, Torg JS, Kirkpatrick J, Sussman S: Manifestations of the battered-child syndrome. *J Bone Joint Surg* 56A:1159–1166, 1974.

16. Rupprecht E, Berger G: Zur differentialdiagnose des multiplen skelet-traumas im kindersalter ("battered child syndrome"). *Radiol Diagn (Berl)* 17:615–625, 1976.

17. Caffey J: The bones: parent-infant trauma syndrome (PITS: Caffey-Kempe syndrome; battered babe syndrome). In *Pediatric X-Ray Diagnosis*, ed 7. Chicago, Year Book Medical Publishers, 1978, vol 2, pp 1335–1351.

18. Barrett IR, Kozlowski K: The battered child syndrome. *Australas Radiol* 23:72–82, 1979.

19. Silverman FN: Radiologic aspects of the battered child syndrome. In Helfer RE, Kempe CH (eds): *The Battered Child*, ed 2. Chicago, University of Chicago Press, 1974, pp 41–60.

20. Dorst JP: Child abuse. *Radiologe* 22:335–341, 1982.

21. Dorst JP: The radiographic manifestations of child abuse. In Rodriguez A (ed): *Handbook of Child Abuse and Neglect*, Flushing, NY, Medical Examination Publishing, 1977, pp 34–63.

22. Radkowski MA, Merten DF, Leonidas JC: The abused child: criteria for the radiologic diagnosis. *RadioGraphics* 3:262–297, 1983.

23. Leonidas JC: Skeletal trauma in the child abuse syndrome. *Pediatr Ann* 12:875–881, 1983.

24. Hilton S: The accidentally injured and abused child. In Hilton SVW, Edwards DK, Hilton JW (eds): *Practical Pediatric Radiology*. Philadelphia, WB Saunders, 1984, pp 443–485.

25. Kogutt MS, Swischuk LE, Fagen CJ: Patterns of injury and significance of uncommon fractures in the battered child syndrome. *Am J Roentgenol (AJR)* 121:143–149, 1974.

26. Galleno H, Oppenheim WL: The battered child syndrome revisited. *Clin Orthop* 162:11–19, 1982.

27. Merten DF, Radkowski MA, Leonidas JC: The abused child. A radiological reappraisal. *Radiology* 146:377–381, 1983.

28. Gosnold JK, Sivaloganathan S: Spinal cord damage in a case of non-accidental injury in children. *Med Sci Law* 20:54:57, 1980.

29. Towbin A: Sudden infant death (cot death) related to spinal injury. *Lancet* 2:940, 1967.

30. McGrory BE, Fenichel GM: Hangman's fracture subsequent to shaking in an infant. *Ann Neurol* 21:82, 1977.

31. Swischuk LE: The beaked, notched, or hooked vertebra: its significance in infants and young children. *Radiology* 95:661–664, 1970.

32. Hiller HG: Battered or not—a reappraisal of metaphyseal fragility. *Am J Roentgenol Radium Ther Nucl Med (AJR)* 114:241–246, 1972.

33. Harris JH Jr: Flexion injuries. In *The Radiology of Acute Cervical Spine Trauma*. Baltimore, Williams & Wilkins, 1978, pp 42–60.

34. Gehweiler JA Jr, Osborne RL Jr, Becker RF: The radiology of vertebral trauma. *Monogr Clin Radiol* 16:261–305, 1980

35. Swischuk LE: Anterior displacement of C2 in children. Physiologic or pathologic? A helpful differentiation. *Radiology* 122:759–763, 1977.

6 Dating Fractures

JOHN F. O'CONNOR, M.D.
JONATHAN COHEN, M.D.

Widespread recognition of the diagnosis of child abuse first depended on unequivocal radiologic evidence of fracture or fractures unsupported by a history of injury. It is still true that, when radiologic evidence of injury to the axial and appendicular skeleton is important in the diagnosis and treatment of abused children, the single most important factor is the relationship between the alleged cause and timing of the trauma. The correlation or lack of correlation of the diagnostic images with the temporal elements in the history is often the first evidence of suspicious trauma. It is usually clear, for example, that if no history of injury is given and a fracture is found, there are at least grounds for neglect and the question then must be raised as to whether an attempt to conceal the actual cause of the injury is being mounted by the historian. Typically, an explanation is provided by the historian, be it parent, guardian, or both, however plausible it may be, for the symptoms or signs that brought the child to medical attention. The ability of caregivers to assess the veracity of the historic comments then depends on the assessment of the injury as it presents clinically or is displayed on various imaging modalities. If, for example, a single injury to a localized portion of the extremity is alleged to have occurred but multiple fractures or foci of periosteal new bone formation are seen, then the caregiver should become suspicious and initiate further investigation. If, on the other hand, all the evidence reveals the fracture to be fresh, and the severity of the alleged injury correlates with the location of the injury and its clinical and radiographic characteristics, the suspicion of child abuse may never arise. It is clear, then, that the ability

of the radiologist or clinician to evaluate the age of the fracture or injury is one of the assessments critical to an initial determination of suspected child abuse. Obviously, the forensic aspects of establishing responsibility and determining the need for intervention by the authorities responsible for the care of the patient rests strongly in the assessments of the clinician and the radiologist regarding the nature and timing of the injury.

It is of interest that the literature on the healing of fractures and the correlation of histologic changes with radiologic images is extensive, but there is very little published information concerning the dating of fractures on the basis of radiographic appearance. Moreover, there is almost no literature on the subject of dating fractures in abused children. This is remarkable when one considers that clinical and medical/legal decisions concerning the management of abused children often are critically dependent upon these observations.

In this chapter, we will attempt to provide some criteria for dating fractures in the appendicular skeleton of children. The chapter will begin with a discussion of the special features of the pathophysiology of fractures in abused children. This will be followed by a discussion of the histologic response as correlated with imaging features of musculoskeletal tissues after injury, with particular emphasis on the soft tissues, periosteum, fracture line definition, endosteal callus formation, and the effects of immobilization or lack of immobilization on these processes. Most of the information will be drawn from our experience and what literature is available concerning the healing of experimental fractures in animals, and what is known about the healing of fractures of known age occurring in infants and children as a result of trauma of established cause. A discussion of old fractures and the possibilities for dating injuries that have already healed will also be included. Finally, general guidelines that allow the dating of fractures will be presented.

Pathophysiology

An understanding of the pathophysiology of fractures in the abused child must take into account three ways in which those fractures differ from normal, run-of-the-mill fractures in children following trauma. Henceforth, these fractures will be referred to as "ordinary fractures" to differentiate them from "abuse fractures." First, the vast majority of abuse fractures occur in infants and are unusual in children 4 years or older. Second, there may be no history whatsoever of injury or, if there is one, it may be a fabricated story alleging a misleading set of circumstances. Most important, the abuse fracture should usually be regarded as a result of a sequence of several injuries rather than a single physical insult. Even when, in retrospect, circumstances allow determination that only one traumatic episode occurred, there usually is a considerable delay between that episode and medical diagnosis and treatment. During that delay, often a matter of days or weeks, the absence of treatment (some type of immobilization of the injured part) constitutes a series of injuries at the fracture site. Of course, when there have been several or many episodes of abuse, the timing of those episodes as they affect the healing process may elicit profound changes in the nature of that process. Any single episode may not only disrupt whatever repair has taken place, but also may provide a stimulus for repair comparable to a fracture de novo.

The natural tendency for one who wishes to understand the pathophysiology of the abuse fracture is to bring into consideration all the knowledge accumulated concerning the radiology, pathomechanics, histology, and experimental studies of ordinary frac-

tures. In so doing, however, he/she must factor into the equation the essential differences that each of those considerations imposes on the situation. Each one of these deserves separate elaboration.

AGE

Radiologists are well aware that any fractures in the acute stage, particularly undisplaced epiphyseal plate fractures, may be difficult to diagnose in an infant. It is common knowledge that predominantly cartilagenous structures at the ends of the bones of children require the radiologist diagnosing skeletal injury to pay careful attention to soft tissue images, and occasionally to require that there be comparable views of the contralateral extremity. Those requirements in an infant suspected of having an abuse fracture are much more stringent than for an infant not under suspicion. Further, the clinician whose suspicions have been aroused in any way should share that suspicion (i.e., any positive or even equivocal historic or physical findings) with the radiologist in order that the appropriate radiologic examination(s) be made. Any guarding of a part, any decrease in movement, any tenderness to palpation merits radiologic investigation. Often a skeletal survey is indicated. The indications for survey examinations have been discussed at length elsewhere in this text (Chapter 2). When any view reveals evidence of one or more fractures that may be more than a few days old, but in particular when fractures of different ages are imaged, the diagnosis of abuse may be firm, but then the chronology of the repair must be reckoned with. Here, the well-recognized rapidity of repair processes in the infant deserves a more detailed consideration than is usually provided in textbooks and articles on fractures in infants and children. In those publications, not much emphasis exists on differences between infants and children as to the locations and character of the fractures (see pathomechanics below), or on reactions of tissue to trauma. For the dating of a fracture radiologically, the general precept has been that periosteal reaction (new bone) will occur at the earliest 1 week after injury, but the usual interval is 10 to 14 days. In young infants, the usual interval is considered somewhat shorter, probably 7 to 14 days. Similarly, the elaboration of callus is much more rapid in the infant than in older children, as is solidification of the callus and remodeling of the healed area.

Histologists are also aware of differences between infants and children with respect to tissue changes after fracture, but this knowledge, based on firsthand observations, is quite limited for two reasons. One is the paucity of available specimens of fractures in infants in the early stages of healing. The other is that such specimens provide only one frame in a motion picture of pathophysiology. As a general rule, a fracture in an infant will elicit a more rapid rate of progress in all the phases of healing, especially in the production of fibrocartilagenous matrix in the callus. Whether the extent of hemorrhage and exudate is in proportion to the size of the injured member or to the age of the individual is problematic because so many other variables enter into those processes, for example, severity of the injury or injuries, displacement of the fracture fragments, and the effectiveness of immobilization. The multiplicity of variables has forced histologists to rely more on experimental evidence than on specimens from humans. That evidence, as it relates to the study of differences between infants and older individuals, is not only sparse but also inherently qualified by the questionable assumptions that the species differences can be ignored, and that animals in infancy are comparable in the areas under study to human infants. However, it is in pathomechanics that the differences in age offer some of the most challenging problems. The study of fractures in recent years has laid great emphasis on such subjects as the energy causing the fracture and the mechanical conditions imposed by the anatomic pattern of the skeletal part, the forces applied and the pattern of displacement of fragments. In relation to abuse fractures these considerations become even more important. So-called high-energy fractures caused by motor vehicle accidents, gunshot wounds, or the like are rare in infants in general, but in cases of abuse fractures the actual traumatic event rarely is known explicitly, at least at the time of the diagnosis. Most ordinary fractures in infants are the result of falls (i.e., low-energy injuries), and this applies to abuse fractures as well. However, with abuse fractures there may be patterns that are characteristic (e.g., buckethandle fractures) or suspicious (e.g., multiple fractures, often involving two extremities). When the pattern also reveals different dates for the fractures, suspicion is enhanced.

HISTORY

The circumstances surrounding the arrival of a child at a medical facility vary greatly. A discussion of these complex circumstances would take this presentation far afield. However, it is imperative that the radiologist eventually obtain a concise history regarding the nature and time of the injury. All too often the radiologist, who infrequently sees the patient, is expected to express an opinion about the dating of injuries solely on the basis of his/her examination of the films. The medical person who elicits the history may not confer with the radiologist at the time when films are ordered and initially read. For this reason, appropriate views may not be ordered. Moreover, equivocal findings may be discounted when they would be given greater or lesser credence if all the circumstances surrounding the history and its details were known. Although the radiologist often provides crucial guidance about the dating of injuries, the final determination is often based upon consultation with other members of the diagnostic team. The radiologist, therefore, will have to keep in mind the reliability of the clinical details furnished at the time the film is read, especially if any finding on them arouses a suspicion of abuse fracture.

REPETITIVE INJURIES

Repetitive injuries, which are considered commonly associated with the diagnosis of abuse fracture, are taken to mean two or more inflicted injuries to the same area of bone, and this term should therefore be restricted to that set of circumstances. Repeated injury to the child affecting different bones is also of importance and often is diagnosed on the initial presentation of the patient when images are pathognomonic of different stages of healing. Repeated injury in that sense does not pose much of a problem in pathophysiology because each injury is repaired according to its inherent chronology. It is true that the radiologist must know, usually from personal experience, what the chronology of repair is likely to be for each individual bone (longest for the largest long bones, shortest for the small cancellous bones). Multiple injury is usually taken to mean injuries to more than one bone (or system or viscus) incurred simultaneously. Excluding that circumstance and also the situations when, because a specific fracture may be left untreated and will be subjected to further motion, the circumscribed entity of repetitive injury is defined as the inflicting, more than once, of significant trauma to the part.

The timing of repetitions of injury and their severity is obviously quite variable. If, for instance, an infant is abused sufficiently to cause a fracture of the femur and the process is repeated the next day, it would be expected that the hematoma around the fracture ends would be amplified considerably. If no significant additional displacement of fracture fragments occurs on either occasion, the repair sequence described above would follow. In contrast, if the repetitive trauma were inflicted one week after the first episode, not only would there be more hemorrhage, but also a tearing of many, if not all, of the newly formed thin-walled vessels and injury of the collagenous fibers that had stabilized the fracture fragments. There would also be further devitalization of the soft tissue and bone at the fracture site, including some of the cells of repair and of inflammation. Thus, an understanding of the processes engendered by repetitive injuries has to be a part of the assessment of an abuse fracture as evaluated by clinician, radiologist, and pathologist. It should be clear to the reader that the three considerations that have just been dis-

cussed, age, history of injury, and presence of repetitive injuries, strongly interact with each other. Each of these factors cannot be viewed in isolation from the other two.

Timetable of Histologic Phases of Fracture Healing

STAGE OF INDUCTION

The stage of induction is defined as the time interval between the instant of injury and the appearance of new bone in the area of the fracture. The duration of the stage of induction varies *inter alia* according to the site of injury, the severity of the trauma, and the patient's age. The most important event governing the duration of the stage of induction is the time it takes for a significant amount of granulation tissue to develop and to produce osteoid. There is controversy regarding the origin of the cells that produce the osteoid (so-called precursor cells, which change into osteoblasts), and emphasis has variably been put on cells of the periosteum or circulating undifferentiated cells. Whereas the division of a particular cell or its assumption of new capabilities (i.e., elaboration of matrix) may be shown to occupy a time frame of hours, the elaboration of a tissue (granulation) requires at least several days, and perhaps a week or more. Actual structures in the tissue, capillaries, strands of collagen, and the precursor cells have to be formed before the definitive elements, osteoid and bone, are produced.

During the stage of induction, hemorrhage occurs following the disruption of many vessels in bone and soft tissues at the fracture site. The hemorrhage may recur whenever the fracture fragments are moved. Hemorrhage, therefore, may occur within moments of the injury or, if it is cyclic, it can recur within several days. Two processes then are initiated—inflammation and resorption of nonviable tissues, including clot. These processes have a timetable of several days at a minimum, but more commonly of 3 or 4 weeks. The inflammation that begins soon after the injury occurs involves widespread swelling of the soft tissues at the site of fracture and is clinically associated with pain and swelling that are accentuated with any attempt to move the injured extremity. With fractures that are undisplaced, the duration of acute inflammation may be a few days. In infants and children this interval is considerably shorter than in adults. Infants and chldren may be free of pain as early as 1 to 2 days after the original injury. As the hemorrhage ceases and the hematoma and edema stabilize the soft tissues, the margins of the fracture that have become necrotic and the soft tissues that have become devitalized start to be resorbed. The ingrowth of new capillaries is required for the transport of inflammatory cells, precursor cells, and fluid as well as of macrophages and osteoclasts to accomplish the work of repair. Histologically, osteoclasts may begin to mobilize and osteolytic activity is usually present within 4 to 7 days of the original injury (1, 2).

Radiologically, the images of soft tissue reveal the presence of the hemorrhage, edema, and the concentration of cells as the first evidence of fracture if no displacement of the fracture fragments has occurred. In infants and children, nondisplaced fractures occur much more commonly than in adults, owing to the flexibility of the child's skeleton and the increased amounts of stretch that are tolerated by the soft tissues. The position and volume of the soft tissue swelling caused by exudation and hemorrhage are shown on radiographs, and the distortion of normal fat collections, including those adjacent to fascia and other connective tissue structures, often is the first diagnostic radiographic evidence of fracture. This precedes the demonstration of callus and generally decreases in amount as callus develops.

STAGE OF SOFT CALLUS

Internal and external soft callus begins to form between 10 and 14 days after injury in older children and adults, but somewhat earlier in infants. The earliest evidence of soft callus formation is the laying down of periosteal new bone. Histologically, the callus is produced by active proliferation of osteoblasts in the cambium layer of the periosteum while the precursor cells also produce some cartilage. Both the new woven bone and the cartilage increase in volume at the fracture site and gradually mature in the pattern of the trabeculae. This sequence is accompanied by a gradual increase in the ingrowth of thin-walled blood vessels and fibrous tissue. The stage of soft callus usually lasts between 3 and 4 weeks or until the bony fragments, when separated, begin to be bridged by lamellar bone. The end of this stage is clinically apparent when the bony fragments are no longer easily moved and beginning obliteration of the fracture line is noted on radiographs.

STAGE OF HARD CALLUS

When the fracture approaches this stage, both periosteal and endosteal bone begin to be converted to lamellar bone, which has an orientation that bridges the fracture site. At this stage the vascularity has increased, especially the blood supply to the endosteum. The osteoclasts are still active in removing necrotic trabeculae or cortex, but by this time nearly all of the hematoma and exudate and much of the inflammatory (granulation) tissue has been resorbed. The removed trabeculae are gradually replaced with fiber bone and then with lamellar bone. Radiographically, the fracture is now solidly united and remodeling of the callus will begin. The average elapsed time for this process in adults after a single, well-immobilized fracture is between 2 and 3 months for the major long bones (1–3).

In children and particularly in infants, such an ordinary fracture caused by an accident and well treated will take much less than 2 months to begin consolidation. Salter noted that "fractures of the shaft of the femur ["ordinary fractures"] may serve as an example of this phenomenon. A femoral fracture occurring at birth will be united in 3 weeks. A comparable fracture at the age of 8 years will be united in 8 weeks and at the age of 12 years, it will be united at 12 weeks. From the age of 20 years to old age, it will be united in approximately 20 weeks" (4).

However, as noted above, these estimates should be regarded as unreliable when applied to abuse fractures mainly because of the likelihood of repetitive injury. In one of our own cases, an untreated birth injury in a neonate with severe spina bifida (and thereby insensitive to pain and subjected to repetitive injuries during handling), a femoral fracture was noted at postmortem to be massively involved in bulky, highly cartilagenous callus but showed no consolidation or hard callus. The baby was 30 days old when she died.

STAGE OF REMODELING

Woven bone is gradually converted to lamellar bone and the original configuration of cortex and medullary cavity is gradually restored with correction of deformity by smoothing of the callus circumferentially surrounding the fracture. When the medullary canal has been reconstituted and the cortex approximates the original configuration of the cortex of the adjacent uninjured bone or a contralateral counterpart, the stage of remodeling is said to be complete. In adults, complete remodeling may not occur; in children, extreme degrees of remodeling are possible and may take place over a period as long as 1 to 2 years following the original injury. Some authors emphasize that remodeling of injuries with extensive deformity may occur throughout the period of growth and may even continue after the closure of the epiphyses (1–3).

Histology of Healing Epiphyseal Plate Injury

The histologic timetable of repair, as mentioned, varies also with the site of injury. Metaphyseal and diaphyseal fractures have the assigned stages of healing described above. However, the process in epiphyseal plate fractures is accompanied by involvement of enchondral bone formation since the usual plane of cleavage or fracture is through the zones of cartilage proliferation and/or the immediate subjacent metaphyseal bone. As stressed elsewhere, autopsy findings in abused children suggest that

these injuries are quite different than epiphyseal plate fractures encountered in everyday practice. Kleinman et al. (5) have noted, for instance, that fractures in abused children are more often found traversing the primary spongiosa or the region immediately adjacent to metaphyseal new bone rather than the cartilagenous physis itself. A prominent feature of the material derived from abused children at autopsy is the failure to show the typical plane of cleavage through the enchondral region. Instead, the plane of cleavage usually traverses the primary spongiosa, and the development of periosteal new bone is not a prominent feature in such cases (5). This will result in some confusion when classic criteria are used to date the fractures in abused children.

The following comments on the histology of epiphyseal plate healing are derived from experimental, biopsy, or autopsy material from children who have had trauma of known cause (6–11). The rate of epiphyseal plate healing will be much faster than healing in cancellous bone or cortical bone. When the fracture occurs in the zone of resting or proliferating cartilage, there is minimal hematoma that is rapidly replaced by granulation tissue. The uninjured cartilage cells proliferate so that there is a relatively rapid increase in the number of cells of each column. This causes a moderate widening of the physis. Resorption of the devitalized tissue occurs in the healing process as in other locations. As this healing process is taking place, there is gradual resumption of normal enchondral ossification. The conversion of hypertrophied cartilage cells to bone occurs simultaneously with the ossification of the fibrous callus. The provisional calcification and invasion of the cartilage by metaphyseal vessels proceeds normally. The vessels rapidly invade maturing cell columns, and repair may lead to restoration of strength in 10 days to a few weeks. When the fracture plane involves the zone of hypertrophied cells as well as the primary spongiosa, the hemorrhage and subsequent invasion of granulation tissue have the appearance of disorganized fibrocartilagenous callus, and that pattern is the one usually encountered in fractures of the metaphysis or diaphysis during the phase of early soft callus formation.

The process of fracture healing (i.e., periosteal as opposed to endosteal callus formation) is always seen at either of the fracture sites under discussion (the physis or metaphysis). It provides a ring of periosteal new bone formation around the fracture site that may be the first indication that the fracture is consolidating. As cellular proliferation and soft callus formation continue on the epiphyseal side of the metaphysis, they cause a widening of the physis and an apparent widening of the fracture line. In epiphyseal plate injuries, the periosteum is usually interrupted on one side and stripped from the metaphysis and diaphysis on the contralateral side. This periosteal stripping will provide the earliest evidence of radiologic healing. A fine line of periosteal new bone (or callus) is laid down and may be seen on images as early as 4 to 7 days after injury in the infant. Epiphyseal plate injuries in the Salter-Harris III and IV categories are so rarely seen in abuse fractures that they need not be discussed in great detail. Suffice it to say that these are injuries to resting cartilage and are usually healed by the development of fibrocartilage. This is particularly true in the case of fractures extending to articular surfaces. If the gap to be bridged is more than a millimeter or two, the relatively soft fibrocartilaginous bridge provides an irregular surface that may lead to the late development of osteoarthritic change. If anatomic reduction has occurred, the fibrocartilaginous bridge may be less than a millimeter in diameter and no discernable effect on articular function will result. When injury extends across all cell layers of the physis and subjacent metaphysis, the healing process is necessarily complex since it involves healing of the physis when it is split longitudinally as well as healing of the gap in the articular cartilage.

Of most importance from the standpoint of restoration of function is the possible bridging of bone between the primary spongiosa of the epiphysis and immediately adjacent metaphyseal osseous structures. If such a bridge develops, asymmetrical growth arrest may result, with attendant deformity. Fortunately, these epiphyseal fractures are rare in victims of child abuse and, although repetitive injuries to the metaphyses of the long bones may result in growth arrest, this is an uncommon consequence.

Radiologic Dating of Healing Abuse Fractures

SOFT TISSUES

Whenever a fracture occurs, there is a variable degree of injury to the soft tissues. As previously mentioned, the hemorrhage and exudate occur immediately after the trauma, and inflammation then develops during the repair process. The first principle in identifying an injury to the skeleton is based on a knowledge of the normal relationships of the fat planes between muscles and in aggregations adjacent to bony or articular structures. The injury to the soft tissue results in infiltration by edema or hemorrhage of the interstitial tissues, and that infiltration usually obliterates the normal relative radiolucency of the deep or superficial planes or displaces the fat planes around the injured bony or articular structures. If there has been no associated articular or osseous injury, these changes typically resolve completely in a few days following the injury. This sequence is useful in indicating that healing of the relatively minor injury to soft tissues has occurred. Restoration of fat planes in the absence of osseous injury is evidence that the injury occurred 3 to 7 days before the time of imaging. When there is associated injury to bone and/or cartilage, the severity of swelling and its tendency to involve the skeletal member circumferentially as well as the delay in return of normal imaging of the fatty structures may serve to differentiate the more serious injury from soft tissue contusion.

THE PERIOSTEUM AND INJURY

In humans and animals alike, the periosteum responds to injury in a nonspecific way that is similar regardless of the mechanism of injury. Periosteal new bone is laid down in response to injury of many different types including burns, frostbite, and infection, as well as trauma. In general, it is proportional to the severity of the injury (i.e., the amount of energy absorbed). It is important in attempting to assess the age of the injury to the skeleton to be aware that other etiologic possibilities exist in addition to trauma, especially when one is imaging a suspected child abuse victim.

Some recent evidence derived from Kleinman et al.'s (5) study of infants at autopsy suggests that periosteal reaction may be less frequent after injury in the abuse fracture than in the ordinary fracture. Why the periosteum should play a different role in the healing of fractures in abused children is difficult to ascertain. It is possible that some abuse fractures have actually occurred after the infant's demise so that hemorrhage would not play a significant role and is not seen. It is also possible that the fractures without periosteal new bone noted in their study may have been so recent that the periosteum had not been activated at the time of the histologic observations. It may be true that chronic repetitive trauma results in continued obliteration or destruction of periosteal new bone even as it develops, resulting in failure to image the usual healing sequence. It is Kleinman's view that the stresses that result in fractures of the delicate trabeculae of the primary spongiosa are, in some cases, insufficient to produce periosteal injury. In any event, the most likely change in assessment of the age of the fracture in an abused child would be to suggest that the fracture is more recent in the absence of periosteal new bone. On the other hand, if periosteal new bone is seen in the abused child, the fracture may be somewhat older than would be expected with a timetable derived from experimental or ordinary fractures.

In the authors' experience, the earliest that periosteal new bone can be imaged with 200–400-speed rare earth or conventional screen–film combinations is between 4 and 7 days after injury. High-detail systems, including nonscreen filming, are the most effective way to image early and minimal change, but the higher radiation dose is seldom justified. Certainly, ultradetail on nonscreen filming should not be used in survey radiography.

A bell-shaped distribution curve characterizing the earliest time of radiographic visualization of periosteal new bone in injured extremities would be most useful, but careful studies such as this have not been performed. Most radiologists depend on their experience to identify unusual circumstances when periosteal new bone has been deposited, or its extent and pattern do not correlate with the clinical history and, therefore, should raise the suspicion of child abuse. In the authors' experience, the peak time for the demonstration of periosteal new bone, especially in children under the age of 1 year, is between 10 and 14 days after injury, but radiographic evidence of periosteal new bone may be seen in infants and even in young children up to 4 years as early as 4 days after injury. Occasionally, the appearance of periosteal new bone may be delayed and, if other findings point to the presence of an abuse fracture, that phenomenon may be ascribed to repetitive trauma or poor nutritional status, especially deficiency of vitamin D and/or calcium.

The quantity, thickness, density, and longitudinal extent of periosteal new bone all increase when there is motion occurring at the fracture site (i.e., when there is a series of repetitive injuries). Each one adds to the periosteal stripping or subperiosteal hemorrhage. It is for this very reason that many abuse fractures are characterized radiologically by extensive amounts of periosteal callus or periosteal new bone around the fracture site. The magnitude of the reaction in itself may raise the suspicion that the lesion is an abuse fracture. The callus, in fact, may be palpated on physical examination and the palpated bony masses may be confused clinically and, on occasion, radiologically and pathologically with other lesions such as neoplasm, osteogenesis imperfecta, or old fracture deformity (see Figure 3.5) (12–19).

FRACTURE LINE DEFINITION

The sharpness of the margins of fracture lines is also a function of the age of the fracture. Recent fractures are usually sharply delineated and the margins of the fracture fragments are sharp and clearly defined. It should be possible, in attempting to piece together the two adjacent segments, to envision reduction of the fracture fragments without evidence of gaps or poor definition. With early healing and especially with lack of immobilization, the margins of the fracture line may become poorly defined, helping to date the injury. As in the cases of periosteal new bone, careful studies and objective criteria for fracture line definition have not been developed and, to a certain extent, this assessment depends on the experience of the radiologist. In the authors' experience, fracture line definition occurs somewhat later than the expected periosteal new bone and may be delayed as long as 14 to 21 days. We disagree with those who say that the loss of fracture line definition is the earliest sign of fracture healing (16).

In abused children, corner fractures and bucket-handle fractures may have less well defined margins and, although no periosteal new bone is present, the margins of the fracture fragments are often poorly defined, thus helping to date the injury. It is probable that chronic repetitive trauma may also contribute to the blunting of the asperities of bucket-handle and corner fractures.

ENDOSTEAL CALLUS FORMATION

As fractures heal, the osteocytes around the trabeculae of cancellous bone begin to produce osteoid and, ultimately, new bone. On radiographic images, this appears as a vague, diffuse increase in density along the fracture line. In the case of impacted fractures, endosteal callus formation may be the only evidence of injury. Fortunately, in most cases of child abuse, impacted fractures are rare and, although endosteal callus is seen in adequately immobilized fractures, it is a less useful parameter of healing and dating than the appearance time of periosteal new bone or evolving fracture line definition. Endosteal callus is frequently inhibited by lack of immobilization. Thus, the fracture line definition may continue to be poor, or the fracture line itself may actually widen due to the resorption of the asperities. In the dating of fractures that have solidly healed, relevant information can be gained by assessing the degree of remodeling of either the deformity that may have occurred or the periosteal callus deposited during repair. When fractures older than 3 months as judged by remodeling data are demonstrated on skeletal surveys, they are most useful as *prima facie* evidence of abuse when associated with no credible history of injury in such cases. Fractures in the stages of healing that transpire between solid union of the fragments and complete remodeling of the bone can be assessed radiographically.

In infants, the degree of remodeling may be a criterion of the age of the fracture. In infants with fractures that were characterized initially by little if any displacement of fracture fragments, there may be only minimal evidence at 1 year postinjury that there was any injury whatsoever. Most abuse fractures of the long bones in infants will have consolidated by 3 months after the fracture was inflicted and often, when there have been few or no repetitions of the injury, consolidation will be evidenced in 4 to 6 weeks. If, as previously noted, there was little or no displacement and the fracture healed rapidly, the only evidence noted may consist of an ill-defined area of radiodensity at the fracture site, and by 2 years even that radiodensity may have disappeared. With a fracture that had considerable displacement of fragments (unreduced) or angular deformity, and especially in a case where repetitive injuries were found, there would be considerable residual callus and deformity at 1 or even 2 years after the injury, even in an infant and especially in a child over the age of 1 year. In such a patient, the deformity may even be permanent. Between these two extremes there are all degrees of remodeling, so that the chronology of an individual case depends on the several variables already discussed.

Guidelines

The dating of skeletal injury and its chronologic relation to the history of injury or exposure to a suspected abuser is, at best,

Table 6.1
Timetable of Radiographic Changes in Children's Fractures[a]

Category	Early	Peak	Late
1. Resolution of soft tissues	2–5 days	4–10 days	10–21 days
2. Periosteal new bone	4–10 days	10–14 days	14–21 days
3. Loss of fracture line definition	10–14 days	14–21 days	
4. Soft callus	10–14 days	14–21 days	
5. Hard callus	14–21 days	21–42 days	42–90 days
6. Remodeling	3 mos	1 year	2 years to epiphyseal closure

[a] Repetitive injuries may prolong categories 1, 2, 5, and 6.

inexact. Although the actual dating of fractures may only be approximated according to the principles outlined, a few things can be said with reasonable certainty. First, it should be noted that a fracture without periosteal new bone formation is usually less than 7 to 10 days of age and is seldom 20 days old. The authors feel very strongly that a fracture with definitive but slight periosteal new bone formation may be as recent as 4 to 7 days old and that, with the exception of anatomic immobilization or internal fixation, a 20-day-old fracture will almost always have well-defined periosteal new bone and, typically, soft callus. It can be further stated that a fracture with a large amount of periosteal new bone or callus is more than 14 days old. Several observations may be made with regard to fracture line definition. In the authors' experience, the loss of marginal sharpness occurs somewhat later than the expected periosteal new bone and may be delayed as long as 14 to 21 days.

Corner fractures or bucket-handle metaphyseal fractures, which may be present for longer periods of time without the development of periosteal new formation, can only be dated by marginal loss of definition of the asperities. In abused chldren, chronic repetitive trauma and lack of immobilization may lead to loss of fracture line definition as the earliest finding.

Special radiologic examinations, including radionuclide bone studies and computed tomography scanning, are usually not helpful in establishing the age of fractures. Radionuclide studies become positive within hours of injury and are probably only useful when activity is decreased long after the injury. The role of magnetic resonance imaging in dating fractures is yet to be established, and chemical shift imaging may actually prove to be a more accurate tool as the modality evolves.

In summary, the inherent differences in ordinary fractures and abuse fractures and the timetable of healing have been reviewed with particular emphasis on the complex histopathologic changes that are taking place as the healing process progresses. A convenient summary of the authors' experience with the healing of ordinary fractures is contained in Table 6.1. Where possible, the important differences in the healing of fractures in abused children have been stressed.

REFERENCES

1. Heppenstall RB: Fracture healing. In Heppenstall RB (ed): *Fracture Treatment and Healing.* Philadelphia, WB Saunders, 1980, pp 35–64.
2. Ogden JA: Uniqueness of growing bones. In Rockwood CA Jr, Wilkins KE, King RE (eds): *Fractures in Children.* Philadelphia, JB Lippincott, 1984, Vol. 3, pp 5–14, 61–63, 71–81.
3. Ham AW: A histological study of the early phases of bone repair. *J Bone Joint Surg* 12:827–844, 1930.
4. Salter RB: Special features of fractures and dislocation in children. In Heppenstall RB (ed): *Fracture Treatment and Healing.* Philadelphia, WB Saunders, 1980, p 190.
5. Kleinman PK, Marks SC, Blackbourne B: The metaphyseal lesion in abused infants: a radiologic-histopathologic study. *AJR* 146:895–905, 1986.
6. Brashear HR Jr: Epiphyseal fractures: A microscopic study of the healing process in rats. *J Bone Joint Surg* 41A:1055–1064, 1959.
7. Ford LT, Key JA: A study of experimental trauma to the distal femoral epiphysis in rabbits. *J Bone Joint Surg* 38A:84–92, 1956.
8. Ford LT, Key JA: A study of experimental trauma

to the distal femoral epiphysis in rabbits II. *J Bone Joint Surg* 40A:887–896, 1958.

9. Smith DG, Geist RW, Cooperman DR: Microscopic examination of a naturally occurring epiphyseal plate fracture. *J Pediatr Orthop* 5:306–308, 1985.

10. Bright RW, Burstein AH, Elmore SM: Epiphyseal-plate cartilage. A biomechanical and histological analysis of failure modes. *J Bone Joint Surg* 56A:688–703, 1974.

11. Nordentoft EL: Experimental epiphyseal injuries. *Acta Orthop Scand* 40:176–192, 1969.

12. Salter RB: Child abuse. In Heppenstall RB (ed): *Fracture Treatment and Healing.* Philadelphia, WB Saunders, 1980, pp 232–233.

13. Lee KE, Pelker RR, Rudicel SA, Ogden JA, Panjabi MM: Histologic patterns of capital femoral growth plate fracture in the rabbit: the effect of shear direction. *J Pediatr Orthop* 5:32–39, 1985.

14. Rudicel S, Pelker RR, Lee KE, Ogden JA, Panjabi MM: Shear fractures through the capital femoral physis of the skeletally immature rabbit. *J Pediatr Orthop* 5:27–31, 1985.

15. Harris WR, Hobson KW: Histological changes in experimentally displaced upper femoral epiphyses in rabbits. *J Bone Joint Surg* 38B:914–927, 1956.

16. Bright RW: Physeal injuries. In Rockwood CA Jr, Wilkins KE, King RE (eds): *Fractures in Children.* Philadelphia, JB Lippincott, 1984, Vol 3, pp 87–89, 105–125, 135–140.

17. Blech EE, Kleinman RG: Child abuse. In Rockwood CA Jr, Wilkins KE, King RE (eds): *Fractures in Children.* Philadelphia, JB Lippincott, 1984, Vol 3, pp 123–125.

18. Ogden JA: Battered child syndrome. In *Skeletal Injury in the Child.* Philadelphia, Lea and Febiger, 1984, pp 196–199.

19. Cumming WA: Neonatal skeletal fractures: birth trauma or child abuse? *J Can Assoc Radiol* 30:30–33, 1979.

7 Visceral Trauma

PAUL K. KLEINMAN, M.D.

In contrast to shaking and other indirect injuries so closely associated with infant abuse, blunt abdominal and thoracic trauma become common only after the child is able to freely move about. There have been few studies that provide adequate indications of the incidence of visceral injury in children who survive the assaults. These patients may lack the stigmata of abuse, such as bruises and lacerations, despite substantial visceral injury (1). Additionally, symptoms can be vague and significant intra-abdominal injuries may be overlooked, or investigative studies may be nondiagnostic. Documentation of abuse may occur only at autopsy.

Perry and Venters reported 99 children dying from violence over a 5-year period in Saint Paul and Ramsey County, Minnesota (2). Twelve of these were deemed homicides, and seven were believed likely to represent examples of the battered child syndrome. Four of the seven died from abdominal visceral injury. Only two died from head injury. With increasing age there is a clear shift in the site of the fatal injury from the brain to the abdomen.

McCort and Vaudagna described 10 infants with visceral injury secondary to abuse (3). The average age was 20 months; seven were males and three females. All injuries involved the abdominal viscera. O'Neill et al. reported an analysis of 110 abused children ranging from 3 weeks to 11 years of age (4). Nine injuries involving the liver, pancreas, intestine, and mesentery were described. All injuries occurred secondary either to blunt blows or to sudden deceleration after the child was thrown. Tank et al. reported 74 infants experiencing blunt abdominal trauma seen between 1951 and 1966 at Children's Hospital Medical Center in Boston (5). Of these, only three were believed to be secondary to parental abuse. Gornall et al. reported 75 cases of visceral injury treated at the Manchester Children's Hospital between 1961 and 1970 (6). Six cases of the battered child syndrome were identified, two of which resulted in death. Touloukian reviewed the literature and reported a mortality rate of 50% for visceral injuries associated with child abuse. In reviewing deaths from abdominal injury in the state of Rhode Island, he found visceral injuries in child abuse accounted for 20% of the total mortalities (7). He detailed the findings in five children dying from massive abdominal injury. The average age was 21 months. All infants had evidence of external injury (8).

Incidence estimates of visceral injury will vary depending on the type of population from which the cases are drawn. Caniano et al. found that only 1% of 256 abused children had visceral injury (9); however, the study group included such varied forms of abuse as sexual abuse and nutritional deprivation. Since many clinically insignificant visceral injuries are likely overlooked or attributed to accident, the true incidence is probably greater than the literature suggests.

As with most forms of abuse, a precise description of the mechanism of injury is rarely provided, but in most cases visceral trauma results from direct blows with a clenched fist, from a kick, or from the effect of rapid deceleration after being hurled. In contrast to skeletal injuries, which in some cases are highly specific for abuse, most visceral injuries can be plausibly explained as accidental. Thus, the significance of the injuries noted radiologically can only be assessed in conjunction with the clinical findings. If an inconsistent history is provided as explanation for a major solid or hollow viscus injury, then the radiologist can and should suggest the possibility of abuse. It is often the radiologist who, being troubled by the discrepancy between the traumatic injury and the lack of appropriate history, raises the possibility of battering.

None of the abdominal or thoracic viscera are spared from intentional trauma; however, the most common injuries involve the hollow viscera, mesenteries, liver, and pancreas.

The Abdomen

THE GASTROINTESTINAL TRACT

The Stomach

The stomach is usually spared from direct injury, although it may show striking gaseous distension when duodenal obstruction is present, or as a result of acute atony in neglected children (10, 11) (see Chapter 9). Gastric rupture has occasionally been reported in abused children (3, 12–14) (Fig. 7.1). The scarcity of reports is similar to that relating to gastric perforation secondary to accidental blunt abdominal injury. Siemens and Fulton indicated that 0.9% to 1.7% of all hollow viscus ruptures involve the stomach (15). The ruptures generally occur in association with large amounts of gastric contents, and a history of injury following ingestion of a meal is often elicited. At laparotomy, the perforations, like those of accidental blunt injury, are usually along the anterior wall or curvatures, and occasionally combined anterior and posterior perforations are noted. The injury may be isolated or associated with other solid and hollow viscus injury. Gastric rupture is a serious injury and if unrecognized can lead to sepsis, shock, and death (13). Radiologic findings will generally be nonspecific, usually with evidence of massive free intraperitoneal air (Fig. 7.1). The dramatic presentation and signs of intra-abdominal sepsis will lead to immediate exploration, precluding any further radiologic studies.

A unique case of a giant gastric ulcer in an abused child was reported by Stroh et al. (16). This penetrating lesser curvature ulcer was noted in a 3½-month-old battered child who presented with hematemesis (Fig. 7.2).

Small Intestine

Perforation. Small intestinal perforation is a well-recognized feature of child abuse and is generally attributed to a blunt blow to the abdomen. The number of reports in the literature undoubtedly fails to reflect the true incidence of this visceral injury. A literature review revealed a total of 21 small intestinal perforations occurring in 17 abused children (3–5, 8, 17–20). The average age of the children was 2 years, with a range of 6 months to 4 years. The distribution of these injuries is depicted in Figure 7.3. Approximately 60% occurred in the jejunum; when specified, the site was usually just distal to the ligament of Treitz. Thirty percent occurred in the duodenum and 10% in the ileum. Two patients had a history of a prior perforation, with inadequate documentation of abuse. One patient was found to have three simultaneous perforations involving the jejunum and duodenum.

The predilection for the duodenum and proximal jejunum supports the concept that fixation either in a retroperitoneal location or just distal to the ligament of Treitz renders the gut susceptible to nonpenetrating injury. This pattern is somewhat at variance with that occurring in primarily adult clinical series as well as in experimental studies. Georghegen and Brush reported 20 cases of intestinal perforation and reviewed the literature on the subject (21). They found little relationship between the site of small intestinal perforation and the degree of fixation or length of small bowel mesentery. They performed a series of experiments in which they dropped 50-pound weights from heights varying from 3.5 to 4.5 feet onto the abdomens of intact etherized dogs. They again found no predilection for sites of fixation such as the duodenum or proximal jejunum.

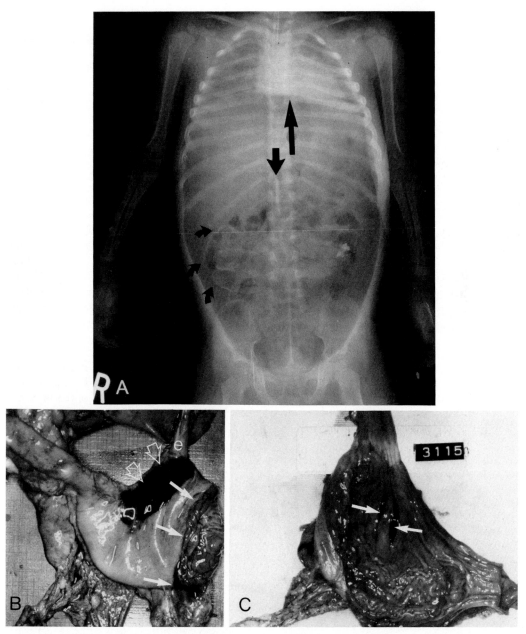

Figure 7.1. Gastric perforation in a 2-year-old abused child. The stepfather admitted to striking the child in the abdomen with his upraised knee. *A*, Massive free air outlines the peritoneal cavity "football" sign. Free air defines the serosal aspect of the small bowel (*curved arrows*), the umbilical ligament (*short solid arrow*), and the anterior diaphragmatic attachment (*long arrow*). *B*, Gross pathologic specimen reveals a large transmural laceration along the proximal greater curvature of the stomach (*solid arrows*). A large contusion is present along the lesser curvature (*open arrows*). *e*, esophagus. *C*, View of the stomach opened along the greater curvature demonstrates several of the 13 mucosal lacerations (*arrows*). (Reproduced with permission from Case MES, Nanduri R: Laceration of the stomach by blunt trauma in a child: A case of child abuse. *J Forensic Sci* 28:496–501, 1983. Copyright ASTM.)

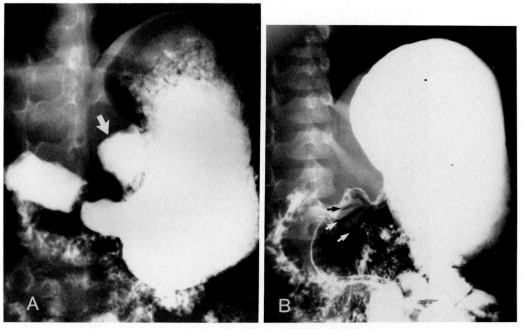

Figure 7.2. Gastric ulcer. *A*, Upper GI series of a 3½-year-old abused child who presented with hematemesis. There is a large penetrating lesser curvature giant ulcer (*arrow*). *B*, Repeat upper GI series following 3 weeks of cimetidine treatment shows mucosal folds (*arrows*) radiating to an almost completely healed ulcer crater. (Reproduced with permission from Stroh A, Zamet P, Bomsel F: Ulcere aigu de stress dans une famille maltraitante. *Arch Fr Pediatr* 40:411–414, 1983.)

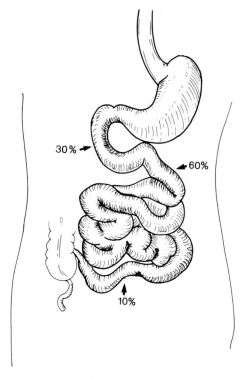

Figure 7.3. Distribution of small intestinal perforations in abused children.

In the abused child, perforations of the duodenum and proximal jejunum occur with direct crushing or compressive forces. Although the resultant sudden increase in intraluminal pressure may result in perforation, experimental data in dogs suggest that the pressure created is insufficient to rupture the bowel (22). It is more likely that shearing between apposing surfaces produces the intestinal perforation. The portions of the small bowel suspended by a mesentery may also be injured by a sudden deceleration, typically occurring after a child is thrown or swung into a solid object. This may result in a disruption of the vascular supply to the small bowel with or without perforation (23).

Free intraperitoneal perforations are generally associated with impressive findings of abdominal pain, distension, leukocytosis, and fever. Delay in seeking attention is itself an indication of extreme neglect. Retroperitoneal perforations resulting from duodenal injury may be insidious and, although associated with signs of sepsis, may not display typical findings of peritonitis. If an uncomplicated intestinal perforation is attended to shortly after the injury, the prognosis is good. Although the patient is extremely ill, intestinal injury may not be suspected because of a misleading history, or neurologic findings that dominate the clinical picture. If other visceral injuries coexist, or if medical attention is delayed, a high mortality is associated with these injuries (8).

The radiologic abnormalities related to intestinal perforation are dependent on the location of the injury. Free intestinal perforations will usually, but not invariably, result in identifiable free intraperitoneal air. The volume of pneumoperitoneum is usually small and, in contrast to that associated with gastric perforations, is difficult to identify in the supine position. A variety of radiologic signs will, on occasion, allow identification of small amounts of free air in the supine position (Fig. 7.4). Collections of free air lying adjacent to gas-filled bowel will define the serosal aspect of the gut (Fig. 7.4B). This will result in visualization of the inner and outer aspects of the bowel wall indicating free air. This pattern can be simulated by two closely apposed gas-filled bowel loops, but careful analysis of the findings should allow differentiation. Free air may also collect in the subhepatic region, or between the liver and abdominal wall, with characteristic patterns (Fig. 7.4A). Air may collect beneath the anterior diaphragmatic attachments, resulting in a vague radiolucency in the xiphoid region on the supine or semi-erect chest film (24). Larger collections of air may outline the falciform ligament and accumulate centrally beneath the anterior abdominal wall, producing the so-called football sign (see Fig. 7.1). An upright film or, if the patient cannot be placed erect, a cross-table lateral or left lateral decubitus view will confirm the presence of free air (Fig. 7.4C). Any patient in whom there is the least suspicion of an intestinal injury should have not only a supine abdomen, but a view with a horizontal beam, preferably upright, to assess for pneumoperitoneum. Retroperitoneal perforations are extremely difficult to detect on plain radiographs; however, if sufficient air leaks into the retroperitoneum, or if gas-forming organisms produce retroperitoneal abscesses, a mottled or bubbly pattern will be evident (3).

If, as often occurs, there is intraperitoneal bleeding, or if ascites is present secondary to abdominal sepsis, a pattern of free fluid in the abdomen will result. This is manifest as diffuse increased density within the abdomen, often with a ground glass appearance (Fig. 7.5A). If massive fluid is present, a central location of the gas-filled loops of bowel may be noted. Differentiation between ascites and a large amount of intraluminal fluid can be difficult both clinically and radiographically, and ultrasonography is ideally suited to aid in this diagnosis (Figs. 7.5B and 7.5C).

Intramural Hematoma. Intramural hematomas of the duodenum and jejunum are the most frequent abdominal injuries documented radiologically in abused children. In contrast to intestinal perforations, which are diagnosed by inference from the finding of free intraperitoneal air, specific radiologic alterations occur in cases of intramural intestinal hematomas, allowing confident diagnosis. Although intestinal perforation can occur from a variety of causes only one of which is trauma, in the child without a bleeding tendency the radiologic diagnosis of an intramural hematoma indicates prior trauma.

The description of intramural intestinal hematomas in the child abuse literature is a relatively recent occurrence. In 1965, Eisenstein et al. described a 38-month-old child with a 6-day history of vomiting (25). A laparotomy 1 day after admission revealed a gangrenous loop of jejunum containing a large intramural hematoma. Bratu et al. described the radiologic findings on an upper gastrointestinal (GI) series in an abused child with a jejunal hematoma (26). Numerous reports of small intestinal hematomas have appeared subsequently, and the entity is well accepted as one of the more classic abdominal injuries in cases of child abuse (6, 20, 27–34). Pathologically, hematomas may be diffuse or, more commonly, localized. When well confined, blood lies mainly in a subserosal location, although extension into the other layers of the bowel

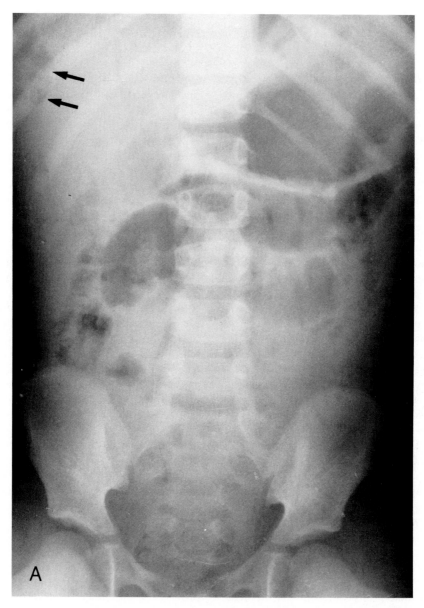

Figure 7.4. Free intraperitoneal air. *A*, Supine abdomen of a 5-year-old abused child. A small collection of air (*arrows*) is noted in the right upper quadrant between the liver and the anterior abdominal wall. *B*, Coned-down view of the right upper quadrant reveals a faint collection of free air in the region of Morrison's pouch (*open arrows*), and combined intraluminal and intraperitoneal air defines the wall of an intestinal loop (*solid arrows*). *C*, An upright film demonstrates free air beneath the diaphragm (*arrows*).

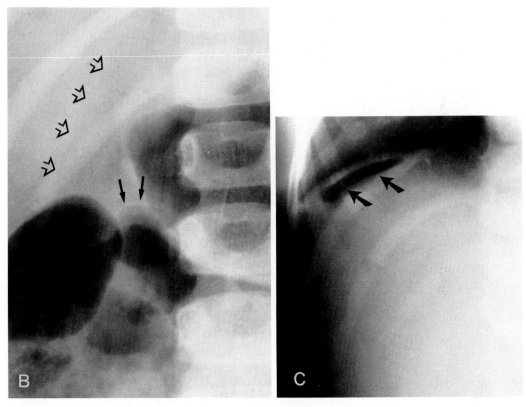

Figure 7.4. *B* and *C*.

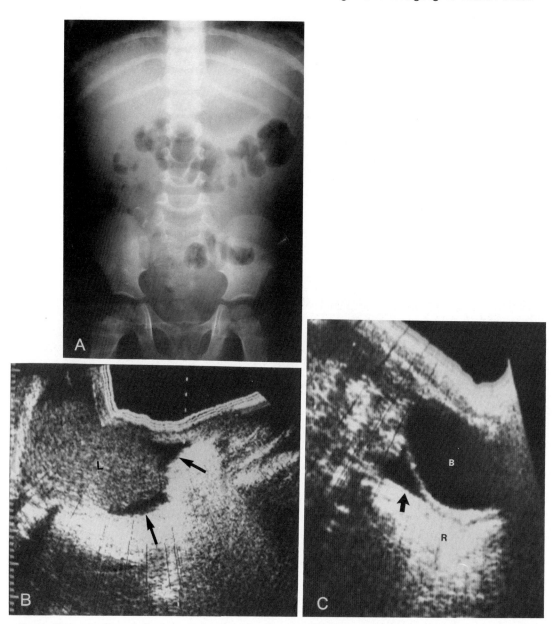

Figure 7.5. Ascites. *A*, Supine abdomen of a 3-year-old abused child reveals increased density within the abdomen with a "ground glass" appearance. Barium from a prior contrast study is incidentally seen in the appendix. *B*, Sagittal ultrasound reveals free fluid (*arrows*) along the inferior margin of the right lobe of the liver (*L*). *C*, Sagittal pelvic ultrasound of another abused infant with a duodenal hematoma reveals intraperitoneal fluid (*arrow*) in the rectovesical space. *B*, bladder *R*, rectum.

wall occurs. In most cases the mucosa is uninvolved, but occasionally ischemic necrosis may occur (35, 36). In the jejunum and ileum, bleeding within the small bowel mesentery may be found in association with the characteristic intramural collections.

Anatomic differences between the duo-denum and the remainder of the small bowel influence the pathogenesis of the hematomas, as well as their resultant radiologic patterns (Fig. 7.6). Great importance has been placed on the relationship of the transverse portion of the duodenum to the spine. It is postulated that a blunt injury

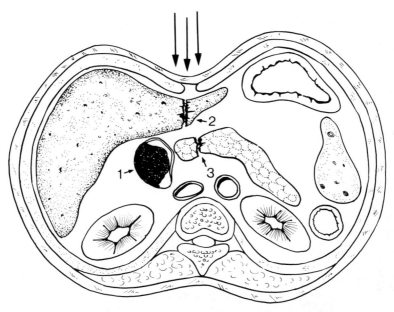

Figure 7.6. Distribution of visceral injuries from blunt trauma. A midline abdominal blow will compress the abdominal viscera against the spine resulting in injury to the duodenum (*1*), left lobe of the liver (*2*), and pancreas (*3*). More laterally positioned blows may result in injury to the right lobe of the liver, the kidneys, and, occasionally, the spleen. Shearing forces generated by a direct blow or sudden deceleration will result in intestinal-mesenteric injuries.

that compresses the duodenum between the anterior abdominal wall and the spine results in duodenal hematoma (20, 22, 29). As the descending duodenum lies to the right of the spine, additional factors must be considered to explain the conspicuous hematomas frequently encountered in this region. The firm fixation of the descending duodenum in a retroperitoneal location renders the bowel susceptible to a compressive blow, particularly if the child is in a fixed position and is unable to recoil from the assault. The duodenum has a rich vascular supply that is well known to protect it from ischemic injury. The many terminal arborizations of the inferior and superior pancreaticoduodenal arteries are potential sites for extravasation of blood. In the descending duodenum, the bleeding is most frequently noted along the lateral aspect of the descending duodenum opposite the site of entry of the nutrient vessels. In the jejunum and ileum, the hematomas are usually noted adjacent to the small bowel mesentery, and associated injury and bleeding in the mesentery may be present.

The clinical findings in patients with duodenal and jejunal hematomas are quite characteristic. Vomiting and abdominal pain are invariably present in those patients coming to diagnosis. As with other injuries in abused children, it is sometimes difficult to date the specific injury, and in some cases vomiting may be delayed for hours or days after the traumatic insult (20). Blood loss can be significant and there may be elevation of the white blood cell count. If there is associated pancreatic injury, the serum amylase will be elevated (20). If there is associated perforation, signs of peritonitis and sepsis will develop. In the past, surgical evacuation of intramural hematomas was frequently carried out. It is now generally accepted that a nonsurgical approach should be followed (37).

The plain film findings in cases of duodenal hematoma may be normal; however, if significant obstruction is present a dilated gas- and fluid-filled stomach will be evident, with little intestinal contents distally (Fig. 7.7). On rare occasion, gas within the proximal portion of the duodenum will de-

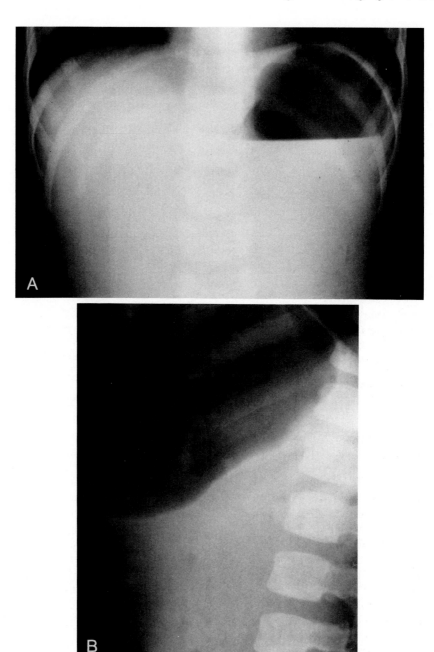

Figure 7.7. Duodenal hematoma. Upright (*A*) and right lateral (*B*) views of the abdomen in a 2½-year-old abused child demonstrate a dilated gas- and fluid-filled stomach. *C*, An upper GI series reveals a partially obstructing filling defect in the second portion of the duodenum (*arrows*). The suggestion of a "coiled-spring" appearance is present. *D*, The coiled-spring appearance (*open arrows*), and smoothly marginated hematoma (*closed arrows*) are seen to advantage on this double-contrast view. *E*, Follow-up study reveals a residual mural mass in the descending portion of the duodenum (*arrows*). (Reproduced with permission from Kleinman PK, Brill P, Winchester P: The resolving duodenal-jejunal hematoma in abused children. *Radiology* 160:747–750, 1986.)

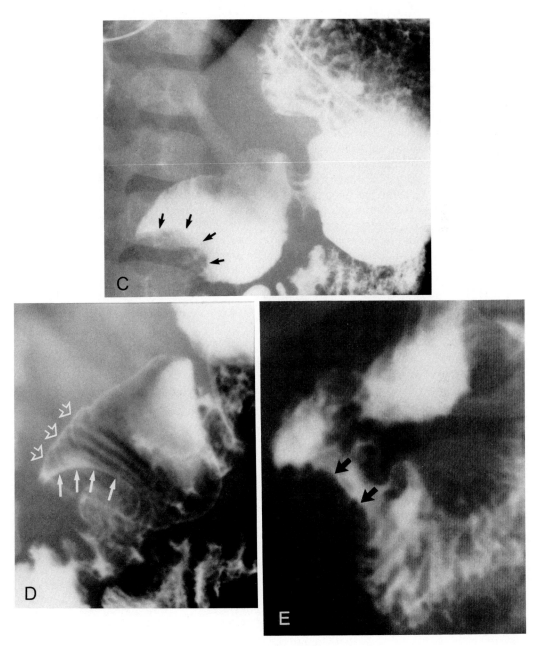

Figure 7.7. *C–E.*

fine the encroaching intraluminal mass (38). Other associated injuries may be manifest by free intraperitoneal air or ascites.

The characteristic pattern on upper GI series is a large intramural mass that encroaches upon the intestinal lumen. The mass is smooth and rounded, and may produce varying degrees of obstruction (Figs. 7.7C, 7.7D and 7.8). With complete obstruction, barium will cap the proximal margin of the mass (Fig. 7.8A). The appearance in these cases is of a nonspecific obstructing mural process. With less obstruction, varying amounts of barium will pass between the mass and the surrounding mucosa resulting in a "coiled-spring" appearance (Figs. 7.7C, 7.7D and 7.9). There has been considerable confusion in the literature regarding the use of this term. Some authors have described an intraluminal mass in association with thickened mucosal folds as an

example of the coiled-spring appearance (39). A careful reading of Felson and Levin's classic article on the subject reveals a clear distinction between simple fold thickening related to accumulation of fluid or blood circumferentially within the bowel wall, and an intraluminal mass over which crowded valvulae conniventes are outlined (40). Felson and Levin attempted to produce the coiled-spring appearance by intramural injection of water, but succeeded only in producing thickened folds without the coiled-spring appearance (40). The prerequisite for the production of the coiled-spring appearance is a large intraluminal mass projecting into the lumen of the bowel (Fig. 7.10). The adjacent mucosal folds are draped over the mass, and there is crowding of the valvulae conniventes; barium trapped within the mucosal folds results in the coiled-spring appearance. A similar appearance is noted in

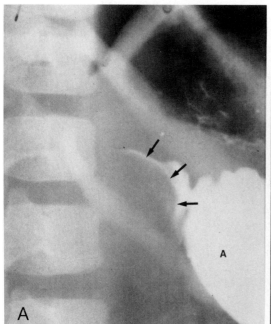
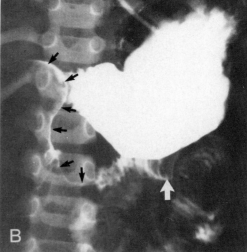

Figure 7.8. Duodenal-jejunal hematoma. *A*, Upper GI series in a 2-year-old abused infant demonstrates initial obstruction secondary to a smooth intraluminal mass protruding into the duodenal bulb (*arrows*). *A*, Gastric antrum. *B*, Delayed film demonstrates tracking of contrast between the mass and the medial aspect of the second portion, and superior aspect of the third portion of the duodenum (*black arrows*). Barium defines an intramural hematoma of the proximal jejunum producing a coiled-spring appearance (*white arrow*). (Reproduced with permission from Kleinman PK, Brill P, Winchester P: The resolving duodenal-jejunal hematoma in abused children. *Radiology* 160:747–750, 1986.)

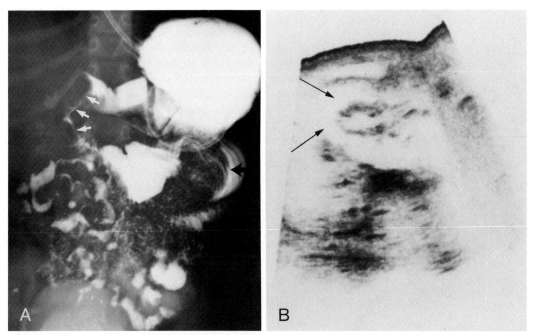

Figure 7.9. Duodenal and jejunal hematomas in a 2½-year-old abused infant with multiple bruises and no history of trauma. *A,* Upper GI series shows barium trapped between the intramural mass and the medial wall of the descending duodenum (*white arrows*). Barium also defines the margins of an intramural jejunal hematoma with a coiled-spring appearance (*black arrow*). *B,* Abdominal ultrasound reveals a large anechoic structure with central echoes consistent with a jejunal hematoma (*arrows*). (Reproduced with permission from Radkowski MA, Merten DF, Leonidas JC: The abused child: Criteria for the radiologic diagnosis. *RadioGraphics* 3:262–297, 1983.)

cases of intestinal intussusception, where normal mucosa of the intussuscipiens is draped over the intussusceptum, producing the coiled-spring effect. Thus, although some degree of fold thickening may be present, it is the intraluminal mass that is the essential component for the production of the coiled-spring sign (41).

In the descending duodenum, the intramural mass characteristically projects from the lateral margin or greater curvature aspect of the duodenum (Figs. 7.8*B* and 7.9*A*), but occasionally the mass may appear to arise from the medial aspect of the duodenum (42). This feature is extremely helpful in evaluating cases of resolving hematomas, because the lateral location of the mural defect will remain constant. As the mural mass extends into the third portion of the duodenum, the mass will arise from the inferior margin of the bowel, and will be outlined superiorly by intraluminal bar-

ium. Beyond the ligament of Treitz, the intramural masses are generally located along the mesenteric portion of the jejunum and may be associated with significant mesenteric vascular injury (Figs. 7.8, 7.9, and 7.11). This will result in bleeding into the peritoneal space and, if intestinal lymphatics are disrupted, chylous ascites may result (1, 43–46) (see Fig. 7.5). Radiologically, it may be difficult to distinguish a blood collection within the mesentery from that within the bowel wall, and it is likely that a combined location is present in some cases (Fig. 7.11). Such a mass may be appreciable at the ligament of Treitz.

If bleeding is diffuse and circumferential within the bowel wall, a pattern of fold thickening may predominate without mural defects, especially in resolving lesions. In such cases, the pattern has been referred to as a stacked-coin appearance (Fig. 7.12*A*). The various signs associated with localized

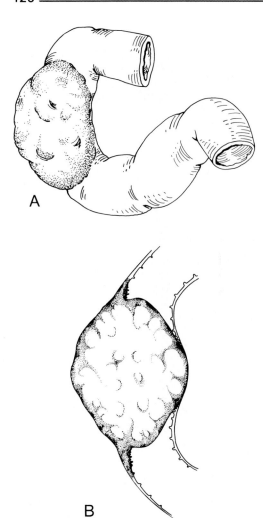

A

B

Figure 7.10. Schematic representation of a duodenal hematoma. Intact duodenum (*A*); coronal section (*B*). The hematoma arises in the lateral aspect of the duodenum. The intraluminal mass encroaches upon the lumen from laterally. Barium will collect between the mass and the crowded mucosal folds, resulting in the coiled-spring appearance.

and diffuse intramural collections of fluid and blood may produce considerable confusion. One should not be diverted by the terminology, but rather should concentrate on the specific anatomic findings of either a localized intramural mass, a finding characteristic of an intramural hematoma, or diffuse fold thickening, a somewhat less specific alteration.

Abdominal ultrasound may provide a

clue to the diagnosis of an acute intramural hematoma of the small bowel (31) (Fig. 7.9). An upper GI series should follow, however, to fully document the lesion. Computed tomography (CT) is best suited for evaluation of accompanying solid organ injury. It may reveal bloody ascites associated with intramural bleeding (Figs. 7.11*C–E*).

Despite resolution of symptoms, characteristic radiologic features may persist for more than a month (41). The changes associated with a resolving duodenal hematoma can be anticipated from the findings in the acute phase (Figs. 7.7*E*, 7.11*A*, 7.11*B*, 7.12, 7.13*A*, and 7.13*B*). As the large intraluminal mass resolves, smaller mural defects, either single or multiple, may be seen generally arising from the greater curvature aspect of the descending duodenum. As liquefaction of the hematoma occurs, the process will tend to spread circumferentially within the bowel, and a pattern of fold thickening may be evident. Identification of the resolving hematoma may be extremely helpful in providing necessary documentation for abuse. Although vomiting is uniformly present, it will eventually resolve spontaneously. The abdominal component of the patient's clinical picture may tend to be dismissed as the symptoms resolve. Further investigation to provide documentation of abuse may be unrewarding, and the child who has suffered a major abdominal injury may remain unidentified as an abuse victim. Thus, just as the skeletal survey is performed to substantiate clinically insignificant but legally crucial documentation of abuse, the upper GI series may provide similar highly specific data. It is our practice to perform an upper GI series in patients suspected of being abused, despite clearing of abdominal symptoms. Resolution of custodial and legal questions is facilitated with such radiologic documentation.

Miscellaneous Lesions.

Strictures. Rarely, patients with blunt abdominal injury will develop small intestinal strictures, presumably secondary to localized mesenteric injury. If the lumen is sufficiently narrow, an element of obstruction will be present (Fig. 7.13*C*).

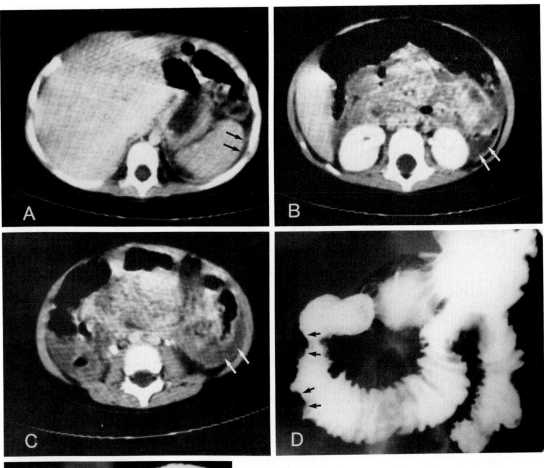

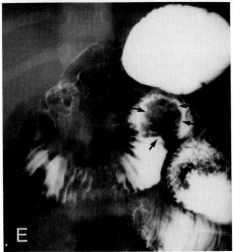

Figure 7.11. Two-year-old abused child with major abdominal trauma. *A–C:* Contrast-enhanced CT sections through the upper, mid, and lower abdomen. Free fluid is noted within the peritoneal cavity (*arrows*) outlining the spleen and collecting within the left paracolic gutter. *D,* Early film from upper GI series demonstrates intramural hematoma producing lobulated masses along the lateral aspect of the descending duodenum (*arrows*). *E,* Later film demonstrates an intramural mass in the region of the ligament of Treitz (*arrows*). Fold thickening is present as the duodenum crosses the spine, probably related to intramural blood. (Reproduced with permission from Kleinman PK, Brill P, Winchester P: The resolving duodenal-jejunal hematoma in abused children. *Radiology* 160:747–750, 1986.)

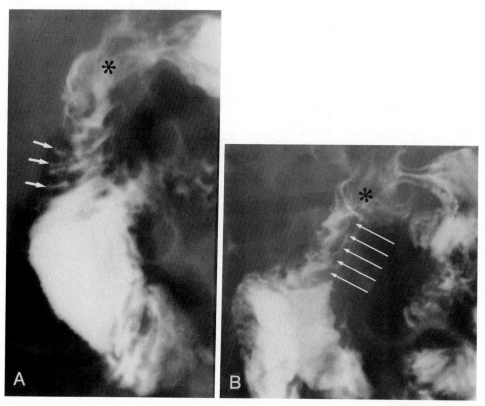

Figure 7.12. Upper GI series in a 2-year-old abused child with history of vomiting, which subsequently resolved. *A,* Barium is trapped between thickened folds of the postbulbar duodenum (*arrows*), resulting in an appearance reminiscent of "stacked coins." There is no obstruction to the flow of contrast. *, duodenal bulb. *B,* A later film shows generalized thickening of the folds in the second portion of the duodenum (*arrows*). *, duodenal bulb. (Reproduced with permission from Kleinman PK, Brill P, Winchester P: The resolving duodenal-jejunal hematoma in abused children. *Radiology* 160:747–750, 1986.)

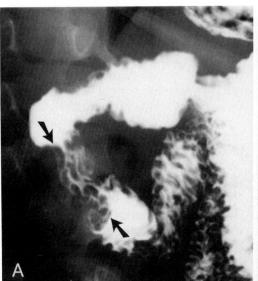

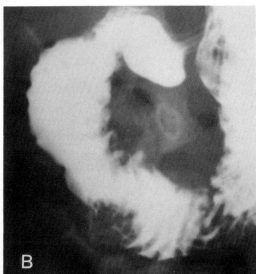

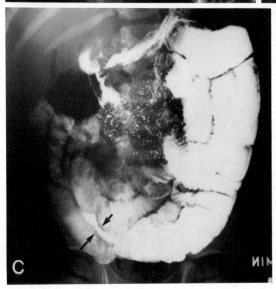

Figure 7.13. Resolving duodenal hematoma. *A*, Upper GI series in a 3-year-old child with abdominal pain and distension, vomiting, and guaiac-positive stools. Lobulated mural defects arising from the lateral aspect of the descending duodenum are noted (*arrows*) in association with thickening of the mucosal folds. *B*, A follow-up study 3 weeks later shows decrease in the size of the mural defects. *C*, Delayed film demonstrates a stenotic area in the distal small bowel (*arrows*) with proximal dilatation. Five months later, the child was found dead at home with multiple visceral and central nervous system injuries judged to be secondary to homicide. (Reproduced with permission from Kleinman PK, Brill P, Winchester P: The resolving duodenal-jejunal hematoma in abused children. *Radiology* 160:747–750, 1986.)

Pneumatosis Intestinalis and Portal Venous Gas. Pneumatosis intestinalis, a common pattern occurring in infants with necrotizing enterocolitis, may occur in abused children

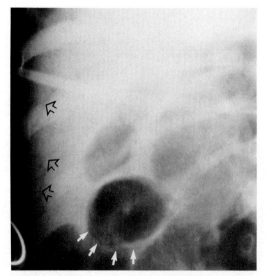

Figure 7.14. Pneumatosis intestinalis. One-year-old neglected child suffering a cardiac arrest of uncertain origin. Pneumatosis intestinalis (*closed arrows*) is noted in the right upper quadrant, associated with portal venous gas (*open arrows*). This may be secondary to intestinal trauma, or to ischemic changes during the cardiac arrest.

(31). A variety of mechanisms of injury may explain this pattern. A rent in the intestinal mucosa may allow bowel contents, including gas-producing organisms, to enter bowel wall. If a patient has suffered an anoxic insult as a result of abuse, an ischemic lesion may result in a similar appearance. This intramural gas will appear as curvilinear, mottled, and occasionally cystic lucencies related to bowel loops (Fig. 7.14). Once air has entered the bowel wall, it may pass to the portal venous system with a characteristic radiographic pattern of branching radiolucencies within the hepatic region.

Foreign Bodies. Bizarre forms of poisoning by forced feeding of harmful foreign objects have been described. The hazards of accidental ingestion of small alkaline batteries are well known (47–54). Temple and McNeese described a case of a 12-year-old child who had ingested a mercury battery from a watch as part of an alleged poisoning attempt by an uncle (55) (Fig. 7.15). Thirty-six hours after ingestion the battery ruptured, and at surgery impending perforation of the gastric mucosa was found. Varying opinions regarding the approach to battery ingestions have been put forth, but the prevailing view seems to point to a conservative, nonsurgical approach in most cases.

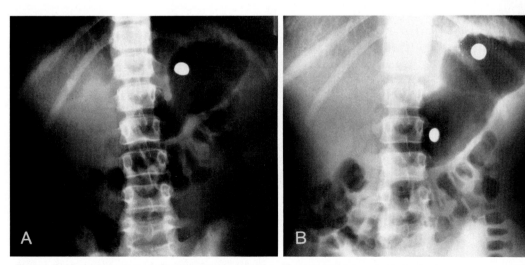

Figure 7.15. Poisoning. *A,* Supine abdomen of a 12-year-old boy who ingested a mercury watch battery as part of an alleged poisoning attempt. An intact battery is noted in the gastric fundus. *B,* Follow-up film 36 hours later demonstrates disassociation of the battery fragments. (Reproduced with permission from Temple DM, McNeese MC: Hazards of battery ingestion. *Pediatrics* 71:100–103, 1983. Copyright 1983.)

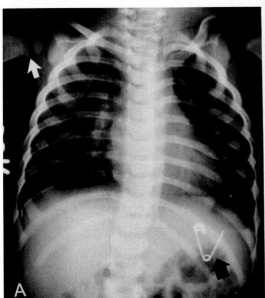 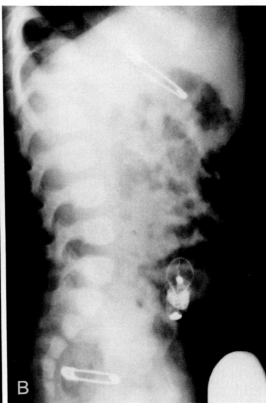

Figure 7.16. Poisoning. *A,* Supine chest of an abused child with a fractured humerus (*white arrow*). An open safety pin is noted within the stomach (*black arrow*). *B,* Lateral view of the abdomen also demonstrates a light bulb, and a closed safety pin in the rectum. The mother had reportedly fed the child these foreign bodies during periods of intoxication. (Reproduced with permission from Baker DH, Berdon WE: Special trauma problems in children. *Radiol Clin North Am* 4(2):289–305, 1966.)

Baker and Berdon described a unique case of abuse characterized by force-feeding a child a variety of foreign bodies including safety pins and a light bulb (56) (Fig. 7.16). The child had multiple healing fractures identified elsewhere. The child's mother was an alcoholic and was reported to have beaten the child only during periods of intoxication. Other examples of poisoning are described in Chapter 9.

Intussusception. A rare manifestion of abuse was described by Walker and Giltman (57). In a review of 24 cases of intussusception, the authors described a battered child in whom an intussusception was unexpectedly discovered during laparotomy.

Colon

The most common injuries to the colon are associated with sexual abuse, a topic addressed in Chapter 9. Colonic injuries due to blunt trauma are rare in abused children. Because the transverse colon passes in front of the spine, a colonic intramural hematoma in association with jejunal injury may occur rarely (8). Cohen et al. described hematomas in the ascending and transverse colon in an abused child with pancreatitis (58). An extraordinary case of colonic perforation in a 2½-year-old abused and neglected child was reported by Gornall et al. (6). He presented with severe peritonitis and died a day following surgery. An explanation for the relative sparing of the colon relates to its mobility and to the fact that large portions either are located in the periphery of the abdomen or are shielded within the pelvis.

A variety of other rare injuries to the colon have been reported. Swadia et al. described a case of multiple needles inserted

into the chest and abdomen by the child's mother (59) (Fig. 7.17). One of the needles perforated the cecum and the child presented with an acute abdomen. Forced lax-ative abuse has been described (60–62). The findings might be expected to produce a dilated colon, but radiographic studies in these patients were not described. A unique

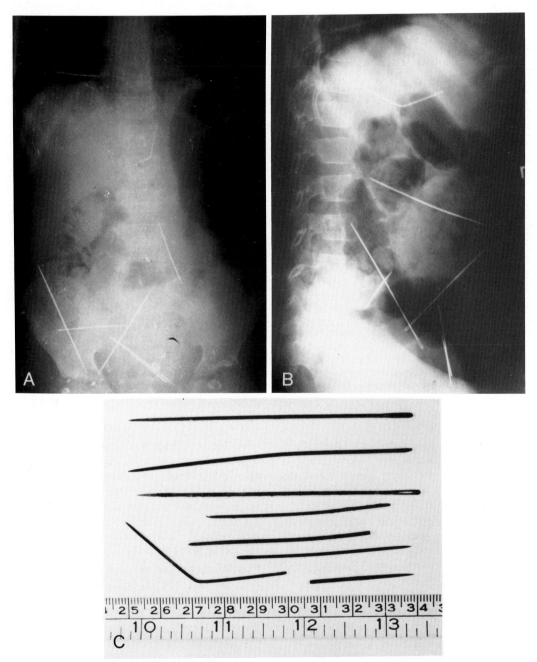

Figure 7.17. Impalement. *A* and *B*, Supine, and lateral abdominal films of an 11-year-old boy demonstrate multiple needles within the chest and abdomen. Seven needles, one broken (*C*), were removed at surgery. One needle had perforated the cecum and the second had pierced the left lobe of the liver. The mother admitted to inserting these needles during the preceding 6 weeks. (Reproduced with permission from Swadia ND, Thakore AB, Patel BR, Bhavani SS: Unusual form of abuse presenting as an acute abdomen. *Br J Surg* 68:668, 1981.)

case of child abuse related to the administration of a lye enema has been described, without radiologic studies (27). The celiac syndrome has been associated with child neglect and abuse (63–64). Neglect of ulcerative colitis resulted in a fatality in a 15½-year-old girl (65). A more detailed discussion of neglect can be found in Chapter 9.

THE PANCREAS

Pancreatitis and Pseudocysts

For many years the pancreas had eluded accurate assessment by standard radiologic techniques. Acute pancreatic injury and its complications were generally defined at surgery or postmortem examination. Although barium contrast studies provided secondary evidence of pancreatic inflammation or mass, manifest as deformity and displacement of contrast-filled bowel, noninvasive direct visualization of the pancreas had been impossible. With the advent of ultrasonography, CT, and magnetic resonance imaging (MRI), disturbances in the gross morphology of the pancreas are now easily and accurately definable. These techniques have greatly enhanced our ability to detect pancreatic pseudocysts in abused children, and the capacity to monitor this condition noninvasively has had a significant impact on medical and surgical management.

In contrast to adults, in whom up to 80% of pancreatic pseudocysts are due to complications of alcoholic pancreatitis (66), the majority of pseudocysts in children are due to blunt abdominal injury. Cooney and Grosfeld, reporting on 15 children with pancreatic pseudocysts and reviewing an additional 60 cases from the literature, found that 60% were due to trauma (67). In 32% the cause was unknown; undoubtedly some of these were secondary to unrecognized blunt abdominal trauma. In 1964, Kilman et al. described a child with a large pancreatic pseudocyst, with incidental fractures of three ribs and a clavicle (68). The authors felt that this was "perhaps" a case of child abuse. In 1967, Kim and Jenkins described a 3-year-old with a large pseudocyst in the retrogastric region (69). Although the child evidenced bruises and scars, and investiga-

tions supported abuse, legal proof of physical abuse was not obtained. On the insistence of the mother, the child was discharged to her care. Four months after discharge the child was brought to another hospital dispensary, dead on arrival. The child had suffered a recent fractured arm, skull fracture, acute subdural hematoma, and multiple contusions. Numerous additional reports of pancreatitis and pseudocysts associated with abuse have appeared, and the entity is sufficiently characteristic that diagnosis has become routine (1, 28, 58, 70–77).

Three critical ingredients are required for the development of pancreatitis: (a) disruption of acinar or ductal integrity, (b) seepage of pancreatic enzymes into tissue spaces, and (c) activation of proteolytic and lipolytic enzymes (78). The pancreas lies in a precarious position extending from the medial aspect of the descending duodenum upward across the spine, ending in the region of the splenic hilus (see Fig. 7.6). It is vulnerable to blunt abdominal trauma, which may result in acinar and ductal injury. Enzymatic autodigestion of the organ and hemorrhage result in a pathologic pattern of hemorrhagic pancreatitis. As the process continues, fluid collections containing pancreatic enzymes develop in and around the organ. Initially, these collections may be loosely confined, but with time a firm fibrous capsule develops. Diffuse fluid collections are generally referred to as effusions, and the more discretely confined collections as pancreatic pseudocysts. Secondary infection of the pancreatic and mesenteric collections also occurs.

Development of pancreatitis may be rapid, occurring within days of the injury, or it may be gradual and insidious. Although there may be minimal symptoms immediately following the injury, a factor that may result in failure to seek attention, a consistent pattern of complaints and physical findings can be expected. Vomiting, abdominal distension, and fever are present in the vast majority of patients. Serum amylase is elevated, but may return to normal despite continued illness. Ascites is often detectable, and paracentesis may yield fluid with an elevated amylase. Pleural effusions, frequent in adults with pancreatic disease, are uncommon in abused children with pseudocysts (75). Bruises, scars, and burns may be noted upon inspection. Skeletal surveys may reveal rib, clavicle, and extremity fractures (68, 70, 72, 73, 75). However, there may be no physical evidence whatsoever to suggest abuse, and the etiology of the process may go undiscovered until additional injury occurs (1).

The abdominal plain film may provide some clue as to the presence of pancreatitis. Several signs have been described that, although associated with pancreatic inflammatory disease, can be noted in other conditions (79). Localized dilatation of bowel loops with air–fluid levels, or "sentinel loops," in the region of the pancreas may be noted with acute pancreatitis. An abrupt termination of a gas-filled proximal transverse colon, or "colon cutoff" sign, is another nonspecific feature of pancreatic inflammation. A mass effect upon the descending duodenum and separation of the stomach from the transverse colon are additional findings that may be evident if sufficient intraluminal gas is present. These latter changes, however, are best evaluated with opaque contrast media.

Historically, the upper GI series has been a useful tool in the evaluation of pancreatic pseudocysts. Most cysts are found to lie in the retrogastric region, often extending into the lesser sac. The resultant effect on the stomach is a mass effect posteriorly (Fig. 7.18). The process may extend into the transverse mesocolon with resultant elevation of the stomach and displacement of the transverse colon (75). Spiculation of the mucosa and/or mass effect upon the medial aspect of the descending duodenum provide additional evidence of pancreatic inflammatory disease. Complete duodenal obstruction may occur with pseudocysts in the head of the pancreas (73). Thickening of the folds in the duodenum and jejunum may reflect associated intramural bleeding, although dissection of pancreatic enzymes to these regions can produce a similar appearance. It is not surprising that duodenal hematomas and traumatic pancreatitis can coexist (8).

In recent years, ultrasonography has become the primary modality for the evaluation of pancreatic pseudocysts in children (1, 73). It not only has provided enhanced identification of pseudocysts, but has further elucidated the natural history of the lesion. Prior to ultrasound, definitive diagnosis and management of pancreatic pseudocysts was achieved at surgery. Extensive experience with ultrasonography in adults has shown that many pancreatic pseudocysts will resolve spontaneously under close scrutiny with serial examinations (80, 81). Experience in childhood supports a conservative approach in most cases, except where there is clinical deterioration or persistent elevation of serum amylase. An enlarging cyst in and of itself presents no specific indication for surgery (73).

In acute pancreatitis, ultrasonography may reveal diffuse enlargement of the gland with decreased echogenicity, presumably related to edema. Pseudocysts are identified as anechoic masses within the pancreas, most frequently within the body and tail (Figs. 7.18C, 7.19, and 7.20). They are visualized behind the stomach and are frequently seen to lie just anterior to the left kidney. If there is significant debris within the cyst, it will gravitate posteriorly and produce multiple echoes in this region. It is often difficult to define the actual thickness of the wall related to surrounding inflammatory and fibrotic changes. Although pseudocysts can occur virtually anywhere within the abdomen, pseudocysts in children have usually been confined to the pancreas and lesser sac.

Computed tomography is well suited for evaluation of the pancreas (28, 33). It can delineate the location, size, and extent of pancreatic pseudocysts. It will also show diffuse pancreatic enlargement, pancreatic ductal dilatation, and peripancreatic inflammatory disease (Fig. 7.20B). However, ultrasonography provides similar data at a substantially lower cost. As there is no ionizing radiation and no need of contrast material, multiple serial studies can be performed without risk. Finally, ultrasonography provides rapid evaluation of ascites, as well as other visceral injury. Since patients may be extremely ill due to multiple sites of trauma,

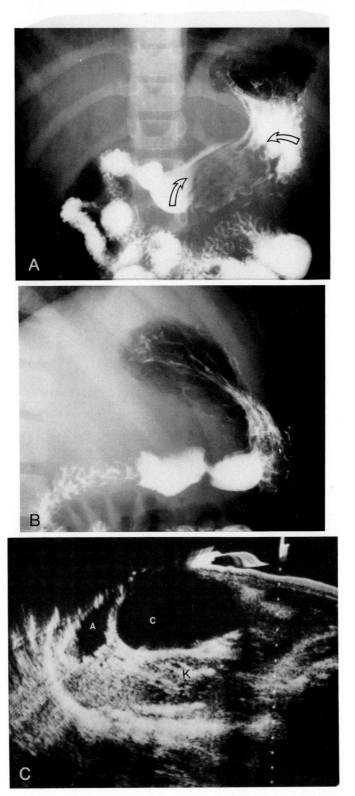

Figure 7.18. Pancreatic pseudocyst. *A* and *B*, Frontal and lateral views of an upper GI series in a 4½-year-old child with vomiting, distension and fever reveal a smooth retrogastric mass (*arrows*). *C*, Left parasagittal ultrasound shows an anechoic mass (*C*) lying anterior to the left kidney (*K*) associated with ascites (*A*). There was no external evidence of trauma and the diagnosis of abuse was confirmed 18 months later when skeletal injuries were documented. (Reproduced with permission from Kleinman PK, Raptopoulos VD, Brill PW: Occult nonskeletal trauma in the battered-child syndrome. *Radiology* 141:393–396, 1981.)

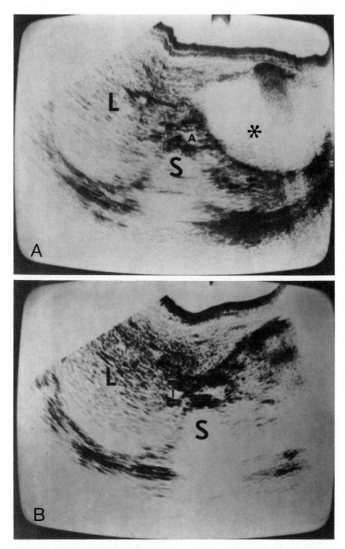

Figure 7.19. Pancreatic pseudocyst with resolution. Ultrasound examination of a 3½-year-old abused child with abdominal pain and vomiting, second degree burns and multiple scars. A, Transverse ultrasound demonstrates a large anechoic mass (*) in the left upper quadrant. There are strong back-wall echoes and good through transmission indicating the cystic nature of the mass. L, liver; S, spine; A, aorta. B, Follow-up study after surgical drainage shows resolution of the cyst. L, liver; S. spine; I, inferior vena cava. (Reproduced with permission from Slovis TL, VonBerg VJ, Mikelic V: Sonography in the diagnosis and management of pancreatic pseudocysts and effusions in childhood. *Radiology* 135:153–155, 1980.)

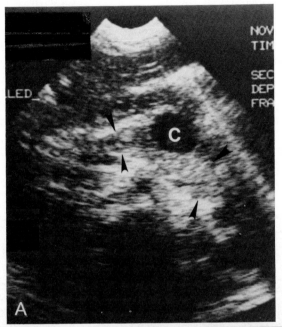

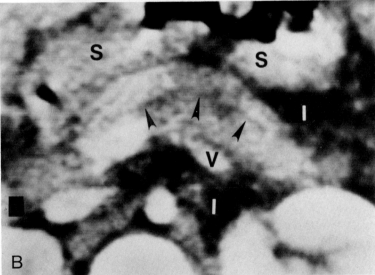

Figure 7.20. Pancreatitis and pancreatic pseudocyst. *A,* Transverse abdominal ultrasound in a 28-month-old abused child demonstrates a normal sized pancreas (*arrowheads*), with a 2.4 cm cystic mass (*C*) anterior to the body. The cyst was believed to be infected, and after 2 weeks of antibiotics a CT scan (*B*) revealed resolution of the cyst, pancreatic ductal dilatation (*arrowheads*) and peripancreatic inflammation (*I*). *S,* stomach, *V,* splenic vein. (Reproduced with permission from Kaufman RA, Babcock DS: An approach to imaging the upper abdomen in the injured child. *Semin Roentgenol* 19:308–320, 1984.)

ultrasound provides the benefit of portable examinations. Thus, ultrasound should be the primary mode of imaging of the pancreas, followed by CT in selected cases.

Systemic release of enzymes following blunt injury to the pancreas may result in fat necrosis at distant sites (82–84). Medullary fat necrosis may be associated with the production of lytic osseous lesions (84–87). Several reports described similar osteolytic lesions in children with pancreatitis secondary to abuse (58, 71, 73, 76). Bone lesions have been noted as early as 2 weeks and as late as 10 weeks following the onset of abdominal symptoms. The symptoms usu-

ally involve the lower extremities, typically the small bones of the feet. Soft tissue swelling and tenderness may be noted over the dorsum of the feet.

Radiologically, there are multiple lytic areas of varying size (Fig. 7.21). The number of lesions may be in excess of 300 (77). The patterns range from a "moth-eaten" appearance to punched-out geographic areas of destruction. With healing, increasing sclerosis is noted, and periosteal new bone is incorporated into the cortex. The lesions have a predilection for the small bones of the feet, as well as for the metaphyseal regions of the long bones. Epiphyseal in-

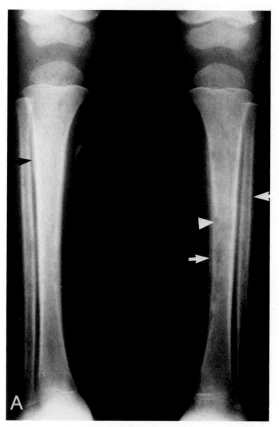

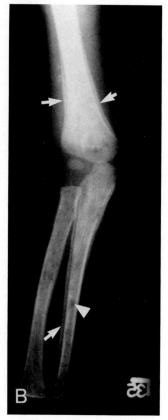

Figure 7.21. Osteolytic lesions secondary to pancreatitis. A 3-year-old abused child with abdominal tenderness and elevated amylase. Initial skeletal survey showed only a healing fractured rib. Views of the lower legs (*A*), forearm (*B*), and two views of the right foot (*C*) reveal permeative, and "moth-eaten" areas of destruction throughout the bony structures. Periosteal new bone formation (*arrows*) is noted at multiple sites. Several "punched out" geographic areas of destruction are seen (*arrowheads*). *D*, Follow-up study 6 months later shows slight increase in overall bone density of feet, but otherwise resolution of the destructive lesions. (Reproduced with permission from Neuer FS, Roberts FF, McCarthy V: Osteolytic lesions following traumatic pancreatitis. *Am J Dis Child* 131:738–740, 1977.)

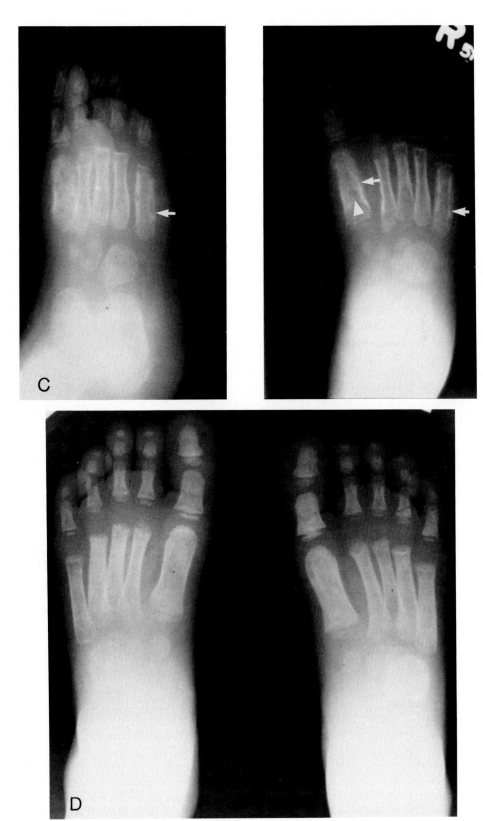

Figure 7.21. *C* and *D.*

volvement is unusual but has been described (58).

These lesions appear to develop following the acute phase of the pancreatic inflammatory process, and resolution is spontaneous regardless of treatment. Radiographic changes persist long after clinical findings have resolved, and mild residual changes may be evident as late as 1 year following diagnosis (77).

These destructive changes bear considerable similarity to the osseous lesions associated with disseminated malignancy. The finding of lytic destructive lesions with associated periosteal reaction will raise the concern of leukemia and metastatic neuroblastoma. As the patient may present with systemic illness with abdominal complaints, care should be taken to avoid confusing these entities. In the child presenting with multiple painful lytic lesions involving the small bones of the extremities, serum amylase determination is mandatory.

LIVER

Hepatic injuries in abused children are generally due to direct injury from blows to the abdomen (see Fig. 7.6), or to impact following sudden deceleration (2–4, 6, 7, 28, 71, 76, 88–90). Rarely, penetrating injuries resulting from needles inserted into the abdomen may be encountered unexpectedly on radiographic examination (59, 91, 92) (see Fig. 7.17). Although on occasion rib fractures may be associated with hepatic injury, in most cases fractures are not identified. The clinical findings will usually be overshadowed by evidence of intestinal perforation, obstruction due to intramural hematoma, or neurologic disturbances. On occasion, the diagnosis of a major hepatic injury may go undetected, with a fatal outcome (2). Hepatic injuries are rare in young abused infants because the assaults in most cases do not include direct blows to the baby. However, a rare example of such injuries has been reported by Simpson (89). He described conviction of a 19-year-old man at the Old Bailey for two separate murders of his 4-month-old and 5-week-old sons. Both children had evidence of extensive trauma, but the major abdominal

injuries were ruptures of the liver with large amounts of free blood in the peritoneal cavity.

It is difficult to assess the incidence of hepatic injury in abused children. Although major injuries will be identified at laparotomy, and on occasion noninvasively with various radiologic studies, it is clear that many small contusions and lacerations involving the liver go undetected. It is vital to diagnose all such cases because, although detection may have little impact on immediate therapy, documentation is of utmost importance for ultimate determination of abuse. Radiologic studies that provide specific indication of hepatic injury include ultrasonography, CT, and radionuclide examinations. Ultrasonography is well suited to the initial evaluation of these patients. Ultrasound provides a rapid survey of the abdominal viscera and easily detects intraperitoneal fluid. Focal areas of increased echogenicity representing hepatic contusion may be identified (Fig. 7.22A). Subcapsular collections of fluid may be identified as homogeneously hypoechoic areas conforming to the outer contour of the liver. Small lacerations are not easily detected with this technique.

Computed tomography provides the most sensitive noninvasive technique to assess for hepatic injury. The high density associated with acute bleeding within the liver parenchyma as well as in the subcapsular region is easily identified on the unenhanced scan. Areas of diminished perfusion following administration of contrast indicate sites of disruption of parenchymal architecture. Computed tomography is particularly helpful in identifying scars within the liver related to prior injury (28). The radionuclide liver–spleen scan has traditionally been used to assess for hepatosplenic injury (Fig. 7.22B). Although it remains a frequently used technique for the evaluation of the spleen, CT is the modality of choice if hepatic injury is strongly suspected. Beauchamp et al. reported a subcapsular hematoma in an abused child detected by liver scintigraphy (88). Beau et al. described disruption of the left hepatic duct secondary to paternal beating of a 3-year-old (93). This injury was documented at surgery with an

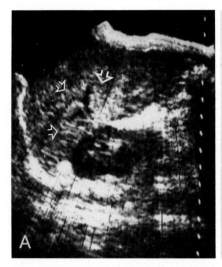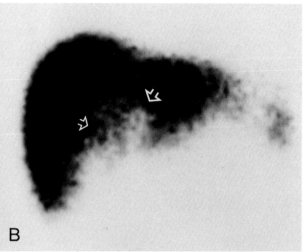

Figure 7.22. Hepatic contusion in a 14-month-old child with irritability, lethargy, and elevated liver enzymes. *A,* Right parasagittal ultrasound reveals increased echoes in the region of the portahepatis (*arrows*). *B,* A technetium-99m sulfur colloid radionuclide scan shows a corresponding area of decreased activity (*arrows*). An initial diagnosis of toxic encephalopathy was made. Formal confirmation of abuse was made at 18 months of age when major additional abdominal and thoracic injuries occurred (see Figures 7.24 and 7.30).

intraoperative colangiogram. Gornall et al. described a 32-month-old battered child who had suffered a complete avulsion of the common bile duct from its attachment to the duodenum (6). Palmer and Weston reported a hepatic portal vein thrombosis in a fatally abused 12-month-old infant (90). Although there was diffuse hepatic parenchymal injury, the precise cause of the thrombosis was uncertain.

THE SPLEEN

It is curious that, despite frequent splenic injury noted in accidental blunt abdominal trauma, injuries of the spleen are rare in abused children (94). Gornall et al. found 18 splenic injuries in 69 children with accidental abdominal injury (6). There was no splenic injury in six battered children with abdominal trauma. No examples of splenic injury were found in the larger series of abused children with abdominal visceral injury (3, 4, 7).

Sty et al. reported an usual case of a 5-year-old abuse victim who demonstrated increased splenic uptake on a technetium-99m (^{99m}Tc) methylene diphosphonate scan performed to detect skeletal injury (Fig.

7.23) (95). A subsequent ^{99m}Tc sulphur colloid scan confirmed a subcapsular splenic hematoma. The mechanism of accumulation of the bone-seeking agent in the splenic hematoma is obscure.

URINARY TRACT

Kidneys

Injuries involving the urinary tract are distinctly uncommon in child abuse. Although the most common lesions involve direct disruption of the renal parenchyma or collecting systems, renal disfunction may occur secondary to more generalized disturbances related to massive injury.

Disruption of the renal parenchyma occurs in the form of contusion, laceration, or gross fracture (1, 4, 96–98). Patients may present with bruising and evidence of trauma elsewhere, but this is not an invariable finding (1). Posterior rib fractures so commonly seen in young abused infants are infrequently encountered with renal injury. A multimodality approach to renal injury will produce the highest yield of renal injuries. Contusion will be manifest on intravenous urography by focal or diffuse decrease in visualization of the collecting system (Fig.

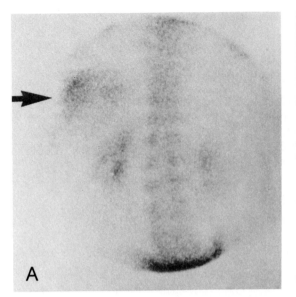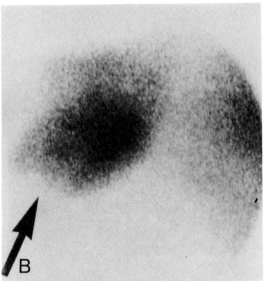

Figure 7.23. Splenic injury. *A,* Technetium 99m methylene diphosphonate bone scan performed in a 5-year-old abused child demonstrates abnormal activity within the spleen (*arrow*). *B,* Technetium-99m sulfur colloid liver spleen scan demonstrates a splenic defect (*arrow*) on the left posterior oblique image. (Reproduced with permission from Sty J, Starshak RJ, Hubbard A: Accumulation of Tc-99m MDP in the spleen of a battered child. *Clin Nucl Med* 7:292, 1982.)

7.24). Radionuclide scintigraphy may increase uptake of tracer with an enlarged kidney. Delayed images will show persistent delayed tracer activity with a normal pattern of excretion on the opposite side (Fig. 7.24). When laceration or fracture is present, contrast material may extravasate into the perirenal space or flow along the renal sinus into the proximal ureter. Kimmel and Sty reported such an abused child with perirenal extravasation of contrast material (97) (Fig. 7.25). Technetium methylene diphosphonate bone imaging resulted in persistent increased activity surrounding the traumatized kidney. Contusion and extravasation were confirmed with intravenous pyelography (IVP) and renal scintigraphy.

As in accidental trauma, underlying structural abnormalities may place the kidneys at risk in abusive attacks. Rosenberg reported a unique case of traumatic avulsion of the vascular supply of a crossed unfused ectopic kidney (98). She described a 3-year-old abused child who presented with bruises on the lower back and laboratory evidence of anemia and hematuria (98). Skeletal survey showed no associated fractures. Abdominal ultrasound revealed left crossed unfused renal ectopia, and intravenous

urography showed visualization of only the normally positioned right kidney (Fig. 7.26). Surgery revealed avulsion of the pedicle of the ectopic kidney. The accompanying retroperitoneal hematoma was evacuated and the ectopic kidney was removed.

Acute renal failure may develop in children with massive battering. In most cases the renal disease relates to myoglobinuria secondary to rhabdomyolysis (99). Intravenous urography will demonstrate a dense nephrogram and a striated appearance of the renal parenchyma due to visualization of the medullary rays (Fig. 7.27). Radionuclide bone scans may reveal intense activity in the kidneys (100) (Fig. 7.28). Other cases of pigmenturia associated with child abuse have been described (95, 101–103).

Bladder and Urethra

The lower urinary tract is generally spared from nonaccidental blunt abdominal injury; however, rupture of the bladder without associated pelvic fracture has been described by Sauer et al. and by Halsted and Shapiro (19, 104). Renal failure in the Halsted and Shapiro case resulted from extravasation of urine into the peritoneal cavity (Fig. 7.29). A bizarre form of abuse has

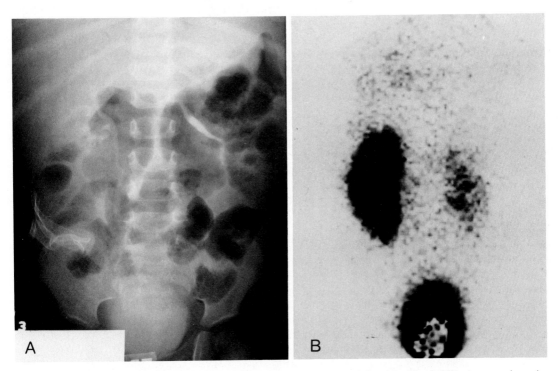

Figure 7.24. Renal contusion. An 18-month-old infant (same patient as Fig. 7.22) who was found unarousable with multiple bruises and abdominal distension. *A,* An IVP demonstrates no definite function of the left kidney. The right kidney is normal. *B,* Delayed view of a ^{99m}Tc DTPA renal scan demonstrates increased activity within an enlarged left kidney consistent with a renal contusion. (Reproduced with permission from Kleinman PK, Raptopoulos VD, Brill PW: Occult nonskeletal trauma in the battered-child syndrome. *Radiology* 141:393–396, 1981.)

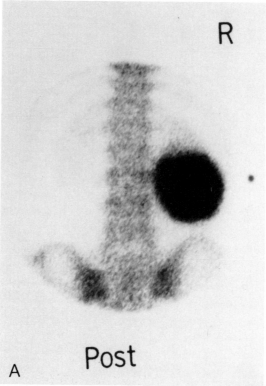

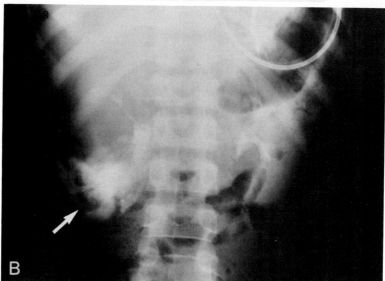

Figure 7.25. Renal fracture. *A,* Posterior view of a ^{99m}Tc methylene diphosphonate bone scan performed to detect skeletal abnormalities in an abused child reveals an abnormal collection of tracer around the right kidney. *B,* An IVP demonstrates perirenal extravasation of contrast material (*arrow*). *C,* Sequential images of a subsequent renal scan demonstrate a fractured right kidney (*closed arrow*) with a photon deficient region representing a perirenal uriniferous collection (*curved arrow*). The left kidney (*open arrow*) is normal. (Reproduced with permission from Kimmel RL, Sty JR: ^{99m}Tc-methylene diphosphonate renal images in a battered child. *Clin Nucl Med* 4:166–167, 1979.)

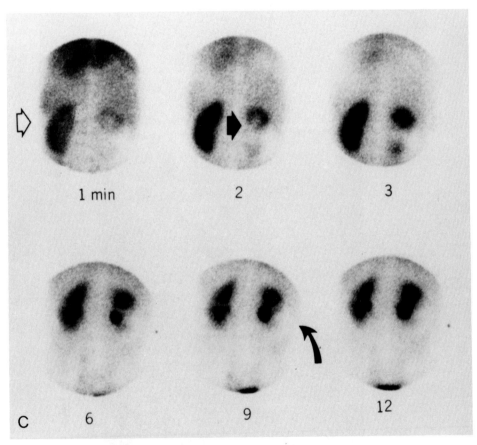

Figure 7.25. *C.*

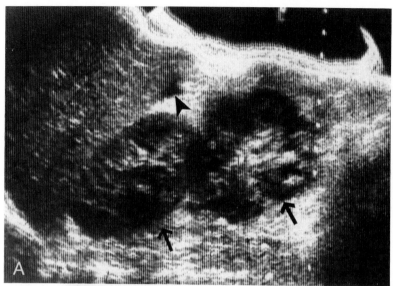

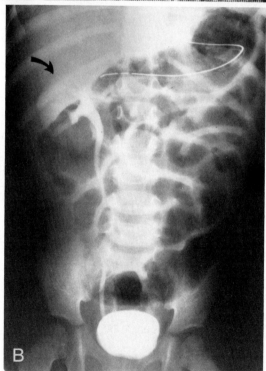

Figure 7.26. Vascular injury of a crossed unfused ectopic kidney. *A*, A sagittal ultrasound in a 3-year-old child with multiple bruises reveals an ectopically positioned left kidney lying adjacent to the lower pole of the normal right kidney (*arrows*). A small amount of ascites is present (*arrowhead*). *B*, An IVP reveals a normal-appearing right kidney (*arrow*) without evidence of a second renal structure. At surgery, avulsion of the blood supply to a crossed unfused ectopic kidney was found, and the kidney was removed. (Reproduced with permission from WB Saunders Co. and Rosenberg HK: Traumatic avulsion of the vascular supply of a crossed unfused ectopic kidney: Complementary roles of ultrasonography and intravenous pyelography. *J Ultrasound Med* 3:89–91, 1984.)

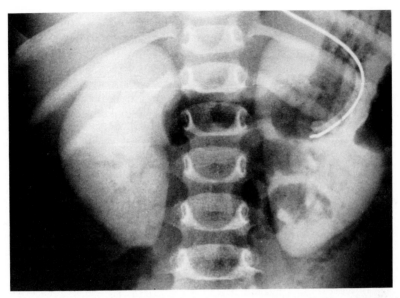

Figure 7.27. Renal failure due to probable myoglobinuria. A 4-hour delayed IVP film in a severely abused 4-year-old child demonstrates bilateral dense nephrograms and faintly visualized collecting systems. (Reproduced with permission from Rosenberg HK, Gefter WB, Lebowitz RL, Mahboubi S, Rosenberg H: Prolonged dense nephrograms in battered children. *Urology* 21:325–330, 1983.)

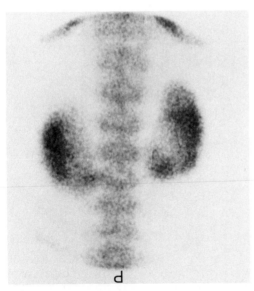

Figure 7.28. Myoglobinuria. ^{99m}Tc DPTA bone scan in an abused patient with myoglobinuria demonstrates abnormal intense renal activity. (Reproduced with permission from Sty JR, Starshak RJ: The role of bone scintigraphy in the evaluation of the suspected abused child. *Radiology* 146:369–375, 1983.)

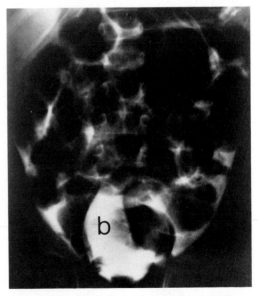

Figure 7.29. Bladder rupture and renal failure. Cystogram performed in a 2-year-old abused child with renal failure reveals extravasation of contrast throughout the peritoneal cavity. The bladder (*b*) is displaced to the right, probably from a pelvic hematoma. (Reproduced with permission from Halsted CC, Shapiro SR: Child abuse: Acute renal failure from ruptured bladder. *Am J Dis Child* 133:861–862, 1979. Copyright 1979, American Medical Association.)

been described in which bilateral hydrone-phrosis was noted in a fatally injured 2-year-old. Autopsy revealed marked hyper-trophy of the bladder with bilateral hydro-nephrosis and hydroureter. It was suggested that the father had tied off the child's penis in order to prevent enuresis (105).

Injuries to the urethra and external geni-talia may occur with sexual abuse, a subject covered in Chapter 9.

The Thorax

Despite the high frequency of rib injuries in abused patients, underlying injuries to the pleura, lungs, and mediastinal structures are only occasionally documented radiolog-ically. It is likely, however, that mild injuries to these regions occur with significant fre-quency, but may simply go undetected.

PLEURA

Pneumothorax

In contrast to accidental thoracic trauma, pneumothoraces secondary to abuse are rare. Bruises may be lacking and radio-graphs may fail to demonstrate associated rib fracture (Fig. 7.30). In such cases, the diagnosis of a spontaneous pneumothorax may be entertained and the possibility of abuse overlooked. Pneumothoraces can be identified in the supine position, but are best appreciated with the horizontal beam in the upright or decubitus position. A large tension pneumothorax will result in medias-tinal shift to the contralateral hemithorax. In the child who presents with massive in-jury, there may be reluctance to obtain such films, but in most cases with proper medical supervision these examinations can be achieved.

Pleural Fluid

Accumulations of pleural fluid may be noted with and without associated rib frac-tures. Fluid collections are usually modest and are best identified in the decubitus po-sition with the affected side down (Fig. 7.31). Pleural fluid may be noted as an

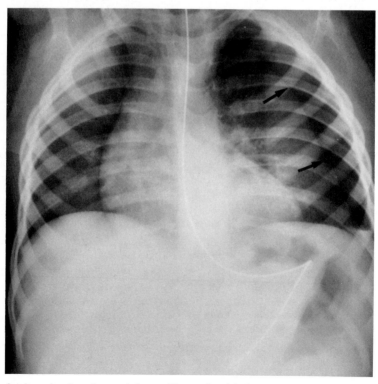

Figure 7.30. Supine chest radiograph in an 18-month-old abused child with thoracic and abdom-inal injuries reveals a left pneumothorax (*arrows*). No rib fractures are identified.

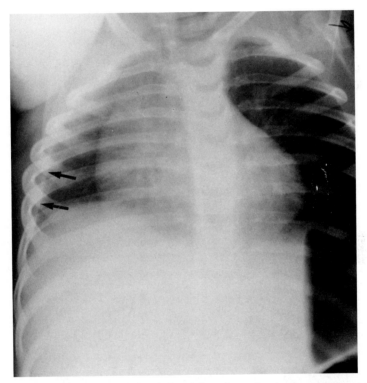

Figure 7.31. Pleural effusion. A right lateral decubitus view of a 1-year-old abused child demonstrates a small right pleural effusion (*arrows*).

incidental finding on ultrasound performed for suspected abdominal trauma. Computed tomography is extremely sensitive in the detection of pleural fluid collections. In patients with massive thoracic injury and associated pleural effusion, thoracentesis may reveal infected hemorrhagic fluid (Fig. 7.32).

Rarely, injury to the thoracic lymphatic ductal system will result in the development of a chylothorax (106). Green described an 8-month-old child with disruption of the thoracic lymphatic drainage resulting in a large right pleural effusion (107). Multiple associated rib and extremity fractures were identified, further documenting abuse. Surgical closure of the lymphatic ductal disruption resulted in cure.

LUNGS

Contusion

It is surprising that pulmonary contusions or areas of atelectasis related to abuse are only rarely described (1) (Fig. 7.32A). Mild degrees of contusion are likely overlooked on suboptimal examinations of the chest.

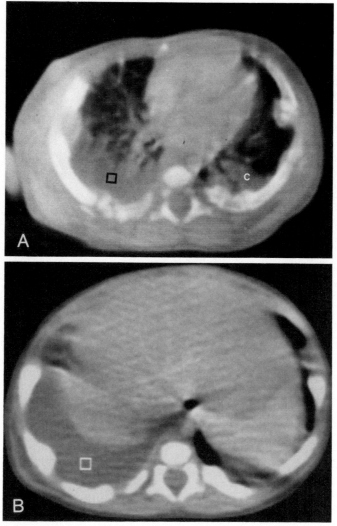

Figure 7.32. CT images (*A* and *B*) through the mid and lower thorax in a 6-month-old abused child with multiple rib fractures. Pleural effusion (*box*) is noted on the right. Pulmonary contusion (*C*) is noted on the left. A right thoracentesis yielded hemorrhagic fluid.

Computed tomography has revealed impressive areas of parenchymal disease with minimal plain film abnormalities. With increasing use of CT in the evaluation of thoracic injury due to abuse, the incidence of recognizable pulmonary contusion will likely increase. Although less common than in adults, pleural effusions may be associated with pancreatitis and pancreatic pseudocyst (75). In a child with abdominal symptoms and pleural effusion, an amylase determination is mandatory.

Pneumonia

Pulmonary infiltrates in the child with other injury may also be due to aspiration or secondary infection. Radiologically it may be difficult to distinguish between these en- tities. A rare case of pulmonary consolidation due to parental poisoning was described by Saulsbury et al. (108). The mother of an 11-month-old boy had introduced a hydrocarbon of the naphtha variety into the child's intravenous line during the patient's hospitalization. The child suffered an abrupt respiratory arrest, and during resuscitation a strong odor of hydrocarbon was noted. Radiographs demonstrated bilateral infiltrates that showed gradual resolution over subsequent days (Fig. 7.33).

MEDIASTINUM

Heart

Cardiac injuries due to abuse are rare and may involve all layers of the heart. In 1952,

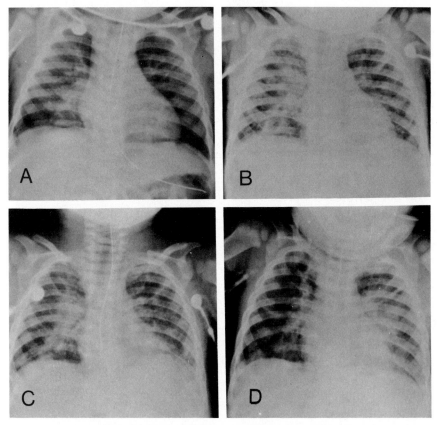

Figure 7.33. Pulmonary infiltrates secondary to poisoning of an infant whose mother injected a naphtha hydrocarbon into the child's intravenous line during a hospitalization. *A,* Admission radiograph was interpreted as normal. Radiographs obtained at 13 hours (*B*), 22 hours (*C*), and 36 hours (*D*) reveal patchy pulmonary infiltrate. (Reproduced with permission from Saulsbury FT, Chobanian MC, Wilson WG: Child abuse: Parenteral hydrocarbon administration. *Pediatrics* 73:719–721, 1984.)

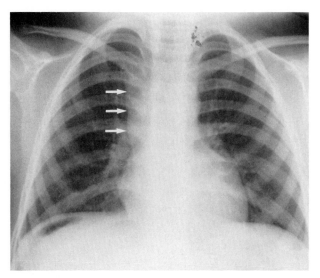

Figure 7.34. Mediastinal hemorrhage. PA radiograph in a 5-year-old abused child demonstrates widening of the right superior mediastinum (*arrows*), probably related to venous bleeding. Free intraperitoneal air is evident below the right hemidiaphragm as a result of a jejunal perforation.

Kugelmann described· endocardial and myocardial hemorrhages in a 5½-year-old abused infant with multiple long bone fractures and a subdural hematoma (109). Marino and Langston described the cardiac findings on postmortem examination in an 18-month-old abused infant dying from head injuries (110). In addition to 50 ml of blood in the pericardium, there was evidence of infarction involving the right ventricular wall and the interventricular septum. A portion of the conducting system also appeared injured. Rees et al. described a 5-year-old girl with congestive heart failure who had been kicked in the chest 2 weeks earlier (111). Cardiac catheterization revealed a ventricular septal defect (VSD). At surgery, in addition to the VSD, a right ventricular apical aneurysm was encountered and repaired.

Penetrating injuries of the heart are rarely encountered secondary to abuse. Ramu reported a child with two sewing needles lodged in the heart and others within the abdomen and extremities (91). The child died as a result of septicemia. Swadia et al. described large metallic needles variously inserted in the abdomen and the chest without any intrathoracic complications (59) (see Fig. 7.17).

Esophagus

Sauer et al. described a 6-month-old infant with an intramural cavity associated with a mucosal rent in the thoracic esophagus (19). This partial esophageal perforation was associated with old and new fractures of a rib, ulna, radius, and the skull, all presumably due to abuse.

Blood Vessels

Major mediastinal vascular injuries are extraordinary in blunt injury in childhood. If sufficient bleeding is present, there will be mediastinal widening (Fig. 7.34).

The Neck

Rare cases of soft tissue injury with radiologic manifestations have been described. McDowell and Fielding reported a 3-month-old boy and a 4-month-old boy both presenting with extensive interstitial emphysema involving the cervical soft tissues, without associated bony injury (112) (Fig. 7.35). Endoscopic examination showed evidence of pharyngeal hemorrhage in one patient, and a perforation with retropharyngeal abscess in the second. Abuse was

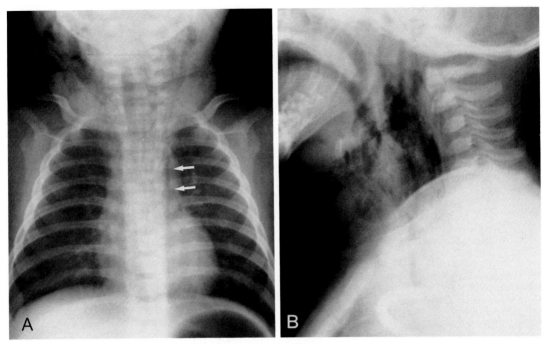

Figure 7.35. Perforation of the hypopharynx in an abused infant. AP view of the chest (*A*) and lateral views of the neck (*B*) demonstrate massive deep and superficial cervical emphysema, greatest in the retropharyngeal region. There is extension of the cervical air to the mediastinum (*arrows*, part A). (Courtesy of D.W. Fielding, Countess of Chester Hospital, Chester, United Kingdom.)

strongly suspected in both cases. Salmon described a 38-month-old child with extensive bruising over the neck, thorax, and limbs (113). Massive deep and subcutaneous emphysema was noted, secondary to a ruptured trachea. The symptoms were said to have occurred following a fall from a tricycle; however, child abuse was strongly suspected. Thomas and Cameron described a 13-month-old child who suffered a midline stab wound to the neck (114). Multiple bruises and lacerations were present. The major injury was a laceration of the left internal jugular vein, which was repaired, followed by an uneventful recovery.

REFERENCES

1. Kleinman PK, Raptopoulos VD, Brill PW: Occult nonskeletal trauma in the battered-child syndrome. *Radiology* 141:393–396, 1981.
2. Perry JF Jr, Venters HD: Childhood deaths due to injury. *Surgery* 62:620–623, 1967.
3. McCort J, Vaudagna J: Visceral injuries in battered children. *Radiology* 82:424–428, 1964.
4. O'Neill JA Jr, Meacham WF, Griffin PP, Sawyers JL: Patterns of injury in the battered child syndrome. *J Trauma* 13:332–339, 1973.
5. Tank ES, Eraklis AJ, Gross RE: Blunt abdominal trauma in infancy and childhood. *J Trauma* 8:439–448, 1968.
6. Gornall P, Ahmed S, Jolleys A, Cohen SJ: Intraabdominal injuries in the battered baby syndrome. *Arch Dis Child* 47:211–214, 1972.
7. Touloukian RJ: Abdominal trauma in childhood. *Surg Gynecol Obstet* 127:561–568, 1968.
8. Touloukian RJ: Abdominal visceral injuries in battered children. *Pediatrics* 42:642–646, 1968.
9. Caniano DA, Beaver BL, Boles ET Jr: Child abuse. An update on surgical management in 256 cases. *Ann Surg* 203:219–224, 1986.
10. Franken EA Jr, Fox M, Smith JA, Smith WL: Acute gastric dilatation in neglected children. *Am J Roentgenol (AJR)* 130:297–299, 1978.
11. Shulman BH, Evans HE, Manvar D, Flicker S: Acute gastric dilatation following feeding of nutritionally abused children. *Clin Pediatr* 23:108, 1984.
12. Schechner SA, Ehrlich FE: Gastric perforation and child abuse. *J Trauma* 14:723–725, 1974.
13. Case MES, Nanduri R: Laceration of the stomach by blunt trauma in a child: a case of child abuse. *J Forensic Sci* 28:496–501, 1983.
14. Tollner U, Henrichs I, Bittner R, Reinhardt G: Rupture of the stomach caused by child-battering. *Monatsschr Kinderheilkd* 132:801–802, 1984.

15. Siemens RA, Fulton RL: Gastric rupture as a result of blunt trauma. *Am Surg* 43:229–233, 1977.
16. Stroh A, Zamet P, Bomsel F: Ulcere aigu de stress dans une famille maltraitante. *Arch Fr Pediatr* 40:411–414, 1983.
17. Jones HH, Davis JH: Multiple traumatic lesions of the infant skeleton. *Stanford Med Bull* 15:259–273, 1957.
18. Boon WH: The battered child syndrome in Singapore. *J Singapore Paediatr Soc* 21:148–159, 1979.
19. Sauer H, Kurz R, Fink M: Uber thoracoabdominale- und knochenverletzungen bei kindesmisshandlungen (battered child-syndrome). *Monatsschr Unfallheilk* 78:533–543, 1975.
20. Woolley MM, Mahour GH, Sloan T: Duodenal hematoma in infancy and childhood: changing etiology and changing treatment. *Am J Surg* 136:8–14, 1978.
21. Georghegen T, Brush BE: The mechanism of intestinal perforation from nonpenetrating abdominal trauma. *Arch Surg* 73:455–464, 1956.
22. Williams RD, Sargent FT: The mechanism of intestinal injury in trauma. *J Trauma* 3:288–294, 1963.
23. Furnemont E: La desinertion traumatique du mesentere: a propos d'une observation. *Ann Radiol* (Paris) 20:517–521, 1977.
24. Kleinman PK, Raptopoulos V: The anterior diaphragmatic attachments: an anatomic and radiologic study with clinical correlates. *Radiology* 155:289–293, 1985.
25. Eisenstein EM, Delta BG, Clifford JH: Jejunal hematoma: an unusual manifestation of the battered-child syndrome. *Clin Pediatr* 4:436–440, 1965.
26. Bratu M, Dower JC, Siegel B, Hosney SH: Jejunal hematoma, child abuse, and Felson's sign. *Conn Med* 34:261–264, 1970.
27. Grosfeld JL, Ballantine TVN: Surgical aspects of child abuse (trauma-X). *Pediatr Ann* 5:106–120, 1976.
28. Kaufman RA, Babcock DS: An approach to imaging the upper abdomen in the injured child. *Semin Roentgenol* 19:308–320, 1984.
29. Stewart DR, Byrd CL, Schuster SR: Intramural hematomas of the alimentary tract in children. *Surgery* 68:550–557, 1970.
30. Silverman FN: Radiologic aspects and special diagnostic procedures. In Kempe CH, Helfer RE (eds): *The Battered Child*, ed 3. Chicago, University of Chicago Press, 1980, pp 215–240.
31. Radkowski MA, Merten DF, Leonidas JC: The abused child: criteria for the radiologic diagnosis. *RadioGraphics* 3:262–297, 1983.
32. Wilkinson RH: Imaging of the abused child. In Newberger E (ed): *Child Abuse*. Boston, Little, Brown, 1982, pp 159–175.
33. Hilton S: The accidentally injured and abused child. In Hilton SVW, Edwards DK, Hilton JW (eds): *Practical Pediatric Radiology*. Philadelphia, WB Saunders, 1984, pp 443–485.
34. Pickett LK: Role of the surgeon in the detection of child abuse. *Conn Med* 36:513–514, 1972.
35. Mahour GH, Woolley MM, Gans SL, Payne VC Jr: Duodenal hematoma in infancy and childhood. *J Pediatr Surg* 6:153–160, 1971.
36. Buchino JJ: Recognition and management of child abuse by the surgical pathologist. *Arch Pathol Lab Med* 107:204–205, 1983.
37. Touloukian RJ: Protocol for the nonoperative treatment of obstructing intramural duodenal hematoma during childhood. *Am J Surg* 145:330–334, 1983.
38. Zahran M, Eklof O, Thomasson B: Blunt abdominal trauma and hollow viscus injury in children: the diagnostic value of plain radiography. *Pediatr Radiol* 14:304–309, 1984.
39. Izant RJ Jr, Drucker WR: Duodenal obstruction due to intramural hematoma in children. *J Trauma* 4:797–813, 1964.
40. Felson B, Levin EJ: Intramural hematoma of the duodenum. A diagnostic roentgen sign. *Radiology* 63:823–829, 1954.
41. Kleinman PK, Brill PW, Winchester P: The resolving duodenal-jejunal hematoma in abused children. *Radiology* 160:747–750, 1986.
42. Bailey WC, Akers DR: Traumatic intramural hematoma of the duodenum in children: a report of five cases. *Am J Surg* 110:695–703, 1965.
43. Boysen BE: Chylous ascites. Manifestation of the battered child syndrome. *Am J Dis Child* 129:1338–1339, 1975.
44. Vollman RW, Keenan WJ, Eraklis AJ: Post-traumatic chylous ascites in infancy. *N Engl J Med* 275:875–877, 1966.
45. Dillard RP, Stewart AG: Total parenteral nutrition in the management of traumatic chylous ascites in infancy. *Clin Pediatr* 24:290–292, 1985.
46. Viswanathan U, Putnam TC: Therapeutic intravenous alimentation for traumatic chylous ascites in a child. *J Pediatr Surg* 9:405–406, 1974.
47. Votteler TP: Warning: Ingested disc batteries. *Tex Med* 77:7, 1981.
48. Willis GA, Ho WC: Perforation of Meckel's diverticulum by an alkaline hearing aid battery. *Can Med Assoc J* 126:497–498, 1982.
49. Blatnik DS, Toohill RJ, Lehman RH: Fatal complication from an alkaline battery foreign body in the esophagus. *Ann Otol Rhinol Laryngol* 86:611–615, 1977.
50. D'Sa EA, D'Sa Barros AAB: Mercury battery ingestion. Letter to the editor. *Br Med J* 1:1218, 1979.
51. Litovitz T, Butterfield AB, Holloway RR, Marion LI: Button battery ingestion: assessment of therapeutic modalities and battery discharge state. *J Pediatr* 105:868–873, 1984.
52. Litovitz TL: Battery ingestions: Product accessibility and clinical course. *Pediatrics* 75:469–476, 1985.
53. Katz L, Cooper MT: Re: Danger of small children swallowing hearing aid batteries. Letter to the editor. *J Otolaryngol* 7:476, 1978.
54. Shabino CL, Feinberg AN: Esophageal perforation secondary to alkaline battery ingestion. *J Am Coll Emerg Physicians* 8:360–362, 1979.
55. Temple DM, McNeese MC: Hazards of battery ingestion. *Pediatrics* 71:100–103, 1983.
56. Baker DH, Berdon WE: Special trauma problems in children. *Radiol Clin North Am* 4(2):289–305, 1966.

57. Walker A III, Giltman LI: Intussusception: a case review. *South Med J* 77:336–339, 1984.
58. Cohen H, Haller JO, Friedman AP: Pancreatitis, child abuse, and skeletal lesions. *Pediatr Radiol* 10:175–177, 1981.
59. Swadia ND, Thakore AB, Patel BR, Bhavani SS: Unusual form of child abuse presenting as an acute abdomen. *Br J Surg* 68:668, 1981.
60. Zahavi I, Shaffer EA, Gall DG: Child abuse with laxatives. *Can Med Assoc J* 127:512–513, 1982.
61. Ackerman NB Jr, Strobel CT: Polle syndrome: chronic diarrhea in Munchausen's child. *Gastroenterology* 81:1140–1142, 1981.
62. Forbes DA, O'Loughlin EV, Scott RB, Gall DG: Laxative abuse and secretory diarrhoea. *Arch Dis Child* 60:58–60, 1985.
63. Manson G: Neglected children and the celiac syndrome. *J Iowa Med Soc* 54:228–234, 1964.
64. Kunstadter RH, Singer MH, Steinberg R: The "battered child" and the celiac syndrome. *Illinois Med J* 132:267–272, 1967.
65. Jackson DL, Korbin J, Youngner S, Carter KJ, Robertson AL: Fatal outcome in untreated adolescent ulcerative colitis: an unusual case of child neglect. *Crit Care Med* 11:832–833, 1983.
66. Thomford NR, Jesseph JE: Pseudocyst of the pancreas. A review of fifty cases. *Am J Surg* 118:86–94, 1969.
67. Cooney DR, Grosfeld JL: Operative management of pancreatic pseudocysts in infants and children: a review of 75 cases. *Ann Surg* 182:590–596, 1975.
68. Kilman JW, Kaiser GC, King RD, Shumacker HB Jr.: Pancreatic pseudocysts in infancy and childhood. *Surgery* 55:455–461, 1964.
69. Kim T, Jenkins ME: Pseudocyst of the pancreas as a manifestation of the battered-child syndrome. Report of a case. *Med Ann District of Columbia* 36:664–666, 1967.
70. Hartley RC: Pancreatitis under the age of five years: a report of three cases. *J Pediatr Surg* 2:419–423, 1967.
71. Keating JP, Shackelford GD, Shackelford PG, Ternberg JL: Pancreatitis and osteolytic lesions. *J Pediatr* 81:350–353, 1972.
72. Pena SDJ, Medovy H: Child abuse and traumatic pseudocyst of the pancreas. *J Pediatr* 83:1026–1028, 1973.
73. Slovis TL, Berdon WE, Haller JO, Baker DH, Rosen L: Pancreatitis and the battered child syndrome: report of 2 cases with skeletal involvement. *Am J Roentgenol (AJR)* 125: 456–461, 1975.
74. Slovis TL, VonBerg VJ, Mikelic V: Sonography in the diagnosis and management of pancreatic pseudocysts and effusions in childhood. *Radiology* 135:153–155, 1980.
75. Bongiovi JJ, Logosso RD: Pancreatic pseudocyst occurring in the battered child syndrome. *J Pediatr Surg* 4:220–226, 1969.
76. Neuer FS, Roberts FF, McCarthy V: Osteolytic lesions following traumatic pancreatitis. *Am J Dis Child* 131:738–740, 1977.
77. Keeney RE: Enlarging on the child abuse injury spectrum. Letter to the editor. *Am J Dis Child* 130:902, 1976.
78. Hillemeier C, Gryboski JD: Acute pancreatitis in infants and children. *Yale J Biol Med* 57:149–159, 1984.
79. Young LW, Adams JT: Roentgenographic findings in localized trauma to the pancreas in children. *Am J Roentgenol Rad Therapy Nucl Med (AJR)* 101:639–648, 1967.
80. Sarti DA: Rapid development and spontaneous regression of pancreatic pseudocysts documented by ultrasound. *Radiology* 125:789–793, 1977.
81. Bradley EL, Clements JL Jr, Gonzalez AC: The natural history of pancreatic pseudocysts: a unified concept of management. *Am J Surg* 137:135–141, 1979.
82. Scarpelli DG: Fat necrosis of bone marrow in acute pancreatitis. *Am J Pathol* 32:1077–1087, 1956.
83. Blauvelt H: A case of acute pancreatitis with subcutaneous fat necrosis. *Br J Surg* 34:207–208, 1946.
84. Boswell SH, Baylin GJ: Metastatic fat necrosis and lytic bone lesions in a patient with painless acute pancreatitis. *Radiology* 106:85–86, 1973.
85. Gerle RD, Walker LA, Achord JL, Weens HS: Osseous changes in chronic pancreatitis. *Radiology* 85:330–337, 1965.
86. Sperling MA: Bone lesions in pancreatitis. *Aust Ann Med* 17:334–340, 1968.
87. Immelman EJ, Bank S, Krige H, Marks IN: Roentgenologic and clinical features of intramedullary fat necrosis in bones in acute and chronic pancreatitis. *Am J Med* 36:96–105, 1964.
88. Beauchamp JM, Belanger MA, Neitzschman HR: The diagnosis of subcapsular hematoma of the liver by scintigraphy. *South Med J* 69:1579–1581, 1976.
89. Simpson K: Battered babies: Conviction for murder. *Br Med J* 1:393, 1965.
90. Palmer CH, Weston JT: Several unusual cases of child abuse. *J Forensic Sci* 21:851–855, 1976.
91. Ramu M: Needles in a child's body (a case report). *Med Sci Law* 17:259–260, 1977.
92. Stone RK, Harawitz A, San Filippo JA, Gromisch DS: Needle perforation of the liver in an abused infant. *Clin Pediatr (Phila)* 15:958–959, 1976.
93. Beau A, Prevot J, Mourot M: Rupture traumatique en deux temps du canal hepatique gauche, chez une enfant victime de sevices. *Ann Chir Infant* 12:47–52, 1971.
94. Wilkinson RH, Kirkpatric JA Jr: Pediatric skeletal trauma. *Curr Probl Diagn Radiol* 6:3–38, 1976.
95. Sty J, Starshak RJ, Hubbard A: Accumulation of Tc-99m MDP in the spleen of a battered child. *Clin Nucl Med* 7:292, 1982.
96. Talbert JL, Felman AH: Identification and treatment of thoracoabdominal injuries in "battered children." *South Med Bull* 58(3):37–43, 1970.
97. Kimmel RL, Sty JR: ^{99m}Tc-methylene diphosphonate renal images in a battered child. *Clin Nucl Med* 4:166–167, 1979.
98. Rosenberg HK: Traumatic avulsion of the vascular supply of a crossed unfused ectopic kidney: complementary roles of ultrasonography and intravenous pyelography. *J Ultrasound Med* 3:89–91, 1984.
99. Rosenberg HK, Gefter WB, Lebowitz RL, Mah-

boubi S, Rosenberg H: Prolonged dense nephrograms in battered children. *Urology* 21:325–330, 1983.

100. Sty JR, Starshak RJ: The role of bone scintigraphy in the evaluation of the suspected abused child. *Radiology* 146:369–375, 1983.

101. Kumar K, Khan AJ, Flicker S, Soborio J, Schaeffer HA, Evans HE: Acute renal failure in battered child syndrome. *J Natl Med Assoc* 72:27–28, 1980.

102. Rimer RL, Roy S III: Child abuse and hemoglobinuria. *JAMA* 238:2034–2035, 1977.

103. Schleyer F, Pioch W: Tod eines kindes am crush-syndrom nach fortgesetztem prugeln. *Monatsschr Kinderheilkd* 105:392–394, 1957.

104. Halsted CC, Shapiro SR: Child abuse: acute renal failure from ruptured bladder. *Am J Dis Child* 133:861–862, 1979.

105. Pfundt TR: The problem of the battered child. *Postgrad Med* 35:426–431, 1964.

106. Silverman FN: Unrecognized trauma in infants, the battered child syndrome, and the syndrome of Ambroise Tardieu. Rigler lecture. *Radiology* 104:337–353, 1972.

107. Green HG: Child abuse presenting as chylothorax. *Pediatrics* 66:620–621, 1980.

108. Saulsbury FT, Chobanian MC, Wilson WG: Child abuse: parenteral hydrocarbon administration. *Pediatrics* 73:719–721, 1984.

109. Kugelmann J: Uber symmetrische spontanfrakturen unbekannter genese beim saugling. *Ann Paediatr (Paris)* 178:177–181, 1952.

110. Marino TA, Langston C: Cardiac trauma and the conduction system. A case study of an 18-month-old child. *Arch Pathol Lab Med* 106:173–174, 1982.

111. Rees A, Symons J, Joseph M, Lincoln C: Ventricular septal defect in a battered child. *Br Med J* 1:20–21, 1975.

112. McDowell HP, Fielding DW: Traumatic perforation of the hypopharynx—an unusual form of abuse. *Arch Dis Child* 59:888–889, 1984.

113. Salmon MA: The spectrum of abuse in the battered-child syndrome. *Injury* 2:211–217, 1971.

114. Thomas M, Cameron A: Rarity of non-accidental penetrating injury in child abuse. *Br Med J* 1:375–376, 1977.

8 Head Trauma

PAUL K. KLEINMAN, M.D.

No single organ is more profoundly affected by child abuse than the brain. The acute life threatening consequences of central nervous system (CNS) injury, as well as the long-term effects on the development of the child, have caused investigators to focus on this subject in numerous medical, psychologic, and sociologic publications. The resilience of the human organism allows virtually complete recovery from most skeletal and visceral injuries. In contrast, acute CNS damage and its effects on intellectual and psychologic function have long-term consequences for the individual and society that we are only just beginning to understand.

A strong association exists between mental retardation and child abuse. Investigators were slow to recognize and study this relationship, however. In 1968, 22 years after Caffey's historic article, an exhaustive review revealed only one study dealing with the influences of abuse upon child development (1). This important study (2) stimulated much research, and the past decade has yielded a flood of information elucidating the influence of abuse upon child development. Although major head injury produces direct, long-term effects on the development of the brain, the respective roles of lesser traumatic injury versus the general influences of an abusive environment on the psychological development of the child are difficult to separate (3). In an early but comprehensive study, Elmer and Gregg (4) found that 30% of abused children had evidence of CNS injury and 57% had an IQ below 80. In 1969, the authors found that 42% of abused infants under 13 months of age showed signs of developmental retardation (5). Martin et al. studied the physical and intellectual characteristics

of a group of 58 previously abused children (6). At a mean of 4.5 years following the abuse, 5% were found to be microcephalic, and 31% had heights or weights below the third percentile. Fifty-three percent had neurologic abnormalities, of which 31% were moderate to severe. Although this study group included less severely injured patients than those studied in prior reports, the number of patients with significant neurologic disfunction was impressive.

If all patients admitted to medical facilities with neurologic injury are studied, abused children generally constitute less than 10% of the total (7, 8). However, if the study is restricted to infants, the group of patients most susceptible to a nonaccidental injury, the proportion of those abused increases dramatically. Billmire and Meyers (9) studied 84 patients ranging from 3 weeks to 11 months of age admitted with the diagnosis of head injury and/or abnormal computed tomography (CT) scans. They found that 64% of all head injuries, excluding uncomplicated skull fractures, were secondary to child abuse. Furthermore, 95% of serious intracranial injuries were the result of intentional injury. Their findings supported those of Helfer et al. (10) and Hobbs (11) and indicate that accidental intracranial injury is rare in infancy.

Prior to CT, estimates of intracranial injury in child abuse were primarily limited to clinical, surgical, and autopsy findings. Weston found intracranial injury in 60% of fatalities due to physical abuse (12). CT has provided data that allow more accurate assessment of the overall incidence of CNS trauma. Merten and Osborne identified CT evidence of intracranial injury in 7% of 716 abused children (13). Tsai et al. found intracranial injury in 19% of 177 abused children

(14). These estimates will vary considerably depending upon the age and the presenting complaints of the abuse population. Centers with large neurologic services and those seeing greater proportions of seriously ill abused infants will generally encounter larger percentages with neurologic injury. Similarly, the frequency with which CT is performed in cases of suspected abuse will influence the percentage of cases with evidence of craniocerebral injury. It is likely that many cases of CNS injury go undetected because clinical findings may be insufficient to warrant CT scanning. The criteria employed in diagnosing CNS injury may also vary between centers; for example, cerebral atrophy may be viewed as a consequence of abuse at one center but not at another. Finally, as will be discussed, there is strong reason to believe that some acute structural alterations of the brain may not be evident on state-of-the-art, high-resolution CT. Increased experience with CT, ultrasound, and the promising new clinical tool of magnetic resonance imaging (MRI) will undoubtedly increase the frequency with which CNS injury is identified in abused patients. These conservative estimates as to incidence of CNS injury in the abused are sufficient to warrant an aggressive approach to identification of all such abnormalities.

The Scalp

Patients with craniocerebral injury frequently have associated swelling of the scalp. When fractures are present in young infants there is often a large subgaleal hematoma, and a substantial amount of blood can be lost into this potential space. The absence of such swelling, however, should in no way exclude the possibility of an underlying fracture, particularly if the injury was sustained more than a few days prior to medical evaluation. Although blunt injury accounts for most instances of subgaleal hematoma, a similar hemorrhage can occur as a result of hair pulling. The hematoma will typically lie at the site of a large hair braid (15). Large subgaleal hematomas

may be appreciated on standard roentgenograms of the skull, and care must be exercised in "bright lighting" all margins of the skull. A subgaleal hematoma may point to an underlying calvarial fracture. CT is well suited to assessing subgaleal blood collections. Simple adjustment of level and window settings at the computer console will allow excellent definition of the soft tissues of the scalp, and density readings will indicate the presence of fresh or old blood in the subgaleal space (see Figs. 8.18 and 8.19).

The Calvarium

Calvarial injury constitutes an important component of the battered child syndrome. Silverman drew attention to Tardieu's description of a skull fracture in an intentionally injured child in 1860, well before the first clinical radiograph (16).

By definition, skull fractures indicate direct impact of the head with a solid object. Although fractures are frequently noted in infants who have been shaken, a fracture signifies that the child has also had a blunt impact injury. It has long been known that a poor correlation exists between skull fractures in general and intracranial injury; this has led most authorities to restrict the use of skull radiography in cases of minor trauma and to utilize CT in situations wherein strong suspicion of CNS injury exists (10, 17, 18). However, the value of skull films in patients suspected of having been abused cannot be overstated. These radiographs often provide firm documentation of nonaccidental injury. The pattern of skull fractures, as well as inconsistencies between the observed fractures and the alleged mechanism of injury, are often instrumental in confirming child abuse.

Billmire and Meyers (9) studied 84 infants less than 12 months of age admitted to the hospital with the diagnosis of head injury and/or abnormal findings on CT scan consistent with trauma. Thirty infants were subsequently found to be abused. There were 55 skull fractures, 87% of which were linear. Two depressed fractures were noted, one in an abused child, the other in a child

hit by a falling television. Four complex multiple fractures were associated with intracranial hemorrhage, and all occurred in battered children.

Hahn et al. (19) reviewed the records of 621 confirmed cases of child abuse treated at the Children's Memorial Hospital in Chicago. Of the 77 (12%) with intracranial injury, 37 (48%) skull fractures were noted. There were 30 linear, 5 depressed, and 2 diastatic fractures. An additional 6 patients without fractures had separation of the sutures. The skull fractures comprised 60% of all fractures noted in the 77 patients with head injury. The parietal bone was the most frequent site of fracture, showing involvement in 86% of the cases. Twenty-seven percent of patients were under 6 months old; 85% were under 2 years old. A blunt blow to the head was thought to cause the intracranial injuries in at least one half of the patients.

James and Schut (20) found 5 skull fractures in 45 cases of suspected abuse. Tsai et al. (14) found evidence of head injury in 45 of 177 abused patients and identified fractures in 17 patients (38%). They found intracranial injury in 65% of those with skull fractures and in 78% of the 28 patients with normal skull series.

Zimmerman et al. (21) found 6 skull fractures in 26 abused children with CNS injury (23%). Cohen et al. (22) studied 37 children with head injury resulting from physical abuse. Eleven patients (30%) had skull fractures, none of which were depressed. Except for epidural hematoma and brain laceration, which were noted only with skull fracture, the patients without fractures suffered the same range of injuries as those with them. The patients without fracture had a higher incidence of subarachnoid hemorrhage (85% versus 45%).

Merten and Osborne (13) found 93 cases of craniocerebral injury in 712 physically abused children. Sixty-seven skull fractures were seen (72%). Fifty-nine (88%) of these were simple linear fractures that were parietal or occipital in location. Diastatic, comminuted, and depressed fractures were uncommon. Intracranial injury was associated with fractures in 56% of cases.

O'Neill et al. (23) reported 110 victims of physical abuse. They identified 32 patients with cerebral trauma. Fifteen patients had demonstrable skull fractures, and in 6 of these cases a subdural hematoma was present. Twelve patients with subdural hematomas had no skull fracture, again dramatizing the poor correlation of skull fracture and underlying cerebral injury.

Hobbs (11) studied 89 children under 2 years of age with skull fractures; 29 of these fractures were due to abuse. Of 60 accidental fractures, 55 were linear, 3 complex, 3 depressed, 4 diastatic (maximum width at presentation 3 mm), and 2 were growing. In contrast, of 29 fractures due to abuse, 6 were linear, 23 were multiple or complex, 12 were depressed, 10 were diastatic, and 6 were growing. The 12 depressed fragments in abused infants were noted to lie within the central area of complex bony injury. In three children, multiple depressed areas suggested repeated blows. There were six parietal and six occipital depressed fractures. A fatal outcome occurred in one-half of the parietal fractures and in all of the occipital fractures. Thus the occipital depressed fracture signified a severe associated intracranial injury. In the accidental cases, no fracture was wider than 5 mm. In the abused children, six fractures measured greater than 5 mm. The maximum width of the fracture in 40 accidental cases was less than 1 mm. None of the fractures in abused infants were less than 1 mm.

Hobbs found that most accidental fractures appeared to result from falls ranging from 3 feet to 5½ feet. He cited examples such as falls from baby chairs placed on tables or from the arms of standing adults. In these situations fractures were generally linear, narrow, and uncomplicated. The severe accidental fractures resulted from falls down stairs or from heights greater than 6 feet. Hobbs found that, in contrast to previous reports, the presence of a growing fracture had a strong association with abuse. He concluded that a growing fracture implies a severe injury, and if a minor injury is alleged in such cases, abuse is likely. Depressed fractures will also point strongly to abuse unless a definite history of a direct

impact with a sharp or pointed object is provided. Hobbs concluded that a depressed occipital bone fracture is virtually pathognomonic of abuse (11).

Kravitz et al. (24) studied a large group of patients under 1 year of age suffering accidental falls from heights ranging from 2 to 5 feet. The incidence of skull fracture in those infants who had experienced their "first fall" was approximately 2%. This study, which included no cases of suspected child abuse, dramatized the rare occurrence of fracture following falls from modest elevations. Helfer et al. (10) reported the results of 246 children who fell from a bed, crib, or sofa at a maximal height of 150 cm. Three skull fractures were identified. Neither in these three patients nor in the remainder of the group was there any significant neurologic injury. One patient suffered a fractured humerus and three sustained fractured clavicles. Although the thrust of this study was to curtail the use of skull radiographs in children under 5 years old falling from modest heights, it provides a basis for viewing significant neurologic injury in the context of a purported minor fall. All cases with complex skull fractures and/or neurologic findings occurring following a fall from a height reported to be less than 90 cm should be viewed as possible instances of abuse.

Although considerable controversy exists regarding the relative roles of radiography and radionuclide scintigraphy in assessing skeletal injury in abused children (see Chapter 2), there is unanimity regarding the insensitivity of radionuclide studies in identifying skull fractures. In those institutions using scintigraphy as the primary screening tool for abuse, such examinations must be supplemented with at least two views of the skull (25, 26).

RADIOLOGIC PATTERNS OF CALVARIAL INJURY

Various classifications of skull fracture patterns are described. For the purpose of this discussion, radiographic appearances will be divided into simple and complex fractures. A simple fracture, often described as linear, consists of a single fracture line that appears to extend in a straight, jagged, or curved fashion (Fig. 8.1). The fracture margins are closely apposed and are separated by no more than 2 mm. Fractures are restricted to one bone in the calvarium (i.e., they do not cross suture lines or synchondroses). Complex fractures are comprised of more than one fracture line and may evidence a branching pattern (Figs. 8.1B and 8.2), or a stellate configuration, in which numerous fractures radiate from a central point. These are most frequently encountered in the occipital or posterior parietal regions (Figs. 8.1, 8.3, and 8.4). If the fracture results in isolation of one or more separate fragments, it is considered comminuted (Fig. 8.3). In comminuted fractures, a fragment may be displaced inward toward the brain; the fracture is then considered depressed (Figs. 8.1 and 8.5). If there is an overlying laceration of the scalp, the fracture is referred to as compound. Any calvarial injury may demonstrate separation or diastasis of the fracture margins (Figs. 8.1, 8.3, 8.4, and 8.6). Sutures may also be diastatic either in association with a fracture or in isolation (Figs. 8.4, 8.6, and 8.7). Diastatic sutural injuries should be distinguished from generalized sutural widening secondary to increased intracranial pressure (Figs. 8.7 and 8.8) or "catch-up" brain growth in neglected children (see Chapter 9).

In infants and young children, follow-up films are mandatory to assess for "growth" of the fracture. Because these fractures may be identified incidentally on skeletal survey, the neurosurgeon may not be involved, and radiographic follow-up may not occur. In such cases the diagnosis of a serious complication, a leptomeningeal cyst, may be delayed (27). With increasing complexity and diastasis of the fracture, there is greater likelihood that underlying dural injury is present. A defect in the dura will allow herniation of the underlying contents, which in as little as 2 months may result in "growth" of the fracture. If the process continues, actual herniation of arachnoid and cerebrospinal fluid through this defect may result in a leptomeningeal cyst.

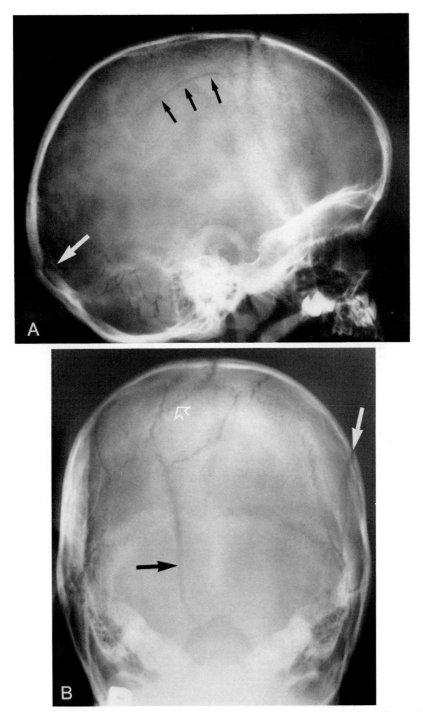

Figure 8.1. Two-year-old abused infant. Lateral skull radiograph (*A*) reveals a linear fracture in the parietal region (*black arrows*). A depressed occipital fracture is also present (*white arrow*). A Towne's projection (*B*) reveals dramatic abnormalities in the occipital region. A branching, diastatic fracture (*black arrow*) crosses the right lambdoid suture (*open white arrow*). The linear parietal fracture (*solid white arrow*) is seen to lie on the left.

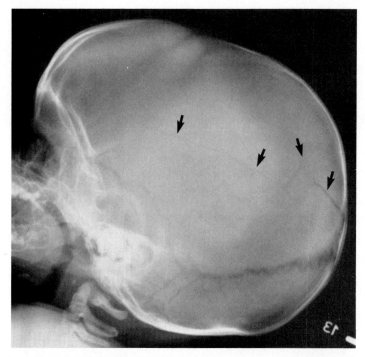

Figure 8.2. Lateral view of the skull of a 7-month-old abused infant reveals a branching fracture (*arrows*) extending from the lambdoid to the coronal sutures. Suture integrity is maintained.

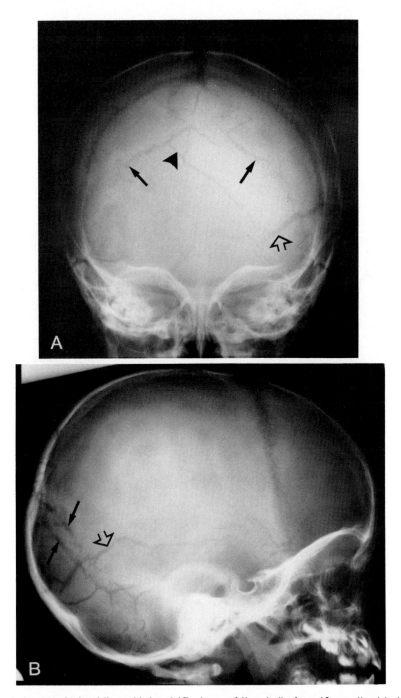

Figure 8.3.   Anteroposterior (*A*) and lateral (*B*) views of the skull of an 18-month-old abused child demonstrate a complex fracture involving the occipital and parietal regions. Note that the diastatic component of the fracture (*open arrow*) crosses the lambdoid suture (*solid arrows*). An isolated comminuted fragment is noted (*arrowhead*).

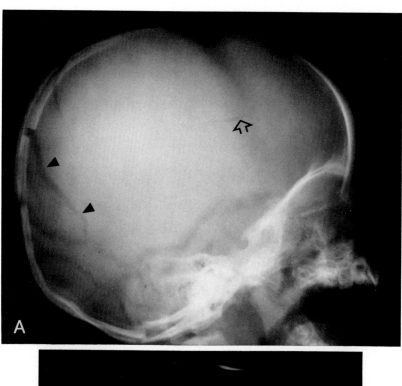

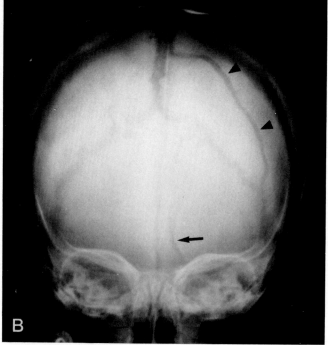

Figure 8.4. Lateral (*A*), AP (*B*), and Towne's (*C*) views of the skull in this 8-month-old abused child demonstrate multiple skull fractures. A diastatic occipital fracture extends from the lambdoid suture to the foramen magnum (*arrows*). A diastatic posterior parietal fracture enters the lambdoid suture (*arrowheads*). A linear fracture enters the coronal suture (*open arrow*). Both coronal and lambdoid sutures are diastatic.

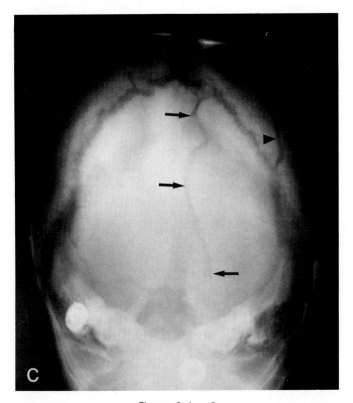

Figure 8.4.   *C.*

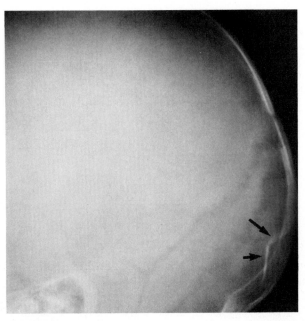

Figure 8.5. A typical depressed skull fracture is noted in the occipital region (*arrows*). There was no evidence of abuse.

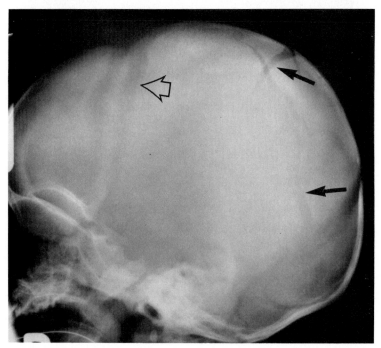

Figure 8.6. Diastatic fractures are noted in the mid and posterior parietal regions (*solid arrows*) in this 3-month-old abused child. Coronal sutural diastasis is secondary to increased intracranial pressure (*open arrow*).

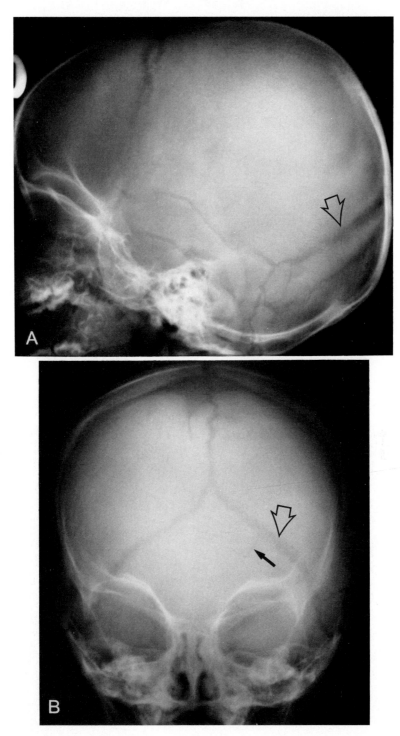

Figure 8.7. Lateral (*A*) and AP (*B*) projections of the skull in an 8-month-old abused infant reveal diastasis of the left lambdoid suture (*open arrow*) in association with a linear fracture (*solid arrow*).

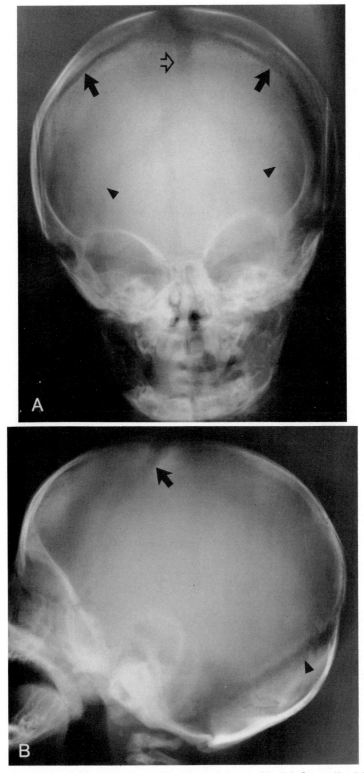

Figure 8.8. Anteroposterior (*A*) and lateral (*B*) views of the skull in this 2-month-old abused infant reveal splitting of the coronal (*solid arrows*), lambdoid (*arrowheads*), and sagittal (*open arrow*) sutures secondary to increased intracranial pressure.

Any patient undergoing CT for suspected trauma, and all infants in whom there is evidence of intracranial pathology that is not clearly the result of trauma, must have images filmed at a bone window setting. These images may reveal previously unsuspected fractures if they course at right angles to the plane of the section (Figs. 8.9–8.11). However, fractures occurring in the same plane or at a shallow obliquity to the CT cut may be undetectable. Fracture detection requires a knowledge of normal cranial suture anatomy as viewed on axial CT sections. Although CT is a useful tool in providing virtually simultaneous identification of osseous and soft tissue injury, it is not a substitute for roentgenograms (28). In cases of depressed skull fracture, the CT scan is of great value in precisely assessing the depth of depression of the fracture fragment(s) (Fig. 8.11C). In patients with "growing" frac-

tures associated with leptomeningeal cysts, the CT scan will provide precise delineation of the mass and the associated bony defect.

A rare form of infantile cranial injury is that caused by animal bites. These may be purely accidental; however, such assaults generally occur with animals that pose particular hazards to infants, such as wolves, and the circumstances surrounding these assaults indicate ignorance at the least, and at worst raise the specter of neglect (29). Such a case is illustrated in Figure 8.12 in which an infant was fatally assaulted, allegedly by dogs of the Rottweiler breed. The injuries were essentially depressed skull fractures with severe underlying cerebral injury.

Facial Injuries

Facial injuries are common in abused children, but in the vast majority of cases they are related to soft tissue bruises and lacerations. Fractures constitute only 2% of all intentional facial injuries (30). Tate (31) found a greater incidence of cutaneous facial injury than long bone and rib fractures in abused children. Despite these interesting statistics, the incidence of radiologically manifest maxillofacial abnormalities is minute (31–33). Most reported injuries involve the mandible. A case of a suspected but nonconfirmed mandibular fracture was reported by Tate (31) in a 4-year-old girl. Palmer and Weston (32) described fractures of the maxilla and mandible in a 3-year-old abused female. Fractures of the mandible may be difficult to identify on the standard films obtained for skeletal survey, but if sufficient displacement is present a fracture will be evident. Fractures of the mandible are almost always bilateral, although only one component may be noted. The mandibular fracture shown in Figure 8.13 occurred as the infant was struck across the face with the back of the assailant's hand. In healing injuries, periosteal reaction may be the only indication of trauma. This new bone formation may in fact reflect subperiosteal hemorrhage rather than an actual disruption of cortical bone (Fig. 8.14). The scarcity of

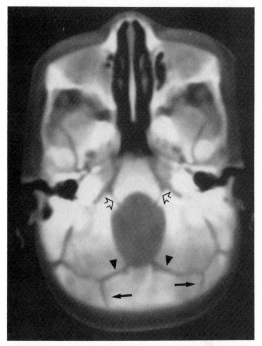

Figure 8.9. CT scan through base of the skull filmed at a bone window setting in a 3-month-old abused infant. There are bilateral occipital fractures (*solid arrows*) intersecting the synchondrosis (*arrowheads*) between the exoccipital and supraoccipital portions of the occipital bone. Also note normal spheno-occipital synchondroses (*open arrows*).

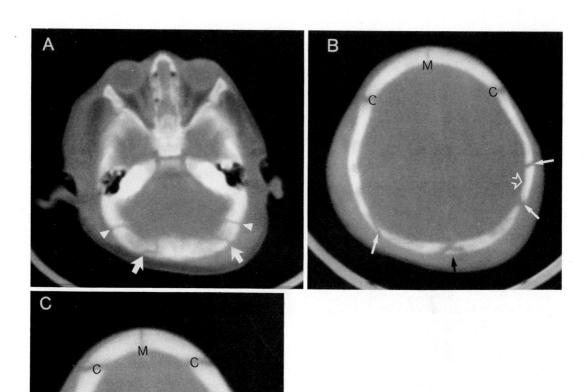

Figure 8.10. CT scan filmed at bone window settings in a 3-month-old abused infant. *A,* Views of the base of the skull demonstrate bilateral occipital fractures (*arrows*). Note normal lambdoid sutures (*arrowheads*). *B* and *C,* Images at higher levels demonstrate extension of these fractures (*white arrows*) toward the vertex. A comminuted fracture fragment (*open arrow*) is present in the left parietal region. Note extensive soft tissue swelling. Also note normal intersutural bone (*black arrow*). *C,* coronal suture; *M,* metopic suture.

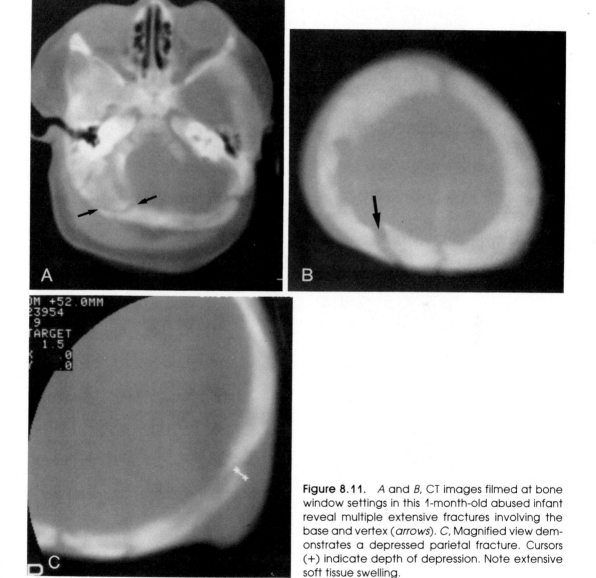

Figure 8.11. *A* and *B*, CT images filmed at bone window settings in this 1-month-old abused infant reveal multiple extensive fractures involving the base and vertex (*arrows*). *C*, Magnified view demonstrates a depressed parietal fracture. Cursors (+) indicate depth of depression. Note extensive soft tissue swelling.

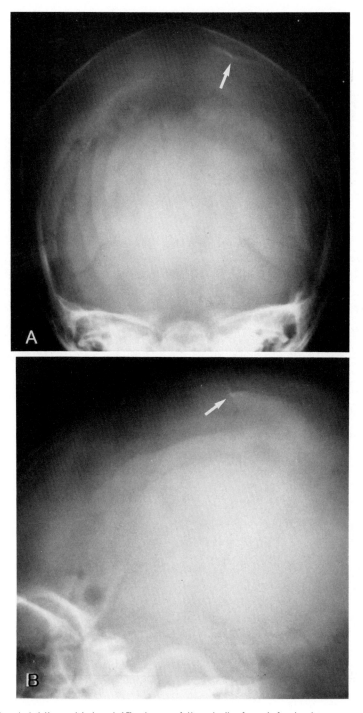

Figure 8.12. Frontal (*A*) and lateral (*B*) views of the skull of an infant who was mauled by two dogs of the Rottweiler breed reveal a depressed skull fracture (*arrow*). The infant had been briefly left alone with the dogs; there was no evidence to support parental abuse.

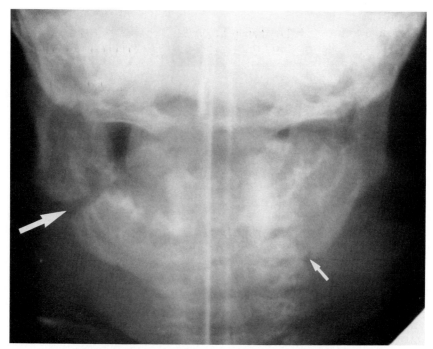

Figure 8.13. Anteroposterior view of the mandible in a 6-month-old infant demonstrates an obvious fracture involving the angle (*large arrow*). A less well-defined fracture is present on the left (*small arrow*). No evidence of healing is present. An endotracheal tube is in place.

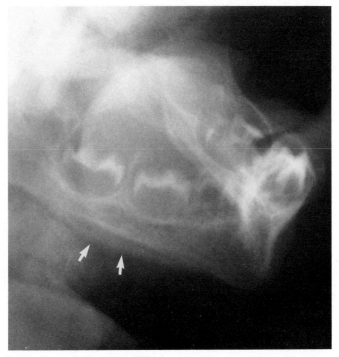

Figure 8.14. Oblique view of the mandible in an abused infant with other extensive injuries demonstrates periosteal new bone formation (*arrows*) along the margin of the mandible without identifiable fracture.

mandibular injuries attests to the massive direct force required to produce these fractures. An unexplained facial fracture in an infant or young child indicates abuse.

Intracranial Structures

THE ROLE OF SHAKING IN CENTRAL NERVOUS SYSTEM INJURY

Although blunt injury plays a major role in intracranial injury in child abuse, it fails to explain the often fatal intracranial alterations noted in infants exhibiting no external evidence of blunt craniocerebral injury. The absence of fracture in the majority of abused infants with intracranial injuries further points to indirect forces as the cause for many of these CNS lesions. In 1968, Weston described three infants with subdural hematomas (12). In each case there was an admission of violent shaking. In 1971, Guthkelch described two infants with subdural hematomas without external evidence of injury (34). In both cases, there was an admission of shaking prior to the development of convulsions. In 1972, Caffey (35) presented his views "On the Theory and Practice of Shaking Infants." In this address to the American Medical Association he provided a concept that attempted to unify various skeletal and CNS lesions with a single mechanism of injury. In 1974, Caffey (36) suggested the terms in "The Whiplash Shaken Infant Syndrome" to describe this subgroup of abused children (36). Following these early reports, gradual acceptance of the role of shaking in production of CNS injuries occurred (37). However, it was not until cranial CT simplified the diagnosis of subdural hematoma, as well as a variety of other traumatic intracranial lesions, that the tremendous importance of this mechanism of injury in abused infants was appreciated (13, 19, 21, 38–46).

Ommaya and others have studied whiplash injury experimentally in subhuman primates (47, 48). They routinely produced extracerebral hemorrhage and cerebral contusion with rapid acceleration. The degree of injury correlated well with the rotational displacement of the head on the neck, expressed as either rotational velocity or rotational acceleration. By applying a firm collar to the neck of these animals, they demonstrated that a translational motion without rotatory component would not produce these injuries. These studies provide a convincing argument that deceleration-type injuries, particularly motor vehicle accidents, produce significant intracranial damage without direct impact. It is harder to extrapolate these data to infants, whose cervical musculature is less well developed and whose head to body mass ratio is greater than that of adults. Violent shaking will produce a combination of rapid rotational accelerations and decelerations, but there are no data available regarding the magnitude of forces generated during violent shaking of infants. However, the frequent occurrence of major intracranial injury without evidence of skull fracture or external injury, the many reported cases of admitted shaking in abused infants, and the specific pathologic lesions that will be discussed all provide compelling evidence that shaking plays a major role in CNS injury. Despite this evidence, reluctance to accept shaking as a cause of subdural hematoma may still be encountered.

THE MENINGES

Subdural Hematoma

Sherwood (49) cited one of the first recorded cases of subdural hematoma as described by Ambroise Pare. The victim was Henry II, who was wounded in a tourney in 1559. Despite this early association with a traumatic insult, a variety of other etiologies for subdural hematomas has been proposed, including infection (pachymeningitis hemorrhagica), degeneration, venous congestion, and spontaneous hemorrhage. Sherwood's review found subdural hematoma to be associated with a variety of systemic illnesses diagnosed as congenital syphilis, rickets, scurvy, tuberculosis, and birth injury. These conditions all share features with the battered child syndrome, and it is likely that some of these cases in fact represented examples of abuse. Trotter (50) was one of the first modern authors to clearly formulate a trauma theory for the development of subdural hematomas. He believed that in most cases trauma was the cause, and that on occasion a bleeding tendency aggravated by trauma led to the lesion. In his 1930 article, Sherwood noted an unexplained healing radial fracture in a 9-month-old girl with a subdural hematoma, retinal hemorrhages, and optic atrophy (49). Alluding to the child's status as a state ward, he suggested that trauma might explain both subdural hematoma and radial fracture. In 1939, Ingraham and Heyl (51) reported on 11 infants with subdural hematomas. One infant, an 8-month-old with convulsions, showed bilateral greenstick fractures of the radius and ulna. There was no history of trauma. In 1944, Ingraham and Matson stated, "it seems justifiable to conclude that some form of trauma is practically a constant etiologic factor.... We should like to emphasize again, however, the inadequacy of the history in many cases of these infants. Because of this, the absence of history of trauma should never influence the diagnosis against a subdural hematoma" (52).

In 1946, Caffey published perhaps the most historically significant work in the vast literature on child abuse (53). He described six patients with subdural hematomas and a combination of 27 fractures and/or areas of periosteal new bone formation. In none of the cases was there any history of injury or associated systemic disease. Caffey was somewhat reluctant to implicate intentional injury in these cases: "The negative history of trauma in so many cases can probably be best explained by assuming that sometimes lay observers do not properly evaluate ordinary but causally significant accidents especially falls on the head, and that other important traumatic episodes pass unnoticed or are forgotten by the time delayed cranial symptoms appear." He added, however: "Also recognized injuries may be denied by mothers and nurses because injury to an infant implies negligence on the part of its caretaker." He pointed out that one case in which the child was clearly unwanted by both parents "raised the question

of intentional ill-treatment of the infant." In the years immediately following this report, he expressed the view that these lesions were a manifestation of maltreatment by custodians (16). Caffey's important contribution to this subject lies not so much in his recognition of this association, since he in fact alluded to the other earlier observations of this relationship, but in his effort to bring together a number of cases documenting a distinct pattern of injury unique to infancy.

During the next two decades, numerous articles appeared confirming the association of subdural hematoma with child abuse (39, 54–72). It is difficult to comprehend how the common association between subdural hematomas and skeletal injuries, and the etiologic factors linking the two, could have eluded the scrutiny of all but a handful of physicians and surgeons dealing with children until Caffey's historic observations.

Pathogenesis. It is generally accepted that subdural hematomas originate from disruption of the delicate bridging veins extending from the surface of the brain to the dura (49, 51, 73). (Fig. 8.15). The injuries most frequently involve the venous structures draining to the sagittal sinus. As a result, the smallest and earliest collections are frequently encountered in the interhemispheric region. As blood accumulates within the subdural space, the brain is displaced further from the dura, a factor that may produce continued bleeding following the initial injury. Because increasing tension is thus placed upon the remaining bridging veins, repeated injury will likely produce recurrent bleeding. Associated cerebral laceration or contusion may contribute to extravasation of blood into the subdural space. If the subdural collection is unrecognized, it will undergo a predictable evolution. The clot initially becomes surrounded by endothelial cells, and invasion of granulation tissue from the dural aspect of the lesion occurs (74). The hematoma begins to liquefy and progresses from a hemorrhagic appearance to a serous one. These membranes, which develop in approximately 2 to 3 weeks, are thicker along their dural aspect and evidence considerable vascularity. There may be a continued increase of the

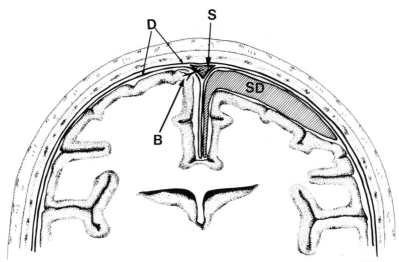

Figure 8.15. Schematic representation of a coronal section of the brain. A subdural hematoma (*SD*) with a convexity and interhemispheric component is noted on the left. These lesions occur with disruption of bridging veins (*B*) extending from surface of the brain to the dural sinuses. *S*, superior sagittal sinus; *D*, dura.

serous fluid within these collections, despite recurrent hemorrhage. Occasionally, the hematoma may go on to calcify.

Radiologic Patterns. Noninvasive cross-sectional imaging of the brain with CT, ultrasound, and MRI has dramatically simplified assessment of subdural hematomas as well as most other intracranial injuries (13, 14, 21, 22, 28, 38, 39, 41, 42, 44, 45, 75–78). Although subdural hematomas may produce secondary alterations as visualized on angiography and pneumoencephalography, these techniques are beyond the scope of the current discussion. From a historic perspective, they provide a background for understanding current imaging techniques, and for this purpose the reader is referred to the excellent publication by Harwood-Nash (79).

Subdural hematomas may be acute or chronic, with a continuum bridging the ends of this spectrum. Zimmerman et al. have popularized the concept of the acute interhemispheric subdural hematoma (21, 45, 80). As has been described, there is a tendency for bleeding to occur between the cerebral hemispheres. Because blood collecting within this region lies adjacent to normal parenchyma, small collections are much more easily identified than similar volumes

of blood over the convexities adjacent to the skull. The pattern is one of a high-density stripe conforming to the interhemispheric region (Figs. 8.16 and 8.17). The collections are usually seen in the posterior interhemispheric space, although similar collections occur anteriorly. Zimmerman et al. (21) noted this pattern in 17 of 26 abused infants (65%) with acute head injury.

Difficulty can be encountered in differentiating the interhemispheric subdural collection from the normal falx cerebri and interhemispheric subarachnoid blood (22, 80, 81). The normal falx cerebri has a relatively dense appearance as compared to the surrounding adjacent brain on the unenhanced scan. This structure may appear strikingly dense if there is surrounding cerebral low density as a result of edema or extracerebral fluid (see Figs. 8.20 and 8.24). In these cases, the density is thin and quite linear, and may extend fully from the parietal to the frontal region above the level of the corpus callosum. This normal pattern bears considerable similarity to the appearance of interhemispheric subarachnoid blood (see below). Features that are useful in the identification of interhemispheric subdural blood are (*a*) a substantial thickness of interhemispheric high density, (*b*)

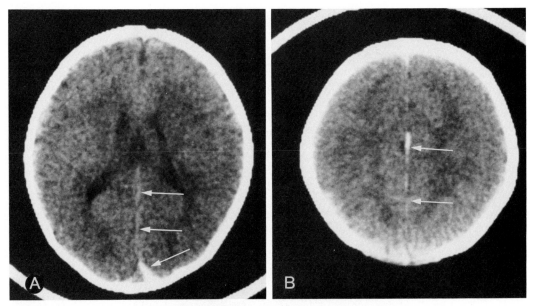

Figure 8.16. Unenhanced CT scans (*A* and *B*) of a 4-month-old abused infant. Note acute interhemispheric subdural hematoma (*arrows*).

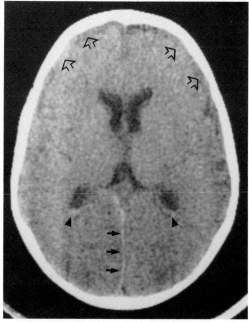

Figure 8.17. Unenhanced CT scan of a 5-month-old fatally abused infant. Note interhemispheric subdural hematoma (*arrows*). Blood is present in the occipital horns (*arrowheads*). Subtle bifrontal acute subdural collections are present (*open arrows*). Interventricular hemorrhage, convexity, and interhemispheric subdural blood was confirmed at autopsy.

asymmetry as the collection relates to the falx, (*c*) a flat medial border and a convex lateral border, *d*) extension over one tentorial surface (21, 80), and (*e*) a patchy or irregular distribution of the high-density interhemispheric collection. Pathologically, it is not unusual to encounter both subarachnoid and subdural blood in the interhemispheric fissure region. Although the sign as described by Zimmerman et al. is useful, it should be applied judiciously in the assessment of CNS injury.

Small acute subdural hematomas over the convexities may be difficult to detect because of the adjacent high density of the cranial vault (Figs. 8.17 and 8.18). Secondary signs such as effacement of cortical sulci and adjacent mass effect will aid in this regard. Small subdurals overlying the central parietal convexity may be overlooked unless the highest CT slice extends through this portion of the vertex (82) (see Fig. 8.21*C*). It may be impossible to differentiate a small subdural hematoma from a cortical contusion. Larger subdural collections will separate the cerebral cortex from the skull, and possess a crescentic configuration. These convexity hematomas are less fre-

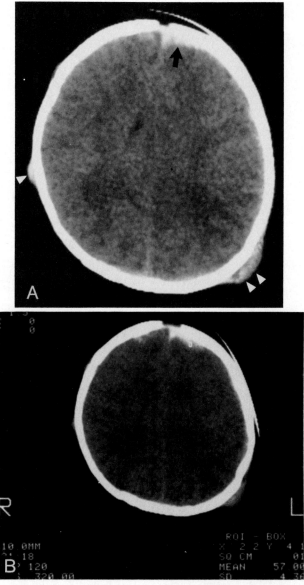

Figure 8.18. *A,* CT scan of 1-month-old abused infant. There is effacement of the ventricular system and sulci due to diffuse cerebral edema. High density is present over the left frontal convexity (*arrow*). *B,* A cursor placed over this region of interest shows a reading of 57 Hounsfield units, consistent with subdural blood. Two subgaleal hematomas are seen (*arrowheads*). Findings were confirmed at autopsy.

quent than the smaller or interhemispheric variety (21).

Below the tentorium, subdural hematomas may be difficult to identify. Bone artifact in the posterior fossa often limits optimal assessment of this region. However, when large subdural collections are present, they are clearly identified tracking along the tentorial surface (Fig. 8.19). Coronal imaging, either directly or with reconstruction, will define these posterior fossa subdural hemorrhages to advantage (Fig. 8.19C). Acute posterior fossa subdural hemorrhages are usually indicative of severe injury and, in contrast to convexity subdurals, are usually associated with massive fractures of the

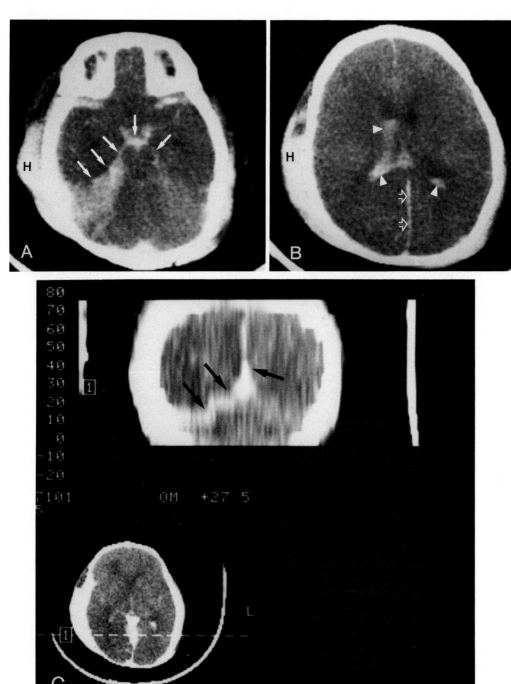

Figure 8.19. *A* and *B*, Axial cranial CT images of 3-month-old abused infant. Subdural and subarachnoid blood is seen tracking along the tentorium and brainstem (*arrows*). Blood is noted in both lateral ventricles (*arrowheads*). Interhemispheric subarachnoid blood is present posteriorly (*open arrows*). It is seen to conform to the gyral pattern of the occipital cortex. This is difficult to differentiate from normal high density of the falx. Extensive subgaleal hematoma (*H*) is present. *C*, Coronal reconstruction reveals blood along the falx and tentorial surfaces (*arrows*). Large posterior fossa subdural hematoma and subarachnoid and interventricular hemorrhage were noted at autopsy.

occipital bone. Routine cranial CT scanning does not adequately assess the posterior fossa. When fractures are present, or if suspicious findings are noted on the initial CT scan, images obtained with the gantry angled for the posterior fossa at 5-mm increments are indicated. Because this is a region where fractures may be difficult to identify on radiographs, bone window imaging is of particular value (see Fig. 8.10). Because MRIs are not degraded by bone artifact, they provide enhanced images in posterior fossa injuries.

Associated cerebral edema is common with acute extracerebral blood collections (Fig. 8.18) (see below). Merten and Osborne (13) found cerebral low density in 24 of 26 (92%) patients with extracerebral collections. As will be discussed, the subdural collection in most cases is a relatively insignificant concomitant of more serious underlying parenchymal brain injury. Rather than requiring specific surgical therapy, the subdural hematoma is often a finding implying severe underlying parenchymal injury that may have long-term neurologic consequences.

Chronic subdural hematomas are generally quite conspicuous and are rarely overlooked. The collections tend to be situated over the frontal convexities and with increasing size extend further posteriorly (Figs. 8.20–8.22, also see Fig. 8.28). They may surround the entire brain when massive. A correlation exists between the density of the collection and the chronicity of the process (83). With relatively recent subdurals, the collections are of high density, approaching that seen in acute cases. With time, the density of the collections diminishes and may begin to approach that of the cerebrospinal fluid. In such cases, these so-called subdural hygromas may be difficult to differentiate from enlargement of the subarachnoid spaces secondary to atrophy or communicating hydrocephalus. Careful measurement of the attenuation of these regions is possible with virtually all CT scanners, and simultaneous measurements over the ventricles and the cerebrospinal fluid (CSF) collections usually resolve the problem. Another helpful feature is a distinct

transition between the subdural collection and the lower density subjacent CSF (Fig. 8.20). The extracerebral spaces are normally prominent in young infants (84) and may in fact be increased in abused infants; this factor further highlights the separation between subdural and subarachnoid fluid.

Cranial ultrasound is of limited value in assessment of small subdural collections. It is of use in following the progression of gross extracerebral collections as well as the development of ventricular enlargement (Fig. 8.22).

As subdural collections are frequently the result of repeated injury, a single scan may provide evidence of both chronic and acute injury (77) (Fig. 8.21). This may be visualized as a localized high-density collection within a larger diffuse low-density process. Serial scans may show the development of new high-density areas in previously relatively low-density regions. When it is not possible to distinguish a chronic subdural from enlargement of the extracerebral spaces, it may be necessary to sample the fluid, percutaneously or by burr hole, and examine its constituents. Based upon the literature, chronic posterior fossa subdural hematomas appear to be rare. In contrast to convexity subdurals, which are often chronic upon discovery, the posterior fossa subdural, commonly associated with a fracture, is presumably so life threatening that it prompts medical attention shortly after injury.

Differential Considerations. Subdural hematomas occur in association with skeletal abnormalities in a variety of conditions that fall into the differential diagnosis of child abuse (see Chapter 11). These conditions include birth trauma, syphilis, tuberculosis, bacterial meningitis and osteomyelitis, vitamin A toxicity, scurvy, rickets, and Menkes' syndrome. A complete history, careful physical examination, and appropriate laboratory tests will exclude these possibilities.

Acute Epidural Hematoma

Acute collections of blood in the epidural space are unusual sequelae of child abuse.

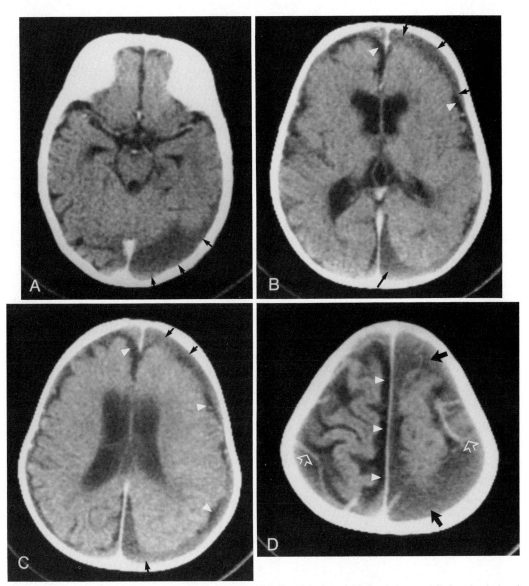

Figure 8.20. Multiple CT (*A–D*) images of a 4-month-old abused infant. Large bilateral subdural hematomas are present (*solid arrows*), and are greater on the left. Careful inspection demonstrates two layers of differing extracerebral density. The denser, outermost layer is subdural hematoma, the inner layer (*arrowheads*) represents subarachnoid fluid. There is associated ventriculomegaly, which probably reflects an element of communicating hydrocephalus. On the highest image (*D*), contrast-enhanced cortical venous structures are visible (*open arrows*).

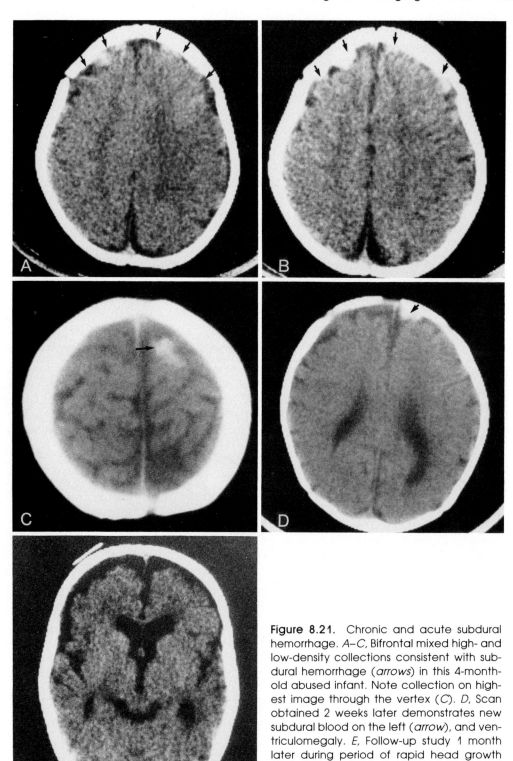

Figure 8.21. Chronic and acute subdural hemorrhage. *A–C,* Bifrontal mixed high- and low-density collections consistent with subdural hemorrhage (*arrows*) in this 4-month-old abused infant. Note collection on highest image through the vertex (*C*). *D,* Scan obtained 2 weeks later demonstrates new subdural blood on the left (*arrow*), and ventriculomegaly. *E,* Follow-up study 1 month later during period of rapid head growth reveals enlargement of the extracerebral CSF spaces and ventriculomegaly, indicating posttraumatic communicating hydrocephalus.

Of 47 patients with intracranial injury manifest by CT, Merten and Osborne (13) found only two cases of epidural hemorrhage (1984). Tsai et al. (14) described a similar large epidural hemorrhage and also noted a small epidural hematoma in a 3½-year-old without associated skull fracture. Other large series (21, 22) failed to describe any cases of epidural hematomas. Most epidural hematomas originate from an arterial source, although occasionally venous bleeding produces the lesion. In contrast to subdurals, which generally do not present an acute life threatening situation, large epidural hematomas are surgical emergencies (85). They are usually associated with skull fractures, another feature contrasting with subdural hematomas. Large epidural hematomas have a characteristic lenticular shape, are often well localized, and exert an impressive mass effect (Fig. 8.23). Smaller epidurals, however, may demonstrate a crescentic appearance and be virtually indistinguishable from acute subdural hematoma (14).

THE BRAIN

Blunt trauma, irrespective of overlying fracture, and indirect injuries associated with rapid acceleration and deceleration are responsible for the vast majority of brain injuries in abused infants and children. These forms of injury account for the greatest morbidity and mortality in cases of abuse and have been the subject of considerable investigation (47, 48, 86–89).

Two major physical factors govern the development of intracranial injury. With a direct blow, a force is applied locally to the calvarium and transmitted to the underlying brain substance. The transmission of this force is accentuated in the young infant, in whom the skull is more easily deformed. As a result, shearing and tearing forces are developed, maximal in the region of impact. If sufficient deformity of the brain occurs so that the contralateral cerebral substance impacts the inner surface of the cranium, a contracoup injury occurs (87).

An alternative explanation is required to explain diffuse cerebral edema and other focal cerebral injuries occurring at sites other than at or opposite the site of direct impact. As the brain shifts within the calvarium, certain regions show relatively restricted mobility because of fixation by the falx or the tentorium, as well as bony regions such as the lesser sphenoid wings. The differential motion of the brain thus creates areas where shearing forces may disrupt the cerebral parenchyma (87). Holbourn (90) analyzed the areas of maximal shear strain within the brain utilizing gelatin models. Those areas subject to the most shear strain were the parasagittal and fronto-orbitotemporal surfaces. The differential density of white and grey matter may also lead to abnormal strains at their interfaces (91). The experimental production of rotatory hyperacceleration injuries in human primates as well as the clinical experience with shaken infants indicates the major role of nondirect head injury in the production of diffuse cerebral damage.

Pathologically, a variety of cerebral lesions have been identified. These include diffuse and focal edema, contusional hemorrhage and tears, laceration, and associated subarachnoid and intraventricular hemorrhage. Characteristic microscopic alterations accompany these gross pathologic findings. Cerebral edema reflects one of the major secondary effects of CNS trauma (92).

The edema is a response to endothelial damage and results in increased permeability of injured blood vessels. Increase in cerebral blood volume also appears to contribute to generalized cerebral swelling (93). At autopsy, the brains are increased in weight, with flattening of the gyral surfaces and compression of the ventricular system. The microscopic alterations noted in cases of pure cerebral edema are nonspecific, and if edema is present without other cerebral injury or extracerebral hemorrhage, differentiation of hypoxic changes from traumatically induced brain swelling may be impossible.

Immediately beneath the site of direct trauma, morphologic abnormalities may be noted. If the injury is associated with a depressed skull fragment, or if marked de-

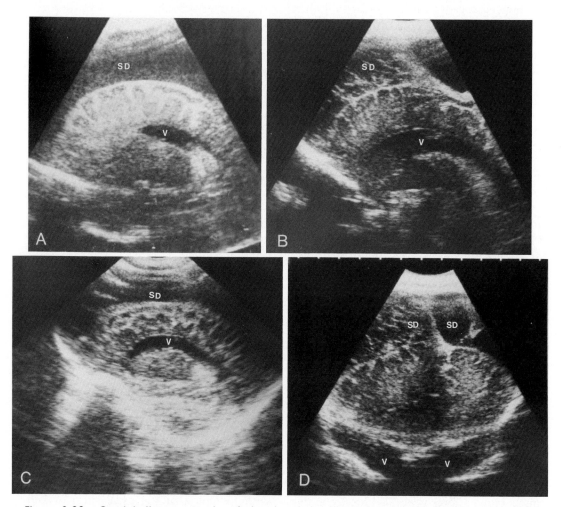

Figure 8.22. Cranial ultrasonography of chronic subdural hematoma in an abused infant. Right (*A* and *B*) and left (*C*) parasagittal images and a coronal image (*D*) reveal large hypoechoic collections (*SD*) over both cerebral convexities. There is mild ventricular enlargement (*V*). Lateral (*E*) and frontal (*F*) views of the skull following introduction of air via a subdural shunt catheter demonstrate extensive gaseous lucency throughout the left subdural space (*arrows*).

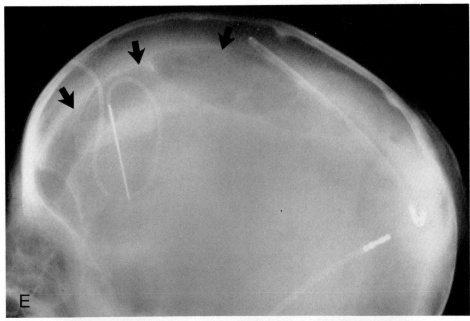

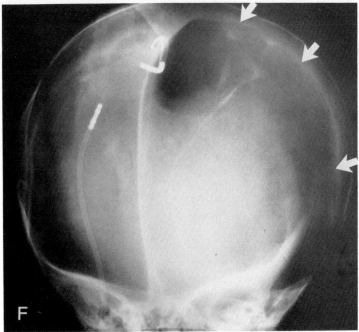

Figure 8.22. *E* and *F.*

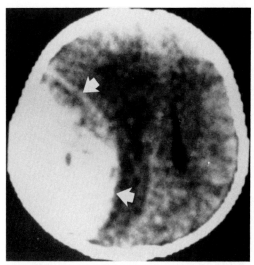

Figure 8.23. Cranial CT of 5-month-old infant reveals a large epidural hematoma. The convex inner margin (*arrows*) is typical of a large epidural bleed. Surrounding cerebral edema and mass effect are present. There was an associated skull fracture. The infant eventually died. (Reproduced with permission from Merten DF, Osborne DRS: Craniocerebral trauma in the child abuse syndrome: Radiological observations. *Pediatr Radiol* 14:272–277, 1984.)

formity of the skull occurs with the blunt insult, direct injury to the underlying cortex will occur. This may be seen either as an actual laceration of the brain or as hemorrhagic cortical contusion. These lesions are most commonly seen in older patients suffering complex skull fractures or penetrating head injury. In contrast, the immature incompletely myelinated brain of infancy appears to respond differently to blunt head injury. Although small hemorrhagic cortical contusions may be seen at the site of direct injury, the most characteristic and commonly encountered feature is a tear or contusional cleft of the cerebral white matter (87). These tears are slit-like or irregularly shaped clefts within the frontal and temporal lobe white matter. These sites of injury are in accordance with the experimental work of Holbourn (90). On occasion they are situated beneath the area of impact; however, in most cases, their location bears little relation to the site of injury. Occasionally, the white matter tears extend to the

cortical grey matter, changing from an orientation at right angles to one parallel to the cortical surface. Little bleeding is noted within these lesions, and they may be overlooked or considered to be postmortem artifact. With increasing cellular reaction and healing, the defects become walled off, and a cystic space is formed. This pattern of healing is a predictable one, and the chronicity of the process can be well assessed. As expected, injuries sustained at different ages may coexist.

Studies have shown that diffuse axonal injury occurs with blunt head trauma (86). Extensive disruption of white matter tracts occurs at the time of injury and is unrelated to increased intracranial pressure or hypoxic damage. The alterations are easily overlooked unless proper staining methods and meticulous histologic analysis are carried out. It is likely that these white matter lesions play an important role in the well-described cerebral atrophy and associated neurologic and developmental deficits evidenced by infants surviving episodes of abuse.

Cortical contusion or white matter lacerations extending to the surface of the brain will be associated with subarachnoid bleeding. Tears of major dural vessels and venous sinuses may also be associated with subarachnoid as well as subdural blood. Parenchymal injuries that extend to the ventricular surfaces will result in intraventricular hemorrhage. As this blood freely diffuses throughout the subarachnoid fluid and is rapidly absorbed, gross evidence of subarachnoid bleeding is a relatively transient phenomenon.

Radiologic Alterations

Cerebral Edema. Cerebral edema may be generalized or focal. Generalized cerebral swelling is the most common CT alteration in all types of pediatric head injury (83, 93, 94). CT reveals obliteration or compression of the ventricles and absence of the subarachnoid spaces in the sylvian fissures, around the brainstem, and over the convexities (see Fig. 8.18). Considerable variation in the size of these CSF-containing spaces occurs in infants and children, and caution must be exercised in assessing the significance of these findings alone. However, if there is no visible ventricular system and the subarachnoid spaces are obliterated in infancy, cerebral swelling can be assumed (84). Diminished density of the brain and loss of the normal grey-white matter differentiation are additional features supporting edema. These latter findings should be assessed only on high-resolution scans obtained under technically satisfactory conditions.

Cerebral edema is more reliably identified when it is focal, as opposed to diffuse. Of 37 abused children with head injury, Cohen et al. identified cerebral edema in 24 (65%) (22). Of these, 18 (75%) had focal or unilateral hemispheric edema. The areas of low density may roughly correspond to a vascular distribution (Fig. 8.24), or they may cross vascular territories. Asymmetric areas of edema may exert considerable mass effect, causing compression of the adjacent ventricular system and a contralateral shift of the midline structures (Fig. 8.25). The adjacent cortical sulci and other cysternal spaces may be obliterated on the ipsilateral side of the lesion. In some cases, when peripheral edema is diffuse and severe, diminished density will be evident throughout the cortical grey and white matter. In contrast, the white matter of the thalamus, brainstem, and cerebellum is spared, resulting in a relatively high density of these regions as compared with the surrounding brain. Cohen et al. (22) have termed this "the reversal sign" (Figs. 8.26 and 8.27).

Although the CT finding of cerebral edema is useful, the absence of edema radiologically should not rule out the possibility of severe intracranial injury. A normal CT scan may, in fact, be seen in children with fatal CNS insults. Elevated intracranial pressure may be significant in victims of severe shaking injury without alterations on CT (41).

Subarachnoid Hemorrhage. Large amounts of subarachnoid blood are relatively easy to identify because portions will

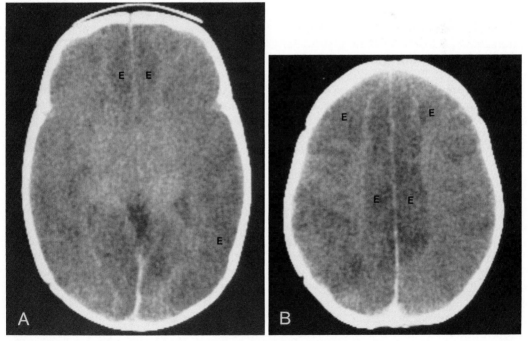

Figure 8.24. Unenhanced CCTs (*A* and *B*) of a 3-month-old abused infant demonstrate patchy areas of low density consistent with edema (*E*), most evident in the anterior cerebral vascular territory. The lateral ventricles are not visualized because of compression.

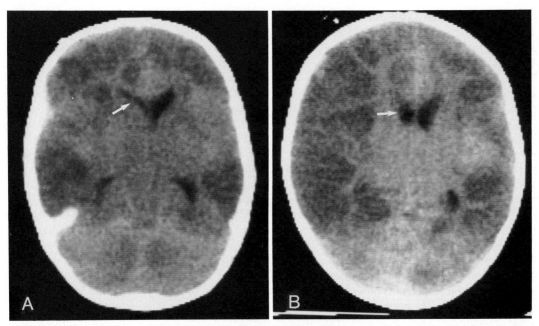

Figure 8.25. Unenhanced CCTs (*A* and *B*) of a 3-month-old fatally abused infant demonstrate extensive cerebral low density (greater on the right). There is compression of the right frontal horn (*arrow*), and a midline shift to the left secondary to the mass effect in the right hemisphere.

commonly surround the brainstem (see Fig. 8.19). Smaller hemorrhages may be manifest only by blood within the interhemispheric region, and considerable difficulty differentiating subarachnoid from subdural blood or the normally dense falx may be encountered (22, 80, 83, 95). These difficulties limit estimates of subarachnoid hemorrhage in abused patients. Cohen et al. found evidence of subarachnoid hemorrhage in 27 of 37 patients (73%) (22). In contrast, Merten and Osborne found subarachnoid hemorrhage in 9 of 36 patients (25%) (13). In contrast to subdural hematomas, interhemispheric blood does not widen the interhemispheric fissure, and thus it is extremely difficult to differentiate this from the normal falx, especially if there is adjacent cerebral low density related to edema (see Fig. 8.24). Zimmerman et al. (80) suggested that extension of anterior interhemispheric hyperdensity to the rostrum of the corpus callosum indicates subarachnoid blood because the normal falx does not extend to this structure. They also indicated that subarachnoid blood does not alter the appearance of the posterior portion of the inter-

hemispheric fissure. A useful sign indicating that hyperdensity between the hemispheres is indeed subarachnoid blood is an undulating margin conforming to the gyral surface of the brain (see Fig. 8.19).

Intraventricular Hemorrhage. Gross intraventricular hemorrhage is usually associated with massive intracranial injury. In the acute phase, it will produce striking high density within the otherwise low-density cerebral ventricles (Fig. 8.27). Smaller amounts of subarachnoid hemorrhage may produce high density only in the posterior aspect of the occipital horns and can be easily overlooked (see Fig. 8.17). Careful assessment may reveal a blood-CSF level. Ultrasonography is a useful adjunct in the detection of intraventricular hemorrhage (96), although at present it appears to be of limited value in the general assessment of craniocerebral injury (22).

Contusional Hemorrhage. Most hemorrhagic contusions noted in abused children are relatively small and, if visible on CT, are characterized by focal areas of high density (Fig. 8.28). They are seen along the cerebral convexities, particularly in the fron-

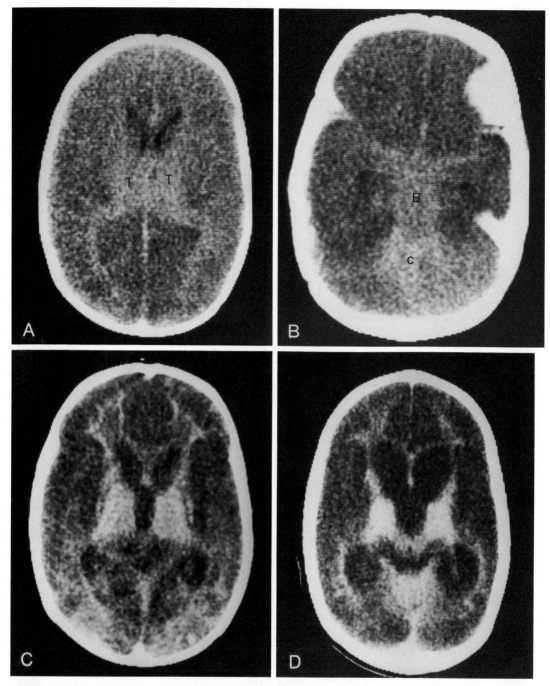

Figure 8.26. CCTs of a 4-month-old abused child; reversal sign. The initial study (*A* and *B*) demonstrates diffuse cerebral low density with relative sparing of thalamai (*T*), brainstem (*B*) and cerebellum (*c*). Follow-up examinations at 2 weeks (*C*) and 1 year (*D*) following injury revealed progressive ventricular dilatation and marked cortical low density due to cortical atrophy. (Reproduced with permission from Cohen RA, Kaufman RA, Myers PA, Towbin RB: Cranial computed tomography in the abused child with head injury. *AJR* 146:97–102, 1986. Copyright by American Society of Neuroradiology (1986).)

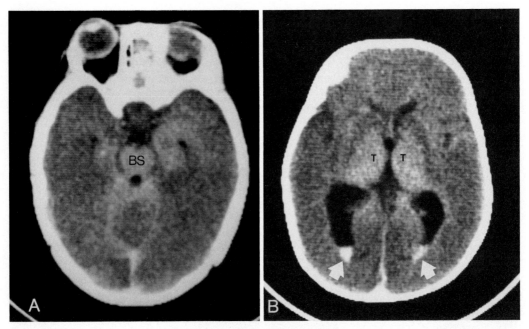

Figure 8.27. Unenhanced CCTs (*A* and *B*) of 4-month-old abused infant demonstrate diffuse cerebral edema with preservation of high density within the brainstem (*BS*) and thalamai (*T*). Fresh blood is noted within the occipital horns of the lateral ventricles (*arrows*).

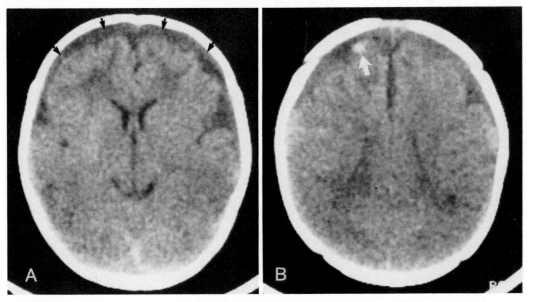

Figure 8.28. Unenhanced CT images (*A* and *B*) of a 2-month-old abused infant demonstrate a frontal cortical contusion (*white arrow*) in association with bifrontal subdural hematomas (*black arrows*).

tal and parasagittal regions, conforming to the sites of greatest stress during acceleration-deceleration movements. They are commonly associated with other craniocerebral injury, such as subdural hematoma. On occasion, such cortical contusions may be quite impressive (44). Major deep hemorrhagic contusion may occur, such as within the thalamus or corpus callosum (13, 77). Hausdorf and Helmke (97) reported a large parieto-occipital hemorrhage detected by ultrasound in a 1-month-old abused infant. With small hemorrhages there is little mass effect unless significant focal cerebral edema is present. In major hemorrhages, expected displacements as a result of the intracranial mass are identified. Parenchymal injury in the posterior fossa is uncommon; however, when complex fractures involving the occipital bone are present, substantial cerebellar injury can be expected. Unfortunately, technical artifacts due to adjacent bony structures in the posterior fossa limit the ability of CT to detect these abnormalities.

Contusional Clefts. Despite the frequent occurrence of white matter tears in infants subjected to blunt head trauma (87), recognition of contusional clefts radiographically in abused children is rare (76, 97). Ordia et al. described a 2-month-old with irritability and seizures (76). Radiographs revealed bilateral skull fractures. In addition to subdural hematomas, CT demonstrated bilateral cleft-like defects in the frontal white matter with surrounding high density (Fig. 8.29). The central portions of these clefts measured in the fluid density range. A follow-up study 9 months later demonstrated a persistent unilateral fluid-filled cleft with a thick, high-density rim. In a second case, a 4½-year-old child with multiple fractures and failure to thrive exhibited similar findings in the frontal white matter.

Hausdorf and Helmke (97) reported on a 1-month-old infant with multiple skull, rib, and extremity fractures. Cerebral ultrasound demonstrated an anechoic region with central dense echoes in the parieto-occipital region. A CT scan at the same time demonstrated frontal lobe edema and a large intracerebral hemorrhage in the left parieto-occipital area. Four weeks later, cranial ultrasound demonstrated enlargement of the left parieto-occipital defect, and bilateral frontal lobe anechoic clefts were evident. Computed tomography at this time demonstrated large white matter clefts in both frontal lobes.

These important reports demonstrate cerebral injuries that are much more common than the literature suggests. There are several reasons why CT appears to have a low sensitivity in the identification of these abnormalities. First, the lesions are usually small, and many are likely beyond the resolving capacity of the technique. Second, density differences produced by the small amount of bleeding associated with these lesions may be insufficient for detection. Ultrasound may well prove to be quite useful in this regard, because differences in acoustic impedance resulting from these abnormalities may be more easily identified than density changes detected by CT. Although MRI provides no greater spatial resolution than CT, it is an extremely useful technique in the identification of disturbances of cerebral white matter. Although for technical reasons MRI is not usually performed in acutely ill infants, future availability of this technique in such patients will likely provide diagnosis of white matter tears and cerebral edema not readily identified by other modalities.

Cerebral Atrophy. Computed tomography provides the link between acute craniocerebral injury in infants and subsequent neurologic and developmental deficits. Although this relationship has long been assumed, CT has elucidated the precise pattern of evolution from acute injury to long-term deficit. Changes of cerebral atrophy may be visible as early as 1 month following an acute injury (22). Depending upon the site and extent of original injury, changes of atrophy may be focal or diffuse. With diffuse cerebral loss there will be generalized enlargement of the ventricular system and of the extracerebral CSF spaces as well (Figs. 8.26, 8.29, and 8.30). The pattern is essentially one of central and cortical encephalomalacia (14, 21, 22, 39, 75). Of 12 patients with cerebral atrophy reported by Zimmer-

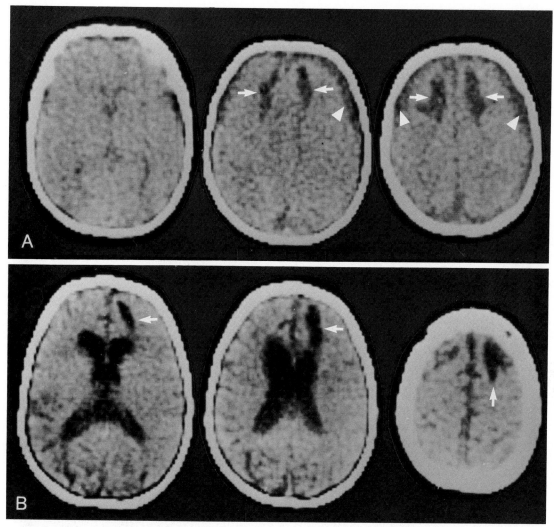

Figure 8.29. *A*, CT scan of 2-month-old infant with irritability and seizures. There are bilateral frontal white matter clefts (*arrows*) in association with chronic subdural hematomas (*arrowheads*). *B*, Follow-up 9 months later shows ventriculomegaly with enlargement of one frontal cleft and disappearance of the contralateral lesion. (Courtesy of D. Sucher and R. Strand, Children's Hospital Medical Center, Boston, Massachusetts.)

man et al. (21), 9 were bilateral and 3 uni-lateral. They found a pattern consistent with cerebral infarction in 50%. Of 13 patients followed up clinically, 5 showed no evidence of neurologic defect, and 2 were blind and evidenced spastic quadriplegia and severe mental retardation. One patient was blind and hemiparetic, two had homonymous hemianopsia and hemiparesis, two had homonymous hemianopsia, and one had hemiparesis.

When diffuse ventricular and CSF space enlargement is present as a result of atrophy, differentiation from communicating hydrocephalus purely on CT grounds may be difficult (see below). Care must be taken not to confuse diffuse atrophy from the normally prominent CSF spaces in infants (84).

Focal atrophic changes will be manifest as enlargement of the ipsilateral ventricular and CSF-containing spaces. There may be a

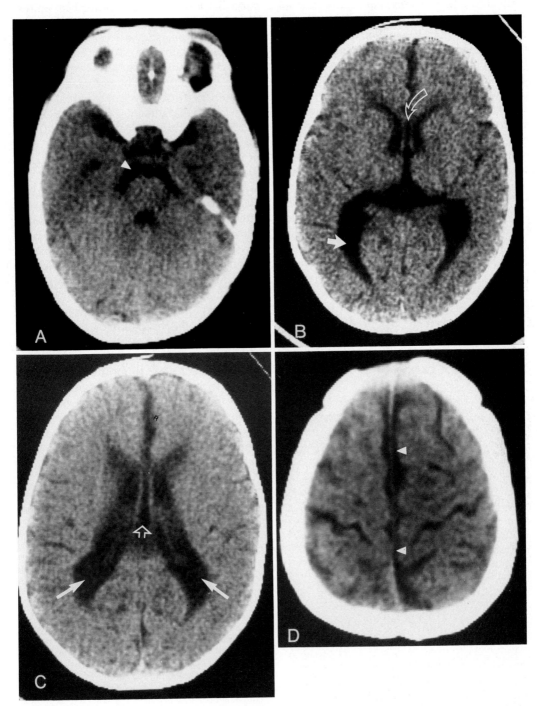

Figure 8.30. Cerebral atrophy. CCT images (*A–D*) of a 6-month-old abused infant demonstrate diffuse enlargement of the ventricles (*arrows*) as well as the extracerebral spaces (*arrowheads*). Note large cavum septum pellucidum and cavum vergae (*open arrow*).

shift of the contralateral structures to the side of atrophy, and, with time, the affected hemicranium may be smaller than the normal side. The CT picture may be quite confusing if both acute and chronic changes are present. Although cranial ultrasound at present is of limited utility in the acute setting (22), it is a valuable tool to follow ventricular size in patients with prior intracranial injury. It is also a useful screening tool in patients with suspected abuse in whom the question of prior craniocerebral injury is raised (Fig. 8.31).

Posttraumatic Hydrocephalus. As a result of intraventricular and subarachnoid hemorrhage, blockage in the CSF pathways may occur. If the obstruction is intraventricular, there will be enlargement of the ventricles with obliteration of the extracerebral CSF spaces (13). When obstruction involves the pacchionian granulations over the cerebral convexities, there will be enlargement of the subarachnoid spaces (see Fig. 8.21). This pattern may be difficult to differentiate on radiographic grounds from central and cortical atrophy. Sequential head circumference measurements, as well as other clinical data, should provide easy differentiation of these two possibilities. On occasion, an element of communicating hydrocephalus may coexist with subdural hematomas, producing both high-density extracerebral collections and enlargement of the underlying extracerebral CSF compartment. In difficult cases, radionuclide cysternography may provide the diagnosis of communicating hydrocephalus.

Miscellaneous Lesions. Hill et al. (98) described *Toxocara canis* infection of the brain in a 2½-year-old child who resided with a large pet dog. The child had been abused because of excessive crying. The relationship between child abuse and the *Toxocara* infection was uncertain, but the author speculated that the child's behavorial disorder may have led to increase in pica, resulting in the ingestion of infected dog feces. Demmler et al. (99) described a 9½-year-old mentally retarded female with a ventriculoperitoneal shunt infection caused by *Neisseria gonorrhoeae*. Computed tomography demonstrated mild ventricular dilatation. On the basis of gonorrheal infection in a sibling, the child was believed to be a victim of sexual abuse with consequent *Neisseria gonorrhoeae* peritonitis.

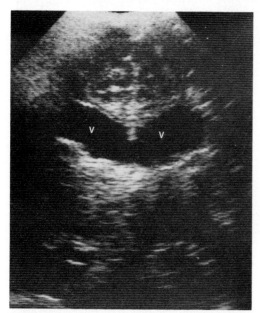

Figure 8.31. Cerebral atrophy in a 3-month-old infant with prior episodes of abuse. Cranial ultrasound through the anterior fontanelle reveals enlargement of the frontal horns of the lateral ventricles (V). The extracerebral spaces are not adequately assessed on this study.

REFERENCES

1. Silver LB: Child abuse syndrome: A review. *Med Times* 96:802–820, 1968.
2. Elmer E: Identification of abused children. *Children* 10:180–184, 1963.
3. Martin HP: The consequences of being abused and neglected: how the child fares. In Kempe CH, Helfer RE (eds): *The Battered Child*, ed 3. Chicago, University of Chicago Press, 1980, pp 347–365.
4. Elmer E, Gregg GS: Developmental characteristics of abused children. *Pediatrics* 40:596–602, 1967.
5. Gregg GS, Elmer E: Infant injuries: accident or abuse? *Pediatrics* 44:434–439, 1969.
6. Martin HP, Beezley P, Conway EF, Kempe CH: The development of abused children-Part I. A review of the literature. Part II. Physical, neurologic, and intellectual outcome. *Adv Pediatr* 21:25–73, 1974.
7. Mayer T, Walker ML, Johnson DG, Matlak ME: Causes of morbidity and mortality in severe pediatric trauma. *JAMA* 245:719–721, 1981.
8. Craft AW, Shaw DA, Cartlidge NEF: Head injuries in children. *Br Med J* 4:200–203, 1972.
9. Billmire ME, Meyers PA: Serious head injury in infants: accident or abuse? *Pediatrics* 75:340–342, 1985.

10. Helfer RE, Slovis TL, Black M: Injuries resulting when small children fall out of bed. *Pediatrics* 60:533–535, 1977.
11. Hobbs CJ: Skull fracture and the diagnosis of abuse. *Arch Dis Child* 59:246–252, 1984.
12. Weston JT: The pathology of child abuse. In Kempe CH, Helfer RE (eds): *The Battered Child*, ed 3. Chicago, University of Chicago Press, 1968, pp 77–100.
13. Merten DF, Osborne DRS: Craniocerebral trauma in the the child abuse syndrome: radiological observations. *Pediatr Radiol* 14:272–277, 1984.
14. Tsai FY, Zee C-S, Apthorp JS, Dixon GH: Computed tomography in child abuse head trauma. *CT:The Journal of Computed Tomography* 4:277–286, 1980.
15. Hamlin H: Subgaleal hematoma caused by hairpull. *JAMA* 205:314, 1968.
16. Silverman FN: Unrecognized trauma in infants, the battered child syndrome, and the syndrome of Ambroise Tardieu. Rigler lecture. *Radiology* 104:337–353, 1972.
17. Leonidas J, Ting W, Binkiewicz A, Vaz R, Scott RM, Pauker SG: Mild head trauma in children. When is a roentgenogram necessary? *Pediatrics* 69:139–143, 1982.
18. Harwood-Nash DC, Hendrick EB, Hudson AR: The significance of skull fractures in children. *Radiology* 101:151–155, 1971.
19. Hahn YS, Raimondi AJ, McLone DG, Yamanouchi Y: Traumatic mechanisms of head injury in child abuse. *Childs Brain* 10:229–241, 1983.
20. James HE, Schut L: The neurosurgeon and the battered child. *Surg Neurol* 2:415–418, 1974.
21. Zimmerman RA, Bilaniuk LT, Bruce D, Schut L, Uzzell B, Goldberg HI: Computed tomography of craniocerebral injury in the abused child. *Radiology* 130:687–690, 1979.
22. Cohen RA, Kaufman RA, Myers PA, Towbin RB: Cranial computed tomography in the abused child with head injury. *AJR* 146:97–102, 1986.
23. O'Neill JA Jr, Meacham WF, Griffin PP, Swayers JL: Patterns of injury in the battered child syndrome. *J Trauma* 13:332–339, 1973.
24. Kravitz H, Driessen G, Gomberg R, Korach A: Accidental falls from elevated surfaces in infants from birth to one year of age. *Pediatrics (Suppl)* 44:869–876, 1969.
25. Sty JR, Starshak RJ: The role of bone scintigraphy in the evaluation of the suspected abused child. *Radiology* 146:369–375, 1983.
26. Merten DF, Radkowski MA, Leonidas JC: The abused child. A radiological reappraisal. *Radiology* 146:377–381, 1983.
27. Gugliantini P, Caione P, Fariello G, Rivosecchi M: Post traumatic leptomeningeal cysts in infancy. *Pediatr Radiol* 9:11–14, 1980.
28. Saulsbury FT, Alford BA: Intracranial bleeding from child abuse: the value of skull radiographs. *Pediatr Radiol* 12:175–178, 1982.
29. Pinckney LE, Kennedy LA: Fractures of the infant skull caused by animal bites. *AJR* 135:179–180, 1980.
30. Becker DB, Needleman HL, Kotelchuck M: Child abuse and dentistry: orofacial trauma and its recognition by dentists. *J Am Dent Assoc* 97:24–28, 1978.
31. Tate RJ: Facial injuries associated with the battered child syndrome. *Br J Oral Surg* 9:41–45, 1971.
32. Palmer CH, Weston JT: Several unusual cases of child abuse. *J Forensic Sci* 21:851–855, 1976.
33. Sims AP: Non-accidental injury in the child presenting as a suspected fracture of the zygomatic arch. *Br Dent J* 158:292–293, 1985.
34. Guthkelch AN: Infantile subdural haematoma and its relationship to whiplash injuries. *Br Med J* 2:430–431, 1971.
35. Caffey J: On the theory and practice of shaking infants. Its potential residual effects of permanent brain damage and mental retardation. *Am J Dis Child* 124:161–169, 1972.
36. Caffey J: The whiplash shaken infant syndrome: manual shaking by the extremities with whiplash-induced intracranial and intraocular bleedings, linked with residual permanent brain damage and mental retardation. *Pediatrics* 54:396–403, 1974.
37. Oliver JE: Microcephaly following baby battering and shaking. *Br Med J* 2:262–264, 1975.
38. Schneider V, Woweries J, Grumme T: Das "Schuttel-Trauma" des sauglings. *MMWR* 121:171–176, 1979.
39. Roussey M, Le Francois MC, Le Marec B, Gandon Y, Carsin M, Senegal J: La tomodensitometrie cranienne chez les enfants maltraites. *Ann Radiol* 25:237–243, 1982.
40. Benstead JG: Shaking as a culpable cause of subdural haemorrhage in infants. *Med Sci Law* 23:242–244, 1983.
41. Bennett HS, French JH: Elevated intracranial pressure in whiplash-shaken infant syndrome detected with normal computerized tomography. *Clin Pediatr* 19:633–634, 1980.
42. Carter JE, McCormick AQ: Whiplash shaking syndrome: retinal hemorrhages and computerized axial tomography of the brain. *Child Abuse Negl* 7:279–286, 1983.
43. Ludwig S, Warman M: Shaken baby syndrome: a review of 20 cases. *Ann Emerg Med* 13:104–107, 1984.
44. Ellison PH, Tsai FY, Largent JA: Computed tomography in child abuse and cerebral contusion. *Pediatrics* 62:151–154, 1978.
45. Zimmerman RA, Bilaniuk LT, Bruce D, Schut L, Uzzell B, Goldberg HI: Interhemispheric acute subdural hematoma. A computed tomographic manifestation of child abuse by shaking. *Neuroradiology* 16:39–40, 1978.
46. Eagan BA, Whelan-Williams S, Brooks WG Jr: The abuse of infants by manual shaking: medical, social and legal issues. *J Fla Med Assoc* 72:503–507, 1985.
47. Ommaya AK, Hirsch AE: Tolerances for cerebral concussion from head impact and whiplash in primates. *J Biomech* 4:13–21, 1971.
48. Ommaya AK, Faas F, Yarnell P: Whiplash injury and brain damage: an experimental study. *JAMA* 204(4):285–289, 1968.
49. Sherwood D: Chronic subdural hematoma in infants. *Am J Dis Child* 39:980–1021, 1930.
50. Trotter W: Chronic subdural haemorrhage of traumatic origin, and its relation to pachymeningitis haemorrhagica interna. *Br J Surg* 2:271–291, 1914.
51. Ingraham FD, Heyl HL: Subdural hematoma in infancy and childhood. *JAMA* 112:198–204, 1939.

52. Ingraham FD, Matson DD: Subdural hematoma in infancy. *J Pediatr* 24:1–37, 1944.
53. Caffey J: Multiple fractures in the long bones of infants suffering from chronic subdural hematoma. *Am J Roentgenol (AJR)* 56:163–173, 1946.
54. Lis EF, Frauenberger GS: Multiple fractures associated with subdural hematoma in infancy. *Pediatrics* 6:890–892, 1950.
55. Smith MJ: Subdural hematoma with multiple fractures. Case report. *Am J Roentgenol (AJR)* 63:342–344, 1950.
56. Meneghello J, Hasbun J: Hematoma subdural y fractura de los huesos largos. *Rev Chil Pediatr* 22:80–83, 1951.
57. Marquezy R-A, Bach C, Blondeau M: Hematome sous-dural et fractures multiples des os longs chez un nourrisson de 9 mois. *Arch Fr Pediatr* 9:526–531, 1952.
58. Kugelmann J: Uber symmetrische spontanfrakturen unbekannter genese beim saugling. *Ann Paediatr* 178:177–181, 1952.
59. Marie J, Apostolides P, Salet J, Eliachar E, Lyon G: Hematome sous-dural du nourrisson associe a des fractures des membres. *Ann Pediatr* 30:1757–1763, 1954.
60. Cohen M, LoPresti J, Burke F, Mateos J, Rubio L, Stevens H: Traumatic periostitis and subdural hematoma. *Clin Proc Child Hosp DC* 12:240–246, 1956.
61. Kinley G, Riley HD Jr, Beck CS: Subdural hematoma, hygroma, and hydroma in infants. *J Pediatr* 38:667–686, 1951.
62. Woolley PV Jr, Evans WA Jr: Significance of skeletal lesions in infants resembling those of traumatic origin. *JAMA* 158:539–543, 1955.
63. Lelong M, Alison F, Rougerie J, Le TV, Caldera R: L'hematome sous-dural chronique du nourrisson. *Arch Fr Pediatr* 12:1037–1084, 1955.
64. Willemin-Clog L, Chapelot J: Accidents hemorragiques intra-craniens avec fracture du crane et des os longs observes chez 3 nourrissons d'une meme fratrie. *Sem Hop Paris* 34:1875–1877, 1958.
65. Klein M-R: L'hematome sous-dural du nourrisson. *Arch Fr Pediatr* 21:425–440, 1964.
66. Neimann N, Beau A, Antoine M, Pierson M, Manciaux N, de Kersauson MC: Les alterations des os long au cours de l'hematome dural chronique du nourrisson. *J Radiol Electr* 39:576–581, 1958.
67. Neimann N, Manciaux M, Sapelier J, Grall R: L'hematome sous-dural chronique du nourrisson. Considerations etiologiques. *Pediatrie* 21:409–425, 1966.
68. Neimann N, Manciaux M, Rabouille D, Zorn G: Les enfants victimes de sevices. *Pediatrie* 23:861–875, 1968.
69. Josserand P, Germain D, Devillard A, Girerd J: Un nouveau cas d'hematome sous-dural associe a des fractures de membres chez un nourrisson. *Pediatrie* 15:647–659, 1960.
70. Russell PA: Subdural haematoma in infancy. *Br Med J* 2:446–448, 1965.
71. Lazorthes G, Bardier A, Martinez-Cobo J: Les epanchements sous-duraux du nourrisson: discussion etiopathogenique a propos de 59 cas. *Presse Med* 71:1903–1905, 1963.
72. Kempe CH, Silverman FN, Steele BF, Droegemueller W, Silver HK: The battered-child syndrome. *JAMA* 181:105–112, 1962.
73. Peet MM, Kahn EA: Subdural hematoma in infants. *JAMA* 98:1851–1856, 1932.
74. Putnam TJ, Cushing H: Chronic subdural hematoma: its pathology, its relation to pachymeningitis hemorrhagica, and its surgical treatment. *Arch Surg* 11(3):329–393, 1925.
75. Ment LR, Duncan CC, Rowe DS: Central nervous system manifestations of child abuse. *Conn Med* 46:315–318, 1982.
76. Ordia IJ, Strand R, Gilles F, Welch K: Computerized tomography of contusional clefts in the white matter in infants. *J Neurosurg* 54:696–698, 1981.
77. Merten DF, Osborne DRS: Craniocerebral trauma in the child abuse syndrome. *Pediatr Ann* 12:882–887, 1983.
78. Frank Y, Zimmerman R, Leeds NMD: Neurological manifestations in abused children who have been shaken. *Dev Med Child Neurol* 27:312–316, 1985.
79. Harwood-Nash DC: Craniocerebral trauma in children. *Curr Probl Radiol* 3(3):3–42, 1973.
80. Zimmerman RD, Russell EJ, Yurberg E, Leeds NE: Falx and interhemispheric fissure on axial CT. II. Recognition and differentiation of interhemispheric subarachnoid and subdural hemorrhage. *AJNR* 3:635–642, 1982.
81. Osborn AG, Anderson RE, Wing SD: The false falx sign. *Radiology* 134:421–425, 1980.
82. Wing SD, Osborn AG, Wing RW: The vertex scan: an important component of cranial computed tomography. *Am J Roentgenol (AJR)* 130:765–767, 1978.
83. Scotti G, Terbrugge K, Melancon D, Belanger G: Evaluation of the age of subdural hematomas by computerized tomography. *J Neurosurg* 47:311–315, 1977.
84. Kleinman PK, Zito JL, Davidson RI, Raptopoulos V: The subarachnoid spaces in children: normal variations in size. *Radiology* 147:455–457, 1983.
85. Hawkes CD, Ogle WS: Atypical features of epidural hematoma in infants, children, and adolescents. *J Neurosurg* 19:971–980, 1962.
86. Adams JH, Graham DI, Murray LS, Scott G: Diffuse axonal injury due to nonmissile head injury in humans: an analysis of 45 cases. *Ann Neurol* 12:557–563, 1982.
87. Lindenberg R, Freytag E: Morphology of brain lesions from blunt trauma in early infancy. *Arch Pathol* 87:298–305, 1969.
88. Strich SJ: The pathology of brain damage due to blunt head injuries. In Walker AE, Caveness WF, Critchley M (eds): *The Late Effects of Head Injury.* Springfield, IL, Charles C Thomas, 1969, pp 501–524.
89. Peerless SJ, Rewcastle NB: Shear injuries of the brain. *Can Med Assoc J* 96:577–582, 1967.
90. Holbourn AHS: Mechanics of head injuries. *Lancet* 2:438–450, 1943.
91. Zimmerman RA, Bilaniuk LT, Genneralli T: Computed tomography of shearing injuries of the cerebral white matter. *Radiology* 127:393–396, 1978.
92. Hardman JM: Microscopy of traumatic central nervous system injuries. In Perper JA, Wecht CH (eds): *Microscopic Diagnosis in Forensic Pathology,* Springfield, IL, Charles C Thomas, 1980, pp 268–326.
93. Zimmerman RA, Bilaniuk LT, Bruce D, Dolinskas

C, Obrist W, Kuhl D: Computed tomography of pediatric head trauma: acute general cerebral swelling. *Radiology* 126:403–408, 1978.

94. Zimmerman RA, Bilaniuk LT: L'examen scanographique en traumatologie cranio-cephalique pediatrique [Computed tomography in pediatric head trauma]. *J Neuroradiol* 8:257–271, 1981.

95. Lim ST, Sage DJ: Detection of subarachnoid blood clot and other thin, flat structures by computed tomography. *Radiology* 123:79–84, 1977.

96. Rumack CM, McDonald MM, O'Meara OP, Sanders BB, Rudikoff JC: CT detection and course of intracranial hemorrhage in premature infants. *Am J Roentgenol (AJR)* 131:493–497, 1978.

97. Hausdorf G, Helmke K: Sonographic demonstration of contusional white matter clefts in an infant. *Neuropediatrics* 15:110–112, 1984.

98. Hill IR, Denham DA, Scholtz CL: *Toxocara canis* larvae in the brain of a British child. *Trans R Soc Trop Med Hyg* 79:351–354, 1985.

99. Demmler GJ, Wells D, Heitkamp JW, Laurent JP, Edwards MS: *Neisseria gonorrhoeae* ventriculoperitoneal shunt infection in a child. *Pediatr Infect Dis* 4:419–420, 1985.

9 Miscellaneous Forms of Abuse and Neglect

PAUL K. KLEINMAN, M.D.

Nonorganic Failure to Thrive

Nonorganic failure to thrive is the failure of normal growth and development secondary to a disturbed social and emotional environment. In its most overt form, where nutrition is simply withheld and starvation results, the child presents in an emaciated and frequently moribund state (1–3). Despite profound malnutrition and deficiency of essential dietary constituents, the skeletal examinations in these patients generally show little more than demineralization. On occasion, well-intentioned parents may institute a variety of cult diets resulting in nutritional diseases. In addition to kwashiorkor and marasmus, rickets has been described in infants and children placed on fad diets (4).

In contrast to the child with frank evidence of starvation, most cases of nonorganic failure to thrive are manifest by varying degrees of growth retardation, delayed skeletal maturation, and retarded motor and intellectual development. The clinical entity has been referred to by a variety of terms including the syndrome of maternal deprivation, psychosocial dwarfism, deprivational dwarfism, abuse dwarfism, and the Kaspar-Hauser syndrome (5–17).

A variety of radiologic findings have been noted in patients with psychosocial dwarfism. The most frequent findings are delayed bone age, osteopenia, and diminished subcutaneous fat. Classically, the delay in bone age is commensurate with the abnormal height age (18, 19). The retarded skeletal maturation is secondary to deficient growth

hormone secretion, simulating idiopathic hypopituitarism; however, in contrast to that entity, growth hormone secretion returns to normal when the children are removed from the abnormal home environment. Transient hypopituitarism should be differentiated from irreversible hypothalmic-pituitary disfunction secondary to traumatic head injury associated with abusive assaults (20, 21).

An important radiologic alteration in psychosocial dwarfs has been described by Capitanio and Kirkpatrick (22). They noted widening of the cranial sutures in a group of children undergoing treatment for deprivational dwarfism (Figs. 9.1 and 9.2). The radiologic features suggested increased intracranial pressure, but the authors noted no abnormal neurologic findings. As the enlarging head circumference paralleled the accelerated growth period, the authors concluded that similar rapid growth of the brain resulted in splitting of the cranial sutures. Other investigators have confirmed Capitanio and Kirkpatrick's observations (23–27).

The age at which the sutural widening is noted ranges from 10 weeks to 6 years. It is most frequently discovered around 2 years of age, the most common age at which psychosocial dwarfism is recognized and treated. The sutures are characteristically normal at diagnosis and sutural widening becomes evident once a considerable weight gain occurs. However, occasionally the sutures may be wide at diagnosis (24). The sutural widening is generalized and varies from a slight diastasis to 4 mm of separation of the bony margins. The appearance of the

201

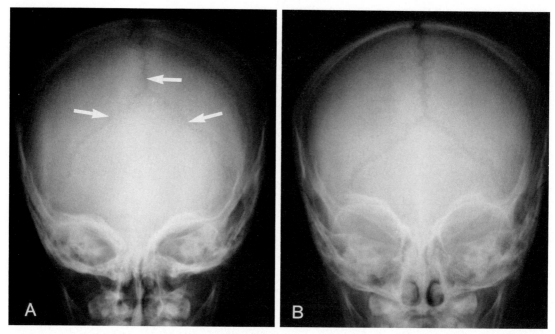

Figure 9.1. Psychosocial dwarfism. *A,* Frontal view of the skull of a 3-year-old child with height and weight below the third percentile reveals normal-appearing sagittal and lambdoid sutures (*arrows*). *B,* Follow-up film 43 days later reveals split sutures. There was no clinical evidence of increased intracranial pressure. (Reproduced with permission from Sondheimer FK, Grossman H, Winchester P: Suture diastasis following rapid weight gain: Pseudopseudotumor cerebri. *Arch Neurol* 23:314–318, 1970.)

sutures can be expected to return to normal in 2 to 3 months.

The significance of this phenomenon is twofold. In the patient with short stature and a normal neurologic examination, the development of cranial sutural widening during the patient's hospitalization should raise the consideration of "catch-up" growth secondary to psychosocial deprivation. Second, sutural widening should not be misinterpreted as a sign of increased intracranial pressure in instances of psychosocial dwarfism. Because these patients may evidence clinical and radiologic signs of the battered child syndrome, the suspicion of intracranial pathology may be raised. Recognition of this finding following accelerated growth, and the absence of increased intracranial pressure, should prevent confusion.

Another unusual phenomenon that occurs in cases of psychosocial dwarfism and in other neglected children is acute gastric dilatation (28, 29). These patients are usually below the third percentile in height and

weight and are noted by caretakers or medical personnel to have a voracious appetite. Marked upper abdominal distension is noted that may simulate hepatosplenomegaly or other intra-abdominal mass. A supine view of the abdomen will support the presence of an upper abdominal mass, and an upright or cross table lateral film will usually reveal an air–fluid level (Figs. 9.3A–C). Ultrasonography will demonstrate an echogenic mass in the upper abdomen (Fig. 9.3D). This condition is a form of gastric atony that occurs in a variety of states, including chronic starvation. It appears to be due to structural and functional changes in the stomach secondary to inadequate nutrition, and classically develops following ingestion of a large meal. Contrast studies may be performed to exclude gastric outlet obstruction, but will show only a dilated stomach with little peristaltic activity. As neglected children may also show signs of physical abuse, the differential diagnosis includes duodenal hematoma, which can pro-

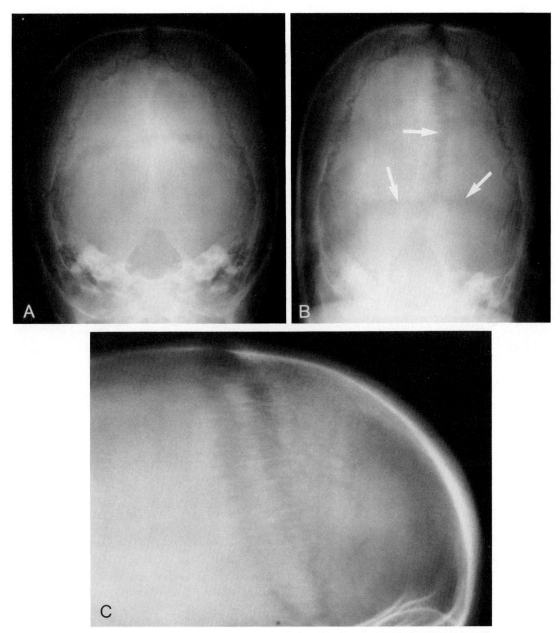

Figure 9.2. *A*, Townes projection of the skull of a 2½-year-old child with failure to thrive reveals normal sutures. A repeat Townes (*B*) and coned lateral view (*C*) 81 days after hospitalization demonstrate split sutures (*arrows*). (Reproduced with permission from Sondheimer FK, Grossman H, Winchester P: Suture diastasis following rapid weight gain: Pseudopseudotumor cerebri. *Arch Neurol* 23:314–318, 1970.)

duce a similar plain film appearance (see Chapter 7).

Neglected children may present with a celiac syndrome characterized by malnutrition and bulky, foul-smelling, greasy stools.

Physical examination reveals height and weight below the third percentile with comparable delays in skeletal maturation. Laboratory studies to document a primary defect in intestinal absorption are unreward-

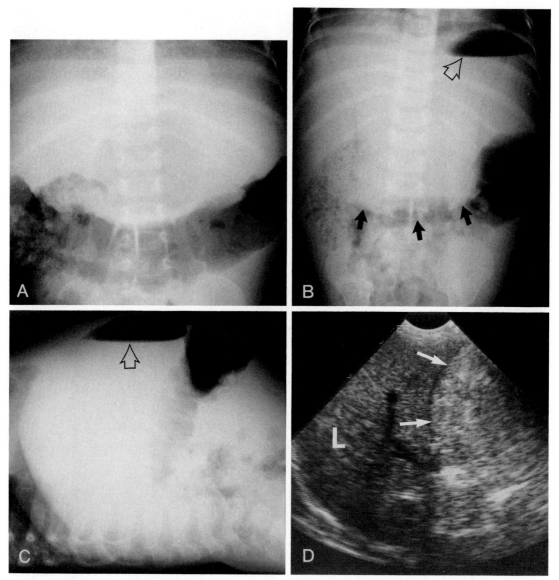

Figure 9.3. Acute gastric dilatation. Supine (*A*), upright (*B*), and cross-table lateral (*C*) views of the abdomen of a 5-month-old infant presenting with an upper abdominal mass. The infant, who was below the third percentile in height and weight, had recently ingested a large meal. The markedly dilated stomach produces a soft tissue mass (*solid arrows*) containing an air–fluid level (*open arrow*) in the mid and upper abdomen. *D*, Sagittal ultrasound image through the upper abdomen shows a structure containing multiple echoes in the infrahepatic region (*arrows*). *L*, liver. The patient was treated with nasogastric suction followed by small frequent feedings.

ing. The child exhibits abnormal behavior, and careful study of the family will reveal disturbed interaction between child and caretaker. Plain films show abdominal distension and dilated loops of small bowel. Gastrointestinal contrast studies are usually unremarkable. Signs of frank physical abuse such as fractures and pancreatic pseudocysts may coexist with the celiac syndrome (30). Institution of proper nutrition and correction of the disturbed caretaker–patient relationship lead to resolution of the gastrointestinal abnormalities. As with other manifestations of psychosocial deprivation, the degree of catch-up growth and maturation depends upon the severity of the original insult.

It is important for the radiologist to recognize that children experiencing psychosocial deprivation may present with a variety of complaints that prompt diagnostic imaging studies to search for organic disease. In addition to those findings noted above, patients may exhibit enuresis, encopresis, self-injury, retarded psychomotor development, and a variety of bizarre behavioral patterns that include eating from garbage cans and drinking from toilet bowls. It should also be stressed that neglected

children are at risk for physical abuse, and thus the radiologist may identify previously unsuspected indications of physical injury. Therefore, in selected younger patients, skeletal surveys may provide clues to the nature of a patient's failure to thrive.

Poisoning and Munchausen's Syndrome

Intentional childhood poisoning can occur in a variety of clinical settings. Injurious substances may be administered with a clear homicidal intent or to produce a factitious disease in a child leading to medical attention, the so-called Munchausen syndrome

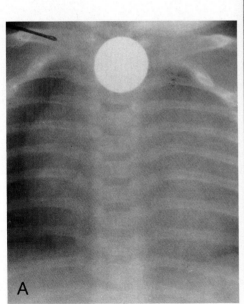
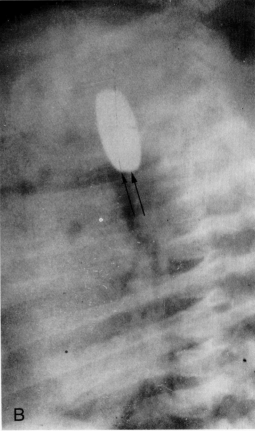

Figure 9.4. Attempted poisoning with foreign body. Frontal (*A*) and lateral (*B*) views of the chest of an infant who had been fed coins by a sibling in a presumed poisoning attempt. The frontal view appears to show only one coin; however, the lateral projection demonstrates two coins (*arrows*) lodged at the level of the aortic knob. (Courtesy of Nancy Geneiser, New York University Medical Center, New York, NY.)

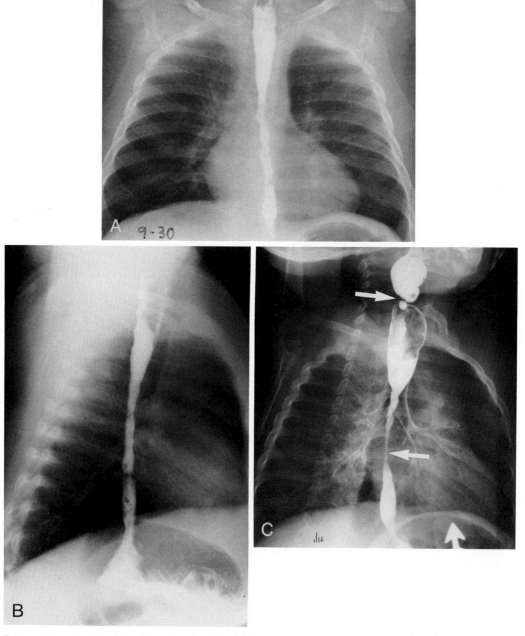

Figure 9.5. Caustic ingestion. The mother of this 6-month-old infant had fed the child scalding milk in an alleged poisoning attempt. Frontal (*A*) and lateral (*B*) views of a barium swallow demonstrate spasm and mucosal irregularity of the mid and distal esophagus. *C*, Follow-up study 10 months later demonstrates high-grade strictures involving the cervical and midthoracic esophagus (*arrows*) with evidence of gross aspiration into the tracheal bronchial tree. The patient was subsequently treated with a colonic interposition. (Courtesy of Nancy Geneiser, New York University Medical Center, New York, NY.)

by proxy. As most poisonings occur with chemical substances producing pharmacologic alterations, diagnostic imaging plays a minimal role in diagnosis (31). However, certain unusual and often bizarre forms of poisoning may prompt radiologic investigation.

A severely disturbed caretaker may forcefeed an infant or child particularly hazardous foreign bodies. These materials include opened safety pins and light bulbs (see Fig. 7.16) and small batteries that carry the threat of gastric or intestinal perforation (see Fig. 7.15). The assailants are usually parents or parent substitutes, but occasionally a "battering child" may be responsible for physical injury (32). Figure 9.4 illustrates an infant who had been fed multiple coins by a sibling presumably in an attempted poisoning. Lye, a well-known agent in accidental poisoning, may also be intentionally administered by an abusive parent (31). Rarely, the feeding of a scalding liquid will lead to an esophageal burn similar to that resulting from a caustic chemical agent (Fig. 9.5). A barium swallow performed in the acute phase will demonstrate esophageal ulceration and spasm. Follow-up studies will reveal varying degrees of esophageal stricture.

Many other substances may be administered to a child to produce physical injury and provoke the concerns of medical personnel. Diagnostic workups may be extensive, and the radiologist may be called upon to perform a variety of imaging studies. Meadow described a 6-year-old victim of the Munchausen syndrome by proxy who was hospitalized for a total of 5 months for his factitious illness (33). During that period he underwent two upper gastrointestinal (GI) series, an intravenous pyelogram, a skeletal survey, and a brain scan, as well as two lumbar punctures, two electroencephalograms, and biopsies of bone, kidney, and skin. As complicated diagnostic problems generally find their way to the imaging department, the radiologist may become involved with and may in fact compound the confusion of these difficult cases.

The various agents employed are most commonly over-the-counter and prescription drugs, but injury has also been produced or feigned by injection of bacterially contaminated material (34–36). Perhaps one of the most disturbing forms of inflicted injury simulating disease occurs in infants who have been intentionally asphyxiated or otherwise abused but are reported to be instances of "near miss" sudden infant death syndrome (37–45). Finally, a parent may produce factitious hemoptysis, hematemesis, and hematuria in a variety of ways utilizing either the child's or his or her own blood.

These various assaults tend to occur in severely disturbed family environments, the same conditions leading to the more commonly observed forms of physical abuse. Therefore, the radiologist must search for "telltale" signs of abuse, and recommend other investigative studies where deemed appropriate.

The Handicapped Child

The child with mental or physical handicap is at increased risk for abuse. The infant or child who is regarded as being less than perfect, and requires special care and support, stresses the home environment and tests the coping ability of the entire family (46, 47). The infant or child may sustain direct physical violence or may simply be neglected, a particular hazard in children with special needs. Patients with paralytic disorders are at special risk for fractures that, if ignored, will result in severe deformity (Fig. 9.6). Caretaker insensitivity to feeding problems may result in aspiration pneumonia, and improper care of urinary diversions and lack of adherence to bladder catheterizations may result in unnecessary urinary tract infection. Premature infants are at special risk for abuse (48, 49). The susceptibility to fracture is particularly increased in very low birth weight infants when nutritional bone disease is present. Helfer et al. described an unusual form of abuse in which four infants, three of them premature, were abused by caretakers who administered medically prescribed exercises in an excessively vigorous manner (50). A

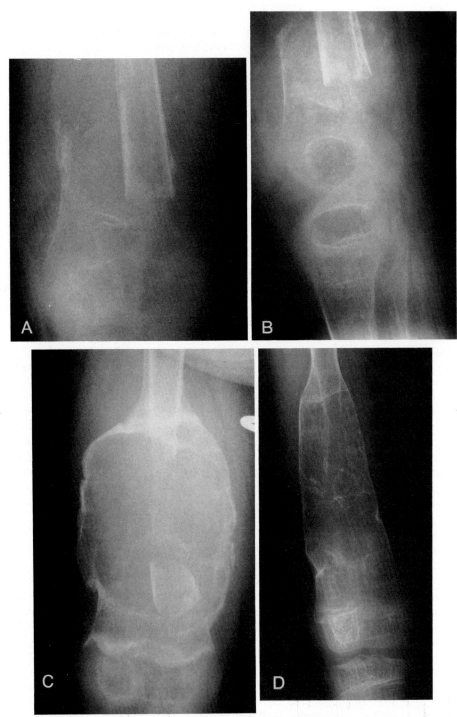

Figure 9.6. Neglected fracture in a handicapped child. This 4-year-old child with severe cerebral palsy sustained a fracture while unattended. The fracture was neglected and was first recognized clinically during the healing stage. A and B, AP and lateral views of the femur demonstrate "telescoping" of the fracture fragments with a massive ossifying soft tissue hematoma. Follow-up studies at ages 4½ years (C) and 6½ years (D) demonstrate progressive reconstitution of a new cortex defined by the hematoma margins, resulting in a severe modeling disturbance.

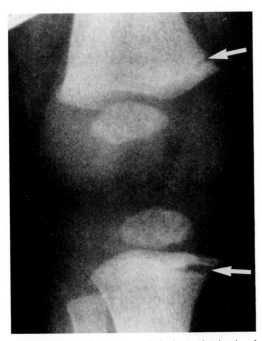

Figure 9.7. Metaphyseal lesions typical of abuse are noted in the distal femur and proximal tibia (*arrows*) of this 4-month-old infant. The parents attributed these injuries to passive range-of-motion exercises. At autopsy, a subdural hematoma was identified.

similar case has been reported by London et al. (51). Radiographs demonstrated typical features of child abuse in the long bones, skulls, and ribs, and examination of the families or baby-sitters revealed psychopathologic tendencies similar to those classified as potentially abusive. Figure 9.7 is a radiograph of the knee of a child reported to have died of the sudden infant death syndrome. Characteristic metaphyseal lesions of abuse were noted. However, the fractures were purported by the parents to be secondary to medically prescribed passive range-of-motion exercises. Computed tomography and postmortem examination revealed an interhemispheric subdural hematoma typical of infant abuse.

Physical abuse has been reported in institutionalized children, and is particularly difficult to diagnose (52). Differentiation from accidental or self-induced injury is often impossible without a witness or admission of the abuser. Figure 9.8 illustrates the findings in an institutionalized patient who developed vomiting and dehydration. An upper GI series and abdominal ultrasound revealed evidence of a duodenal hematoma

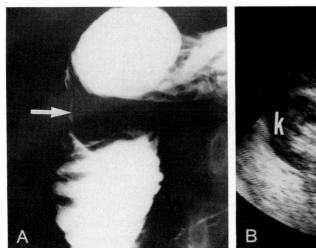
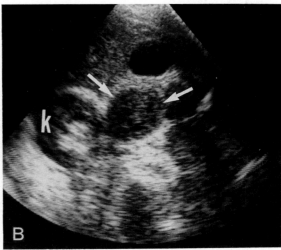

Figure 9.8. Duodenal hematoma in an institutionalized patient. A 17-year-old retarded patient presented with intermittent vomiting for 10 days. *A,* An upper GI series demonstrates evidence of fold thickening and an intraluminal mass (*arrow*) in the second portion of the duodenum. *B,* A transverse abdominal ultrasound demonstrates a well-defined echogenic mass (*arrows*) anterior and medial to the right kidney (*k*). A follow-up ultrasound revealed the mass to be smaller and hypoechoic, consistent with a liquefying hematoma. An occult injury was suspected, but never documented.

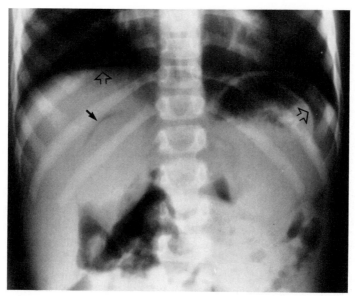

Figure 9.9. Sexual abuse. Subdiaphragmatic (*open arrow*) and subhepatic (*solid arrow*) intraperitoneal air is noted in this female rape victim. (Reproduced with permission from Dorst JP: Child abuse. *Radiologie (Berlin)* 22:335–341, 1982.)

(see Chapter 7). There was no history of injury, and the cause of this characteristically traumatic lesion was undetermined.

Sexual Abuse

Despite the common occurrence of sexual abuse, diagnostic imaging plays a minimal role in the assessment of this disturbing condition. Diagnosis is generally based upon history and physical examination with supporting laboratory studies. When present, most signs of trauma are restricted to the labia, vestibule, vagina, and anus. A rectal perforation may be noted with attendant radiologic manifestations (53). Rarely, the rape victim may manifest free intraperitoneal air (Fig. 9.9) (54). Foreign bodies may be utilized in the sexual assault, and plain films of the abdomen may provide useful information. When major anorectal trauma is present, radiologic studies are invaluable in assessing acute injury as well as postoperative problems. Black et al. described a 3-year-old whose mother had perforated his rectosigmoid with a coathanger (55). Following sigmoid resection, the patient developed a rectovesical fistula and a subsequent

rectourethral stricture. Radiologic studies were invaluable in assessing the complex anatomic alterations.

The radiologist is most likely to encounter instances of sexual abuse unknowingly during diagnostic procedures performed to evaluate suspected medical illness. Sexually abused children are likely to manifest regressive behavior and conversion hysteria (56). Thus the child with recent onset of enuresis may undergo voiding cystourethrography. The sexually abused child with constipation or encopresis may have a barium enema. The radiologist should be familiar with the physical signs suggesting anal-genital trauma and should, where appropriate, inform the referring physician of his/her findings. It should be emphasized that abused children may volunteer crucial evidence of abusive assaults to the examining physician. When incriminating verbal information is uncovered by the radiologist, it should be precisely documented in the medical record (57).

REFERENCES

1. Adelson L: Homicide by starvation. The nutritional variant of the "battered child". *JAMA* 186:458–460, 1963.

2. Davis JH, Rao VJ, Valdes-Dapena M: A forensic science approach to a starved child. *J Forensic Sci* 29:663–669, 1984.
3. Trube-Becker E: Zur totung von kleinkindern durch nahrungsentzug. *Dtsche Z Gerichtl Med* 64:93–101, 1968.
4. Roberts LE, West RJ, Ogilvie D, Dillon MJ: Malnutrition in infants receiving cult diets: a form of child abuse. *Br Med J* 1:296–298, 1979.
5. Nau E, Cabanis D: Kaspar-hauser-syndrom. *MMWR* 108:929–931, 1966.
6. Whitten CF, Pettit MG, Fischhoff J: Evidence that growth failure from maternal deprivation is secondary to undereating. *JAMA* 209:1675–1682, 1969.
7. Solky HJ, Gardner LI, Money J: Abuse dwarfism. Letters to the editor. *Am J Dis Child* 132:724, 1978.
8. Koel BS: Failure to thrive and fatal injury as a continuum. *Am J Dis Child* 118:565–567, 1969.
9. Gardner LI: The endocrinology of abuse dwarfism: with a note on Charles Dickens as child advocate. *Am J Dis Child* 131:505–507, 1977.
10. Silver HK, Finkelstein M: Deprivation dwarfism. *J Pediatr* 70:317–324, 1967.
11. Hufton IW, Oates RK: Nonorganic failure to thrive: a long-term follow-up. *Pediatrics* 59:73–77, 1977.
12. Money J: The syndrome of abuse dwarfism (psychosocial dwarfism or reversible hyposomatotropism): behavioral data and case report. *Am J Dis Child* 131:508–513, 1977.
13. Patton RG, Gardner LI: Influence of family environment on growth: the syndrome of "maternal deprivation." *Pediatrics* 30:957–962, 1962.
14. English PC: Failure to thrive without organic reason. *Pediatr Ann* 7:774–781, 1978.
15. Pelikan L, Mores A, Koluchova J, Siroky J, Farkova H: Tezky deprivacni syndrom u dvojcat po dlouhodobe socialni izolaci. *Cesk Pediatr* 24:980–983, 1969.
16. Chesney RW, Brusilow S: Extreme hypernatremia as a presenting sign of child abuse and psychosocial dwarfism. *Johns Hopkins Med J* 148:11–13, 1981.
17. Money J, Wolff G, Annecillo C: Pain agnosia and self-injury in the syndrome of reversible somatotropin deficiency (psychosocial dwarfism). *J Austism Child Schizophr* 2:127–139, 1972.
18. Powell GF, Brasel JA, Blizzard RM: Emotional deprivation and growth retardation simulating idiopathic hypopituitarism. I. Clinical evaluation of the syndrome. *N Engl J Med* 276:1271–1278, 1967.
19. Powell GF, Brasel JA, Raiti S, Blizzard RM: Emotional deprivation and growth retardation simulating idiopathic hypopituitarism. II. Endocrinologic evaluation of the syndrome. *N Engl J Med* 276:1279–1283, 1967.
20. Miller WL, Kaplan SL, Grumbach MM: Child abuse as a cause of posttraumatic hypopituitarism. *N Engl J Med* 302:724–728, 1980.
21. McKiernan J: Precocious puberty and non-accidental injury. *Br Med J* 2:1059, 1978.
22. Capitanio MA, Kirkpatrick JA: Widening of the cranial suture: a roentgen observation during periods of accelerated growth in patients treated for deprivation dwarfism. *Radiology* 92:53–59, 1969.
23. De Levie M, Nogrady MB: Rapid brain growth upon restoration of adequate nutrition causing false radiologic evidence of increased intracranial pressure. *J Pediatr* 76:523–528, 1970.
24. Gloebl HJ, Capitanio MA, Kirkpatrick JA: Radiographic findings in children with psychosocial dwarfism. *Pediatr Radiol* 4:83–86, 1976.
25. Sondheimer FK, Grossman H, Winchester P: Suture diastasis following rapid weight gain: pseudopseudotumor cerebri. *Arch Neurol* 23:314–318, 1970.
26. Afshani E, Osman M, Girdany BR: Widening of cranial sutures in children with deprivation dwarfism. *Radiology* 109:141–144, 1973.
27. Tibbles JAR, Vallet HL, Brown B, Saint J, Goldbloom RB: Pseudotumor cerebri in deprivation dwarfism. *Dev Med Child Neurol* 14:322, 1972.
28. Franken EA Jr, Fox M, Smith JA, Smith WL: Acute gastric dilatation in neglected children. *Am J Roentgenol (AJR)* 130:297–299, 1978.
29. Shulman BH, Evans HE, Manvar D, Flicker S: Acute gastric dilatation following feeding of nutritionally abused children. *Clin Pediatr (Phila)* 23:108, 1984.
30. Manson G: Neglected children and the celiac syndrome. *J Iowa Med Soc* 54:228–234, 1964.
31. Dine MS, McGovern ME: Intentional poisoning of children — an overlooked category of child abuse: report of seven cases and review of the literature. *Pediatrics* 70:32–35, 1982.
32. Adelson L: The battering child. *JAMA* 222:159–161, 1972.
33. Meadow R: Munchausen syndrome by proxy. *Arch Dis Child* 57:92–98, 1982.
34. Hodge D III, Schwartz W, Sargent J, Bodurtha J, Starr S: The bacteriologically battered baby: another case of Munchausen by proxy. *Ann Emerg Med* 11:205–207, 1982.
35. Kohl S, Pickering LK, Dupree E: Child abuse presenting as immunodeficiency disease. *J Pediatr* 93:466–468, 1978.
36. Halsey NA, Tucker TW, Redding J, Frentz JM, Sproles T, Daum RS: Recurrent nosocomial polymicrobial sepsis secondary to child abuse. *Lancet* 2:558–560, 1983.
37. Bass M, Kravath RE, Glass L: Death-scene investigation in sudden infant death. *N Engl J Med* 315:100–105, 1986.
38. Rosen CL, Frost JD Jr, Bricker T, Tarnow JD, Gillette PC, Dunlavy S: Two siblings with recurrent cardiorespiratory arrest: Munchausen syndrome by proxy or child abuse? *Pediatrics* 71:715–720, 1983.
39. Morris B: Child abuse manifested as factitious apnea. *South Med J* 78:1013–1014, 1985.
40. Meadow R: Munchausen syndrome by proxy: the hinterland of child abuse. *Lancet* 2:343–345, 1977.
41. Meadow R: Munchausen by proxy and brain damage. *Dev Med Child Neurol* 26:669–676, 1984.
42. Berger D: Child abuse simulating "near miss" sudden infant death syndrome. *J Pediatr* 95:554–556, 1979.
43. Hick JF: Sudden infant death syndrome and child abuse. *Pediatrics* 52:147–148, 1973.
44. Minford AMB: Child abuse presenting as apparent "near-miss" sudden infant death syndrome. *Br Med J* 282:521, 1981.
45. Roberts J, Golding J, Keeling J, et al: Is there a link

between cot death and child abuse? *Br Med J* 289:789–791, 1984.

46. Murphy MA: The family with a handicapped child: a review of the literature. *Dev Behav Pediatr* 3:73–82, 1982.

47. Jaudes PK, Diamond LJ: Neglect of chronically ill children. *Am J Dis Child* 140:655–658, 1986.

48. McCormick MC, Shapiro S, Starfield BH: Injury and its correlates among 1-year-old children. *Am J Dis Child* 135:159–163, 1981.

49. Klein M, Stern L: Low birth weight and the battered child syndrome. *Am J Dis Child* 122:15–18, 1971.

50. Helfer RE, Scheurer SL, Alexander R, Reed J, Slovis TL: Trauma to the bones of small infants from passive exercise: a factor in the etiology of child abuse. *J Pediatr* 104:47–50, 1984.

51. London R, Noronha PA, Levy HB: Bone trauma caused by passive exercise. Letter to the editor. *J Pediatr* 105:172–173, 1984.

52. Tomkiewicz S: Violences et negligences envers les enfants et les adolescents dans les institutions. *Child Abuse Negl* 8:319–335, 1984.

53. Schiff AF: Attending the child "rape" victim. *South Med J* 72:906–910, 1979.

54. Dorst JP: Child abuse. *Radiologe (Berlin)* 22:335–341, 1982.

55. Black CT, Pokorny WJ, McGill CW, Harberg FJ: Ano-rectal trauma in children. *J Pediatr Surg* 17:501–504, 1982.

56. Kempe C, Helfer RE: Incest and other forms of sexual abuse. In *The Battered Child*. ed 3. Chicago, University of Chicago Press, 1980, pp 198–211.

57. Myers JEB: Role of physician in preserving verbal evidence of child abuse. *J Pediatr* 109:409–411, 1986.

10 The Postmortem Examination

PAUL K. KLEINMAN, M.D.

Radiology plays an important role in the investigation of suspected homicide in infants and children (1–9). Although most forensic experts on the subject recognize the vital role of radiology in supporting a determination of fatal child abuse, in practice there is great variation in the type of radiographic examinations performed. Cameron, a pathologist with a special interest in child abuse, has advocated complete skeletal surveys with coned-down views of any areas in question (4). In reality, most postmortem radiologic evaluations fall short of this mark; these unfortunate practices can be explained by a variety of factors.

First, In the United States, a significant number of death investigations are carried out by politically appointed lay-coroners. Most medical examiner offices are underfinanced and understaffed, with workloads that may reach staggering proportions. In 1972, it was estimated that the quality of death investigation in 80% of cases lagged 200 years behind that of other civilized countries (10). Considering this state of affairs, it is difficult to imagine any consistency in the quality of postmortem radiography in cases of suspected child abuse. An outmoded x-ray machine using outdated x-ray film with warped, dirty screens, developed by hand in chemicals maintained at improper temperatures will provide images that in the best of hands may be nondiagnostic.

Second, because an infant's body may fit "neatly" onto a 14 × 17 inch x-ray film, it is still common practice to attempt to encompass the entire skeleton on one or two radiographs. The resultant images are degraded by under- and overexposure, distortion due to poor geometry, and scatter. Improper positioning due to rotation and inadequate extension of bony articulations further limit the final product.

Third, in general, when antimortem radiographs are obtained, they are not initially reviewed by pediatric radiologists. As radiology should direct the pathologist to regions of skeletal abnormality, failure to identify these findings leads to the loss of potentially incriminating material. Once the body has been transferred to the funeral home or buried, the process becomes complicated by a variety of factors.

Finally, optimal investigation of infant death requires a close working relationship between the medical examiner and the pediatric radiologist. Constraints imposed by physical factors, time, money, professional bias, and sheer ignorance have resulted in little progress in the postmortem investigation of suspected child abuse. Even when sufficient resources are available, and forensic pathologists and pediatric radiologists have a close working relationship, distinguishing homicide from accidental or "natural" death may be extremely difficult. The investigation should be performed with a strict protocol in a professional and scientific manner. Although the process may supply forensic evidence to support a determination of homicide, it should also be viewed as one that may provide consolation to the parents who have lost a child to an illness, accident, or the sudden infant death syndrome (SIDS).

The Examination

It is clear from the foregoing discussion that the postmortem examination and analysis of the radiologic studies should be performed by individuals familiar with pediatric pathology. Physicians with minimal experience in this area should be willing to seek the advice of authorities more knowledgeable in the field. Studies of suspected cases of SIDS or possible infant homicide are best carried out in centers not only accustomed to dealing with pediatric pathology, but also familiar with the interpersonal, political, and legal aspects of these difficult problems. To ensure the highest quality radiologic studies, the skeletal surveys are best performed during routine working hours. Ideally a technician trained in pediatric radiography should perform the study. However, when studies are carried out on weekends, or if a pediatric technician is not available, a protocol outlining standard film sequences and techniques should be available to the technical staff. Many radiologists find it more convenient to bring the body to the x-ray department and obtain the necessary examinations in a standard x-ray room. This is the preferred approach if equipment in the morgue is inadequate. However, excellent films can be obtained with commonly available portable equipment if simple measures are taken.

1. A modest portable x-ray unit will usually provide adequate exposure to obtain quality radiographs in infants and small children. As the time of the exposure and dose administered are not considerations, techniques can be adjusted to obtain the best exposure.
2. Regular-speed film–screen combinations will provide finer detail than low dose rare earth systems employed clinically. Direct exposure of film packaged in cardboard envelopes can be utilized to film the extremities.
3. Care should be taken to avoid expired film, and the film cassettes should be cleaned regularly, a practice that will minimize film artifact.
4. If an automatic processor is utilized, developer and fixer should be changed regularly and the temperature should be maintained at a correct level. Although hand developing, if properly performed, will provide excellent film processing, it is cumbersome, time consuming, and susceptible to processing artifact.
5. All radiology departments have some form of quality control, and this monitoring should extend to the radiographic equipment in the morgue.

RADIOLOGIC STUDIES

The radiologist should be apprised of the circumstances surrounding the patient's death, and should review the medical record when available. A careful review of available radiographs should be carried out. Ideally, the hospitalized patient should have undergone a skeletal survey and perhaps other diagnostic studies prior to death. These films may be sufficient, and if no evidence of injury is present no further studies preceding the autopsy are necessary. However, if the antemortem films are at all limited in quality, or if they were obtained more than 5 days before death, postmortem films are indicated. Areas of definite or suspected abnormality not fully assessed on antemortem films should be reevaluated prior to autopsy. Performance of the "babygram" is to be condemned, and a protocol similar to that performed in antemortem skeletal surveys (see Table 2.4) should be utilized. Although radiographic studies can be performed following the autopsy, serious artifacts can be produced in the thorax, abdomen, spine, and skull, and thus filming prior to autopsy is preferable. Additionally, if radiographic abnormalities are identified following the autopsy, the pathologist may have to return to the site to remove those bony areas in question. A similar problem arises if the radiologist reviews the films after the body has been released to the funeral home or buried. Obtaining the pathologic material at this point may be difficult, and is impossible in cases of cremation.

THE INFANT POSTMORTEM EXAMINATION

Postmortem radiologic evaluation is particularly important in infants. The extent of

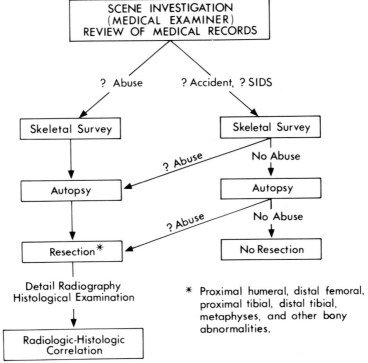

Figure 10.1. Decision tree for the evaluation of unexplained infant death.

the radiologic studies will depend upon the circumstances surrounding the death, and the radiologic findings may in turn direct the pathologist to special areas of interest (see Fig. 10.1). In contrast to older children, in whom most traumatic injuries are either evident clinically or revealed by a thorough history and review of medical records, traumatic injuries are frequently occult and unexpected in the abused infant. In older children who die unexpectedly, the principle diagnostic considerations are accidental injury, overwhelming sudden illness, and homicide. In infants, SIDS or crib death is usually a major differential diagnosis.

SUDDEN INFANT DEATH SYNDROME

The typical infant dying of SIDS is between 1 and 4 months of age, a common age for infant abuse. Characteristically, the child is placed in its crib following feeding and is subsequently found dead. A paucity of pathologic findings is encountered (11). There may be subacute inflammation of the tracheobronchial mucosa. Petechiae are usually present on the visceral pleura and in the greater fissures as well as the epicardium and thymus. Examination of the central nervous system is usually unrevealing.

SIDS is a common form of infant death, accounting for approximately 100 cases per year in the commonwealth of Massachusetts. Although the diagnosis can be strongly suspected based upon the history provided by the family, the diagnosis cannot be certified without a complete investigation at the scene and a thorough postmortem examination (10). A variety of studies have shown that child abuse can simulate SIDS or "near miss" SIDS, and they stress the importance of a thorough investigation (12–19). The sudden unexpected death of an infant is a tremendous tragedy and creates a great sense of loss within the family. A National Foundation for Sudden Infant Death Society exists and, among other activities, supports the grieving families of these infants. As with other aspects of the investigation and autopsy, the radiologic studies should be performed according to a standard protocol, and the results should be included in the final medical examiner's report. Discussing the autopsy findings with the grieving parents may ease the pain of the tragic experience (10).

REMOVAL OF SPECIMENS

Removal of postmortem skeletal material must be performed with the utmost care to preserve damaged tissues and prevent artifact. The specimen should be removed in a manner that will allow optimal delineation of the lesions pathologically, as well as provide correlation with the radiologic abnormalities. Resection technique will also vary depending upon the anatomic site of interest.

Metaphyses

In most cases of infant homicide, resection of the metaphyses will yield the greatest number of abnormalities. Specimens removed should include all those regions demonstrating suspected or definite radiologic alterations. In addition, a variety of metaphyses are injured with sufficient frequency in abused infants that routine resection should be performed in selected cases, even in the absence of radiologically demonstrable abnormality. These regions include the distal femurs, proximal tibias, distal tibias, and proximal humeri. Ideally, the bone should be sectioned completely across its long axis, and the metaphysis, physis, and epiphysis should be entirely removed (Fig. 10.2). This may result in some visual deformity of the body, and an alternative approach entailing a hemisection of these same regions may be chosen. This latter technique entails sawing through the long axis of the end of the bone in either a sagittal or coronal plane, followed by a transverse cut that meets the first plane of division. In essence the end of the bone is bivalved, and the resultant specimen consists of half the metaphyseal-epiphyseal region with a cut edge in either the coronal or sagittal plane (Fig. 10.3). The choice of a sagittal or coronal division is based upon the radiologic appearance.

Other Regions

Other regions will generally lend themselves to an en bloc resection. Posterior rib fractures should be removed along with the ipsilateral vertebral elements. Portions of the scapula, especially the acromion, the sternum, the spinous processes, and long bone fractures, should be removed to include all regions demonstrated to be abnormal radiographically. Care should be taken to avoid separation of any adjacent cartilaginous elements. In cases of vertebral injury the spine can be divided in a midsagittal plane, and a hemisection, including normal vertebra above and below the fracture, should be removed.

Specimens should immediately be placed in formalin, and specimen radiography can be performed at any time prior to decalcification.

SPECIMEN RADIOGRAPHY

Most of the specimens are relatively small and lend themselves well to high-resolution radiography. Direct exposure of industrial-type film provides the best anatomic resolution; however, this type of film and the necessary special processing facilities are generally not available to most radiology departments. "Cardboard" cassettes containing relatively slow film designed for direct exposure are available commercially, and can be developed in standard automatic processors. At the University of Massachusetts a system is utilized that was originally designed for mammographic procedures. Spatial and contrast resolution are comparable to direct exposure film. Exposure should be obtained with a small focal spot and low kilovoltage technique. Specimens should be examined in at least two projections. Metaphyseal lesions are often quite subtle, and it may be necessary to tip the lesion into several obliquities to obtain an image that best documents the anatomic alterations (Fig. 10.2C). If a film–screen combination is utilized, the film cassettes should be free of debris because a relatively minute foreign particle can produce a major artifact on these relatively small images.

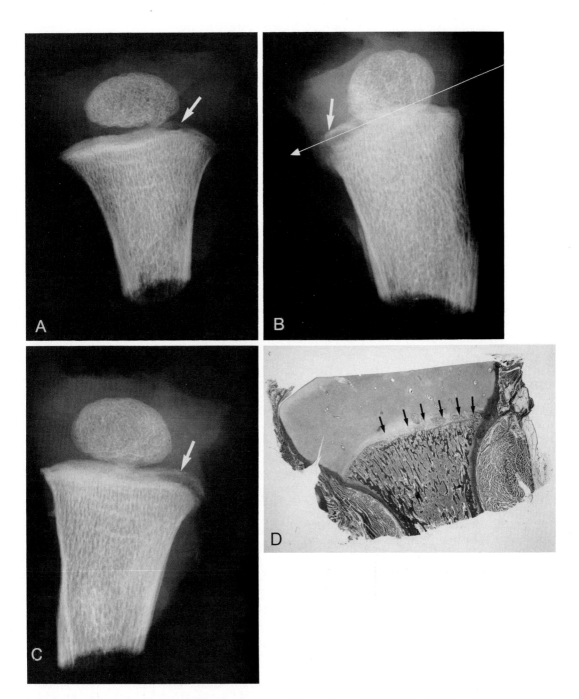

Figure 10.2. Proximal tibial metaphyseal injury in an abused infant. *A,* AP view of postmortem specimen reveals a questionable metaphyseal fragment (*arrow*). *B,* A lateral projection shows the lesion (*short arrow*) to be posteriorly situated. Based upon the location of the fragment, an angulated AP projection can be deyised (*long arrow*) that will optimally image the fragment. *C,* The resultant angle AP image reveals a typical "bucket-handle" lesion (*arrow*). *D,* Histologic sectioning in the AP plane provides excellent correlation with radiographs. Note fracture (*arrows*).

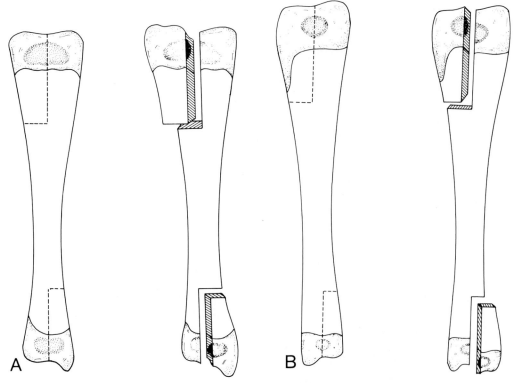

Figure 10.3. Hemisectional removal of tibial metaphyses. *A,* Frontal view. Proximal and distal metaphyseal-epiphyseal specimens are removed by sagittal sectioning. *B,* Lateral view. Proximal and distal metaphyseal specimens are removed by coronal sectioning.

HISTOLOGICAL PREPARATION

Once specimens have been fixed in formalin and decalcified, the specimens should be sectioned in a plane based upon any radiologically demonstrable abnormalities (see Figs. 2.8 and 2.11). In the case of bucket-handle lesions, histologic sections performed coronally in the same plane as the resection will provide exquisite correlation with the radiologic abnormalities (Fig. 10.2D). In some cases, it may be elected to section the specimen at a plane other than that utilized in the radiographic projection, to maximally define anatomic alterations. This is the case in instances of posterior rib fracture, where an axial histologic plane should be utilized (see Fig. 4.3). This will delineate the relationship of the tubercle and head of the rib to the transverse process and vertebral body, respectively. This relationship is important in understanding the pathogenesis of posterior rib fractures (see Chapter 4). In general, histologic sections should be made through the long axis of the bone to display the metaphyseal-epiphyseal relationships. Vertebral body and spinous process fractures are best sectioned in a sagittal plane (Fig. 10.4).

Staining with hematoxylin and eosin is generally sufficient, although special stains for connective tissue and iron may be utilized in certain cases. It must be emphasized that histologic preparation of skeletal material is difficult and requires considerable technical expertise. This is especially true with fragile infant bones containing both osseous and cartilaginous material. It is easy for inexperienced or careless technical personnel to irretrievably damage a potentially critical specimen. If trained technologists are not available at the site of autopsy, the material should be sent to a facility where sufficient technical expertise can be found.

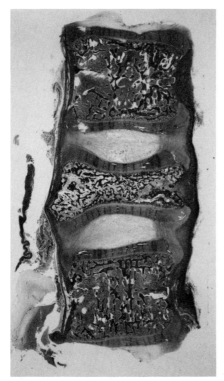

Figure 10.4. Low-power sagittal photomicrograph of the middorsal spine of an abused infant reveals a healing compression fracture.

Radiologic-Pathologic Correlation

After all material has been processed, the pediatric radiologist and pathologist should jointly review the findings. Skeletal pathology, particularly in the growing infant, is a demanding field, and the pathologist should be well versed in this area. Artifacts of preparation produce confusing histologic findings that can be interpreted as abnormalities by the inexperienced microscopist.

All sections should be carefully reviewed. It is essential that multiple serial sections of each specimen be obtained, because abnormalities may be relatively localized. A correlation of the histologic abnormalities with the radiographic changes will often allow the construction of a three dimensional image of the morphologic alteration. In cases of localized injury, the radiograph may point the pathologist to the particular area of interest on the histologic section. In cases in which definite radiologic abnormality is present, and no histologic changes are seen, it will be necessary to obtain further deeper sections through the paraffin block of material. Instituting these procedures will require closer cooperation between the radiologist and the medical examiner, but the likelihood of enhanced detection of infant homicide demands this enlightened approach.

REFERENCES

1. Knight B: How radiography aids forensic medicine. *Radiography* 50:5–10, 1984.
2. Kanda M, Thomas JN, Lloyd DW: The role of forensic evidence in child abuse and neglect. *Am J Forensic Med Pathol* 6:7–15, 1985.
3. Wecht CH, Larkin GM: The battered child syndrome — a forensic pathologist's viewpoint. *Med Trial Tech Q* 28:1–24, 1981.
4. Cameron JM, Rae L: The radiological diagnosis. In: *Atlas of the Battered Child Syndrome*. London, Churchill Livingstone, 1975, pp 20–50.
5. Gee DJ: Radiology in forensic pathology. *Radiography* 41:109–114, 1975.
6. Kerley ER: The identification of battered-infant skeletons. *J Forensic Sci* 23:163–168, 1978.
7. Adelson L: The fatally abused child — infanticide and the lethal maltreatment syndrome ("battered children"). In *The Pathology of Homicide*. Springfield, IL, Charles C Thomas, 1974, pp 617–662.
8. Fatteh AV, Mann GT: The role of radiology in forensic pathology. *Med Sci Law* 9:27–30, 1969.
9. Norman MG, Smialek JE, Newman DE, Horembala EJ: The postmortem examination on the abused child. Pathological, radiographic, and legal aspects. *Perspect Pediatr Pathol* 8:313–343, 1984.
10. Helpern M, Rupp JC, Bornstein FP, Curran WJ: Medical examiners and infant deaths. Letters to the editor. *N Engl J Med* 287:1050–1052, 1972.
11. Valdes-Dapena: The pathologist and the sudden infant death syndrome. *Am J Pathol* 106:118, 1982.
12. Christoffel KK, Zieserl EJ, Chiaramonte J: Should child abuse and neglect be considered when a child dies unexpectedly? *Am J Public Health* 139:876–880, 1985.
13. Berger D: Child abuse simulating "near-miss" sudden infant death syndrome. *J Pediatr* 95:554–556, 1979.
14. Morris B: Child abuse manifested as factitious apnea. *South Med J* 78:1013–1014, 1985.
15. Geelhold GC, Pemberton PJ: SIDS, seizures or 'sophageal reflux? Another manifestation of Munchausen syndrome by proxy. *Med J Aust* 143:357–358, 1985.
16. Hick JF: Sudden infant death syndrome and child abuse. *Pediatrics* 52:147–148, 1973.
17. Minford AMB: Child abuse presenting as apparent "near-miss" sudden infant death syndrome *Br Med J* 282:521, 1981.
18. Roberts J, Golding J, Keeling J, Sutton B, Lynch MA: Is there a link between cot death and child abuse? *Br Med J* (Clin Res) 289:789–791, 1984.
19. Bass M, Kravath RE, Glass L: Death-scene investigation in sudden infant death. *N Engl J Med* 315:100–105, 1986.

11 Differential Diagnosis of Child Abuse

PAULA W. BRILL, M.D.
PATRICIA WINCHESTER, M.D.

The differential diagnosis of the skeletal lesions of child abuse includes a variety of conditions causing fractures, periosteal reaction, irregular metaphyses, or cone-shaped epiphyses alone or in combination (Table 11.1). In some conditions associated radiologic findings allow differentiation from abuse. In others extraskeletal nonradiologic manifestations of the disease provide the diagnostic clues. Abnormalities of the long bones and ribs will be considered in this chapter. The spine and skull are discussed in Chapters 5 and 8, respectively.

Normal Variants

Periosteal new bone formation along the shafts of the long bones, and spurring and cupping of the metaphyses are frequently found in healthy infants during the early months of life (1). These findings, first seen at 2 to 3 months, usually resolve by 8 months of age. The periosteal new bone formation is identical to that seen in trauma, whereas the metaphyseal changes differ from trauma in the absence of bony fragments.

There are numerous normal variants that can simulate small fractures at many sites. The diagnosis of abuse may be erroneously considered when these are misinterpreted as pathologic. The reader is referred to *Caffey's Pediatric X-Ray Diagnosis* for illustrations and discussions of the various pseudofractures (2, pp 416–477).

Birth Trauma

When infants are seen with fractures during the early weeks of life, birth trauma must be considered as a possible cause. Clavicle fractures are by far the most frequent and are often missed in the delivery room and nursery (Fig. 11.1). Healing clavicle fractures due to birth injury are often found incidentally on chest radiographs done for other purposes. The parents are usually unaware of the fracture. Sometimes the hard swelling of callus formation around an undetected clavicular birth fracture brings the child to medical attention. Both of these presentations are common, and neither is suspicious.

The humerus is the most frequently fractured long bone in birth injury (3, 4). The fracture is usually in the midshaft. Fractures of the shafts of lower extremities from birth trauma are usually associated with an underlying neuromuscular or bone disease.

Traumatic dislocations probably do not occur at birth, and bony displacements suggesting dislocation are actually due to fractures through the region of the growth plate (5) (Fig. 11.2). A metaphyseal fragment resembling the corner fracture of child abuse may or may not be present. Most epiphyseal injuries are associated with breech delivery, and because the incidence of breech delivery has decreased in recent years, this type of birth injury has become rare. Most infants with epiphyseal plate fractures are symptomatic, and although establishment of the correct diagnosis is often delayed, swelling

Table 11.1
Differential Diagnosis of Skeletal Lesions in Children

Disease	Shaft fracture	Periosteal reaction	Metaphy-seal irregularity	Generalized osteopenia	Comments
Child abuse	+	+	+	−	
Birth trauma	+	+/−	+/−	−	Clavicle and humerus most frequent fractures
Congenital indifference to pain	+	+	+	−	Normal neurologic exam except for lack of pain and occasional temperature sensation
Myelodysplasia	+	+	+	−	Spinal dysraphism
Osteogenesis imperfecta	+	−	+/−	++	Wormian bones, blue sclerae, dentinogenesis imperfecta
Osteomyelitis	−	+	+	−	Often multifocal in infancy
Congenital syphilis	−	+	+	−	
Rickets	+	+	+	+	Stress fractures
Scurvy	−	+	+	++	
Vitamin A intoxication	−	+	−	−	Increased intracranial pressure
Caffey's disease	−	++	−	−	Mandible usually involved
Leukemia	−	+	−	+	Bone changes extremely variable
Prostaglandin E$_1$ therapy	−	+	−	−	
Methotrexate therapy	+	−	+/−	++	Unlikely to occur with current regimens
Menkes' syndrome	−	+	+	+/−	Wormian bones, low serum copper, bladder diverticula, tortuous vessels

and/or lack of movement of the affected parts are usually appreciated in the immediate neonatal period.

Fractures at birth have been noted to develop callus within 2 weeks (3, 5). Usually callus is evident within a few days (4). Absence of callus at the site of a fracture after the age of 2 weeks is strong presumptive evidence that the fracture did not occur during delivery.

Rib fractures due to birth trauma are rare (6). They are seldom detected at the time of their occurrence and are seen weeks later as callus becomes palpable, a presentation similar to the more frequent clavicle fracture. When bones are normally mineralized, rib fractures found incidentally on a chest radiograph without a plausible history of severe direct trauma are usually due to abuse.

After inflicted thoracic trauma the victim is often brought to the emergency room with a history of having received cardiopulmonary resuscitation (CPR) following an apneic episode. When rib fractures are found, the medical staff may mistakenly accept them as the consequence of CPR. Although CPR has been associated with rib fractures in adults, fractures of normally mineralized ribs of children are rarely, if ever, a result of CPR (6, 7).

Congenital Indifference to Pain

A rare syndrome inherited as an autosomal recessive trait, congenital indifference to pain is associated with lesions that mimic skeletal trauma of child abuse. Affected children have normal intelligence, and their neurologic examinations are normal except for insensitivity or indifference to painful

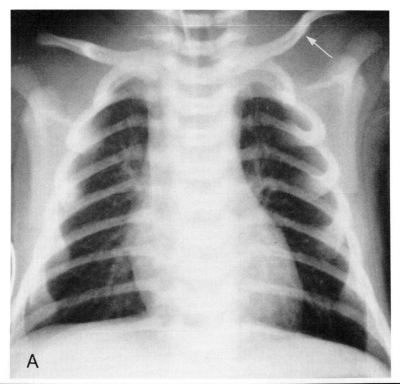

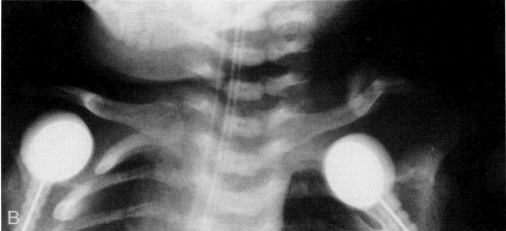

Figure 11.1. Birth trauma: left clavicular fracture. *A*, 3700-g infant born by vaginal delivery. There is a very subtle nondisplaced fracture of the clavicle (*arrow*). *B*, At 12 days of age dense callus is clearly seen at the fracture site.

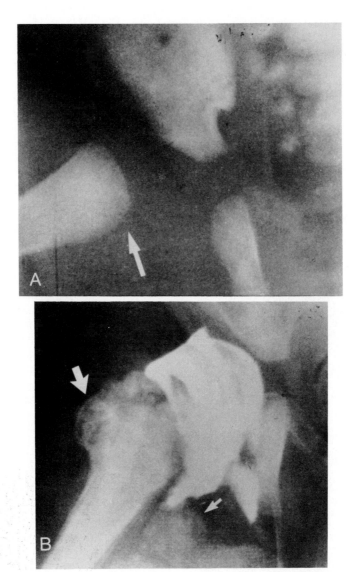

Figure 11.2. Birth trauma—Salter Type I: fracture of proximal femur. *A,* Frog-lateral view of the right hip of a neonate reveals superolateral displacement of the femur (*arrow*). *B,* An arthrogram performed 3 weeks later demonstrates superolateral displacement of the femoral neck with respect to the normally seated head. There is early callus formation (*large arrow*) and inferomedial extravasation of contrast (*small arrow*). (Reproduced with permission from Ogden JA, Lee KE, Rudicel SA, Pelker RR: Proximal femoral epiphysiolysis in the neonate. *J Pediatr Orthop* 4:285–292, 1984.)

stimuli. Light and deep touch and proprioception sensations are normal, although temperature perception is diminished in a few affected patients. Because of the lack of pain, both minor and major trauma to the growing skeleton may go undetected until marked deformity is present. Repeated unrecognized injuries to the growth plate lead to epiphyseal slips and nonunion. Radiographs of an affected area may show fractures and epiphyseal separations in various stages of repair. In addition to ordinary fractures, metaphyseal injuries are common during early childhood (8). Metaphyseal chronic osteomyelitis is also frequent during childhood, perhaps because of the increased incidence of skin infections secondary to the multiple burns and lacerations that these children incur. Aseptic necrosis in weight-bearing joints and osteochondritis are common (9) (Fig. 11.3). By adolescence, repeated

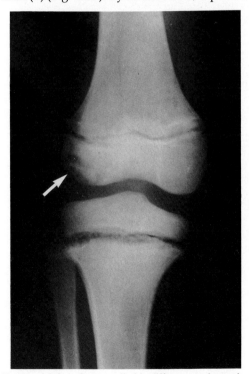

Figure 11.3. Congenital indifference to pain. Frontal film of the knee of a 9-year-old boy. The epiphyseal plates, especially the tibial, are widened. There is irregularity on the metaphyseal side of the tibial growth plate. Aseptic necrosis is present in the lateral femoral condyle (*arrow*).

malposition secondary to microtrauma to the pain-insensitive joint can result in neuropathic arthropathy. Radiographically the bony changes are at times difficult to distinguish from those of child abuse. Careful sensory neurologic examination and clinical history are necessary to establish the diagnosis of congenital indifference to pain.

Myelodysplasia and Associated Bone Trauma

Lumbosacral spinal dysraphism associated with underlying spinal cord and nerve root abnormalities results in sensory loss in the lower extremities and varying degrees of paralysis. In severe motor involvement muscle contractures may develop in infancy so that diapering and routine handling result in shaft fractures (Fig. 11.4). These fractures may go undetected unless marked displacement is present or callus is palpated (10).

In older children without total paralysis, ambulation is encouraged. Braces and crutches contribute to abnormal stress at the joint, the growth plate, and the metaphysis resulting in Salter epiphyseal plate fractures (see Chapter 2). Repeated minor trauma leads to metaphyseal infraction, periosteal separation, and hemorrhage into the growth plate (11). The metaphyses become dense and irregular, the growth plate appears wide, and periosteal reaction is visible during healing (Fig. 11.5). Similar epiphyseal-metaphyseal injuries occur in myelodysplastic infants undergoing vigorous physical therapy for contractures. Although progression to Charcot's arthropathy is a potential complication, complete healing is possible. Since these bone changes occur in the lower extremities in children with known spinal dysraphism, the differentiation from child abuse is simple.

Osteogenesis Imperfecta

The basic defect in osteogenesis imperfecta is an abnormality in the molecular structure of collagen. The disease has been

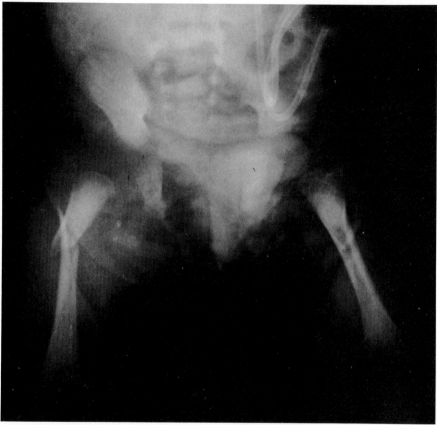

Figure 11.4. Myelodysplasia. Frontal film of the pelvis and femurs of a 12-month-old infant. There is an angulated fracture of the right femoral shaft with marked deep soft tissue swelling. Ventriculoperitoneal shunt tubing is seen in the left lower abdomen. The pedicles in the sacrum and lower lumbar spine are widely spaced, and the spinous processes are absent.

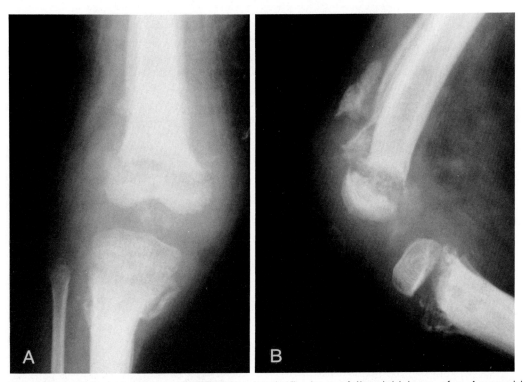

Figure 11.5. Myelodysplasia. AP (A) and lateral (B) views of the right knee of a 4-year-old myelodysplastic patient reveal fragmentation, sclerosis, and irregularity of the metaphyseal-epiphyseal regions. The growth plates are widened, and extensive periosteal new bone formation is present involving the femur and tibia.

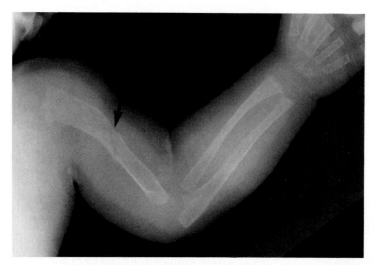

Figure 11.6. Osteogenesis imperfecta. Upper extremity of an 8-month-old infant with generalized osteopenia. There is a fracture through the midshaft of the humerus (*arrow*). Expansion and lateral bowing of the proximal humerus are due to previous healed fractures.

classified into four major clinical types with multiple fractures a major feature in most cases. Extraskeletal manifestations, age of onset of fractures, and mode of inheritance vary in the different types (12). Types 1, 3, and 4 enter into the differential diagnosis of child abuse.

Type 1 disease was previously classified as osteogenesis imperfecta tarda and is inherited as an autosomal dominant. Patients have blue sclerae, and some have dentinogenesis imperfecta. Fractures start in infancy or later childhood (Figs. 11.6 and 11.7). Infants have multiple wormian bones in the skull. There may be a family history of deafness due to otosclerosis.

Type 2, the lethal perinatal form, is characterized by multiple fractures, severe dwarfism, and blue sclerae. The femurs are short, thick, and "crumpled." Inheritance is autosomal recessive.

In Type 3 the bones may not appear deformed early in life, but there is cortical thinning and a tendency to fracture. Bowing deformities after healing are more marked than with Type 1. The sclerae are blue in infancy and usually become normal by adolescence; dentinogenesis imperfecta is common. Inheritance is heterogeneous; both dominant and recessive patterns have been observed in different families.

Type 4 patients have osteoporosis with or without fractures. At the time of the first

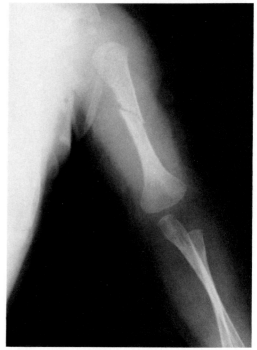

Figure 11.7. Osteogenesis imperfecta. Frontal film of the left arm of a 5-day-old infant shows a midshaft fracture of the humerus. The cortex is thin for a full-term infant, indicative of generalized osteoporosis.

fracture, osteoporosis may not yet be evident. The sclerae are not blue. Inheritance is autosomal dominant.

Fractures usually involve the shafts of

long bones, but metaphyseal fractures resembling those of child abuse have been reported. Astley described seven patients ages 1 day to 3 years who had osteogenesis imperfecta with metaphyseal fractures, usually of the upper extremities (13). There was no confusion with child abuse because of the presence of obvious osteoporosis and wormian bones.

Easy bruisability is frequent in osteogenesis imperfecta, and when seen in combination with fractures, the diagnosis of child abuse is often considered. Generally osteogenesis imperfecta can be easily distinguished from child abuse by the presence of blue sclerae, osteopenia, thin cortices, and the tendency to bowing and angulation of healed fractures. In infancy, however, osteopenia may not be apparent, and healing may be normal. In such instances the differential diagnosis can often be resolved if there are associated extraskeletal manifestations such as blue sclerae or dentinogenesis imperfecta, or if affected family members can be identified.

Osteomyelitis

Osteomyelitis in young infants may cause multifocal metaphyseal lesions with periosteal reaction. Systemic signs and symptoms are often lacking, and even local signs may be minimal when the patient is first examined. Metaphyseal lucencies tend to be less well defined than in abuse, and corner fractures are not present. The radionuclide bone scan usually shows increased uptake at affected sites in both conditions.

Fracture through the growth plate may be caused by trauma, or may occur as a complication of metaphyseal osteomyelitis (Fig. 11.8). At the onset of osteomyelitis bone destruction is not visible radiographically, and the distinction from traumatic fracture must be made on clinical grounds. With time the bone destruction of osteomyelitis or the simple callus of trauma becomes obvious.

In infantile meningococcemia, septic emboli to epiphyseal vessels may damage the growth plate at multiple sites (14). Although the lesion at the growth plate is not usually recognized during the acute illness, short-ening of the affected limbs becomes evident months or years later. The most striking lesion is a central epiphyseal fusion resulting in a cone-shaped or ball-in-socket epiphysis (Fig. 11.9). There is no osteopenia. Identical late lesions can result from trauma, accidental or intentional. Differentiation from abuse is made on the basis of the history of meningococcemia in early infancy.

Congenital Syphilis

Syphilitic infection of the infant's skeleton is diffuse and can involve the long bones, the skull, and even the small bones of the hands and feet in severe cases. Lesions in the spine have not been described. The distribution is irregular. The tibia, femur, and humerus are the bones most often involved.

The spirochetes cross the placenta and are implanted in the fetal tissue. Destructive and productive changes of osteomyelitis are seen in the metaphyses and diaphyses after birth, most commonly between the first and sixth month of life. The epiphyseal ossification centers are spared. Syphilitic granulation tissue is found in the areas of destruction, but, in addition, nonspecific trophic changes are frequently present in the metaphyses soon after birth. Bands of decreased density are seen parallel to the epiphyseal growth plate in the long bones. Productive diaphysitis is frequent, involving a portion of or the entire length of a long bone (2, pp 835–841).

The destructive lesions in the metaphyses vary in degree from small corner rarefactions to deep zones of diminished density to large defects that also involve the cortex. A medial tibial metadiaphyseal defect is referred to as the Wimberger sign. Similar lytic lesions can be seen at the same location in severe bacterial osteomyelitis.

Pathologic fractures in the infected metaphyses are not unusual and mimic the skeletal findings of the abused child (15, 16) (Fig. 11.10). Periosteal reaction is also not specific for congenital syphilis and can be confused with healing trauma. The serologic test for syphilis is most helpful in confirming the diagnosis of congenital lues.

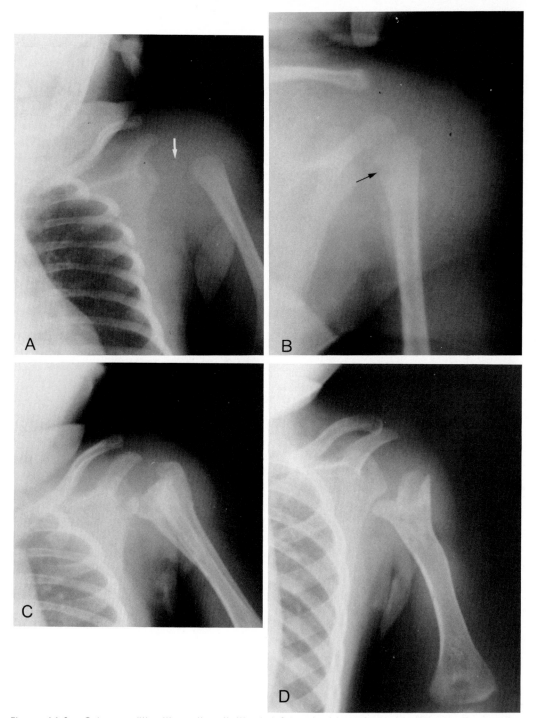

Figure 11.8. Osteomyelitis with septic arthritis. *A,* A 3-week-old previously healthy infant presented with the acute onset of swelling of the shoulder. The joint capsule is distended, causing lateral displacement of the humeral head (*arrow*). In addition, there is lateral displacement of the shaft from the head as a result of a fracture through the growth plate. *B,* Four days later, following aspiration of the joint, the shaft is no longer displaced. The ossification center of the humeral head is no longer visible, because of either destruction by lytic pus or demineralization secondary to hyperemia. Lytic areas are present in the metaphysis (*arrow*). Periosteal new bone cloaks the proximal shaft and is also present along the axillary border of the scapula. The metaphyseal destructive lesions distinguish osteomyelitis from child abuse. *C,* Changes of healing are evident 1 month later during treatment with intravenous antibiotics. Exuberant dense periosteal reaction (involucrum) surrounds the proximal and midhumeral shaft (sequestrum). The periosteal reaction along the scapula has become better defined as healing progresses. *D,* Six months later there is complete healing of the infection with severe residual deformity. The humeral head has been completely destroyed and the shaft is inferiorly and medially displaced. The metaphysis is wide,

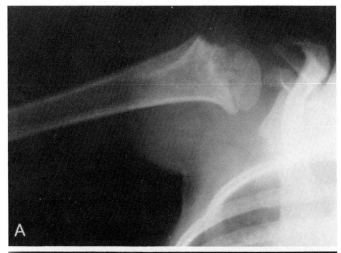

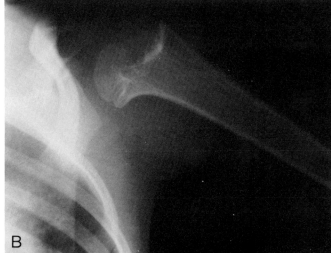

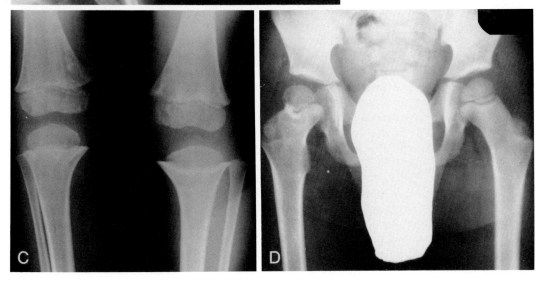

Figure 11.9. Late sequelae of infantile meningococcemia. Films obtained at 3 years of age because of gait disturbance; history of meningococcemia at 11 months. The spectrum of the multifocal growth disturbance is illustrated in radiographs of the right (*A*) and left (*B*) shoulders, knees (*C*), and hips (*D*). There is partial fusion of the growth plates in both humeri, the proximal right femur, and the proximal left tibia. The characteristic coned epiphyseal deformity is best seen in the left tibia and right proximal femur. There are ossification defects in the diametaphyseal region of the knees and right femoral neck. There is marked shortening of the right femoral neck. Only the left hip is normal. (Courtesy of J. Sarfraz, Walton, New York.)

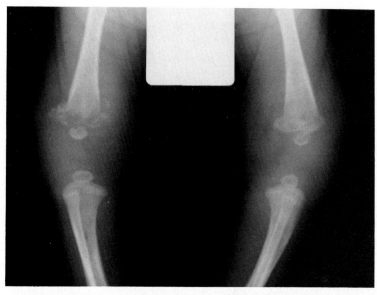

Figure 11.10. Congenital syphilis. Frontal film of the lower extremities of 2-week-old infant. The distal femoral metaphyses appear fragmented, indicating pathologic fractures in areas of infection. Periosteal new bone formation is seen along the lateral aspects of both distal femurs.

Rickets

Metaphyseal irregularity, fractures, and periosteal reaction are seen in both rickets and child abuse. The earliest lesion of rickets in young infants consists of cupping and fraying of the costochondral junctions and long bone metaphyses. In the long bones the zone of provisional calcification (ZPC), normally sharply defined, becomes indistinct. After a few weeks decreased bone density and cortical thinning become apparent. The distance between the epiphysis and shaft of the long bone increases not because of a true separation of these structures, but because the bone continues to grow by deposition of uncalcified osteoid (Fig. 11.11). At this stage there is little resemblance to the lesions of child abuse, but as healing takes place mineralization in the zone of provisional calcification, separated by radiolucent osteoid from the main shaft, may be mistaken for fracture. In rickets, accompanying signs such as decreased bone density and poor definition of epiphyses and round bones should allow differentiation from child abuse. Both healing rickets and trauma may cause periosteal new bone formation. As with the metaphyseal lesions, a search

for other radiographic signs of rickets allows differentiation from traumatic periostitis. Fractures of long bone shafts resembling those of accidental trauma may occur with both rickets and child abuse, but the sharply defined symmetrical transverse stress fractures or "Looser's zones" in the shafts of long bones are seen in rickets or other osteomalacic conditions and not with child abuse.

The premature infant receiving total parenteral nutrition is especially susceptible to rickets, probably because of the inability to provide adequate calcium and phosphorus by the intravenous route (17, 18) (Fig. 11.12). In this setting multiple fractures of ribs and long bones are more apparent than metaphyseal irregularities. The diagnosis of child abuse is not a serious differential consideration when the fractures are noted while the patient is under close observation in the neonatal intensive care unit. However, diagnostic difficulties can occur if fractures are first observed after the premature infant has been discharged.

Although complete healing is the rule after rickets, distortion and sclerosis of the affected spongiosa may persist for years, and occasionally there are residual deform-

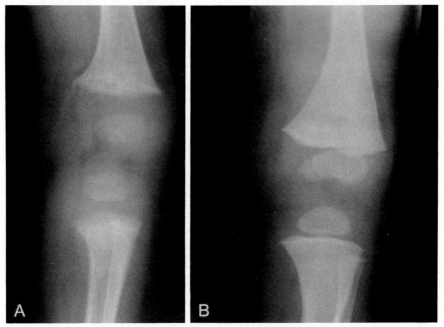

Figure 11.11. Rickets. *A,* Frontal film of the knee of an 18-month-old boy who had been fed only powdered skim milk without vitamin D supplementation since age 2 weeks. The bones are demineralized. The distance between the epiphysis and shaft of the distal femur and proximal tibia is increased. The metaphyses are frayed. *B,* After 3 months of treatment with vitamin D there is almost complete healing. Note the close approximation of the epiphyses to their adjacent metaphyses.

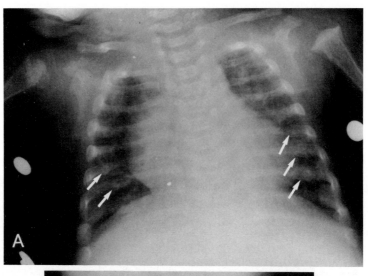

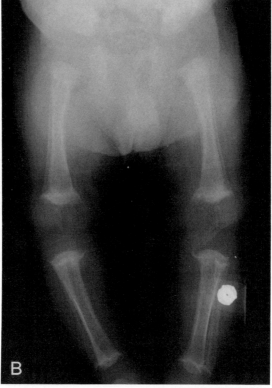

Figure 11.12. Rickets of prematurity. *A,* Chest radiograph of a 3-month-old former premature infant shows osteopenia and multiple healing posterior rib fractures (*arrows*). The metaphysis of the right humerus is irregular, and periosteal reaction is present along both humeral shafts. *B,* Lower extremities of same patient. Metaphyseal irregularity and osteopenia are seen in all the long bones. There is periosteal reaction along the femoral shafts.

ities from fractures. If old fracture deformities are found in a skeletal survey for child abuse, the significance will be altered if there is a well-documented history of rickets.

Scurvy

Scurvy is caused by insufficient ingestion of vitamin C. It is much rarer than rickets, and in the pediatric age group is found primarily in infants who receive pasteurized or boiled milk formulas without vitamin supplements. The onset is seldom before age 6 months.

Some of the radiographic changes are attributable to the suppression of normal cellular activity. Others result from a hemorrhagic tendency caused by deficient intracellular cement in capillary endothelium. There is normal deposition of calcium in the zone of provisional calcification , but the cortex and spongiosa become atrophic. Radiographs show relatively increased density of the zone of provisional calcification and the periphery of the epiphyseal ossification centers. The spongiosa just beneath the zone of provisional calcification is disorganized and appears abnormally radiolucent. Fractures occur through the zone of provisional calcification and the subjacent metaphysis. Subperiosteal and soft tissue hemorrhages are frequent and may be very large. They are most evident radiographically during the healing phase, when large calcific cloaks are seen along the shafts of the affected long bones (2, pp 674–678) (Fig. 11.13).

The metaphyseal changes of scurvy are very similar to those of child abuse. In scurvy, however, there are additional diagnostic clues. Bone atrophy, seen as thin cortices and osteopenia adjacent to the zone of provisional calcification and the central portion of the epiphyseal ossification centers, is a regular feature of scurvy. Similarly, the combination of sclerotic zone of provisional calcification and a dense ring around the epiphyseal bone is seen only in scurvy. In most abused infants general nutrition is adequate and bone mineralization is normal. Fractures of long bone shafts are fre-

quent in abuse and rare in scurvy. Damage to the growth plate during the acute phase of scurvy may result in a cone-shaped epiphysis and growth disturbance.

Vitamin A Intoxication

The early clinical findings of chronic hypervitaminosis A are nonspecific and include anorexia, irritability, and itching. Weeks to months after the onset of excessive administration of vitamin A, hard, tender swellings are found over the extremities, and the diagnosis of child abuse may be considered when radiographs show periosteal reaction in the underlying bone (Fig. 11.14A). The periosteal reaction is thick and undulating. Any tubular bone may be affected, but the ulnae and metatarsals are the most characteristic sites. Normal metaphyses and the absence of fractures help to distinguish hypervitaminosis A from child abuse. In acute vitamin A intoxication there is increased intracranial pressure causing widening of the cranial sutures (Fig. 11.14B).

Following cessation of vitamin A administration the cortical thickening resolves within several months. Despite the absence of a radiographically demonstrable epiphyseal or metaphyseal lesion during the clinical illness, late deformities have been documented. Enlargement and premature fusion of epiphyses may cause significant limb shortening that is usually asymmetrical.

In addition to the growth disturbance associated with vitamin A intoxication, meningococcemia, osteomyelitis, and scurvy described above, cone-shaped epiphyses may be seen in other conditions that are less likely to be confused with child abuse (19). These include sickle cell anemia, prolonged immobilization, achondroplasia, and osteopetrosis. In the digits cone-shaped epiphyses may be seen as normal variants.

Caffey's Disease

Caffey's disease (infantile cortical hyperostosis) is a rare disease of young infants in which painful periosteal reaction and cor-

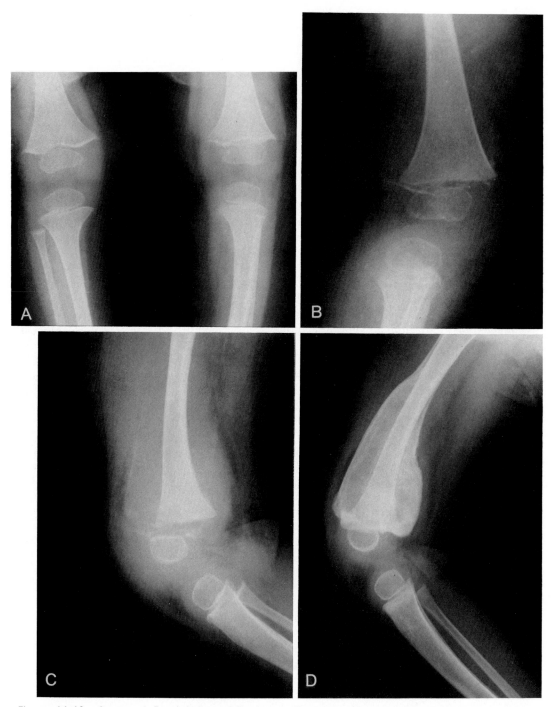

Figure 11.13. Scurvy. *A,* Frontal view of the knees. The zone of provisional calcification and the periphery of the epiphyses appear relatively dense compared with the adjacent demineralized bone. The cortices are thin. *B,* Oblique view of the left knee during vitamin C treatment 5 days later. There is a fracture separating the zone of provisional calcification from the metaphysis of the femur. *C,* Lateral view of the left knee 3 days after Figure 11.13*B.* With continued treatment peripheral calcification is seen in a subperiosteal hemorrhage along the anterior femoral shaft. The epiphysis is displaced anteriorly by the fracture through the zone of provisional calcification. *D,* Lateral view of the left knee 5 weeks after Figure 11.13*C.* The subperiosteal hemorrhage is densely calcified and cloaks the femoral shaft.

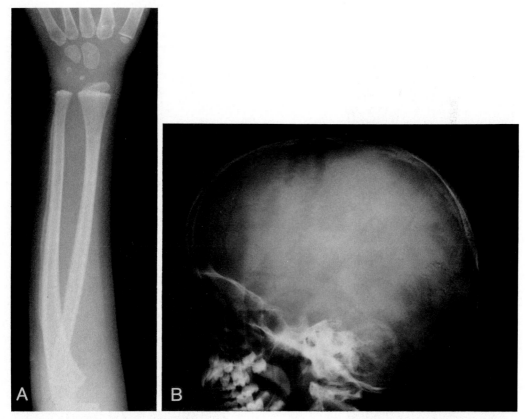

Figure 11.14. Vitamin A intoxication. *A,* Frontal view of the forearm of a 4-year-old boy. Periosteal reaction along the ulnar shaft is thick and undulating. *B,* Lateral view of the skull of the same patient. The widening of the coronal sutures reflects increased intracranial pressure.

tical thickening are found in multiple bones (2, pp 841–849). Its cause is unknown. Virtually all bones can be involved, but the mandible, clavicle, and ulna are the most frequently affected sites (Fig. 11.15). The mandible is involved in about 75% of cases. Onset after the age of 6 months is very rare.

The combination of periosteal reaction and normally mineralized bones occurs in both Caffey's disease and child abuse, but the absence of fractures and metaphyseal irregularity as well as the characteristic sites of involvement and age of onset in Caffey's disease usually allow easy differentiation of the two conditions.

Complete healing is the rule in Caffey's disease, although late sequelae have been reported. The late sequelae in Caffey's disease are usually the result of acquired synostosis of two involved adjacent bony shafts (e.g., radioulnar synostosis). The late sequelae of child abuse are usually the result of damage to the growth plate.

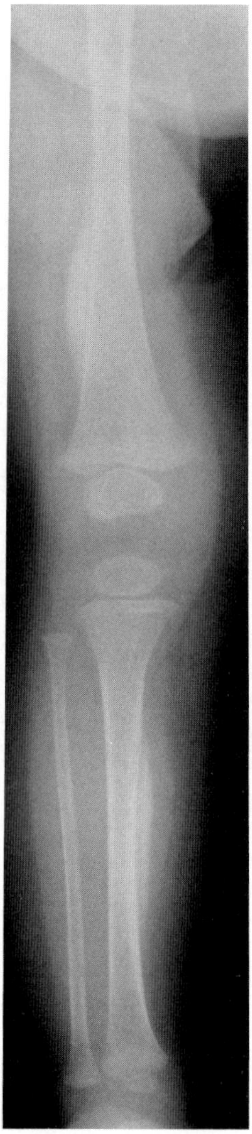

Leukemia

The osseous changes of leukemia in infancy are due to a combination of nutritional disturbance and leukemic invasion (20). Diffuse demineralization and periosteal reaction occur frequently (Fig. 11.16). Localized osteolytic lesions are usually multiple. Scler-

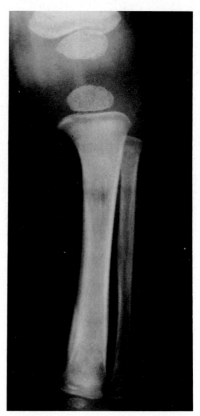

Figure 11.15. Caffey's disease. Thick periosteal reaction is noted along the shafts of the femur and tibia in this 8-month-old infant with Caffey's disease.

Figure 11.16. Leukemia. Frontal view of leg of infant with acute leukemia. Metaphyseal lucent bands, periosteal reaction, and osteopenia are evident.

otic lesions are unusual. "Leukemic lines" are narrow radiolucent metaphyseal bands that can be distinguished from the metaphyseal lesions of child abuse by the accompanying osteopenia and the absence of bony fragments.

Drug-Induced Bone Changes

Prostaglandin E_1 may be used in the treatment of ductus-dependent congenital heart disease to maintain patency of the ductus arteriosus. Its use frequently causes periosteal reaction of the ribs and long bones that resolves within 6 months to 1 year after discontinuation of the drug (21). The radiologic findings are identical to traumatic periostitis. The diagnosis is made on the basis of history.

Fractures and osteopenia have been reported in children treated with methotrexate for leukemia and Burkitt's lymphoma (22).

The history and presence of osteopenia allows differentiation from abuse (Fig. 11.17). Such fractures are seldom seen today because of lower doses of methotrexate in current treatment protocols.

Menkes' Syndrome (Kinky-Hair Disease)

Metaphyseal fractures identical to those seen in child abuse are present in Menkes' syndrome, a rare X-linked recessive disorder in which there is defective gastrointestional absorption of copper. Serum copper and ceruloplasmin levels are reduced. Long bone metaphyses have spurs with or without fracture (23) (Fig. 11.18A). Periosteal reaction may be present, and osteopenia is frequent after 6 months of age. Large numbers of wormian bones may be seen in the skull (Fig. 11.18B). Irregular, tortuous cerebral and abdominal arteries have been demonstrated angiographically (23, 24).

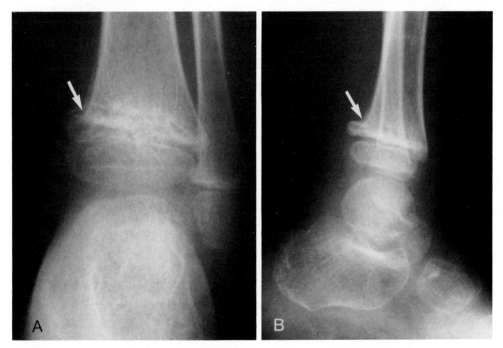

Figure 11.17. Leukemia treated with methotrexate. AP (A) and lateral (B) views of the ankle of this 4-year-old child with acute leukemia reveal a healing tibial metaphyseal fracture (arrows). Methotrexate was included in the drug protocol and may have contributed to the generalized osteopenia.

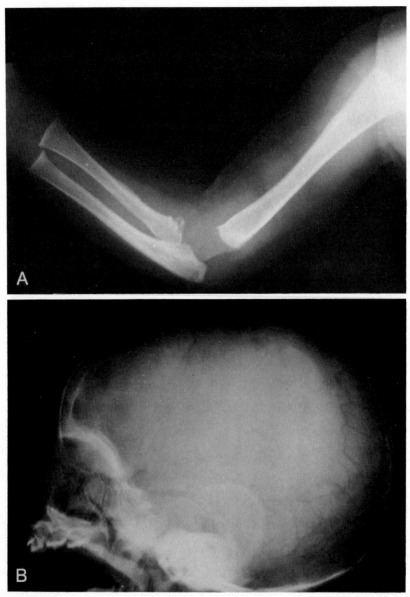

Figure 11.18. Menkes' syndrome. *A,* Upper extremity of a 3-month-old infant. There is a fracture through a spur in the proximal radial metaphysis. *B,* Lateral view of the skull of the same infant. Numerous wormian bones are seen posteriorly. (Courtesy of N. Genieser, New York University Medical Center, New York, NY.)

Menkes' syndrome is differentiated from child abuse primarily on clinical grounds. The hair is thin, coarse, and lacking in pigment. Affected infants have seizures, psychomotor retardation, and failure to thrive. The diagnosis is confirmed with demonstration of low serum copper.

REFERENCES

1. Glaser K: Double contour, cupping and spurring in roentgenograms of long bones in infants. *Am J Roentgenol (AJR)* 61:482–492, 1949.
2. Silverman FN: *Caffey's Pediatric X-Ray Diagnosis: An Integrated Imaging Approach,* ed 8. Chicago, Yearbook Medical Publishers, 1985, pp 416–477, 674–678, 835–841, 841–849.

3. Cumming WA: Neonatal skeletal fractures. Birth trauma or child abuse. *J Can Assoc Radiol* 30:30–33, 1979.

4. Madsen ET: Fractures of the extremities in the newborn. *Acta Obstet Gynecol Scand* 34:41–47, 1955.

5. Ekengren K, Bergdahl S, Ekstrom G: Birth injuries to the epiphyseal cartilage. *Acta Radiol (Diagn)* 19:197–204, 1978.

6. Thomas PS: Rib fractures in infancy. *Ann Radiol (Paris)* 20:115–122, 1977.

7. Feldman KW, Brewer DK: Child abuse, cardiopulmonary resuscitation, and rib fractures. *Pediatrics* 73:339–342, 1984.

8. Silverman FN, Gilder JJ: Congenital insensitivity to pain: a neurologic syndrome with bizarre skeletal lesions. *Radiology* 72:176–190, 1959.

9. Siegelman SS, Heimann WG, Manin MC: Congenital indifference to pain. *Am J Roentgenol (AJR)* 97:242–247, 1966.

10. Waltenspuhl VJ: Traumatisch bedingte knochenlasionen bei meningomyelocelen. *Ann Paediatr* 200:280–304, 1963.

11. Gyepes MT, Newbern DH, Neuhauser EBD: Metaphyseal and physeal injuries in children with spina bifida and meningomyeloceles. *Am J Roentgenol (AJR)* 95:168–177, 1965.

12. Sillence DO, Senn A, Danks DM: Genetic heterogeneity in osteogenesis imperfecta. *J Med Genet* 16:101–116, 1979.

13. Astley R: Metaphyseal fractures in osteogenesis imperfeta. *Br J Radiol* 52:441–443, 1979.

14. Patriquin HB, Trias A, Jecquier S, Marton D: Late sequelae of infantile meningococcemia in growing bones of children. *Radiology* 141:77–82, 1981.

15. Fiser RH, Kaplan J, Holder JC: Congenital syphilis mimicking the the battered child syndrome. *Clin Pediatr* 11:305–307, 1972.

16. Solomon A, Rosen E: The aspects of trauma in the bone changes of congenital lues. *Pediatr Radiol* 3:176–178, 1975.

17. Toomey FE, Hoag R, Batton D, Vain N: Rickets associated with cholestasis and parenteral nutrition in premature infants. *Radiology* 142:85–88, 1982.

18. Gefter WB, Epstein DM, Andy EK, Dalinka MK: Rickets presenting as multiple fractures in premature infants on hyperalimentation. *Radiology* 142:371–374, 1982.

19. Caffey J: Traumatic cupping of the metaphyses of growing bones. *Am J Roentgenol Radium Ther Nucl Med (AJR)* 108:451–460, 1970.

20. Nixon GW, Gwinn JL: The roentgen manifestations of leukemia in infancy. *Radiology* 107:603–609, 1973.

21. Ringel RE, Brenner JI, Haney PJ, Burns JE, Moulton AL, Berman MA: Prostaglandin-induced periostitis: a complication of long-term PGE1 infusion in an infant with congenital heart disease. *Radiology* 142:657–658, 1982.

22. Schwartz AM, Leonidas JC: Methotrexate osteopathy. *Skeletal Radiol* 11:13–16, 1984.

23. Adams PC, Strand RD, Bresnan MJ, Lucky AW: Kinky-hair syndrome: serial study of radiological findings with emphasis on the similarity to the battered child syndrome. *Radiology* 112:401–407, 1974.

24. Wesenberg R, Gwinn JL, Barnes GR: Radiological findings in the kinky-hair syndrome. *Radiology* 92:500–506, 1969.

12 Child Abuse and the Law

RICHARD BOURNE, J.D., Ph.D.

Physicians involved in the detection of child abuse and neglect must be familiar with the law in this area. Often the medical professional has questions about patient consent for assessments, recording in the medical record, filing of mandated child abuse reports with state agencies, civil and criminal court actions, privilege and confidentiality, and courtroom testimony (1).

Despite questions about the law and the need for legal understanding, doctors often resent the intrusion of lawyers into their domain. For example, they may perceive statutory requirements as interfering with the physician–patient relationship: they, not judges, should make decisions affecting patient care. On the other hand, attorneys may resent what they perceive as medical lack of cooperation with the legal process.

The fact is, however, that sensitive management of family violence cases requires both medical and legal input (2). Hospitals often develop multidisciplinary trauma teams to work with abusers and victims. Pediatricians assess the child clinically, radiologists study x-rays to determine the nature and degree of inflicted injury, social workers interview parents, psychologists conduct projective testing to see whether themes of violence or exploitation emerge, and lawyers decide whether sufficient evidence exists to criminally prosecute or to remove the child from biologic parents (3).

Hospitals are not the only institutions that become involved. They often work closely with police departments, district attorneys' offices, courts, and protective service agencies. Sometimes a particular institution must participate in case management because of a legal mandate; at other times involvement is discretionary and depends on the desires of professionals treating the family.

Although the law of child abuse is often vague and ill defined, three basic issues are:

1. When should the state intervene in family life (e.g., is there a need to file a child abuse/neglect report) (4)?
2. How should the state intervene (e.g., should protective agencies supply services to the family, or is there a need to place the child victim in foster care or to bring criminal charges against the alleged perpetrators)?
3. What procedural requirements exist in order to fulfill professional responsibility to patients and the state (e.g., how should one document abuse in the medical record and is there an obligation to supply this record to the patient or his/her attorney)?

Beginning with the issues of consent and record keeping, this chapter covers the principal legal requirements in the area of child physical and sexual abuse, with an emphasis on those materials relevant to radiologists. General information is also provided to allow the radiologist to understand customary practices and procedures in dealing with suspected abuse and neglect. It is important to remember, however, that law in this area varies by state. For specific questions of practice, it is necessary to consult with a lawyer knowledgeable about child protection.

Legal Consent

A minor child cannot usually consent to medical treatment. Only the child's parents

243

or legal guardians have this authority. In most states, however, statutory exceptions exist to this general rule. Among the common exceptions are:

1. An emergency. In an emergency (when, for example, a child with subdural hematomas is brought to the hospital by police ambulance), physicians may take whatever medical steps are necessary to diagnose and treat even if parents/guardians are unavailable, although if time permits staff should make every reasonable effort to contact those able to consent.
2. Emancipated minor. If a minor is or has been married, has children, is a member of the armed forces, or is financially independent or living separate and apart from his/her parents, the child can often consent to medical intervention. As the minor approaches the 18th or 21st birthday, greater legal respect is accorded the child's wishes concerning medical intervention; that is, the parents may have less decision-making authority over an older teen than they do over a toddler.
3. Specific medical issues. Some states permit a minor who is pregnant, or a child who has suffered abuse/neglect, to be treated without parental consent. Hospitals may not bill parents, or release the child's medical records to them, without the written approval of the minor patient. Physicians should inquire as to which "medical" procedures bypass parent control and which demand parental sanction (in Massachusetts, for example, hospitals may take photographs, including x-rays of traumatic injuries, despite parental protest).

Intervention requires the consent of only one parent or guardian, but if conflict exists between parents or guardians, it is probably wise to consult a hospital lawyer or administrator. If a child is in the legal custody of a state protective agency, or resides with foster parents, the agency or foster parents, rather than the minor's biologic parents, may have the authority to make decisions. On the other hand, such authority may depend on whether the medical procedure is necessary or elective, short or long term, has severe risks or is relatively benign; it may also matter whether the biologic parents voluntarily surrendered legal custody or whether the state obtained control through court action (5). If the parent or legal guardian refuses to consent to a diagnostic procedure or to treatment that the physician thinks necessary, the physician or others (e.g., state protective services) may petition a court to order the intervention or compel parental compliance.

Medical Records

Many different audiences may obtain access to records, including the patients, parents and legal guardians, police, and the courts (6). Take care, therefore, in deciding what is recorded and when and how reports are dictated and transcribed.

1. Be certain that reports are neatly typed, dated, and clearly signed, with a supervisor cosigning if hospital practice so dictates.
2. Describe, separately and in detail, the precise radiologic alterations found.
3. Avoid conclusions that are not carefully supported by specific facts; factual data are as important as the interpretations that flow from them.
4. Do not rule out a conclusion unless certain it is invalid or medically impossible (e.g., hesitate to state: "This fracture could not result from child abuse.").
5. Consult with colleagues before dictating, and document the consultation in the report.
6. If an error is made in the report, correct it in the later text rather than removing and destroying the incorrect statement.
7. Record as soon after patient contact as possible.
8. Respect patient privacy by not releasing the record without the written permission of the patient or his/her legal guardian (unless a court-ordered subpoena forces release; see below) (7).

Reporting Statutes

All 50 states now have reporting statutes (8). These statutes have as their primary purpose the identification of child abuse and neglect and, secondarily, the protection of children through state monitoring of families and the provision of services.

Statutes usually begin by defining groups of mandated reporters—those professionals who must report suspected abuse/neglect to departments of social service. Common mandated groups are teachers, psychologists, social workers, guidance counselors, physicians and nurses, and law enforcement personnel.

The basis for notification of state authorities is not knowledge but reasonable suspicion or belief. That is, a person does not need to know that abuse or neglect exists in order to report. Indeed, it is often difficult to distinguish inflicted injury, disease, and accident. If, given the medical or social data, a mandated reporter believes abuse or neglect is a reasonable explanation, he/she must report.

In many states, if a mandated reporter fails to report child abuse when a filing is required, the professional risks imposition of a fine or criminal sanction. There is also risk of civil liability. In a 1976 California court case, *Landeros v. Flood* (9), a physician and hospital were successfully sued because of the physician's failure to report child abuse. A child appeared in a hospital emergency room with bruises and injuries clearly resulting from a battering. The youngster was treated medically, but no abuse report was filed by those mandated to report. Shortly thereafter the child received additional trauma and subsequently died. Although clearly the physician had not inflicted the injuries, his failure to report was seen as the "intervening cause" of the child's death. Had he filed, the state might have intervened to protect, thereby preventing the reinjury.

Legally, it is always better for a mandated reporter to file an abuse/neglect report, even if the allegation later proves erroneous, than to fail to file. All states have an immunity provision in the reporting statute, holding the professional free from civil or criminal liability should a filed report not be substantiated. If this immunity did not exist, physicians and others would hesitate to report a "suspicion." They would understandably fear suits by parents claiming invasion of privacy, intentional infliction of emotional distress, defamation, and other civil wrongs.

Some states have privacy statutes protecting the confidentiality of the physician–patient relationship. A question arises, then, as to whether the abuse reporting requirement overrides this "privilege." It does. The law generally considers the health, safety, and welfare of children to be a greater priority than professional confidentiality.

Several other legal questions arise. First, if various professionals have examined a child, who should assume the reporting responsibility? The best person to report is usually that professional who has had direct contact with the child and who is most knowledgeable about the presenting problem. In most cases this is the pediatrician or family practitioner, although other specialists, including orthopedic surgeons, ophthalmologists, neurologists, and dentists, may have sufficient suspicion to report a case. On the other hand, if a social worker elicits from a family social information that makes him/her think abuse is occurring, then that social worker should assume the full responsibility.

The role of the radiologist in cases of suspected abuse is usually that of a consultant acting with limited clinical and laboratory information. When the radiologic findings point to the possibility of abuse, he/she has the responsibility to indicate this in the written radiology report as well as in a direct verbal communication to the referring physician or physician representative. Radiologists rarely, if ever, file abuse reports because, in the vast majority of cases, discussion of the case with the primary physician will lead to appropriate action. However, if after these discussions the referring physician is unwilling to file a report despite strong radiologic evidence pointing to abuse, the radiologist has the legal responsibility to do so.

Second, if some other person or institution has filed a report on the same episode of abuse, must the radiologist file a duplicate report? The answer is "no," but if new radiologic indications of abuse are observed a new report must be filed. This finding must be reported despite the existing involvement of a department of social services.

Third, what happens if information about past abuse is revealed—for example, a fracture that had occurred months before? If the abuse or neglect is too "old," protective services departments are unlikely to respond. If the radiologist believes that the child remains at risk, or if a past injury continues to cause current medical or psychologic problems, a report must be filed, despite a time lag. If in doubt, a report should probably be filed (for protection of the child and legal protection for the radiologist) or, minimally, the department of social services should be contacted for a "reading" of reporting responsibilities.

Finally, what if the physician observes a relatively minor injury? Is there still a duty to report? If an injury is not medically serious, but reasonably reflects abuse or neglect, the filing requirement persists. All traumatic injuries, except those clearly due to accident or disease, demand a report. Studies show, interestingly, that the designation of an injury as abuse often depends as much on the race and social class of the family as it does on the nature of the harm (10). For example, if a poor minority family appears in a hospital emergency room, staff are more likely to perceive a child's fracture as "abuse." An affluent majority family appearing with the same fracture often elicits the diagnosis of "accident." The greater the social distance between the examining professional and the patient being assessed the greater the likelihood of abuse/neglect being found. The reporting decision should be based upon the reasonable cause of the injury and not on family characteristics (3).

Mandated reporters are required to report many different types of abuse and neglect. "Abuse" includes physical, emotional, and sexual injury or exploitation. "Neglect" covers physical harm (such as failure by caretakers to feed, clothe, or shelter a child),

emotional deprivation (failure to nurture or attend to psychological needs), a lack of monitoring (for example, allowing a child to play on rooftops or on crowded streets), and medical or educational neglect (not taking a child for necessary medical examinations or encouraging truancy) (11). The initial obligation of a mandated reporter is usually to telephone the intake unit of the state department of social services. This unit has the responsibility of deciding whether or not the facts communicated by a reporter constitute abuse or neglect, that is, whether sufficient reason exists for the filing of a report.

Assuming that the intake unit accepts (or "screens in") the oral report, the reporter must usually follow up with a written report within a given time period. The state agency then has an obligation to investigate the allegation of abuse—to speak with parents, child, professionals, and others in order to determine whether or not the state can corroborate the allegations. State law usually limits the amount of time protective services has to investigate, distinguishing between a possible emergency (where immediate outreach is required) and a nonemergency (where 7 days or more may be allowed for the department to conduct an assessment).

If the state fails to corroborate the allegation of abuse/neglect by a reporter, the case is usually closed. On the other hand, if after investigation the reporter's concerns are substantiated, the state has a legal obligation to monitor the family and child, to provide services and supports for protection (e.g., to offer parents respite care, an infant stimulation program, or services of a visiting nurse), and to remove the child from biologic parents if such is essential to prevent a recurrence of serious harm. In some states, reporters also notify the police or district attorney's office so that a criminal investigation of the abuse/neglect might occur; in other states, protective services might refer the case to the criminal justice system if the abuse/neglect has violated criminal law or involves serious and permanent harm, commercial exploitation (e.g., using a child for pornography or prostitution), or repeated infliction of injury.

Professionals are often reluctant to file abuse/neglect reports despite the legal mandate. They feel that possible criminal sanction is an overly harsh response, that filing will alienate the family and cause withdrawal from care, that the state agencies are inefficient and ineffective and their involvement will fail to provide adequate protection. It is important to remember, however, that the legal basis for reporting is whether the case facts fit the statutory standard ("reasonable cause" to believe abuse or neglect exists), not whether the state response is helpful. The professional who is wary of state intervention should attempt to guide and influence the state's response. That is, he/she should file a report and attempt to channel protective outreach rather than to avoid a legal responsibility and risk criminal and/or civil sanction.

Legal Actions and Procedures

Radiologists may be called to testify in both civil and criminal actions concerning child abuse (12). In a civil action, a plaintiff or aggrieved party brings to court an alleged wrongdoer or defendant. Divorce, child custody, and neglect (care and protection) petitions are typical examples. The burden of proof is on the plaintiff, and usually the evidence must reach a particular level or quality, that is, the plaintiff has to demonstrate that the preponderance of the evidence favors his/her position or that he/she has proved the case by "clear and convincing" evidence. In the courtroom, for better or worse, it is evidence or proof that matters, not reality or "fact" (13).

In most civil cases the plaintiff is seeking money (damages) from the defendant. Sometimes the plaintiff seeks another objective, such as visitation rights with, or legal custody of, a child. In a neglect or abuse petition, the state department of social services or another party (e.g., a hospital) seeks to remove legal custody of a child from the biologic parents in order to place the youngster in an out-of-home setting. This step is usually taken only when no other intervention or service is able to protect the child from risk of serious harm. Most child abuse experts believe it is preferable to leave a child with his/her parents whenever possible and, if removal is necessary, seek to place a child with extended family or friends rather than in foster care or an institution.

In a criminal case, the state is the "plaintiff" and brings charges against a defendant who has allegedly committed a criminal offense. The state must meet the highest burden of proof—"beyond a reasonable doubt"—in its presentation of evidence. To do so it often requires testimony from expert witnesses. Similarly, a defense attorney attempting to obtain a "not guilty" verdict may call on the testimony of medical experts.

There are two types of expert witnesses: those whose knowledge of a field is so respected that they are asked for their opinions at a hearing; and those who are competent, but whose testimony is desired primarily because of their first-hand involvement with the facts of the case. The determination of expertise, although based on the professional's background, training, and experience, is made by the judge. What are the consequences of being "qualified" as an expert witness? First, an expert may give an opinion—for example, whether a fracture was more likely caused by an accident or an inflicted injury. A layperson, or nonexpert, is unable to testify as to opinions because he/she lacks the ability to offer valid interpretations. Second, an expert need not have direct involvement with the facts of a case in order to render a judgment. Hypothetical questions (e.g., "Assuming X, Y, and Z were true, what would your opinion be?") are often the means of eliciting the expert's point of view. Nonexpert witnesses generally must have personal involvement (seeing, hearing, smelling) in order to testify without hearsay objections (14).

An expert witness is not necessarily believed, that is, his/her testimony is not always accepted as truth or fact merely because he/she is competent in a particular area. Indeed, a hearing often consists of a "war" between experts, with different professionals offering conflicting opinions for the plaintiff's or defendant's case. The attorney for the opposing party may spend much time "impeaching the credibility" of the witness by attempting to show that the expert is less knowledgeable about an area than is alleged, had made inconsistent statements over time, or is biased because of a personal acquaintance with a party or because of the fee being received for his/her support (15).

A professional usually learns that his/her appearance is requested at a deposition or hearing by receipt of a letter, phone call, or subpoena. A deposition, by the way, is a technique of "discovery" whereby one party to an action learns more about the other party's case. Depositions are usually held in a lawyer's office, with a stenographer present. The "deponent" answers questions asked by both sides, the answers being used at trial at the lawyers' discretion.

A subpoena is a document served upon a person who is not a party to a case, requiring him/her to appear and give testimony. Often it is a subpoena *duces tecum*, requiring the witness to bring certain records, charts, or other tangible evidence such as photographs or x-rays. Failure to obey a subpoena can be grounds for the issuing party to bring contempt proceedings.

If the letter, phone call, or subpoena comes from a patient (or the patient's attorney) and requests the physician's participation, the physician should obtain a written release from the patient, signed and dated, specifically permitting information, opinions, and materials to be divulged to a named party/agency. The physician should also check with the patient to make certain that the attorney is his/her representative on the matter in question (16).

A professional must be very careful in disclosing medical, social, and psychological information because of state privacy statutes and the possibility of a "privileged" relationship. Many states have psychotherapist-patient, social worker–client, and physician-patient privileges whereby, if a person approaches the professional in his/her professional capacity, any communications made in confidence are protected and may be revealed only with the written consent of the patient or client.

This release of information becomes still more complex if the patient is a minor. Under most circumstances the minor's parent or legal guardian has decision-making authority. With certain types of cases (e.g., the treatment of venereal disease) a minor may consent to his/her own medical care and may request that the parent/guardian not be informed. In many states, moreover, if the minor is "mature" or "emancipated" (financially independent and living separately from parents, a parent, married, a member of the armed forces, etc.) he/she may also consent, decide, or waive regardless of parental wishes (see above).

If the request for participation in a deposition or hearing comes from someone other than a patient, the physician should attempt to contact the patient in order to inform him/her of the request and to obtain a written release to testify. If the patient cannot be contacted or refuses permission to testify, then the professional should so inform the issuing party/agency and consider claiming a privileged relationship. That is, assuming the existence of statutes requiring confidentiality of information between professional and patient, the professional should refuse to share private information. The physician might write a letter of objection to the deposing attorney, explaining why he/she is unable to release the requested record. Or, if the legal action involves a court hearing, the physician should communicate his/her inability to reveal to the opposing attorney and, if necessary, to the judge. (If the physician has private counsel, his/her lawyer may file a motion to quash the subpoena.) After the professional claims a privileged relationship, the judge can always waive the privilege and "force" the person to testify, but under such circumstances the witness is usually protected and cannot be sued for divulging confidential material.

As mentioned previously, if a physician is filing a child abuse/neglect report, privileged relationships are not respected nor are they a constraint if the physician is initiating a Care and Protection (court) petition alleging that his/her patient has mistreated a child. In custody disputes where a confidential relationship exists, the judge often weighs the value of maintaining privacy versus the value of the information in determining the "best interests of the child," and gives preference to one or the other consideration.

Testifying in Court

After receiving a request/subpoena to testify, the physician should first consult an attorney if legal services are available. The lawyer may find out why the physician is being subpoenaed, whether his/her testimony is essential, what issues are relevant, and what questions are likely to be asked by both sides. If the date or time is inconvenient, it is often possible to make changes such as calling the physician on a different day, rearranging the order of witnesses, or allowing the physician to remain on standby notice.

The subpoenaed physician should review the entire medical record so that he/she becomes as knowledgeable as possible about the case. His/her lawyer should be informed if he/she notices that the assessments performed were inadequate or incomplete or if the conclusions are controversial.

It is important that the radiologist prepare for his/her role in court by bringing the requested radiographs and reports and by organizing the films according to the order of presentation (17). Technically, if a radiologist works in a hospital setting, only the "keeper" of medical records has the authority to release information because the records belong not to the physicians but to the institution. Although attorneys and courts desire the original radiographs and reports, often copies "authenticated" by the hospital as accurate and complete are acceptable as evidence. Find out who has the authority to release and whether copies, not originals, are sufficient. Make certain that the court has a viewbox or other equipment necessary for proper demonstration. It is also helpful for the radiologist to bring a copy of his/her resume so that the attorney attempting to qualify his/her as an expert witness is better informed about training, background, and experience.

The court demands respect. Pay attention to appearance by dressing appropriately. Usually a suit is preferred, although a white doctor's jacket may enhance credibility. The physician's demeanor should be serious and reserved; he/she is not acting as a partisan for a particular point of view, but as an objective and neutral expert who is communicating "truth."

At a hearing or trial, the questions a "friendly" attorney asks are called "direct examination" while the questions asked by the "hostile" (opposing) counsel are called "cross-examination." On "direct," the lawyer must ask his/her questions in an objective way (e.g., "When did you first become involved in this case?" "When did you review the skeletal survey?" "What opinion did you render?"). On "cross," leading questions are permitted (e.g., "Isn't it true that you failed to recommend further x-rays when such were medically indicated?"). That is, on cross-examination the lawyer himself/herself makes statements or becomes "argumentative."

When asked a question, pause before answering in order to consider the form and content of the response. This pause also gives opposing counsel the opportunity to "object" to the question. All objections must occur prior to the witness's answer or the objection is "waived." If opposing counsel objects to a question, wait until the judge either "sustains" the objection or requests an answer.

When answering a question, follow these rules:

1. Do not use jargon or overly complex language that the court cannot understand; if professional terms are necessary, explain their meaning in simple words.
2. Answer only the specific questions asked; do not "narrate" or go into unnecessary detail.
3. If making a conclusion, be certain that the facts necessary to support the conclusion are provided and that the link between facts and conclusions is clear.

4. If a question is asked that goes beyond personal knowledge or expertise say, "I don't know" or, "I am unable to answer that question." A witness should never give a response that makes him/her feel uncomfortable. For example, if opposing counsel demands a "yes" or "no" answer, and the witness is unable to answer so simply, this should be stated.
5. Do not become argumentative or lose dignity and control. If an attorney is badgering the witness, he/she should look up at the judge for sympathy and support. Most judges are aware that expert witnesses are giving of their time, appreciate their help, and will eventually come to their support.
6. If his/her mind goes blank, or if he/she forgets a fact, a witness may ask to "refresh his/her recollection" by referring to the medical record or personal notes. As long as, after referring to these sources, the physician's memory is stimulated and he/she is testifying from knowledge, no hearsay problem arises. If reference is made to personal notes, all attorneys may view them; it is usually better to rely on pretrial preparation than on scribblings brought into a courtroom.

The radiologist should have reviewed all of his/her films and radiographic data prior to trial. In child abuse cases it is particularly important to note all fractures and other osseous and soft tissue abnormalities and to date their occurrence if that is possible. Attorneys are especially interested in etiology, because a diagnosis of "accident" or "inflicted injury" may determine case disposition. Multiple fractures of different ages may permit a more convincing conclusion than a single, acute fracture, but the nature or location of the fracture (e.g., "corner" fracture, "bucket-handle" lesion, rib fractures) and the consistency between the injury and parental explanation/history are important data. A defense attorney, of course, will attempt to prove that the injuries resulted from disease or accident rather than from abuse or neglect, and the professional must be prepared to defend his/her diagnosis (18).

The radiologist, after "qualifying" as an expert, is often asked the following questions: What studies were performed (bone scans, skeletal surveys, cranial computed tomography)? When were they performed and by whom? What do they reveal (number of fractures, age of fractures, likely cause, amount of force required to produce)? If the physician is unsure of the medical validity of his/her responses, he/she should consult with colleagues, seniors, and experts in the field in order to corroborate impressions and bolster confidence.

In my experience, physicians and other professionals are often reluctant to make clear-cut and unequivocal statements in a courtroom and are much more likely to give "truer" readings informally and off the record. Although clearly one should never present opinions unjustified by the data, it is essential to avoid overcaution. When a child appears with characteristic radiologic patterns of abusive injury, and abuse is the only reasonable explanation, the expert should so state that under oath in the courtroom.

REFERENCES

1. Bourne R, Newberger EH: *Critical Perspectives on Child Abuse.* Lexington, MA, Lexington Books (D.C. Heath and Company), 1979.
2. Miller GE: Practical legal aspects of child abuse cases for the health professional. In Rodriguez A (ed): *Handbook of Child Abuse and Neglect.* Flushing, NY, Medical Examination Publishing, 1977.
3. Newberger EH, Bourne R: The medicalization and legalization of child abuse. *Am J Orthopsychiatry* 48, 1978.
4. Bourne R, Newberger EH: Family autonomy or coercive intervention? Ambiguity and conflict in the proposed standards for child abuse and neglect. *Boston University Law Rev* 57, 1977.
5. Page SL: The law, the lawyer, and medical aspects of child abuse. In Newberger EH (ed): *Child Abuse.* Boston, Little, Brown, 1982.
6. Hirsh HD, Bromberg J: Physician responsibilities in keeping medical records. *Malpractice Digest* Nov-Dec, 1979.
7. Roach WH Jr, Chernoff SN, Esley CL: *Medical Records and the Law.* Rockville, MD, Aspen Publishers, 1985.
8. Schwartz A, Hirsh HL: Child abuse and neglect: a survey of the law. *Med Trial Tech Q* 28(Winter):293–333, 1982.
9. *Landeros v. Flood.* 1976. 131 Calif. Rptr. 69.
10. Bourne R: Family violence: Legal and ethical issues. In Newberger EH, Bourne R (eds): *Unhappy Fami-*

lies. Littleton, MA, P.S.G. Publishing Company, 1985.

11. Wald M: State intervention on behalf of 'neglected' children: a search for realistic standards. *Stanford Law Rev*, 27, 1975.

12. Owen ST, Hershfang HH: An overview of the legal system: Protecting children from abuse and neglect. In Ebeling NB, Hill DA (eds): *Child Abuse and Neglect*. Littleton, MA, John Wright (P.S.G., Inc.), 1983.

13. Ross SH: Child abuse and the juvenile courts. 46 Ala. Law 35–6, JA, 1985.

14. Frumer LR, Broder AJ, Minzer MK: *Examination of Medical Experts* (2 vol). Bender, 1973.

15. Danner D: *Expert Witness Checklists*. Rochester, NY, Lawyers Co-op, 1983.

16. Rice NR, Sayers SM: Compliance with medical records subpoenas: legal dilemma for Mass. health professionals. *Boston Bar J* Sept, 12–22, 1983.

17. Shayne NT: *Medical Evidence*. NY, Practising Law Institute, 1980.

18. Tinkham T: Child abuse revisited. *Med Trial Tech Q* 29(Summer):33–43, 1982.

13 Psychosocial Considerations

PETER F. TOSCANO, Ph.D.

Over the past 20 years pediatricians, psychiatrists, psychologists, and social workers have displayed increasing cooperation in the management of child abuse cases. This team approach reflects the growing appreciation that maltreatment cases are seldom clear-cut, and that violence against children encompasses a spectrum of physical and psychosocial concerns that reflect different issues and risks for particular children in individual families (1, 2). Handling such cases is further complicated by the responses of professionals dealing with abused children and their caretakers. Ranging from outright disbelief to anger and outrage, these responses may affect patient management and blur the roles and objectives of the individuals involved (3).

Radiologists should be viewed as consultants who are responsible for performing and analyzing diagnostic imaging studies. Their goal is to elucidate physical trauma in cases of suspected abuse. However, an appreciation of the context in which these studies are ordered, and a special knowledge of the situations and individuals with whom the professional may be dealing, are critical in achieving optimal diagnostic imaging studies. This chapter is aimed at giving radiologists and other professionals concerned with the radiologic imaging documentation of child abuse an overview of psychosocial concerns that may affect the management of individuals presenting for evaluation.

General Considerations

The violence, neglect, and indifference to children illustrated in the various forms of child maltreatment stand in dramatic contrast to present-day perceptions of the nurturing and love usually shown by caretakers to dependent children. Therefore, they often evoke strong emotional reactions in professionals immediately involved. Some individuals find even the entertainment of the possibility that an adult would batter a child to be completely out of their frame of reference. When faced with very real evidence that an injury may have been inflicted, the physician may find himself/herself so overcome by anger and hostility toward the potential perpetrator that objective medical evaluation is jeopardized. Also, fear of confrontation with a parent or caretaker or uncertainty regarding the differential diagnosis further contribute to an emotionally charged situation. The physician needs to be aware of his/her own feelings and to deal with them in a straightforward fashion (1).

The first step in managing potential maltreatment cases is to recognize that violence against children exists and to maintain a high degree of suspicion in dealing with childhood problems and injuries. Since parents and caretakers are not likely to acknowledge maltreatment as a possible cause of the child's condition, objectivity may require a reversal of the health care professional's stance of compassion, support, and reassurance (1, 3).

The difficulties that health care providers may have in dealing with maltreatment cases have been addressed by numerous authors (1–5). After the immediate medical problem is treated, concern may center on the initial differential consideration of inflicted injury or neglect, especially when the physical evidence is not blatant. Schmitt and Kempe observed that many physicians are reluctant to report abuse because they are unable to identify the abuser (4). However, they pointed out that, in at least 50% of such cases, it is impossible to determine who actually caused the child's injuries and, further, that it is not the physician alone who is to make that determination. In addition, the physician may fear the liability of a false accusation; however, the laws mandating the report also protect him/her from liability if the suspicions are unfounded (see Chapter 12). In the end, such uncertainties exist in most cases of abuse and are a source of stress for experienced as well as inexperienced professionals.

Often such cases involve a large expenditure of time and emotion that are compensated neither by financial reimbursement nor by the appreciation of the individuals involved. Indeed, the physician's initial communication of a possible diagnosis of child maltreatment may elicit anger and hostility in the parents and result in significant familial disruption once reported. This, coupled with possible uncertainties in the differential diagnosis and concerns for the effectiveness of the legal and social networks involved, understandably may increase hesitation in diagnosis and reporting (1, 6).

Current societal attitudes about child maltreatment are embedded in a historical context of disregard for children's rights and centuries of child-rearing practices that included infanticide, abandonment, and severe beating as customary practices (7). It has only been within the last 100 years that children have been considered more than just the property of parents. It is important to recognize that contemporary confusion and conflict regarding the rights of children and the roles of professionals and the state in family life are understandable in light of centuries of ambiguity about who children are and by whom they should be protected.

Awareness of these complex issues should increase the health professional's sensitivity and skill in dealing with abused children and their families. A failure to recognize these issues may place the child in further jeopardy. Children who are brought to a physician for treatment of a manifestation of abuse are at greater risk for reinjury if the situation is not dealt with comprehensively. In the event that the child is reinjured, it is likely that the parents or caretakers will seek medical help elsewhere (8).

The Role of Diagnostic Imaging

Although the radiology department may come in contact with children exhibiting a range of child maltreatment conditions, the most common ones involve physical injuries resulting either from inflicted trauma or "accidents" relating to neglect. The radiologist may be involved with such cases in two general ways. First, radiographic study may be ordered by the primary clinician who already suspects inflicted injuries. Second, the radiologist may detect a lesion that might not be suspected clinically and must alert the referring physician to the possibility of child abuse. The primary role of the radiologist in each case is that of a diagnostician who can determine accurately the presence and extent of injury in order to aid in its management (9, 10).

Initial communication between the radiologist and the referring physician is critical in order to direct most appropriately the proper radiographic investigations to assess specific injury (9). While it is assumed that the individuals bringing the child for evaluation as well as the patient have been interviewed, the radiologist may need to seek further clarifying information directly or through a nurse or social worker. It is important for the radiologist to have an accurate history including information as to how the injury allegedly occurred, and to be aware of pertinent physical findings, because it is often a discrepancy between the history and the radiographic findings that leads to the suspicion of child abuse (11). However, caution should be exercised not to pursue a line of questioning aimed at identifying motives, perpetrators, and the like; this will be the role of others involved in the investigation.

Information obtained from radiographic studies is often integral in the diagnosis of child abuse and may be used in legal proceedings. It should be documented clearly and accurately in the medical record. Communication of the findings to the referring physician should be performed in a manner that optimizes medical treatment and promotes the immediate protection of the child as well. Again, such diagnostic judgments should be based upon accurate information and should reflect those variables associated with the likelihood of inflicted trauma or neglect (9, 10).

Once maltreatment is suspected and/or supported by radiographic study, a more definitive diagnosis of child abuse and/or neglect needs to be made. As Silverman pointed out (10), even in those instances in which radiographic signs can be particularly specific about the time of the injury, the nature of the forces producing it, and the like, no information is provided as to the circumstances surrounding the abuse, who the individual(s) responsible may be, or the motives of the perpetrator(s). The potential risk to the child can only be assessed in consideration of a broader data base, including other medical information, history of the family, and perhaps psychiatric and/or psychological assessment of the individuals involved.

Many clinics and hospitals have protocols for handling child maltreatment cases that provide guidelines for the medical and psychosocial evaluation of the child, information on reporting cases to the local protective service agency, and general case disposition. Major medical centers may have formally organized interdisciplinary diagnostic teams composed of a primary care physician, nurse, social worker, psychiatrist, and other medical consultants with specified roles (e.g., diagnostic radiologist) (8, 12). Where these exist, information from the radiographic examination and follow-up consultation may be a sufficient contribution to the overall evaluation. When a diagnostic team is not available, it is necessary for the physician who sees the child initially and suspects maltreatment to help organize and work with other professionals in the hospital or community. When the radiologist is the first to suspect abuse, communication with the referring physician is the critical factor initiating protection of the child from further injury. The physician's responsibility is to report suspected abuse and neglect, not to determine the guilt or innocence of the individuals involved. Judges, attorneys, social workers, and others all have their roles to play in such protective service issues.

Psychosocial and High Risk Factors

Child maltreatment can take many forms, including nonorganic failure to thrive in infants and other forms of child neglect as well as physical, emotional, and sexual abuse. Often, more than one form is encountered in a given case or family. Individuals responsible for maltreatment are often the primary caretakers, such as natural and foster parents, but other custodians such as relatives, baby-sitters, and day care workers may be implicated. Most often the perpetrator is not a stranger. In approaching such cases, it is important to keep in mind those variables that have been found to characterize these populations.

Radiologists and technologists may come in contact with pediatric cases exhibiting a range of child maltreatment conditions. These usually involve physical injuries resulting from direct, inflicted trauma or "accidents" resulting from neglectful situations. The latter are particularly important because child neglect is the most prevalent of the categories of child maltreatment and may indeed be more responsible than physical abuse for situations resulting in serious injury and death (13).

Most often child neglect is unintentional and inadvertent, and appears in chaotic families with significant amounts of familial and marital discord (2, 14). High rates of intellectual inadequacy, physical problems and illness, and alcohol and drug addiction have been found in neglecting families (15, 16). There may be a lack of knowledge and judgment about parenting because of low intelligence of the caretaker, or loss of touch with the reality of the situation as a result of an emotional disorder. Also, parental overconcern and anxieties regarding the parenting role may interfere with the child's development through overinvolvement with and overcontrol of various situations (17). However, more recent empirical work has deemphasized the importance of such parent-specific characteristics and has refocused attention on high levels of parental stress as more significant contributory factors. Such stress appears related to the parents' own traumatic histories, current social isolation, and conditions of poverty (2, 14, 18).

Historically, much effort has been placed upon an analysis of the allegedly disturbed psychological profiles of adult child abusers. Notions of the actual causes and patterns of abuse have remained entangled in distorted perceptions of bizarre and macabre acts and significantly disturbed psyches of the perpetrators (14). This has occurred despite the widely held consensus by experts in the field that perhaps only 5% to 6% of abusers exhibit extreme symptomology, as may be evidenced in psychotic conditions, or profound sociopathic, sadistic, and/or homicidal tendencies (19–21). As Steele pointed out, although the latter may account for the more severe, atypical cases of abuse and infanticide, most abusive behavior is better considered as an abnormal pattern of caretaker-child interaction related to psychological characteristics that can exist concurrently with but quite independently of any psychiatric disturbance (21). Recent investigations have found a preponderance of stress-related symptoms such as depression and health problems in abusive parents, suggesting poor coping patterns that impair parental competence (22, 23).

Among those parental characteristics that have historically been linked to child abuse is a reported history of abuse and/or neglect in the parent's own background (21, 24). More recent empirical studies, however, have questioned these findings on methodologic grounds, and further work is needed to clarify the relationship (25, 26). Parental difficulties in responding empathetically to their children, unusually high demands and/or distorted perceptions of their child's behavior, and social isolation and lack of support have been discussed as significant characteristics contributing to potentially abusive situations (21, 24, 27, 28).

Analysis of the characteristics of the abused child has been more limited and of more recent concern. Premature and low birth weight children have been found to be especially at risk for abuse (29, 30), as are those who have various congenital deficiencies, abnormalities, chronic or recurrent illnesses, or conditions requiring hospitalization, or who are fussy or "temperamentally difficult" (25, 31, 32). In addition, there is limited evidence suggesting that mentally retarded children and overtly "different" or handicapped children may be at greater risk for neglect than abuse (31, 33).

Abused children tend to display more disruptive, aggressive behaviors than children from nonproblem families (23, 34). The behavior patterns of abuse victims resemble those often displayed by behavior problem children from distressed families who exhibit high rates of physical and verbal aggression toward both parents and peers (23, 35). Whether these behavioral patterns provoke or result from parental abuse is unclear.

Analysis of interactional patterns within families of abused children has demonstrated significant relationships between all forms of severe family conflict and child abuse. Abusive parents emit negative behaviors (such as physical negativism, threats, and yelling) toward each other and toward others in the family (23, 36). Abusive parents use fewer positive and more negative techniques of child management (14, 34). Overall parent-child interactions are less frequent and proportionately more negative than in control groups (36).

In summary, the literature underscores the necessity of taking into account parental characteristics, child vulnerabilities, overall family functioning, and stress from environmental factors in looking at the development and display of child maltreatment. A number of factors emerge in defining vulnerable families and children. In all categories of child maltreatment, lower socio-economic level families are overrepresented. Whether this is because they are more apt to be detected or because poverty is a source of stress that leads to an increased vulnerability is not clear. Families with few external social support systems (i.e., isolated families) as well as those in which there is violent marital discord are at greater risk. Parents or caretakers who themselves have been abused as children may be more apt to abuse their own children.

Exceedingly high or distorted parental expectations of what a child "should" be like at certain developmental phases are associated with abuse. Specific parental characteristics such as intellectual limitations, mental or physical illness, and alcohol and drug abuse are risk factors, especially for neglect. Families with low-frequency, predominantly negative parent-child interactions or those in which role confusions exist are vulnerable. Finally, infants who are premature, temperamental, or have feeding or bowel problems, or children who are physically different or behaviorally difficult to manage, may be the objects of abuse and/or neglect.

The American Medical Association recently wrote in its guidelines concerning child abuse and neglect: "It may be impossible to predict accurately which *individuals* are at high risk as victims or perpetrators, but often it is possible to identify groups of people who are at greater risk" (37).

Dealing with the Child

The child's behavior during examination will be affected by variables such as age and developmental level, customary behavioral characteristics, the degree and type of injury, the age of the injury, what has taken place immediately prior to the examination, and who accompanies the child. Although it is common for most children to be fearful when faced with medical procedures, abused children have been observed to be particularly hypervigilant, frightened, withdrawn, and extremely passive when first seen for physical examination (12). Separa-

tion from the parents may result either in excessive anxiety or the complete absence of it (37). These initial reactions may dissipate somewhat as the child becomes familiar with the environment and indeed may be replaced by a range of negative, provocative, and aggressive behaviors that also may reflect the anxiety aroused by the situation (12, 37).

The nature and extent of the interaction with the child for purposes of radiographic evaluation will be influenced by these considerations as well as the need for eliciting cooperation and, on some occasions, information about the injury(ies). A general approach that stresses warmth, empathy, and caring for the child is best suited for the situation. Except in emergencies or with young infants, attempts at developing rapport and a relationship with the child may prove most useful in alleviating anxieties and gaining cooperation (6, 37). This may be done by explaining the medical purpose of the evaluation and describing the specific procedures to be used in language appropriate to the child's developmental level, and attempting to answer the child's questions. The use of age-appropriate materials (e.g., dolls, pictures, books) may help to illustrate certain procedures and make explanations more meaningful to the child. With distressed infants and young children, the presence of a parent or a known adult may prove comforting.

Detailed questioning of the child about the circumstances surrounding the injury(ies), the perpetrators, and the like will be unnecessary in most cases. It should be assumed that an interview with the child has already been performed by the referring physician. If there is a need for further clarifying information, this should be accomplished by asking simple, direct questions aimed at obtaining a history that is consistent with the injury(ies) (e.g., "How did you do this?"). Allowing the child to use dolls, puppets, pictures, drawings, and the like may enhance communication, especially with very young children or ones with language and speech delays. On occasion, if the radiologist is the first professional to be faced with an abnormality of possible traumatic origin, it may be necessary to obtain further information. In most instances, this history should be sought from the adult who accompanies the child for examination. Inquiring as to whether the child has had any injuries may be sufficient to elicit the needed information. However, caution should be taken to avoid an atmosphere of accusation and guilt (see next section for specific comments).

Statements by the child and the behavioral observations made during the evaluation should be met by the radiologist in a nonjudgmental manner. Although empathetic expressions are appropriate, care should be taken to avoid assumptions about the feelings or perceptions of the child regarding the situation. Even children who have been chronically abused at the hands of caretakers may show significant attachment to them and may react negatively to implications of separation (12). Often, maltreated youngsters feel they are to blame for the abusive or neglectful situation and express their concerns as a confession of guilt (e.g., "I was a bad girl so Mommy hit me— I promise to be good; don't make me go away!") (38).

Although the rapport established with the child and communications elicited are primarily geared to facilitate an optimal radiographic study, information obtained during this contact may prove useful, along with other data, in confirming maltreatment. This interchange should be carefully documented in the medical record and communicated to the referring physician. This is especially important if the child readily states that a particular adult was the cause of the injury, because such statements by the victim are almost always true (39). In addition, it is important to note any atypical reactions on the part of the child and/or caretaker. Upon ending the older child's radiographic examination, he/she should be told what to expect next in the course of the evaluation and reassured whenever possible about normal findings, since abused children often feel damaged. Specific radiologic findings are best related to the child or to the parent through the primary referring physician within the context of an overall medical and psychosocial evaluation.

Dealing with the Parent/ Caretaker

Personnel involved with the diagnostic imaging of the child may actually have minimal contact with the parents or caretakers. The suspicion of child maltreatment may have already been raised and protective measures taken. The child may be brought to the imaging department by a protective service worker or by hospital transport personnel. Extensive history and details surrounding the suspected abuse and/or neglect may be provided to the primary care physician and passed on as part of the imaging consultation. Pertinent radiologic findings and observations made during the evaluation are then submitted as part of the overall report to the child protective agency. Medical personnel may thus have no contact with the caretakers unless a parent-sharing conference is held, or they are called upon for court testimony.

In those cases where the parent or caretaker actually accompanies the child to the emergency room or pediatric setting with a particular complaint, a complete and detailed history as to how the injury allegedly occurred should have been obtained by the primary physician and, again, this information should be shared with the radiologist. In most cases, even when the radiologist may be the first to suspect inflicted trauma, detailed interviewing is best done by individuals who will maintain a more ongoing relationship with the family and be involved with follow-up care.

The behavior of the parents or caretakers who present an abused and/or neglected child to a physician for care is variable. They may express great anxiety about their child's well being, but this may arise as much from guilt or fear of repercussions as from concern over the actual physical condition of their child (3). Attempts at reassuring them about their child's condition may not provide relief. The anxiety the parents exhibit may stem more from worries about themselves than from concerns for the child. Their anxiety may make them emotionally unavailable to the child, causing the child to have a sense of isolation in a potentially frightening medical situation (12). Abusive parents characteristically have difficulties in responding empathetically to their children (27). This factor, in addition to poor coping skills and lack of social supports, can make them vulnerable to the demands of the situation (22, 23, 28).

Detailed questioning about the medical condition of their child is almost always inappropriate, and may lead to defensiveness, anger, and potentially aggressive outbursts. The parents may take the child and leave the situation altogether. If there is an immediate need for further clarifying information, it should be sought in a direct but nonconfrontational manner. The physician's goal at this point of the evaluation process is to gather the best possible radiographic evidence and keep an open mind. Full skeletal surveys may be met with parents' inquiries about the need for such extensive filming. Personnel best handle such concerns by stating that this is routine and necessary for the proper diagnosis of their child's condition. This tends to minimize emotional responses and promotes the continued cooperation of the parent or caretaker, a critical factor in optimal evaluation.

Informing parents or caretakers that child maltreatment is in the differential diagnosis of their child's condition can be the most difficult part in the management of such cases, especially if a family member is the suspected perpetrator. The time and place for such discussion should be carefully considered. Parents and caretakers always need to be informed of the decisions made by the physician(s) involved, particularly when a protective service worker has been called (1, 8). In instances where more than one physician has taken part in the evaluation, as occurs with evidence collected in radiologic study, an agreement needs to be reached as to who will do the reporting to the protective service agency, and who will discuss the findings with the parents or caretakers. Although a mutual responsibility exists, the referring or primary care physician is in the best position to give a more comprehensive overview of the concerns, maintain an ongoing relationship with the child and family, and help develop an appropriate intervention plan (8, 40).

It is important for the physician to be aware of feelings generated by the situation. Uncertainty as to the diagnosis may raise feelings of doubt; this together with the fear of eliciting anger may result in hesitancy and evasiveness in fully communicating concerns to the referring physician (3). Anger and hostility toward the parents for injuring their child may emerge in the medical personnel involved and interfere in the management of the case (41).

A nonjudgmental, nonhostile, and honest approach is the best means of gaining the cooperation of the individuals involved (1, 8). It is often helpful for the primary physician to explain the facts as presented in the medical evaluation and the opinion that they do not appear accidental, or that the "accident" may have occurred under neglecting conditions. Findings of the radiologic study should be discussed in the context of the other information gathered on the case. Conveying specific or technical details should be avoided at this time and perhaps be used in subsequent comprehensive meetings, with the radiologist present if this would prove useful to the eventual outcome of the case. Explaining that the physician is being mandated to report such situations to protective authorities can further objectify the situation. Engaging the parent in continued evaluation in order to remove the child from jeopardy is the goal, not eliciting a confession from the suspected perpetrator (8).

The parents may react with anger and/or alienation. Indeed, an aggressive outburst against the interviewer may ensue. If this is anticipated, appropriate security personnel should be alerted prior to the interview. Defensive denial of the situation is common, and attempts to break through the denial should be limited at this time. In contrast, the parents may evidence relief that an intolerable situation has been identified and that help may be available (3). If the parents or caretakers are not willing to cooperate voluntarily in a further assessment of the situation, a court order may be needed to retain the child for a social hospitalization if protective services are not available (8).

If handled properly, when parents or caretakers are informed of the suspected diagnosis and helped to see that the recommendation of further evaluation is in the best interest of all concerned, they will probably cooperate with at least the initial investigation of the protective service agency. This initial step has the primary goals of protecting the child from further abuse and/ or neglect and beginning to develop an intervention plan for the child and family. Information received from the radiologist can be invaluable in initiating this phase and in proper management of the case.

Summary and Conclusions

Previous sections have outlined that child maltreatment is a pervasive family problem with complex etiologic variables and dynamics. Its detection and documentation very often take place within a medical setting, and an awareness of risk factors is critical. Interdisciplinary input and the careful coordination of information from various medical specialties optimizes the diagnosis of abuse. The radiologist can play a central role in its initial detection and documentation, and occasionally in subsequent intervention. Careful communication with the referring physician is important to clarify details of these roles and the extent of his/her activity in the overall handling of the case.

Dealing with maltreatment cases is made complex by the range of emotions frequently elicited in medical personnel, as well as in the child, parents or caretaker involved. The initial primary goals include attending to the immediate medical needs of the child and protection of the child from further injury. A general approach that stresses warmth, empathy, and caring for the child will optimize the medical evaluation of the child. Parents need to be handled in a nonhostile, nonjudgmental manner aimed at gaining their cooperation with recommendations for further evaluation and/ or intervention. The physician must keep in mind that his/her role is a medical one that includes the responsibility of reporting suspected abuse and neglect, not one of determining the guilt or innocence of the individuals involved.

REFERENCES

1. Ellerstein NN: The role of the physician. In Ellerstein NN (ed): *Child Abuse and Neglect*: *A Medical Reference*. New York, John Wiley and Sons, 1981.
2. Mrazek D, Mrazek P: Child maltreatment. In Rutter M, Hersov L (eds): *Child and Adolescent Psychiatry—Modern Approaches*, ed 2. Oxford, England, Blackwell Scientific Publications, 1985.
3. Rosenzweig HD: Some considerations of the management of child abuse: a psychiatric consultant's perspective. In Newberger EH (ed): *Child Abuse*. Boston, Little, Brown, 1982.
4. Schmitt BD, Kempe CH: The pediatrician's role in child abuse and neglect. *Clin Probl Pediatr* 5:3, 1975.
5. Helfer RE: Why most physicians don't get involved in child abuse cases and what to do about it. *Child Today* 4:28, 1975.
6. Campbell J, Humphreys J: *Nursing Care of Victims of Family Violence*. Reston, VA, Reston Publishing Company, 1984.
7. Robin M: Sheltering arms: The roots of child protection. In Newberger EH (ed): *Child Abuse*. Boston, Little, Brown, 1982.
8. Bittner S, Newberger EH: Pediatric understanding of child abuse and neglect. In Newberger EH (ed): *Child Abuse*. Boston, Little, Brown, 1982.
9. Kuhn JP: Radiology of internal injuries. In Ellerstein NN (ed): *Child Abuse and Neglect*: *A Medical Reference*. New York, John Wiley and Sons, 1981.
10. Silverman FN: Radiologic aspects and special diagnostic procedures. In Kempe CH, Helfer RE (eds): *The Battered Child*, ed 3. Chicago, The University of Chicago Press, 1980.
11. Swischuk LE: Radiology of the skeletal system. In Ellerstein NN (ed): *Child Abuse and Neglect*: *A Medical Reference*. New York, John Wiley and Sons, 1981.
12. Gray J, Kempe R: The abused child at time of injury. In Martin HP, Kempe CH (eds): *The Abused Child*: *A Multidisciplinary Approach to Developmental Issues and Treatment*. Cambridge, MA, Ballinger Publishing Company, 1976.
13. Cantwell HB: Child neglect. In Kempe CH, Helfer RE (eds): *The Battered Child*, ed 3. Chicago, The University of Chicago Press, 1980.
14. Wolfe DA: Child-abusive parents: an empirical review and analysis. *Psych Bull* 97:462–482, 1985.
15. Black R, Mayer J, Cezakian A: The relationship between opiate abuse and child abuse and neglect. In Lowinson JH (ed): *Critical Concerns in the Field of Drug Abuse*. New York, Marcel Dekker, 1978.
16. Martin M, Walters J: Familial correlates of selected types of child abuse and neglect. *J Marr Fam* 44:267–276, 1982.
17. Kempe RS, Cutler C, Dean J: The infant with failure-to-thrive. In Kempe CH, Helfer RE (eds): *The Battered Child*, ed 3. Chicago, The University of Chicago Press, 1980.
18. Newberger EH, Reed RB, Daniel JH, Hyde JN, Kotelchuk M: Pediatric social illness. *Pediatrics* 60:178–185, 1977.
19. Friedman RM, Sandler J, Hernandez M, Wolfe DA: Child abuse. In Mash EJ, Terdal LG (eds): *Behavorial Assessment of Childhood Disorders*. New York, Guilford Press, 1981.

20. Kempe CH: A practical approach to the protection of the abused child and the rehabilitation of the abusing parent. *Pediatrics* 51:804–812, 1973.

21. Steele B: Psychodynamic factors in child abuse. In Kempe CH, Helfer HE (eds): *The Battered Child*, ed 3. Chicago, The University of Chicago Press, 1980.

22. Conger R, Burgess R, Barrett C: Child abuse related to life change and perceptions of illness: some preliminary findings *Fam Coordinator* 28:73–78, 1979.

23. Lahey BB, Conger RD, Atkeson BM, Treiber FA: Parenting behavior and emotional status of physically abusive mothers. *J Consult Clin Psychol* 52:1062–1071, 1984.

24. Spinetta JJ, Rigler D: The child-abusing parent: a psychological review. *Psychol Bull* 77:296–304, 1972.

25. DeLissovoy V: Toward the definition of abuse-provoking child. *Child Abuse Negl* 3:341–350, 1979.

26. Cicchetti D, Aber JL: Abused children-abusive parents, an overstated case? *Harvard Educ Rev* 50:244–255, 1980.

27. Belsky J: Child maltreatment. *Am Psychol* 35:320–335, 1980.

28. Helfer RE: The etiology of child abuse. *Pediatrics* 51:777–779, 1973.

29. Elmer E, Gregg G: Developmental characteristics of abused children. *Pediatrics* 40:596–602, 1967.

30. Klein M, Stern L: Low birth weight and the battered child syndrome. *Am J Dis Child* 122:15–18, 1971.

31. Glasser D, Bentovim A: Abuse and risk to handicapped and chronically ill children. *Child Abuse Negl* 3:565–575, 1979.

32. Friedrich WN, Boriskin JA: The role of the child in abuse: a review of the literature. *Am J Orthopsy-chiatry* 46:580–590, 1976.

33. Martin HP: The neuropsychodevelopmental aspects of child abuse and neglect. In Ellerstein NS (ed): *Child Abuse and Neglect*. New York, John Wiley and Sons, 1981.

34. Bousha DM, Twentyman CT: Mother-child interactional style in abuse, neglect, and control groups. *J Abnorm Psychol* 93:106–114, 1984.

35. Main M, George C: Responses of abused and disadvantaged toddlers to distress in agemates: a study in the day care setting. *Dev Psychol* 21:407–412, 1985.

36. Lorber R, Felton DK, Reid JB: A social learning approach to the reduction of coercive processes in child abusive families: a molecular analysis. *Adv Behav Res Ther* 6:29–45, 1984.

37. American Medical Association: AMA diagnostic and treatment guidelines concerning child abuse and neglect. *JAMA* 254:796–800, 1985.

38. Martin HP, Beezeley P: Personality of abused children. In Martin HP, Kempe CH (eds): *The Abused Child: A Multidisciplinary Approach to Developmental Issues and Treatment*. Cambridge, MA, Ballinger Publishing Company, 1976.

39. Schmitt BD: The child with nonaccidental trauma. In Kempe CH, Helfer RE (eds): *The Battered Child*, ed 3. Chicago, The University of Chicago Press, 1980.

40. Harper G, Irvin E: Alliance formation with parents: limit-setting and the effect of mandated reporting. *Am J Orthopsychiatry* 55:550–560, 1985.

41. Helfer ME, Helfer RE: Communicating in the therapeutic relationship: concepts, strategies, and skills. In Kempe CH, Helfer RE (eds): *The Battered Child*, ed 3. Chicago, The University of Chicago Press, 1980.

14 Technical Considerations and Dosimetry

VASSILIOS RAPTOPOULOS, M.D.
ANDREW KARELLAS, Ph.D.

This chapter addresses the reader unfamiliar with medical imaging procedures and is designed to provide only a brief and simplified description of how a diagnostic image is produced and of the various procedures used in the evaluation of suspected child abuse.

The terms *roentgenology* (from Wilhelm Roentgen, who discovered x-rays) or *radiology* (from radiant energy) have traditionally been applied to the branch of medicine dealing with the use of x-rays in diagnosis. In the past two decades important changes have taken place, and the present state of the art utilizes sophisticated and ingenious new techniques that employ other energy forms in addition to x-rays. With the introduction of nuclear medicine, ultrasonography, computed tomography (CT), and magnetic resonance imaging (MRI), radiology has expanded to include these new modalities. In addition, new techniques, such as percutaneous drainage procedures, have expanded the role of radiology beyond its strictly diagnostic confines. For these reasons, the term *medical imaging* is considered to better define the contemporary complexities of the specialty, and is rapidly gaining popularity (1–3).

Modern medical imaging has undergone an unparalleled explosion in the development of imaging hardware and techniques. Diagnostic information previously thought unattainable is now recordable. This has resulted in an overall yield of information and accuracy never before imagined, as well as a significant decrease in exploratory surgery and, in some instances, the need for surgical treatment. However, this rapid evolution has created gaps between the capabilities of the techniques, their appropriate implementation, and their acceptance by referring physicians. Thus, the need to integrate and synthesize imaging data and update the imaging workup has reached major proportions, and the radiologist plays an important role in triaging the clinical problem with the appropriate imaging scheme(s). This is reflected by the explosion and constant revision of algorithms, a kind of diagnostic decision tree that attempts to guide the most appropriate workup of a patient's symptoms (1–5).

The appropriate use of available tests is particularly important for pediatric patients, especially for children suspected of being victims of child abuse. It is much more important to avoid unnecessary use of medical x-rays in children than in adults. Furthermore, the potentially lethal implications of child abuse and the sociological, psychological, and legal aspects related to this condition dictate the need for a speedy and accurate diagnosis. A brief description of these modalities and procedures follows, with special emphasis on traumatic injuries.

The Medical Image

As x-rays or other forms of energy pass through the body, they interact with different tissues in a variety of ways. This differential interaction depends on the type of energy applied as well as the density, thickness, and chemical composition of the different organs and tissues. The signals produced are detected and recorded in a number of ways and are eventually displayed and viewed as a medical image.

X-RAYS AND OTHER FORMS OF ENERGY

X-rays were discovered in 1885 by Wilhelm Konrad Roentgen, a professor of physics at the University of Wurzburg, Germany. The discovery was initiated by Roentgen's observations of fluorescence (glowing) of a piece of barium platinocyanide lying several feet from a well-sealed, high-voltage cathode discharge tube. While studying this phenomenon, he noted that within the shadow of his hand he could see the bones of his fingers and, eventually, he recorded this image on a photographic plate. The implications of this discovery were widely recognized, and in 1901 Roentgen received the first Nobel prize in physics for his studies of the physical properties of x-rays. By the turn of the century several other physicists had made important contributions to our knowledge of x-rays, and eventually the Curies discovered that physically identical radiation (gamma rays) is emitted by the nuclei of certain radioactive elements.

X-rays are generated in an evacuated glass tube by boiling electrons off a hot filament (cathode). These electrons are accelerated by a high electric potential toward a target (anode) and, when they strike the anode, dissipate their energy and produce heat and x-rays. X-rays and gamma rays are discrete entities, called photons or quanta, carrying energy but no charge. Their electromagnetic component is similar to light, but their smaller wavelength makes them highly penetrating, invisible rays. They are electrically and magnetically neutral, travel with the speed of light, have a wide range of wavelengths and photon energies, and cause fluorescence of certain substances. They also liberate minute amounts of heat upon passage through matter, and produce

chemical and biologic changes mainly by excitation and ionization (ionizing radiation) (6, 7).

In contrast to ionizing radiation, no significant adverse biologic effects from medical diagnostic ultrasound waves have been reported. These are acoustic waves with frequencies above what the human ear can detect. They are generated by electric stimulation of a piezoelectric crystal (transducer) that produces high-frequency vibrations (acoustic waves) (8, 9).

In MRI, a strong magnetic field in conjuction with radiowaves is used to produce an image. As with ultrasound, no significant adverse biologic effects have been reported from these forms of energy (10).

THE DIAGNOSTIC IMAGE

From a practical standpoint, a diagnostic medical image is only as good as the diagnostic information provided (11). As a rule, the basic types of information obtained from the images are contrast resolution, spatial resolution, motion, and function (6, 7).

Contrast Resolution

Contrast resolution is the ability of the imaging modality to record different substances. This generally depends on three separate components: subject (patient) contrast, recording device contrast, and background interference.

Subject Contrast. In x-ray imaging, subject contrast depends upon the thickness of the different substances, their density, their atomic number, and the energy of the radiation. In ultrasonography, the subject contrast is produced by the different acoustic properties of different tissues. In nuclear imaging, it is determined by the differential concentration of radioactive elements accumulated in a specific organ or body tissue, and in MRI the subject contrast depends on both concentration and chemical environment of specific atoms with magnetic properties (6–10).

Recording Devices Contrast. In conventional radiology this contrast depends mainly on the characteristics of the different types of films or fluorescent screen used, the amplification techniques employed, and the film-processing techniques. In ultrasonography, CT, MRI, nuclear medicine, and digital radiography, the image is either electronically displayed or is digitized. Consequently, film contrast plays a less important role since the different densities of the image can be manipulated on television monitors (6–10).

Background. Film fog, scatter radiation, electronic noise, and background radiation are all terms indicating unwanted information produced or detected that alters radiographic densities. The contrast resolution generally improves as the ratio of signal (useful information) to noise (interfering signals) increases. A major limitation in discerning subtle differences in subject contrast arises from the limited number of x-rays detected. This effect is called quantum noise, a major factor contributing to degradation in the diagnostic quality of x-ray images (6–10).

Of the different imaging modalities, MRI produces the highest contrast resolution for soft tissues (approximately 25 times that of x-rays), followed by CT (approximately 10 times that of x-rays).

Spatial Resolution and Sharpness

Spatial resolution refers to the ability of an imaging system to define the smallest possible distance between two objects; sharpness refers to the clarity of a border. X-ray film provides the highest spatial resolution of all imaging modalities, having the ability to resolve 5–15 line pairs per millimeter. A system having a resolution of 5 line pairs per millimeter would be able to resolve high-contrast objects spaced 0.1 mm apart. Fluoroscopy follows with an overall resolution of 2–6 line pairs per millimeter. The spatial resolution of ultrasonography depends on numerous factors, including whether the different structures are above one another (axial resolution) or next to each other (lateral resolution). It also depends on the distance the sound has to travel and the acoustic frequency used. Thus, high-resolution ultrasonography can resolve 0.2-mm

structures positioned 2 cm from the skin, whereas for further depths this resolution can decrease to 1.5 mm. Computed tomography has a resolving power of 0.7–1.2 mm. Presently, the spatial resolution of MRI is even poorer, and that of nuclear imaging ranges only between 5 and 10 mm (6–10).

Motion and Function

Physiologic or pathologic changes over a short or long period of time can be detected by serial images, continuous imaging, and detection of the distribution, concentration, or excretion of various substances introduced into the body (6–10).

Imaging Modalities

The various modalities used in diagnostic imaging are defined by the type of energy used and/or the methods applied to record the information obtained.

PLAIN FILM RADIOGRAPHY

As the x-ray beam passes through the body, its intensity is differentially attenuated by objects of different density and thickness. This pattern of attenuation is recorded on x-ray film, which is customarily viewed on an illuminated surface. The substances that can be detected by their distinctly different absorptions are, in order of decreasing density, metal, bone, soft tissue, fat, and air. All the soft tissues of the body, including muscle, connective tissue, cartilage, blood, and internal organs, have approximately the same density, referred to as water density. A number of contrast media can be used to alter the density of some of these organs, and thus enhance their visualization. Numerous exposure techniques and positioning of the patient are utilized depending on the size and part of the body examined as well as the specific indication for which the x-ray examination is done (5–7).

Film alone is very rarely used to detect x-rays that exit the body. Instead, a thin plate of a scintillating material (intensifying screen) is placed in contact with the film in a light-tight cassette. This material interacts with x-rays and produces visible light, which in turn exposes the film. Typically, from one absorbed x-ray photon more than 1000 light photons will be produced. In addition, intensifying screens have a higher stopping power for x-rays compared to that of films (50% versus 2% detection efficiency). This amplification effect allows for a drastically reduced x-ray exposure to the patient as compared to using film alone. The new generation of rare earth screens allows for an additional two- to threefold reduction in radiation dose without a significant loss in the quality of the radiographic image (5–7, 12, 13).

Other significant advances in x-ray equipment include improvement in the homogeneity (energy) and collimation of the x-ray beam; short exposure times of a few milliseconds; and built-in controls such as phototimers and computerized technique guides (5–7, 14). All these innovations are of particular benefit to pediatric radiology because they result in significant reduction of radiation exposure, either directly or indirectly.

Plain radiography is the initial mode for evaluating most clinical conditions and serves as screening for other imaging modalities or procedures. It contributes the bulk of the workload of an integrated imaging department. This is especially true for overt or suspected traumatic injuries.

TOMOGRAPHY OR LAMINOGRAPHY

This modality produces radiographic images of a body plane several millimeters thick. This is accomplished by deliberately blurring the portions of the body above and below the plane of interest. It provides good spatial resolution of the area scanned, but it exposes the patient to greater radiation and is influenced by patient motion more than plain radiography (6, 7).

FLUOROSCOPY AND DIGITAL RADIOGRAPHY

In this technique, x-rays pass through the body and their transmission pattern is elec-

tronically intensified (image intensifier) and converted to a closed-circuit television signal by a video camera. This signal is then fed into a television monitor for direct viewing. Images can be recorded on film by intermittent x-ray exposure (6, 7). The signal can also be fed to videotape or digitized and stored in computer memory. Fluoroscopy enables observation of voluntary or involuntary motion of parts of the body or organs. It is used in numerous procedures, including gastrointestinal studies and angiography.

If the fluoroscopic image is digitized (digital fluoroscopy), it is either displayed on a monitor instantaneously or may be retrieved from the computer memory later. Digital fluoroscopy is used very effectively in digital subtraction angiography (DSA), in which two such digitized images are produced, one before intravascular injection of a contrast agent and another after the injection. The computer then subtracts one image from the other and the resulting image displays only the structures (vessels) with the contrast agent. This technique has enabled radiologists to image arteries by using an intravenous injection, avoiding the more invasive intra-arterial injections.

Another approach to digital radiography is to use multidetector arrays. This is an emerging technology and its use is not widespread. At present, digital radiography has a considerably poorer spatial resolution than film radiography. Among its advantages is the ability to manipulate the image (magnify, minify, expand, or decrease contrast densities). This provides a chance for wide-variation exposure latitude, which may eliminate the need for repeat examinations due to exposure error (15).

COMPUTED TOMOGRAPHY

Computed tomography images are, in a sense, slices through the vertical axis that are conventionally viewed as though looking through the body from the feet up toward the head. A narrow, fan-shaped x-ray beam is passed through the patient. The amount of transmitted radiation is measured by an array of detectors and a computer is used to calculate the relative x-ray absorption in each point (pixel) of a slice. This information is used to produce a gray-scale image that is displayed on a television-type monitor. Typically, a CT image consists of approximately 500 × 500 pixel elements (pixels) each displaying a shade of gray that is represented by a number called the CT number of Hounsfield units. Water has a CT number of 0, fat between −20 and −70, and air a value below −200. The different soft tissues have CT numbers from +20 to +70, and compact bone a number over +200. The high contrast sensitivity of CT allows detection of density differences as small as 0.5%, as opposed to 4–5% for conventional x-ray radiography. The use of contrast media further enhances the ability to differentiate tissues that do not provide adequate density difference. For this reason, oral or intravenous contrast materials are used very commonly (6, 16).

In small children and infants CT has some limitations. The patients usually need to be sedated because motion sharply degrades the image. Because of the small size of the patient and relative lack of body fat, the spatial and contrast resolution is considerably poorer than in adults. Finally, for the same radiation dose rate, the surface dose for a child is relatively higher than for an adult because of the child's smaller body diameter. New advancements in producing faster CT scanners (1–2 sec per slice) and improving the contrast resolution have expanded the use of CT in children during the past 2 to 3 years.

NUCLEAR IMAGING (RADIONUCLIDE IMAGING)

All the above modalities use x-rays that pass through the body and record the amount of absorbed radiation. An image can also be produced after administration of a radioactive substance (radioisotope) that concentrates in an organ or tissue. The radiation emitted in the form of gamma rays can be measured by special detectors, digitized, and displayed on television screens. Dynamic, time-related changes in the concentration or flow of these isotopes can also

be measured or depicted on graphs. Because of its poor spatial resolution (5–20 mm), nuclear imaging is more useful for studying pathophysiologic functions than anatomic relationships. Of the radioisotopes, technetium-99m, indium-111, gallium-67, and iodine-123 are most commonly used. Only traces of these elements are used, and they are attached to specific substances, body fluids, or cells, depending upon the specific information sought. In the pediatric patient suspected of being traumatized, bone scans may show activity before radiographic evidence of injury is apparent. Nuclear imaging can also detect traumatic injury or other derangements of internal organs (17).

ULTRASONOGRAPHY (SONOGRAPHY)

In this modality, ultrasonic waves produced in a transducer pass through the body, where they are absorbed, deflected, reflected, and scattered. Although absorption and deflection are not useful in imaging, the reflected and scattered waves (echoes) returning to the same transducer vibrate the crystal. This produces an electric signal. For the sound wave to be reflected as an echo it must meet an interface of different acoustic properties. The percentage of sound that will be reflected depends on the difference in the acoustic properties (acoustic impedance) of the substances on each side of an interface. The degree of vibration the echo produces on the crystal, and thus the intensity of the electric signal, depend on the intensity of this echo. Since the acoustic impedance of a substance depends on its density, the electric signal produced is proportional to the difference in composition on each side of an interface. These signals are electronically amplified, digitized, and displayed on a television-type monitor.

The introduction of real-time ultrasound has made the use of this modality extremely flexible. Placement of the transducer at the end of a wire eliminates the need for specific alignment of the patient with the equipment, a maneuver needed in every other imaging modality. By obtaining 20–30 images per second, the image changes continuously and motion can be seen. These images can be recorded on videotapes or can be "frozen" on the screen and photographed (8, 9).

Ultrasonography is primarily a soft tissue imaging technique, and its basic property is the ability to distinguish solid structures, which produce numerous echoes, from cystic (fluid-filled) structures, which do not produce echoes because of the lack of interfaces. Bone and air are acoustic barriers, so ultrasound is limited in the evaluation of the skeletal system and the lungs. It is widely used in the evaluation of the abdomen, the heart (echocardiography), and the infant brain (neurosonography). The disadvantages of ultrasound include the relative lack of easily identifiable landmarks and the great dependency of the technique on the operator. On the other hand, it is a fast, relatively inexpensive modality that is highly flexible and safe. Ultrasound, more than any other imaging modality, is considered an extension of the physical examination because of the required close contact of the examiner with the patient. This is particularly advantageous in the child suspected of being abused who may feel considerable anxiety when left alone on a large x-ray table or CT scanner. Furthermore, ultrasound does not require the use of sedation.

MAGNETIC RESONANCE IMAGING

In clinical MRI applications, hydrogen atoms are forced to align parallel or antiparallel with a strong magnetic field. This alignment is subsequently modified by radiowaves, causing intermittent excitations (change of alignment) and deexcitations (return to original alignment) of the hydrogen nuclei. During deexcitation, these atoms generate a signal that is converted to a tomographic-type image in any desired plane. As expected, MRI images represent a mapping of the hydrogen concentration in the body, but most importantly they represent the chemical environment around these hydrogen atoms. Because of this additional chemical information, MRI can image le-

sions hitherto not defineable by other modalities. Its contrast resolution is about 10 times that of CT. Although the value of MRI in brain imaging has been established, technical refinements are still underway for body imaging. Among the disadvantages of this modality are the high cost, the relatively long time required for acquisition of data, the inability to detect calcium, and the limited spatial resolution, which is of the order of 1 mm (10, 18). However, many of these disadvantages were cited in the early years of clinical use of CT and have largely been circumvented in a relatively short period of time.

Imaging Procedures

In pediatric imaging, all procedures are and should be tailored to the specific information desired. Thus, close scrutiny of the indications for the different examinations as well as close monitoring of the techniques themselves is required. A brief description of the most commonly used procedures for evaluation of pediatric trauma follows.

THE SKELETAL SYSTEM

Plain Radiography

Plain x-ray films of the bones are widely used for the detection of traumatic bone injuries. They provide excellent spatial and contrast resolution and can detect the progress of bone healing. Furthermore, the mechanism of injury as well as an approximation of the age of the injury may be assessed, providing significant medical and legal evidence. A skeletal survey is commonly used in patients suspected of child abuse. In this series of films, selected views of all bones are taken (see Chapter 2). Questionable areas may then be evaluated by coned-down views and additional projections. An alternative to the skeletal survey is the radioisotope bone scan.

Radionuclide Bone Scan

In this technique technetium-99m methylene diphosphonate (^{99m}Tc-MDP) or a related agent is injected intravenously and images of the skeletal systems are obtained 3 hours later. The agent concentrates in the bone and especially in areas of high metabolic activity, such as fractures, tumors, and infections. Comparison radiographs of abnormal areas are usually required. In experienced hands, bone scanning is an excellent screening method for suspected traumatic injuries, especially occult trauma (17). There is controversy as to whether bone scan or skeletal survey should be performed as the procedure of choice for children suspected of abuse. The issue is addressed in depth elsewhere in this book (see Chapter 2).

Arthrography

In arthrography, visualization of the internal architecture of the joints is achieved by injection of contrast medium and/or gas under fluoroscopic guidance. Radiographic exposures in multiple projections are taken, usually with fluoroscopic assistance. Occasionally, conventional tomography or CT may be used. Arthrography is usually employed in evaluation of traumatic joint processes, usually of active and older children and adolescents. However, in cases of suspected abuse, the examination may be useful in defining nonossified, cartilaginous portions of the joints, including differentiation of epiphyseal separation from dislocation.

THE CENTRAL NERVOUS SYSTEM

Skull Series

Fractures of the skull can be readily identified by plain radiography. Although two views of the skull are usually included in the skeletal survey, multiple views constituting a skull series (4–5 films) are employed when a skull fracture is suspected.

Computed Tomography of the Brain

Computed tomography is the procedure of choice to detect intracranial trauma. Bleeding is readily identified by its high density, and approximation of the time of the injury can be assessed by the known change in the density of hematomas with the passage of time. Brain contusion, edema, herniation, atrophy, and hydrocephalus can also be identified by this technique (19).

Neurosonography

In infants and children under the age of 2, the intracranial structures can be evaluated by sonographic scanning through the anterior fontanelle. In patients suspected of having intracranial trauma, ultrasound can detect hematomas within the brain tissue or ventricles. Although it can also detect extracerebral hematomas (subdural or epidural), small collections located high over the cerebral surfaces may be missed. However, because of the flexibility, availability, and speed with which the procedure can be performed, it should be considered in infants with suspected intracranial injury (9, 19–21).

Cerebral Angiography

In this procedure a catheter is threaded from a groin artery and placed selectively in a great vessel of the neck under fluoroscopic guidance. A concentrated solution of iodinated contrast medium is then injected, and rapid-sequence films are obtained during and shortly after the injection. The images are recorded directly on film, or they are computer processed and manipulated for optimal image quality (digital angiography). The process can be repeated by selectively catheterizing the rest of the neck vessels. With the widespread use of CT, angiography is rarely used today in traumatic brain injury.

Myelography

In this procedure a needle is inserted into the subarachnoid space from the back, usually in the region of the lumbar spine. An iodinated contrast medium, usually water soluble or, rarely, lipid soluble (Pantopaque), is then injected. The latter has to be aspirated after termination of the examination. After the injection, the patient is manipulated under fluoroscopic visualization so the contrast flows to different levels. The method accurately assesses the subarachnoid space and can define abnormalities of the spinal cord. Computed tomography can be used as an adjunct to the procedure, following the introduction of water-soluble contrast.

Magnetic Resonance Imaging

The use of MRI in child abuse has not been adequately assessed as yet. This technique has proved to be considerably more accurate than CT in detecting intracranial abnormalities, expecially in the posterior fossa and in the spine. In general, injuries including hematomas, edema, posttraumatic hydrocephalus, and cerebral atrophy are readily diagnosed (10, 18).

THE CHEST

Plain Radiography

Plain radiography of the chest in the frontal projection provides significant information because of the inherent different natural contrast densities of the thorax, which include bone (ribs), air (lungs), and soft tissue (heart, mediastinum, and great blood vessels) densities. Thus, rib fractures, pleural effusion or pneumothorax, pulmonary contusion or hemorrhage, and mediastinal air or hematoma are usually easily identified. Lateral films, and on occasion oblique views, may be obtained if further evaluation of abnormalities noted on the frontal films is desired. Plain chest radiography is the procedure of choice in suspected chest trauma.

Computed Tomography

Numerous complicated abnormalities seen on plain chest x-rays can be further evaluated by CT. With this modality accurate localization of a pleural, parenchymal, or mediastinal abnormality can be achieved, and often the pathologic process can be clearly detected (16).

Ultrasonography

Ultrasound has limited use in the pulmonary system because the air density of the lung and the bone density of the ribs inhibit propagation of the sound. However, ultrasonography is extensively used for the evaluation of the heart and pericardium (echocardiography). Furthermore, ultrasound detects abnormalities of the chest wall and is useful in evaluating small pleural effusions (9, 21).

Angiography

Angiographic procedures may be performed when vascular trauma is suspected. Such injuries, however, are rarely caused by child abuse.

THE ABDOMEN

Plain Radiography

Plain films of the abdomen provide significant information by detecting enlargement of organs, abdominal calcifications, displacement of gas-filled bowel loops, free fluid (blood) in the abdominal cavity, and free air from a ruptured hollow viscus. A supine abdominal film encompasses a region extending from the pelvis to the diaphragm. If significant trauma is suspected, views with a horizontal x-ray beam (upright, cross-table lateral, or lateral decubitus) should always accompany the supine film for the detection of free intraperitoneal air. Unless symptoms suggest trauma to a specific organ, plain abdominal films are used as the first step in the evaluation of suspected abdominal trauma.

Ultrasonography

The pediatric abdomen is ideal for evaluation by ultrasonography because of its relatively small size as compared to adults. Ultrasound can be used as a screening method to evaluate the whole abdomen and also when specific symptoms referring to a particular organ are evident. The liver, the largest solid organ, can be evaluated with high accuracy, and intrahepatic and subcapsular hematomas can be diagnosed. Abnormalities of the gallbladder and biliary tree can also be accurately evaluated. Similarly, ultrasound is very accurate in detecting traumatic injuries to the pancreas (rupture, traumatic pseudocyst, pancreatitis), spleen

(rupture, contusion, subcapsular hematoma), and kidneys (rupture, perirenal hematomas). In these cases, should conservative treatment be instituted, the progress of healing can be monitored. Free intra-abdominal fluid (such as blood) can be detected more accurately by ultrasound than by any other technique available. Retroperitoneal, intraperitoneal, and abdominal wall or pelvic hematomas may also be identified (9, 21).

Computed Tomography

Although the new scanners are considerably faster and provide higher resolution, CT is not the primary mode of investigation of intra-abdominal injury in most infants and young children. This is because CT images in small pediatric patients are usually of considerably poorer quality than in adults. This modality is usually utilized to further clarify questionable abnormalities indicated by ultrasound. However, high-resolution CT is probably the modality of choice in the occasionally massively traumatized infant or child. The appropriate uses of these two modalities in abdominal trauma depend not only upon the age of the patient, but also on the type of equipment available and the expertise of the diagnostic imagers (16, 22, 23).

Gastrointestinal (GI) Studies

Barium sulfate mixtures administered orally may be used to visualize the esophagus, stomach, and duodenum (upper GI series) and small bowel (small bowel follow-through). For the visualization of the colon, these substances are administered rectally, in the form of an enema (barium enema). Deviation of the GI tract by enlarged organs, masses, or hematomas is detected by this method. Rupture of a viscus is usually suggested on the plain film, but when the rupture is confined these contrast studies can identify the site of rupture. Finally, intramural hematomas, commonly occurring in the duodenum, are best evaluated with GI studies. On occasion, where risk of perforation is present, iodine solutions are used instead of barium suspensions.

Genitourinary Procedures

Intravenous Pyelography (IVP) or Excretory Urography. This is the primary technique by which the urinary system is visualized. After an intravenous injection of an organic iodinated contrast medium, sequential films of the abdomen are obtained. Early films show opacification of the kidneys; delayed films show the collecting systems of the kidneys, the ureters, and the bladder. Traumatic injuries to any of these structures can be detected. In addition, intra-abdominal hematomas may alter the position or shape of these structures. With the advent of ultrasonography and CT, which provide a wider range of information, the use of excretory urography as a screening study for the abdomen is falling from favor.

Cystography. A catheter is introduced into the bladder, which is filled with iodinated contrast medium under fluoroscopic monitoring. Films are obtained as needed. Traumatic rupture of the bladder can thus be detected.

Voiding Cystourethrography (VCUG). After a cystogram is performed, the catheter is removed and the voiding mechanism is viewed with fluoroscopy. Films are taken as needed.

Retrograde Urethrography. In cases of pelvic fractures with suspected urethral rupture, catheterization of the bladder is contraindicated. In such cases retrograde urethrography may be performed. In this examination contrast is injected through the urethral opening, again under direct fluoroscopic visualization.

Retrograde and Antegrade Pyelography. The urinary collecting systems can be opacified and recorded on x-ray films after direct injection of iodine solutions. In retrograde pyelography, the orifice of the ureter is catheterized under direct vision through a cystoscope. In antegrade pyelography a needle in inserted directly into the upper collecting system of the kidney under fluoroscopic, sonographic, or CT guidance.

Angiography

Positioning of a catheter in the aorta or inferior vena cava, or selectively in different

vessels such as the renal, mesenteric, hepatic, and splenic vessels, is performed under fluoroscopic guidance. Rapid-sequence films are taken while injecting iodinated contrast material. The vessels can also be visualized with intra-arterial or intravenous digital subtraction angiography. Intra-arterial digital angiography has the advantage of using a considerably smaller amount of contrast medium than intravenous digital or conventional arteriography (15). In trauma, angiography is used to identify the site of bleeding. In severe cases, embolization of the bleeding vessel can be achieved after selective catheterization. This may control further blood loss and is particularly advantageous in cases of uncontrolled pelvic trauma.

Nuclear Imaging

In contrast to plain radiography and other imaging modalities in which numerous structures can be evaluated at the same time, only specific organ anatomy or function is evaluated with nuclear imaging. In traumatic injuries, the following procedures have proven to be clinically useful (17).

Liver–Spleen Scans. Technetium-99m sulfur colloid is injected and concentrated in the reticuloendothelial system of the liver and spleen. This technique quite accurately detects traumatic injuries of these organs. Furthermore, in contrast to ultrasonography and CT, where the images are in the form of slices, radionuclide tests provide an assessment of the whole organ. For splenic trauma in which nonsurgical treatment is advocated, monitoring of the healing process is well achieved with spleen scans.

Radionuclide Renal Studies. A number of agents tagged with technetium-99m can be utilized in order to evaluate different aspects of the urinary system. Dimercaptosuccinic acid (^{99m}Tc-DMSA) best assesses cortical abnormalities, including renal fracture. Diethylenetriamine pentaacetic acid (^{99m}Tc-DTPA) evaluates the collective systems. Glucoheptonate gives information about both renal cortex and collective systems.

Red Blood Cell Scans. The patient's own red blood cells are labeled with technetium-99m and reinjected intravenously. The technique can identify sites of moderate bleeding, expecially from the GI tract.

Indium White Blood Cell Scans. The patient's own white cells are labeled in vitro with indium-111 oxine and reinjected intravenously. These white blood cells concentrate in areas of inflammation, such as abscess and infected hematoma.

Gallium Scans. Gallium-67 citrate also concentrates in areas of infection as well as in tumors.

Benefits and Risks of Diagnostic Imaging in Children

Diagnostic imaging plays a significant role in the investigation of many conditions in infants and children, including physical abuse. Although the risks from imaging procedures are usually minimal, they are real and must be balanced against the benefits. Furthermore, because the imaging techniques are costly, the potential benefit from an examination has to be weighed against its cost. Unfortunately, both risk-to-benefit and benefit-to-cost ratios have not been concretely established because, to an extent, they are both subjective in nature. The radiologist is best able to assess these factors, and to determine when the need for accurate diagnostic data outweighs the potential risk of exposure to ionizing radiation, physical or psychological trauma, adverse reaction to contrast media, or other complications from procedures utilized.

RADIATION RISKS

In the United States the major portion of the average person's exposure to man-made radiation arises from ionizing medical radiation related to therapeutic and diagnostic use of x-rays. The risks may be direct or delayed. Among the direct effects of radiation are radiation sickness and changes in the skin, lungs, and bowel (24, 25). These changes, however, do not occur at the low radiation dose used for diagnostic purposes.

Delayed effects of ionizing radiation include genetic changes, leukemia, cancer development, and cataract production. The in-

formation on the delayed effects of low-dose (diagnostic) radiation is mainly inferential, projected from larger dose studies. However, in the absence of complete data, it is accepted that a conservative approach is best, assuming a linear relationship without a threshold between dose and effect. If this assumption is correct, there is no safe dose (24–30). The potential risk from low-dose radiation has been actively addressed by government regulatory agencies as well as by equipment manufacturers and the medical establishment. The combination of strict regulations, significant equipment refinements, development of innovative procedures, and gains in medical knowledge has not only reduced radiation exposure but also produced images with more information than the ones obtained with higher dose levels.

REDUCTION OF RADIATION EXPOSURE

Reduction of radiation exposure can be achieved by attention to equipment and technique, and by good clinical judgment (5, 28, 31–37).

Attention to Equipment

Although government regulations for basic equipment performance standards exist, large variations among different radiographic units are very common. These become important considerations when small pediatric patients are examined with equipment designed for adults. At the University of Massachusetts Medical Center, for example, a new pediatric radiology suite is now installed that is estimated to reduce the radiation exposure from fluoroscopy by approximately 90%, without loss of diagnostic information. The advancements in equipment include improvements in x-ray generators, filtration of the x-ray beam, collimation devices to reduce unnecessary exposure to areas not needing evaluation, and the use of appropriate films, rare earth intensifying screens, image intensifiers, and phototimers. Recent advances in digital radiography further reduce radiation exposure by using detectors that have high stopping power for x-rays.

Attention to Technique

Use of appropriate technique is obviously very important. This includes selecting exposure factors that may give similar image quality with less radiation dose. Similarly, appropriate shielding of patients may reduce unnecessary exposure to critical organs and should be applied, whenever possible, in all pediatric patients. Fast exposure rates reduce motion artifacts and therefore the risk of unnecessary repeat examinations.

Good Clinical Judgment

Clinical judgment and careful planning are more subjective, but are important factors in radiation exposure and should be carefully applied by both the referring physician and the radiologist. Considerations regarding the necessity of the examination, and the availability of an alternative examination that does not use ionizing radiation, such as ultrasound, should be explored. Furthermore, a judgment should be made about the appropriateness of a repeat examination or the timing of intervals for follow-up examinations. Finally, one should know the quality of equipment available for use in children. Today this information is frequently solicited by concerned patients or their guardians. Both referring physicians and radiologists should be prepared to answer their questions.

RADIATION EXPOSURE AND DOSE

Wide variation in radiation exists not only between the different procedures but also for the same procedure from one institution to another. The wide variation in size of the pediatric patient complicates the matter further. Despite the bulk of literature on radiation exposure and dose, there are only a few, relatively incomplete references or tables stating the exact dose from the different procedures (5, 25, 38). This information is even scantier for pediatric patients (34, 35, 39). A sample of radiation exposures, reflecting the state of the art in radiation reduction schemes, is listed in Table 14.1.

The unit of radiation exposure dose is the roentgen (R) and that of the radiation absorbed dose is the rad or Gray (Gy) (1 Gray

Table 14.1.
Skin (Input) Radiation Exposures[a]

Examination	Patient age	Exposure (mR)
Chest: P.A. (Pigg-o-stat)	2 years	1.4
Lateral		2.4
Chest: P.A. (tabletop)	Premature	1.1
Lateral		2.3
Chest: P.A.	Adult	1.4
Lateral		2.6
Abdomen decubitus (with grid)	13 years	21.0
	3 years	13.5
Pelvis	2 months (chubby)	1.7
	2 months (small)	1.4
Skull: Lateral (with grid)		6.8
P.A.		9.5
Sinuses lateral	6 years	3.8
Cervical spine lateral		2.4
Humerus	12 years	2.8
	3 years	1.3
Elbow	10 years	1.7
Wrist	10 years	1.2
Hand	10 years	1.0
Tibia and fibula (in cast)	10 years	1.0
Legs (3' ortho)	4 years	2.6
Ankle	10 years	1.8
Feet	10 years	1.5
	2 years	1.0

[a] Adapted from Wesenberg et al. (13). Most tables provide dosimetry measurements that are substantially greater than these impressive figures.

= 100 rad). The average total body dose absorbed by each individual from the natural environment is about 0.100 rad per year. At 10,000 feet above sea level this rate is approximately twice as much because of increased exposure to cosmic radiation. With modern equipment and techniques, most pediatric radiographic procedures can be performed at local doses far below that of the yearly natural background dose. Notable exceptions are fluoroscopy and CT, in which the dose in the area being imaged can easily exceed 1 rad. Special fluoroscopic procedures, such as angiography, may easily require 10–20 rad and CT procedures 1–3 rad (34, 35).

Recent developments have shown that the fluoroscopic dose can be reduced dramatically by new techniques (13, 36, 37). Reduction techniques for pediatric imaging have also been suggested for radioisotope studies (40). Although for nearly all pediatric x-ray examinations less radiation is required than for adults, this is not true for all nuclear imaging techniques. For example, in a typical technetium-99m bone scan the metaphyseal growth complex can receive 6 to 8 times greater radiation dose than the corresponding part of an adult skeleton (40, 41). This occurs because the uptake of the isotope in the growth plate region is very high, and is an important consideration when a choice has to be made between an x-ray skeletal survey versus a radionuclide scan in children.

OTHER RISKS AND FINANCIAL CONSIDERATIONS

In addition to the potential risk from radiation, a variety of other risks are posed, some of which are easily minimized. Procedures requiring sedation include CT, MRI, and nuclear imaging. Angiography and interventional procedures in infants and small

Table 14.2.
Cost Considerations

Procedure	Relative cost[a]	Procedure	Relative cost
Skeletal system		Abdomen	
Skull series	2x	Abdomen, plain films	1x
Spine	2x	Upper GI series	3x
Face	2x	Barium enema	3x
Skeletal survey	3x	Intravenous urogram	3x
Bone scan	3–4x	Cystography	2x
		Voiding cystourethrogram	2x
Nervous system		Liver spleen scan	3–5x
Myelography	5–9x	Gallium scan	4–6x
Brain scan	4x	Renal scan	3–5x
CT head	5–7x		
		Other	
Chest		Ultrasound	3x
Chest x-ray	1x	CT body	7–10x
Tomography	2x	Angiography	9–15x
		Biopsy (imaging guided)	4–5x
		Percutaneous drainage	6–9x
		Surgery	740x

[a] One (1) x equals the cost of the usual chest x-ray examination ($35–50).The cost of other procedures is expressed in multiples of x.

children usually require general anesthesia. Most radiology departments are maintained at relatively cool temperatures, and this may affect small children and infants, who are especially sensitive to hypothermia. Thus, close attention should be paid to thermal equilibrium of these patients. The risk of anaphylactic allergic reaction from medications and contrast media, which is extremely difficult to prevent, is very small in children but should always be kept in mind.

The cost of imaging procedures has escalated not only because of the expense of the highly sophisticated equipment needed, but also because of the need for highly specialized personnel (1, 4, 42). It is very difficult to assess a cost-to-benefit ratio when dealing with a patient, especially a sick child. Even more subjective psychological factors are involved when dealing with pediatric trauma, especially in an abused child. Although considerable variations do exist among different institutions, it appears that the difference in charges for most procedures are more or less proportional in different institutions. In Table 14.2, charges relative to a chest x-ray are listed. This can be used as a guideline for relative cost when considering different procedures that may yield approximately the same result, or when considering an algorithmic approach to a given clinical problem (1, 2, 4). Included in this table are only those imaging procedures that are commonly used in the evaluation of trauma, in particular, child abuse.

REFERENCES

1. McNeil BJ, Abrams HL: *Brigham and Women's Hospital Handbook of Diagnostic Imaging.* Boston, Little, Brown, 1986.
2. Sraub WH: *Manual of Diagnostic Imaging: A Clinician's Guide to Clinical Problem Solving.* Boston, Little, Brown, 1984.
3. Zeman RK: Symposium on new imaging technology: pitfalls and controversies. *Radiol Clin North Am* 23:379–586, 1985.
4. Eisenberg RL, Amberg JR: *Critical Diagnostic Pathways in Radiology. An Algorithmic Approach.* Philadelphia, JB Lippincott, 1981.
5. Committee on Radiological Units, Standards, and Protection: *Medical Radiation: A Guide to Good Practice.* Washington, DC, American College of Radiology, 1985.
6. Curry TS III, Dowdey JE, Murr RC Jr: *Christensen's Introduction to the Physics of Diagnostic Radiology.* Philadelphia, Lea and Febiger, 1984.
7. Selman J: *The Fundamentals of X-ray and Radium Physics.* Springfield, IL, Charles C Thomas, 1985.
8. Kremkau FW: *Diagnostic Ultrasound. Principles, Instrumentation and Exercises.* Orlando, FL, Grune & Stratton, 1984.

9. Stewart HF, Stratmeyer ME (eds): *An Overview of Ultrasound: Theory, Measurement, Medical Applications, and Biological Effects.* USDHEW Publication (FDA) 82–8190. Bureau of Radiological Health. Washington, DC, US Government Printing Office, 1982.

10. Partain CL, James AE Jr, Pollo FD, Price RR: *Nuclear Magnetic Resonance Imaging.* Philadelphia, WB Saunders, 1983.

11. Jaffe CC: Medical imaging, vision and visual psychophysics. *Med Radiography Photography* 60:1–48, 1984.

12. Cohen G, Wagner LK, McDaniel DL, Robinson LH: Dose efficiency of screen-film systems used in pediatric radiography. *Radiology* 152:187–193, 1984.

13. Wesenberg RL, Amundson GM, Fleay RF: Ultra-low dose routine radiography utilizing a rare-earth filter. *Radiology* 149(P):38, 1983.

14. Robb WL: Technological seduction: Diagnostic imaging technology facing new demands. *AJR* 145:1112–1114, 1985.

15. Hillman BJ, Newell JD II: Symposium on digital radiography. *Radiol Clin North Am* 21:175–378, 1985.

16. Moss AA, Gamsu G, Genant HK: *Computed Tomography of the Body.* Philadelphia, WB Saunders, 1983.

17. Early PJ, Sodee DB: *Principles and Practice of Nuclear Medicine.* St. Louis, CV Mosby, 1985.

18. Alfidi RJ, Haaga JR. Symposium on magnetic resonance imaging. *Radiol Clin North Am* 22:763–969, 1984.

19. Rumack CM, Johnson ML: *Perinatal and Infant Brain Imaging: Role of Ultrasound and Computed Tomography.* Chicago, Year Book Medical Publishers, 1984.

20. Babcock DS, Han BK: *Cranial Ultrasonography of Infants.* Baltimore, Williams & Wilkins, 1981.

21. Haller JO, Shkolnik A: *Ultrasound in Pediatrics.* New York, Churchill Livingstone, 1981.

22. Federle MP: Symposium on CT and ultrasonography in the acutely ill patient. *Radiol Clin North Am* 21:423–606, 1983.

23. Greenbaum EI: *Radiology of the Emergency Patient: An Atlas Approach.* New York, John Wiley & Sons, 1982.

24. Doll R: Radiation hazards: 25 years of collaborative research. Sylvanus Thompson Memorial Lecture, April 1980. *Br J Radiol* 54:179–186, 1981.

25. Bureau of Radiological Health: *Health Physics in the Healing Arts.* USDHEW Publication (FDA) 73–8029, Washington, DC, US Government Printing Office, 1973.

26. Fabrikant JI: The BEIR-III report: Origin of the controversy. *AJR* 136:209–214, 1981.

27. Hutchison GB: Late neoplastic changes following medical irradiation. *Radiology* 105:645–652, 1972.

28. Margulis AR: The lessons of radiobiology for diagnostic radiology. Caldwell Lecture, 1972. *Am J Roentgenol (AJR)* 117:741–756, 1973.

29. Oppenheim BE, Griem ML, Meier P: The effects of diagnostic x-ray exposure on the human fetus: an examination of the evidence. *Radiology* 114:529–534, 1975.

30. Saenger EL: Radiologists, medical radiation, and the public health. Annual oration in memory of FW O'Brien. *Radiology* 92:685–699, 1969.

31. Committee on Radiology, American Academy of Pediatrics: Radiation protection in diagnostic radiography of children. *Pediatrics* 51:141–144, 1973.

32. Rossi HH: Limitation and assessment in radiation protection. Lauriston S. Taylor Lecture. *AJR* 144:1–8, 1985.

33. Villforth JC: Medical radiation protection: a long view. *AJR* 145:1114–1118, 1985.

34. National Council on Radiation Protection and Measurements: *Radiation Protection in Pediatric Radiology.* NCRP Report No. 68. Washington, DC, US Government Printing Office, 1981.

35. Fearon T, Vucich J: Pediatric patient exposures from CT examinations: GE C/T 9800 scanner. *AJR* 144:805–809, 1985.

36. Bureau of Radiological Health: *The Selection of Patients for X-Ray Examinations.* USDHEW Publication (FDA), 621–447/951. Washington, DC, US Government Printing Office, 1980.

37. Wesenberg RL, Amundson GM: Fluoroscopy in children: low-exposure technology. *Radiology* 153:243–247, 1984.

38. Bureau of Radiological Health: *Patient Exposure from Diagnostic X Rays.* An analysis of 1972–1974 NEXT Data. USDHEW Publication (FDA) 77–8020. Washington, DC, US Government Printing Office, 1977.

39. Bureau of Radiological Health: *Quantification of Current Practice in Pediatric Roentgenography for Organ Dose Calculations.* USDHEW Publication (FDA) 79–8078. Washington, DC, US Government Printing Office, 1979.

40. Shore RM, Hendee WR: Radiopharmaceutical dosage selection for pediatric nuclear medicine. *J Nucl Med* 27:287–298, 1986.

41. Thomas SR, Gelfand MJ, Kereiakes JG, Ascoli FA, Maxon HR, Saenger EL, Feller PA, Sodd VJ, Paras P: Dose to the metaphyseal growth complexes in children undergoing 99mTc-EHDP bone scans. *Radiology* 126:193–195, 1978.

42. Linton OW: Radiology in the medical swirl. *AJR* 145:1118–1120, 1985.

SUPPLEMENTARY BIBLIOGRAPHY

In addition to the references appearing at the end of each chapter, this supplementary bibliography is provided. In total, these references represent an exhaustive search of the world's medical literature for the radiologic manifestations of child abuse and neglect.

Akbarnia BA, Akbarnia NO: The role of orthopedist in child abuse and neglect. *Orthop Clin North Am* 7:733–742, 1976.

Akbarnia BA, Silberstein MJ, Rende RJ, Graviss ER, Luisiri A: Arthrography in the diagnosis of fractures of the distal end of the humerus in infants. *J Bone Joint Surg* 68A:599–602, 1986.

Allen HD, ten Bensel RW, Raile RB: The battered child syndrome. Part 1—Medical aspects. *Minn Med* 51:1793–1799, 1968.

Aoki N, Masuzawa H: Subdural hematomas in infants (response to Rekate HL article). *J Neurosurg* 62:316–317, 1985.

Aoki N, Masuzawa H: Subdural hematomas in abused children: report of six cases from Japan. *Neurosurgery* 18:475–477, 1986.

Bai KI, Rao KVS, Subramanyam MVG: The battered-child syndrome. *The Clinician* 37:199–203, 1973.

Ball TI: The pediatric radiologist looks at child abuse. *J MAG* 74:232–234, 1985.

Barmeyer GH, Alderson LR, Cox WB: Traumatic periostitis in young children. *J Pediatr* 38:184–190, 1951.

Barta RA Jr, Smith NJ: Willful trauma to young children: a challenge to the physician. *Clin Pediatr* 2:545–554, 1963.

Bell WE, McCormick WF: Head trauma ("battered child syndrome"). In *Increased Intracranial Pressure in Children. Major Problems in Clinical Pediatrics.* 1972; vol 8, pp 142–146.

Ben-Yossef L, Schmidt TL: Battered child syndrome simulating myositis. *J Pediatr Orthop* 3:392–395, 1983.

Berant M, Jacobs J: A "pseudo" battered child. *Clin Pediatr* 5:230–237, 1966.

Bergman AB, Larsen RM, Mueller BA: Changing spectrum of serious child abuse. *Pediatrics* 77:113–116, 1986.

Berrey BH: Postinfantile cortical hyperostosis with subdural hematoma: report of case and review of the literature. *Pediatrics* 6:78–85, 1950.

Bhattacharyya AK: Multiple fractures. *Bull Calcutta Sch Trop Med* 14:111–112, 1966.

Bhattacharyya AK, Mandal JN: Battered child syndrome: a review with a report of two siblings. *Indian Pediatr* 4:186–194, 1967.

Birrell RG, Birrell JHW: The "maltreatment syndrome" in children. *Med J Aust* 2:1134–1138, 1966.

Blount JG: Radiologic seminar CXXXVIII: The battered child. *J Miss State Med Assoc* 15:136–138, 1974.

Bognar I, Bodanszky H, Bohar A: "A megkinzott gyermek syndroma" es "a megrazott gyermek syndroma." *Orv Hetil* 117:2544–2547, 1976.

Bolz WS: The battered child syndrome. *Del Med J* 39:176–180, 1967.

Bowen DAL: The role of radiology and the identification of foreign bodies at post mortem examination. *Forensic Sci Soc* 6:28–32, 1966.

Braun IG, Braun EJ, Simonds C: The mistreated child. *Calif Med* 99:98–103, 1963.

Brown RH: The battered child syndrome. *J Forensic Sci* 21:65–70, 1976.

Bwibo NO: Battered child syndrome. *East Afr Med J* 48:56–61, 1971.

Caffey J: Significance of the history in the diagnosis of traumatic injury to children. Howland Award address. *J Pediatr* 67:1008–1014, 1965.

Caffey J: The parent-infant traumatic stress syndrome (Caffey-Kempe syndrome) (battered babe syndrome). *Am J Roentgenol Radium Ther Nucl Med (AJR)* 114:218–229, 1972.

Calder IM, Hill I, Scholtz CL: Primary brain trauma in non-accidental injury. *J Clin Pathol* 37:1095–1100, 1984.

Cameron JM: The battered baby syndrome. *Practitioner* 209:302–310, 1972.

Cameron JM: Radiological and pathological aspects of the battered child syndrome. In Smith SM (ed): *The Maltreatment of Children.* Baltimore, University Park Press, 1978, pp 69–81.

Chodkiewicz J-P, Redondo A, Clouin-Moral M: Les enfants battus hospitalises en neurochirurgie (problemes cliniques et medico-legaux). *Med Leg Domm Corp* 7:21–26, 1974.

Christoffel KK: Homicide in childhood: a public health problem in need of attention. *Am J Public Health* 74:68–70, 1984.

Claus HG: Knochenveranderungen nach Kindesmisshandlung. *Radiologe* 10:241–248, 1970.

Clearinghouse on Child Abuse and Neglect Information, P.O. Box 1182, Washington, DC 20013 (Radiologic examinations and child management. Search date: 2/25/81) (Photographs, x-rays and evidence: Laws. Data base edition, Spring 1982) (Radiologists and child abuse and neglect. Data base edition, Spring 1982)

Cochrane WA: The battered child syndrome. *Can J Public Health* 56:193–196, 1965.

Connell JB: The devil's battered children. *J Kans Med Soc* 64:385–399, 1963.

Conway JJ: Radionuclide bone imaging in pediatrics. *Pediatr Clin North Am* 24:701–712, 1977.

Corcelle L, Theodorides M: Syndrome de Silvermann: a propos d'une observation familiale. *Bull Soc Ophtalmol Fr* 67:644–647, 1967.

Council on Scientific Affairs: AMA diagnostic and treatment guidelines concerning child abuse and neglect. *JAMA* 254:796–803, 1985.

Cremin BJ: Battered baby syndrome. Letter to the editor. *S Afr Med J* 44:1044, 1970.

Curran WJ: Failure to diagnose battered-child syndrome. *N Engl J Med* 296:795–796, 1977.

Dave AB, Dave PB, Mishra KD: Child abuse and neglect (CAN) practices in Durg District of Madhya Pradesh. *Indian Pediatr* 19:905–912, 1982.

David TJ: Diaphragmatic hernia and pleural effusions. *Arch Dis Child* 53:968, 1978.

DiMaio VJM, Bernstein CG: A case of infanticide. *J Forensic Sci* 19:744–754, 1974.

Durrant P, Fowler I, Truscott R: Child abuse: appearing in court. A practical course on court procedure. *Health Visitor* 54:195, 198, 1981.

Dykes LJ: The whiplash shaken infant syndrome: what has been learned? *Child Abuse Negl* 10:211–221, 1986.

Edwards DK: Court testimony in cases of nonaccidental trauma. In Hilton SVW, Edwards DK, Hilton JW (eds): *Practical Pediatric Radiology*. Philadelphia, WB Saunders, 1984, pp 487–496.

Ellerstein NS, Norris KJ: Value of radiologic skeletal survey in assessment of abused children. *Pediatrics* 74:1075–1078, 1984.

Elliott LS: Child abuse: the radiologist's pivotal position. *Appl Radiol* 8:74–79, 1979.

Elvidge AR, Jackson IJ: Subdural hematoma and effusion in infants: review of fifty-five cases. *Am J Dis Child* 78:635–658, 1949.

Evans KT, Knight B, Whittaker DK: Child abuse. In *Forensic Radiology*. Oxford, Blackwell Scientific, 1981, pp 130–152.

Evers K, DeGaeta LR: Abdominal trauma. *Emerg Med Clin North Am* 3:525–539, 1985.

Fabre A, Canet J: Fractures multiples et "syndrome des enfants battus." *Gaz Med Fr* 74:4481–4492, 1967.

Fleming JC, Pysher TJ, Leonard JC: Myocardial localization of technetium-99m MDP in an infant. *Clin Nucl Med* 11:369–370, 1986.

Fontana VJ: Battered children. *N Engl J Med* 289:1044, 1973.

Fontana VJ: When to suspect child abuse. *Med Times* 101:116–122, 1973.

Fontana VJ, Donovan D, Wong RJ: The "maltreatment syndrome" in children. *N Engl J Med* 269:1389–1394, 1963.

Fontana VJ, Robison E: Observing child abuse. *J Pediatr* 105:655–660, 1984.

Fordham EW, Ramachandran PC: Radionuclide imaging of osseous trauma. *Semin Nucl Med* 4:411–429, 1974.

Friedman MS: Traumatic periostitis in infants and children. *JAMA* 166:1840–1845, 1958.

Friendly DS: Ocular manifestations of physical child abuse. *Trans Am Acad Ophthalmol Otolaryngol* 75:318–332, 1971.

Frye TR, Shores RM, Slovis TL, Young LW, Helfer RE: Radiological case of the month. *Am J Dis Child* 138:323–324, 1984.

Gans B: Unnecessary x-rays? *Br Med J* 1:564, 1970.

Garrow I, Werne J: Sudden apparently unexplained death during infancy. III. Pathologic findings in infants dying immediately after violence, contrasted with those after sudden apparently unexplained death. *Am J Pathol* 29:833–851, 1953.

Geissl G: Battered child syndrom. *MMW* 120:1284, 1978.

George JE: Spare the rod: a survey of the battered-child syndrome. *Forensic Sci* 2:129–167, 1973.

Giedion A: Das wiederholte Skeletttrauma beim Saugling und Kleinkind im Rontgenbild. *Praxis* 57:191–196, 1968.

Girardet D: Etude epidemiologique des fractures du crane chez les enfants de moins de 18 mois. *Helv Paediatr Acta* 37:35–47, 1982.

Gnehm HE: Le syndrome de l'enfant battu. *Helv Paediatr Acta* 31(suppl 31):1–27, 1973.

Gordon I, Turner R, Price TW (eds): Evidence and the expert witness. In *Medical Jurisprudence*, ed 3. London, E & S Livingstone, LTD, 1953, pp 311–336.

Gormsen H, Vesterdal J: Barnemishandling. "The battered child syndrome." *Ugeskr Laeger* 130:1203–1209, 1968.

Gostomyzk JG, Rochel M: Befunde bei Kindesmisshandlung und Vernachlassigung. *Beitr Gerichtl Med* 31:102–109, 1973.

Grace A, Kalinkiewicz M, Drake-Lee AB: Covert manifestations of child abuse. *Br Med J* 289:1041–1042, 1984.

Greengard J: The battered-child syndrome. *Am J Nurs* 64:98–100, 1964.

Greengard J: The battered child syndrome. *Med Sci* 15:82–91, 1964.

Gregersen M, Vesterby A: The value of forensic examination in child abuse and neglect. *Med Sci Law* 23:106–108, 1983.

Greinacher I: Rontgenbefunde beim sogenannten battered-child-syndrom. *Fortschr Rontgenstr* 113:704–710, 1970.

Griffiths DL, Moynihan FJ: Multiple epiphysial injuries in babies ("battered baby" syndrome). *Br Med J* 2:1558–1561, 1963.

Gross RH: Child abuse: are you recognizing it when you see it? *Contemp Orthop* 2:676–678, 1980.

Guarnaschelli J, Lee J, Pitts FW: "Fallen fontanelle" (caida de mollera): a variant of the battered child syndrome. *JAMA* 222:1545–1546, 1972.

Gwinn JL, Barnes GR Jr: Radiological case of the month. *Am J Dis Child* 109:457–458, 1965.

Gwinn JL, Lewin KW, Peterson HG Jr: Roentgenographic manifestations of unsuspected trauma in infancy. A problem of medical, social, and legal importance. *JAMA* 176:926–929,1961.

Harcke HT Jr: Bone imaging in infants and children: a review. *J Nucl Med* 19:324–329, 1978.

Harcourt B, Hopkins D: Ophthalmic manifestations of the battered-baby syndrome. *Br Med J* 3:398–401, 1971.

Harcourt B, Hopkins D: Permanent chorio-retinal lesions in childhood of suspected traumatic origin. *Trans Ophthalmol Soc UK* 93:199–205, 1973.

Heins M: The "battered child" revisited. *JAMA* 251:3295–3300, 1984.

Helfer RE: A review of the literature on the prevention of child abuse and neglect. *Child Abuse Negl* 6:251–261, 1982.

Helfer RE, Pollack CB: The battered child syndrome. *Adv Pediatr* 15:9–27, 1968.

Henderson JG: Subdural haematoma and "battered baby." Letter to the editor. *Br Med J* 3:678, 1968.

Hilton SW, Edwards DK: Radiographic diagnosis of nonaccidental trauma (child abuse). *Appl Radiol* 14:13–24, 1985.

Horodniceanu C, Grunebaum M, Volovitz B, Nitzan M: Unusual bone involvement in congenital syphilis mimicking the battered child syndrome. *Pediatr Radiol* 7:232–234, 1978.

Humphreys RP, Gilday DL, Ash JM, Hendrick EB, Hoffman HJ: Radiopharmaceutical bone scanning in pediatric neurosurgery. *Childs Brain* 5:249–262, 1979.

Jones JN, Schwarz HJ, Shoop JD: Selected pediatric abnormalities. *Curr Probl Diagn Radiol* 6:52–59, 1976.

Joseph R, Brault A, Job J-C, Ribierre M: Fractures multiples du nourrisson traumatismes meconnus, ou fragilite osseuse sans dysmorphie? *Arch Fr Pediatr* 17:849–864, 1960.

Kaufmann HJ: Differentialdiagnose periostaler reaktionen im sauglings- und kleinkindesalter. *Radiol Clin (Basel)* 31:337–356, 1962.

Kempe CH: The battered child and the hospital. *Hosp Pract* 4:44–57, 1969.

Kempe RS, Cutler C, Dean J: The infant with failure-to-thrive. In Kempe CH, Helfer RE (eds): *The Battered Child*, ed 3. Chicago, The University of Chicago Press, 1980, pp 163–182.

Kirchner SG, Lee YT: X-ray of the month. *J Tenn Med Assoc* 66:1053–1056, 1973.

Kirks DR: Radiological evaluation of visceral injuries in the battered child syndrome. *Pediatr Ann* 12:888–893, 1983.

Kirschner RH, Stein RJ: The mistaken diagnosis of child abuse. A form of medical abuse? *Am J Dis Child* 139:873–875, 1985.

Klein DM: Central nervous system injuries. In Ellerstein NS (ed): *Child Abuse and Neglect: a Medical Reference*. New York, John Wiley & Sons, 1981, pp 73–93.

Kleinman PK, Akins CM: The "vanishing" epiphysis: sign of Salter Type I fracture of the proximal humerus in infancy. *Br J Radiol* 55:865–867, 1982.

Knight B: The battered child. In Tedeschi CG, Eckert WG, Tedeschi LG (eds): *Forensic Medicine: A Study in Trauma and Environmental Hazards*, vol. 1: *Mechanical Trauma*. Philadelphia, WB Saunders, 1977, pp 500–509.

Kottgen U: Kindesmisshandlung ("battered child syndrome"). *Med Klin* 61:2025–2028, 1966.

Kottgen U: Kindesmißhandlung. *Monatsschr Kinderheilkd* 115:186–197, 1967.

Kottgen U, Greinacher I, Hofmann S: Zur rontgendiagnostik der kindesmißhandlung (battered child syndrome). *Kinderchir* 6:384–392, 1968.

Lagarde CL: John Caffey (1895–1978). *J Radiol* 60:75–77, 1979.

Leake HC III, Smith DJ: Preparing for and testifying in a child abuse hearing. *Clin Pediatr* 16:1057–1063, 1977.

Lee DA: Munchausen syndrome by proxy in twins. *Arch Dis Child* 54:646–647, 1979.

Luke JL, Lyons MM, Devlin JF: Pediatric forensic pathology. I. Death by homicide. *J Forensic Sci* 12:421–430, 1967.

MacKeith R: Speculations on some possible long-term effects. In Franklin AW (ed): *Nonaccidental Injury to Children*. New York, Churchill Livingstone, 1975, pp 63–68. Presented by Tunbridge Wells Study Group on Concerning Child Abuse: papers.

Mackler SF, Brooks AL: Diagnosis and treatment of skeletal injuries in the battered child syndrome. *South Med Bull* 58:27–32, 1970.

Mallet JF, Padovani JP, Rigault P: Le syndrome de Silverman ou syndrome des enfants battus. *Ann Pediatr (Paris)* 31:117–125, 1984.

Manzke H, Rohwedder H-J: Traumatische Knochenveranderungen beim Saugling, insbesondere nach Misshandlungen. *Monatsschr Kinderheilkd* 115:197–199, 1967.

Manzke H, Rohwedder H-J: Rontgenologie traumatischer Skelettveranderungen beim Saugling und Kleinkind. Battered child syndrome. *Chir Praxis* 15:631–640, 1971.

Maroteaux P, Fessard C: La maladie des enfants battus. Syndrome de Silverman. *Concours Med* 91:6704–6711, 1969.

Matin P: Bone scintigraphy in the diagnosis and management of traumatic injury. *Semin Nucl Med* 13:104–122, 1983.

Maxeiner H: Subdural hemorrhage following trauma by shaking. *Beitr Gerichtl Med* 44:451–457, 1986.

McClelland CQ, Heiple KG: Fractures in the first year of life. A diagnostic dilemma? *Am J Dis Child* 136:26–29, 1982.

McClelland CQ, Rekate H, Kaufman B, Persse L: Cerebral injury in child abuse: a changing profile. *Childs Brain* 7:225–235, 1980.

McNeese MC, Hebeler JR: The abused child: a clinical approach to identification and management. *Clin Symp* 29:2–36, 1977.

McRae KN, Ferguson CA, Lederman RS: The battered child syndrome. *Can Med J* 108:859–866, 1973.

Medynska L: Zespol dziecka maltretowanego. *Pediatr Pol* 49:767–772, 1974.

Meier A: Geburtstraumatische epiphysenlosung am proximalen femurende. *Arch Kinderheilkd* 116:267–276, 1939.

Meller JL, Little AG, Shermeta DW: Thoracic trauma in children. *Pediatrics* 74:813–819, 1984.

Merten DF: Introduction: The battered child syndrome: the role of radiological imaging. *Pediatr Ann* 12:867–868, 1983.

Mestel AL, Trusler GA, Thomson SA, Moes CAF: Acute obstruction of small intestine secondary to hematoma in children. *Arch Surg* 78:25–32, 1959.

Milgram JW, Lyne ED: Epiphysiolysis of the proximal femur in very young children. *Clin Orthop* 110:146–153, 1975.

Miller DS: Fractures among children. I. Parental assault as a causative agent. *Minn Med* 42:1209–1213, 1959.

Miller TQ: The role of the radiologist on the child abuse team. *J Natl Med Assoc* 74:647–651, 1982.

Montoya C, Donoso P: Traumatismos repetidos con fracturas multiples en un lactante. *Rev Chil Pediatr* 35:33–38, 1964.

Morris TMO, Reay HAJ: A battered baby wih pharyngeal atresia. *J Laryngol Otol* 85:729–731, 1971.

Morse CW, Sahler OJZ, Friedman SB: A three-year follow-up study of abused and neglected children. *Am J Dis Child* 120:439–446, 1970.

Norton LE: Child abuse. *Clin Lab Med* 3:321–342, 1983.

O'Doherty NJ: Subdural haematoma in battered babies. *Dev Med Child Neurol* 6:192–193, 1964.

Oliver JE: Appendix: Review of world literature on extent of child abuse. In Smith SE (ed): *The Maltreat-*

ment of Children. Baltimore, University Park Press, 1978, pp 415–447.

Ommaya AK, Yarnell P: Subdural haematoma after whiplash injury. *Lancet* 2:237–239, 1969.

Ozonoff MB: Emergency radiology in childhood. *Emerg Med Clin North Am* 3:563–584, 1985.

Pashayan H, Cochrane WA: Maltreatment syndrome of children. *Nova Scotia Med Bull* 44:139–142, 1965.

Paterson CR: Vitamin D deficiency rickets simulating child abuse. *J Pediatr Orthop* 1:423–425, 1981.

Pickett WJ III, Johnson JF, Enzenauer RW: Case report 192: Neonatal fractures mimicking abuse secondary to physical therapy. *Skeletal Radiol* 8:85–86, 1982.

Radkowski MA: The battered child syndrome: pitfalls in radiological diagnosis. *Pediatr Ann* 12:894–903, 1983.

Raekallio J: Histological estimation of the age of injuries. In Perper JA, Wecht CH (eds): *Microscopic Diagnosis in Forensic Pathology.* Springfield, IL, Charles C Thomas, 1980, pp 3–16.

Reeb KG, Melli MS, Wald M, Wesenberg R: A conference on child abuse. *Wis Med J* 7:226–229, 1972.

Reece RM, Grodin MA: Recognition of nonaccidental injury. *Pediatr Clin North Am* 32:41–60, 1985.

Rekate HL: Subdural hematomas in infants (letter). *J Neurosurg* 62:316–317, 1985.

Riddervold HO, Smith TH: Rontgenfunn ved Barnemishandling—The battered child syndrome. *Tidsskr Nor Laegeforen* 101:155–156, 1980.

Rodgers BM: Trauma and the child. *Heart Lung* 6:1052–1056, 1977.

Rogers D, Tripp J, Bentovim A, Robinson A, Berry D, Goulding R: Nonaccidental poisoning: an extended syndrome of child abuse. *Br Med J* 1:793–796, 1976.

Rupprecht E, Berger G: Zur Differentialdiagnose des multiplen Skelettraumas im Kindersalter ("battered child syndrome"). *Radiol Diagn (Paris)* 17:615–625, 1976.

Santhanakrishnan BR, Shetty MV, Raju VB: PITS syndrome. *Indian Pediatr* 10:97–100, 1973.

Santhanakrishnan BR, Sridhar VS, Sriram R, Shetty MVK, Raju VB: Child abuse. *Indian Pediatr* 16:57–60, 1979.

Schmitt BD: The battered child syndrome. In Touloukian RJ (ed): *Pediatric Trauma.* New York, John Wiley & Sons, 1978, pp 177–216.

Schmitt BD: Colic: excessive crying in newborns. *Clin Perinatol* 12:441–451, 1985.

Schneegans E, Haarscher A, Zimmermann G: Fractures spontanees multiples associees a des lesions cerebrales graves. *Arch Fr Pediatr* 6:758–760, 1953.

Seelemann K: Beobachtungen uber kindesmiBhandlungen. *Monatsschr Kinderheilkd* 119:60–65, 1971.

Selander P: Kroppslig misshandel av smabarn. *Nord Med* 70:1192–1194, 1963.

Shopfner CE: Periosteal bone growth in normal infants: a preliminary report. *Am J Roentgenol (AJR)* 97:154–163, 1966.

Shulman BH, Terhune CB: Epiphyseal injuries in breech delivery. *Pediatrics* 8:693–700, 1951.

Silverman FN: Problems in pediatric fractures. *Semin Roentgenol* 13:167–176, 1978.

Simpson K: The use of radiography in the investigation of crime. *Radiography* 46:14–16, 1980.

Smalley RH: X-ray consultation (battered child syndrome). *New Physician* 19:929–930, 1970.

Smith SM, Hanson R: 134 battered children: a medical and psychological study. *Br Med J* 3:666–670, 1974.

Smyth FS, Potter A, Silverman W: Periosteal reaction, fever and irritability in young infants. A new syndrome? *Am J Dis Child* 71:333–350, 1946.

Sneed RC, Bell RF: The dauphin of Munchausen: factitious passage of renal stones in a child. *Pediatrics* 58:127–130, 1976.

Solomons G: Annotations. Child abuse and developmental disabilities. *Dev Med Child Neurol* 21:101–106, 1979.

Staak M, Wagner T, Wille R: Zur diagnostik und sozialtherapie das vernachlassigten kindes. *Monatsschr Kinderheilkd* 115:199–201, 1967.

Starbuck GW: The recognition and early management of child abuse. *Pediatr Ann* 5:27–41, 1976.

Sternowsky HJ, Schaefer E: Traumatische pankreatitis mit peripheren osteolysen als hinweis auf kindesmiBhandlung. *Monatsschr Kinderheilkd* 133:178–180, 1985.

Storey B: The battered child. *Med J Aust* 2:789–791, 1964.

Stover B: Radiologic diagnosis of the battered child syndrome. *Monatsschr Kinderheilkd* 134:322–327, 1986.

Sty JR, Starshak RJ: Abnormal Tc-99m MDP renal images associated with myoglobinuria. *Clin Nucl Med* 7:476, 1982.

Sullivan E, Smith DF, Fox MAV, LoPresti JM, Lovrien E, Newsome ME: Symposium: Battered child syndrome. *Clin Proc Child Hosp* 20:229–239, 1964.

Swischuk LE: The battered child syndrome: radiologic aspects. *South Med Bull* 58:24–26, 1970.

ten Bensel RW, Raile RB: The battered child syndrome. *Minn Med* 46:977–982, 1963.

Teng CT, Singleton EB, Daeschner CW Jr: Skeletal injuries of the battered child. *Am J Orthop* 6:202–207, 1964.

Thach BT: Sudden infant death syndrome. Old causes rediscovered? *N Engl J Med* 315:126–128, 1986.

TMA x-ray of the month. *J Tenn Med Assoc* 66:1053–1056, 1973.

Touloukian RJ: Battered children with abdominal trauma. *GP* 40:106–109, 1969.

Tredwell SJ, Van Peteghem K, Clough M: Pattern of forearm fractures in children. *J Pediatr Orthop* 4:604–608, 1984.

Tufts E, Blank E, Dickerson D: Periosteal thickening as a manifestation of trauma in infancy. *Child Abuse Negl* 6:359–364, 1982.

Welch KJ: Abdominal injuries. In *Pediatric Surgery,* ed 3. Chicago, Year Book Medical Publishers, 1979, vol 1, pp 125–149.

West S: Acute periosteal swellings in several young infants of the same family, probably rickety in nature. *Br Med J* 1:856–857, 1888.

Weston WJ: Metaphyseal fractures in infancy. *J Bone Joint Surg* 39B:694–700, 1957.

Whiplash injury in infancy. *Med J Aust* 2:456, 1971.

Wilkinson RH: Radiographs. *Pediatr Clin North Am* 24:685–699, 1977.

Wilson JC Jr: Fractures and dislocations in childhood. *Pediatr Clin North Am* 14:659–682, 1967.

Worlock P, Stower M, Barbor P: Patterns of fractures in accidental and non-accidental injury in children: a comparative study. *Br Med J (Clin Res)* 293:100–102, 1986.

Index

Page numbers in **_bold italics_** indicate figures, those followed by "t" indicate tables.